D1257118

# WOLVERINE

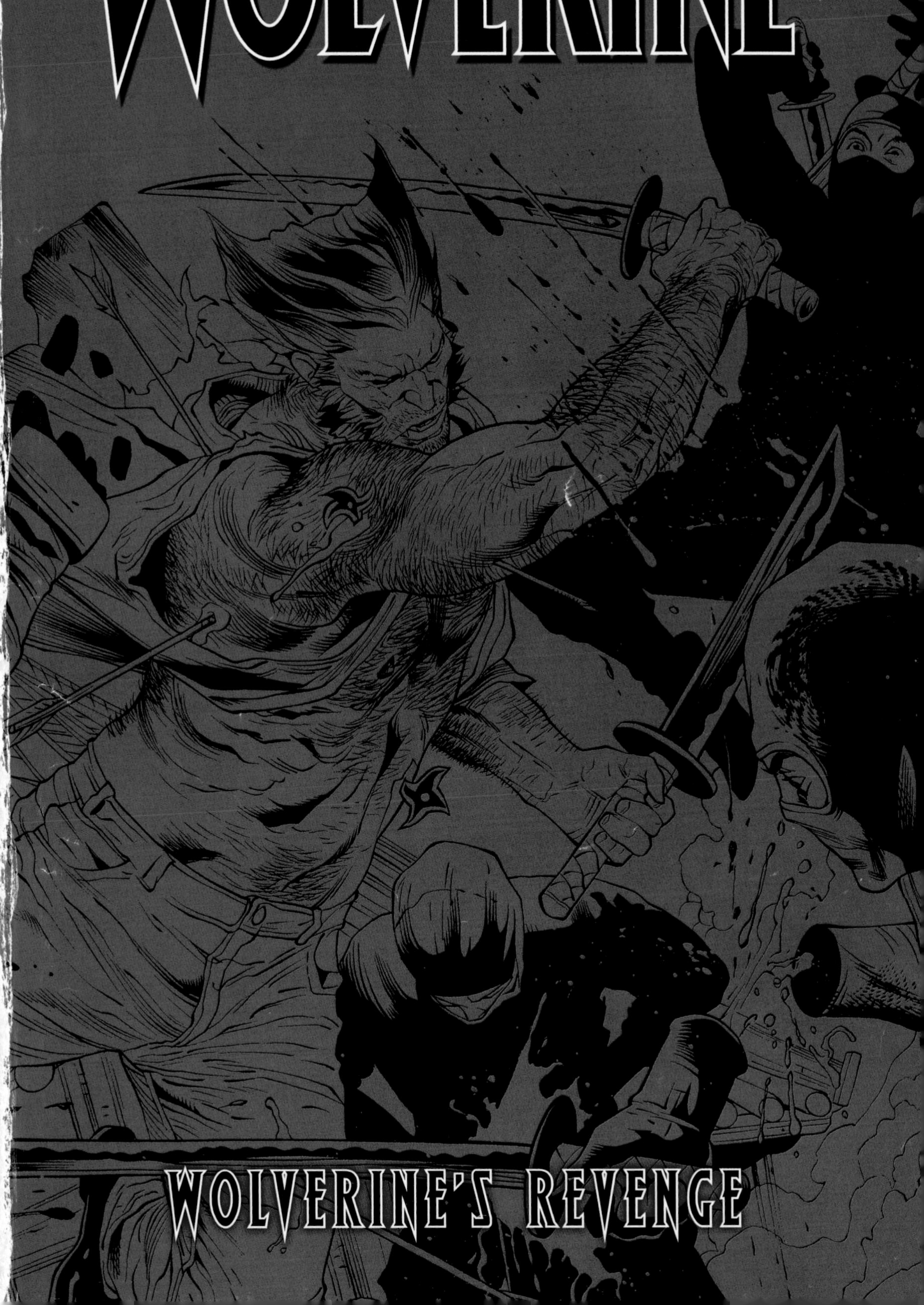

## WOLVERINE'S REVENGE

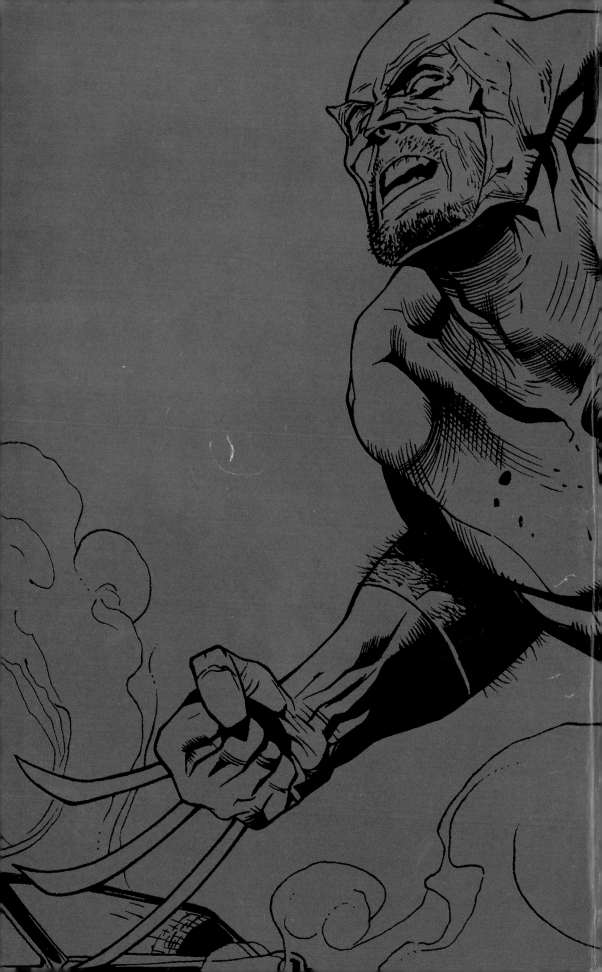

# WOLVERINE'S REVENGE

WRITER **JASON AARON**

PENCILS **RENATO GUEDES**
(ISSUES #10-14)

& **GORAN SUDZUKA**
(ISSUES #15-16)

INKS **JOSE WILSON MAGALHAES**
(ISSUES #10-14)

& **GORAN SUDZUKA**
(ISSUES #15-16)

COLORS **MATTHEW WILSON**

LETTERS VC'S **CORY PETIT**
COVER ART **JAE LEE** WITH **JUNE CHUNG**
ASSISTANT EDITOR **JODY LeHEUP**
EDITOR **JEANINE SCHAEFER**
GROUP EDITOR **NICK LOWE**

Collection Editor CORY LEVINE
Editorial Assistants JAMES EMMETT & JOE HOCHSTEIN
Assistant Editors ALEX STARBUCK & NELSON RIBEIRO
Editors, Special Projects JENNIFER GRÜNWALD
& MARK D. BEAZLEY
Senior Editor, Special Projects JEFF YOUNGQUIST
Senior Vice President of Sales DAVID GABRIEL
SVP of Brand Planning & Communications
MICHAEL PASCIULLO
Book Design JEFF POWELL

Editor in Chief AXEL ALONSO
Chief Creative Officer JOE QUESADA
Publisher DAN BUCKLEY
Executive Producer ALAN FINE

WOLVERINE: WOLVERINE'S REVENGE. Contains material originally published
in magazine form as WOLVERINE #10-16. First printing 2011. Hardcover ISBN#
978-0-7851-5279-8. Softcover ISBN# 978-0-7851-5280-4. Published by MARVEL
WORLDWIDE, INC., a subsidiary of MARVEL ENTERTAINMENT, LLC. OFFICE OF
PUBLICATION: 135 West 50th Street, New York, NY 10020. Copyright © 2011 and
2012 Marvel Characters, Inc. All rights reserved. Hardcover: $24.99 per copy in the
U.S. and $27.99 in Canada (GST #R127032852). Softcover: $16.99 per copy in the
U.S. and $18.99 in Canada (GST #R127032852). Canadian Agreement #40668537.
All characters featured in this issue and the distinctive names and likenesses thereof,
and all related indicia are trademarks of Marvel Characters, Inc. No similarity between
any of the names, characters, persons, and/or institutions in this magazine with
those of any living or dead person or institution is intended, and any such similarity
which may exist is purely coincidental. **Printed in the U.S.A.** ALAN FINE, EVP - Office
of the President, Marvel Worldwide, Inc. and EVP & CMO Marvel Characters B.V.;
DAN BUCKLEY, Publisher & President - Print, Animation & Digital Divisions; JOE
QUESADA, Chief Creative Officer; JIM SOKOLOWSKI, Chief Operating Officer; DAVID
BOGART, SVP of Business Affairs & Talent Management; TOM BREVOORT, SVP of
Publishing; C.B. CEBULSKI, SVP of Creator & Content Development; DAVID GABRIEL,
SVP of Publishing Sales & Circulation; MICHAEL PASCIULLO, SVP of Brand Planning
& Communications; JIM O'KEEFE, VP of Operations & Logistics; DAN CARR, Executive
Director of Publishing Technology; SUSAN CRESPI, Editorial Operations Manager;
ALEX MORALES, Publishing Operations Manager; STAN LEE, Chairman Emeritus. For
information regarding advertising in Marvel Comics or on Marvel.com, please contact
John Dokes, SVP Integrated Sales and Marketing, at jdokes@marvel.com. For Marvel
subscription inquiries, please call 800-217-9158. **Manufactured between 9/12/2011
and 10/10/2011 (hardcover), and 9/12/2011 and 4/9/2012 (softcover), by R.R.
DONNELLEY, INC., SALEM, VA, USA.**

10 9 8 7 6 5 4 3 2 1

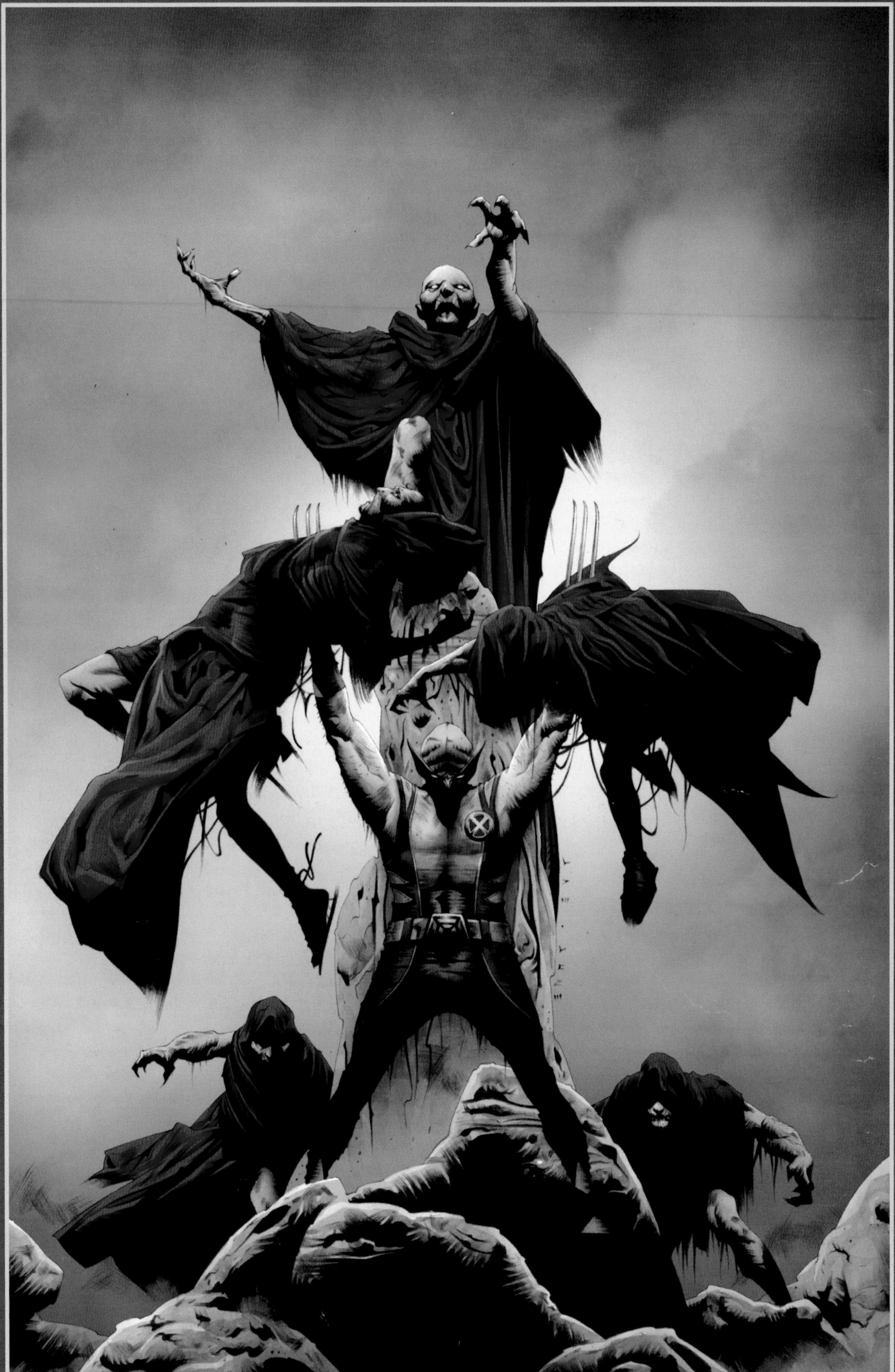

# 10

*Many years ago, a secret government organization abducted the man called Logan, a mutant possessing razor sharp bone claws and the ability to heal from any wound. In their attempt to create the perfect living weapon, the organization bonded the unbreakable metal Adamantium to his skeleton. The process was excruciating and by the end, there was little left of the man known as Logan. He had become...*

# WOLVERINE

## PREVIOUSLY...

A mysterious organization known as The Red Right Hand sent Wolverine's soul to hell and charged his demonically possessed body with the murder of his friends and loved ones. After enduring horrific torture at the hands of the devil himself, Logan was able to escape hell and retake possession of his body with the help of his fellow X-Men and his girlfriend, Melita Garner. Back in control and thirsty for blood, Wolverine set out to take his revenge.

Logan's first target was the manipulative mutant shape-shifter known as Mystique, the woman responsible for betraying him to the Red Right Hand. When Logan finally tracked her down, the pair waged a violent battle in which Mystique revealed the whereabouts of the Red Right Hand's headquarters before dying by Logan's hand.

Now, Logan is after his next target...

## WOLVERINE'S REVENGE!

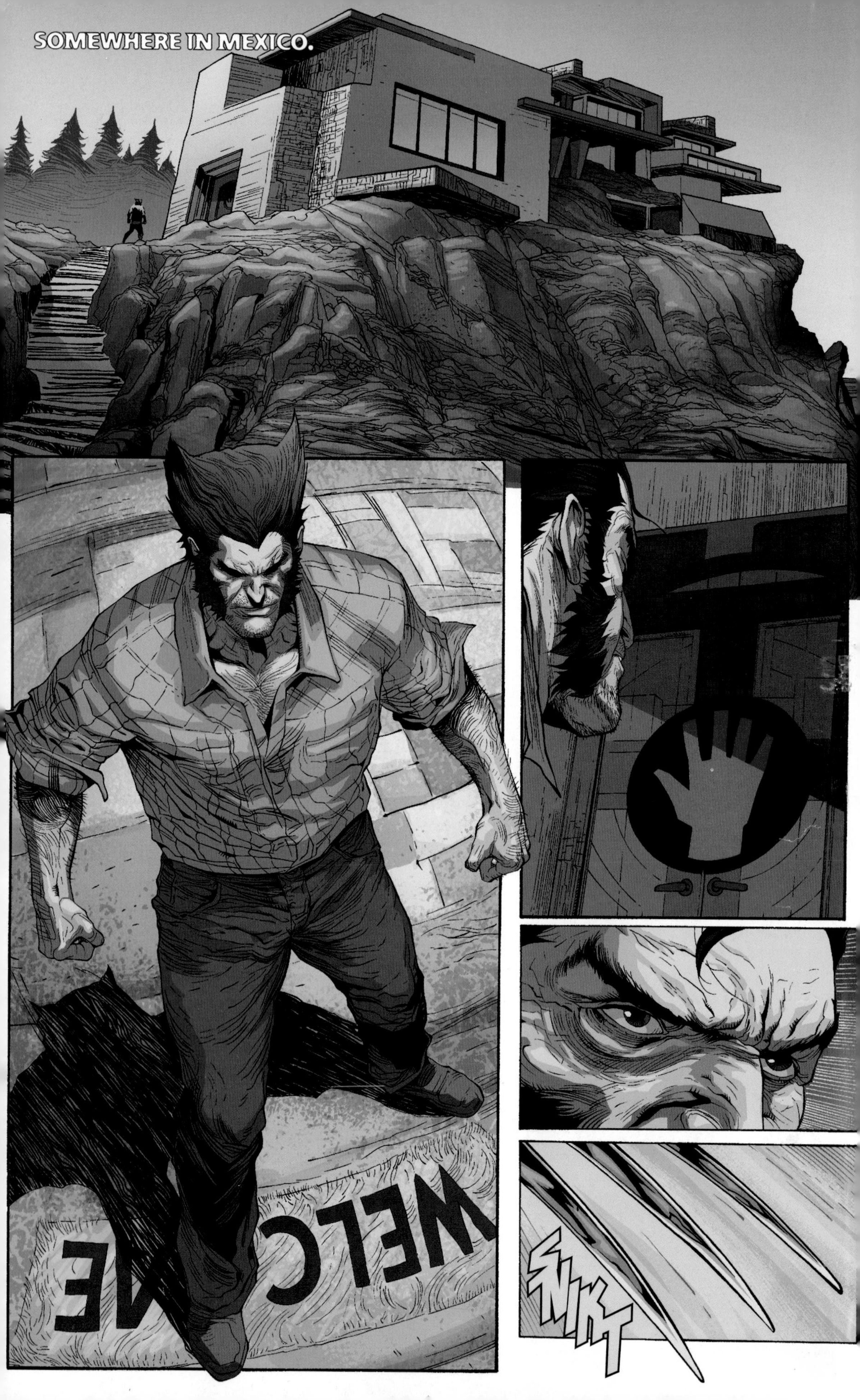
SOMEWHERE IN MEXICO.
SNIKT

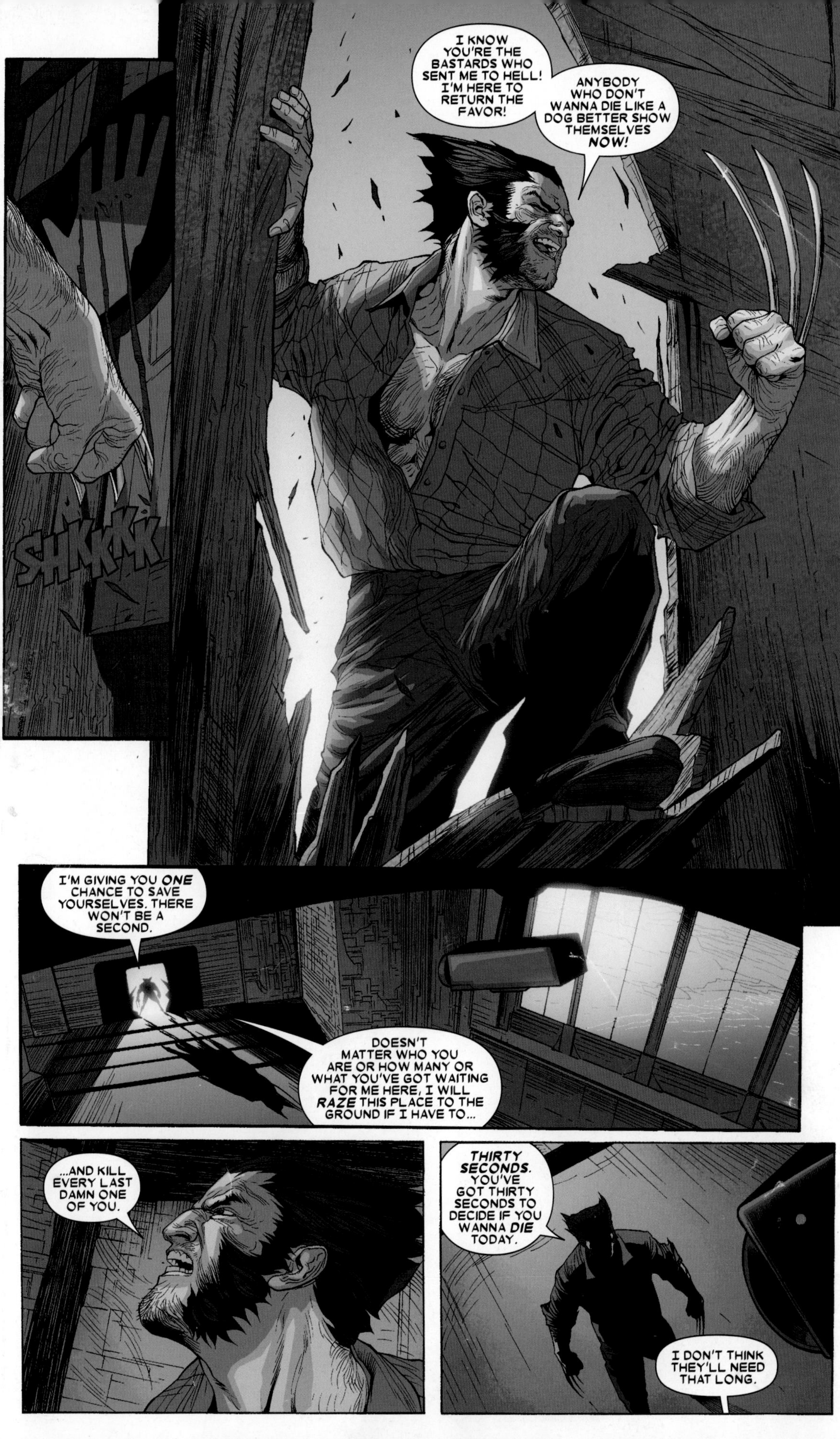
SHHKKKK
I KNOW YOU'RE THE BASTARDS WHO SENT ME TO HELL! I'M HERE TO RETURN THE FAVOR!
ANYBODY WHO DON'T WANNA DIE LIKE A DOG BETTER SHOW THEMSELVES *NOW!*
I'M GIVING YOU *ONE* CHANCE TO SAVE YOURSELVES. THERE WON'T BE A SECOND.
DOESN'T MATTER WHO YOU ARE OR HOW MANY OR WHAT YOU'VE GOT WAITING FOR ME HERE, I WILL *RAZE* THIS PLACE TO THE GROUND IF I HAVE TO...
...AND KILL EVERY LAST DAMN ONE OF YOU.
*THIRTY SECONDS*. YOU'VE GOT THIRTY SECONDS TO DECIDE IF YOU WANNA *DIE* TODAY.
I DON'T THINK THEY'LL NEED THAT LONG.

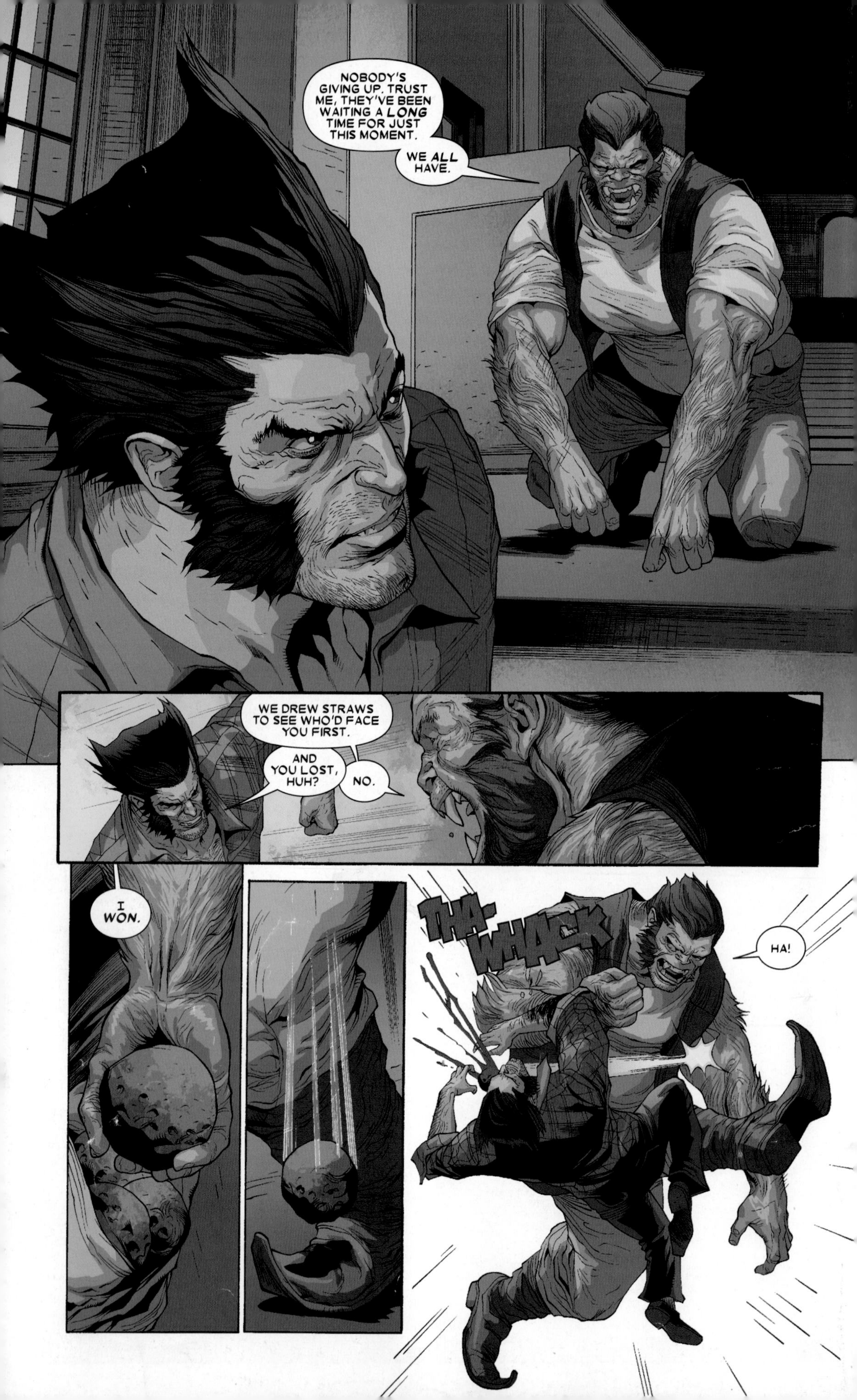
NOBODY'S GIVING UP. TRUST ME, THEY'VE BEEN WAITING A LONG TIME FOR JUST THIS MOMENT.
WE ALL HAVE.
WE DREW STRAWS TO SEE WHO'D FACE YOU FIRST.
AND YOU LOST, HUH?
NO.
I WON.
THA-WHACK
HA!

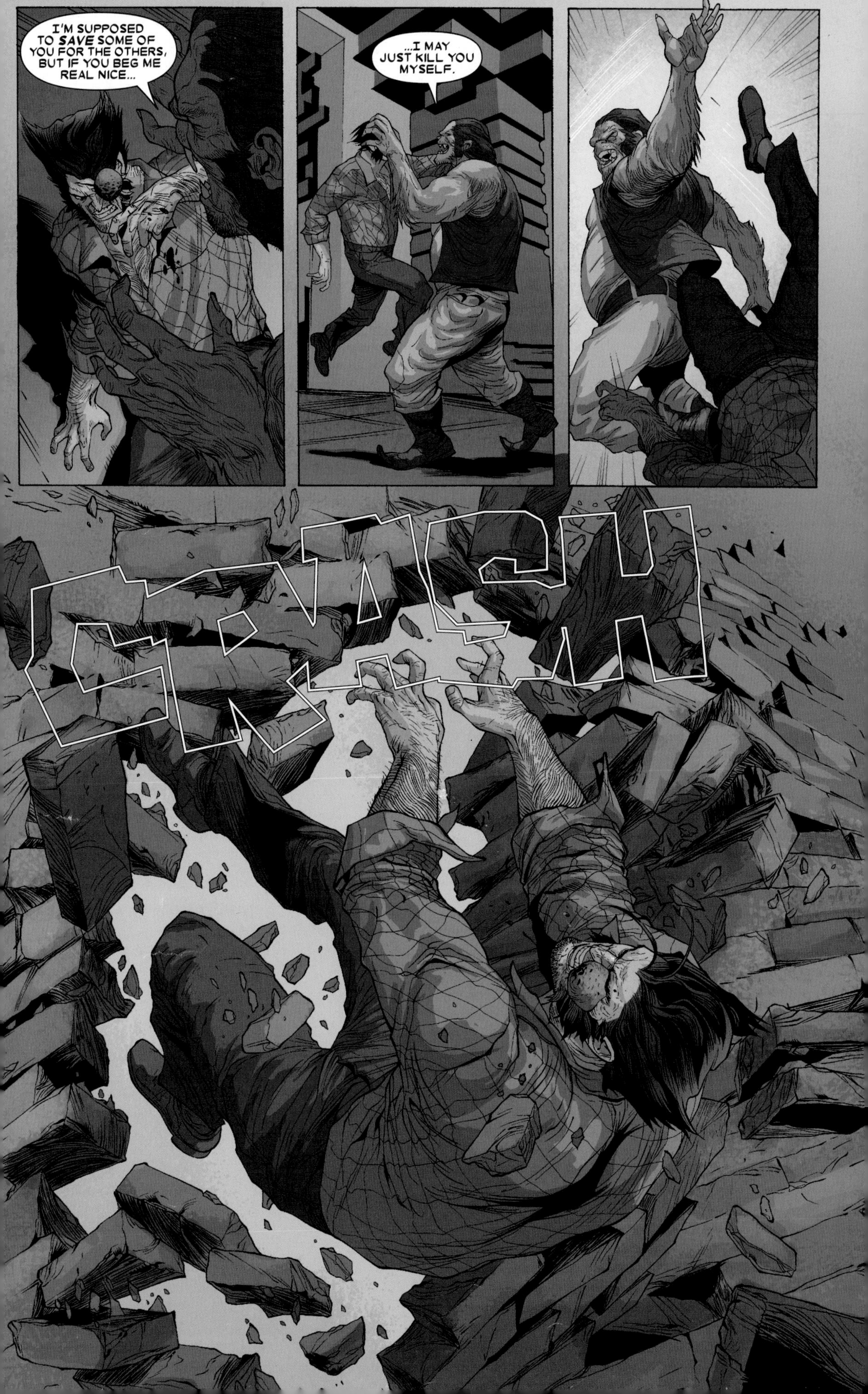
I'M SUPPOSED TO SAVE SOME OF YOU FOR THE OTHERS, BUT IF YOU BEG ME REAL NICE...
...I MAY JUST KILL YOU MYSELF.
SMASH

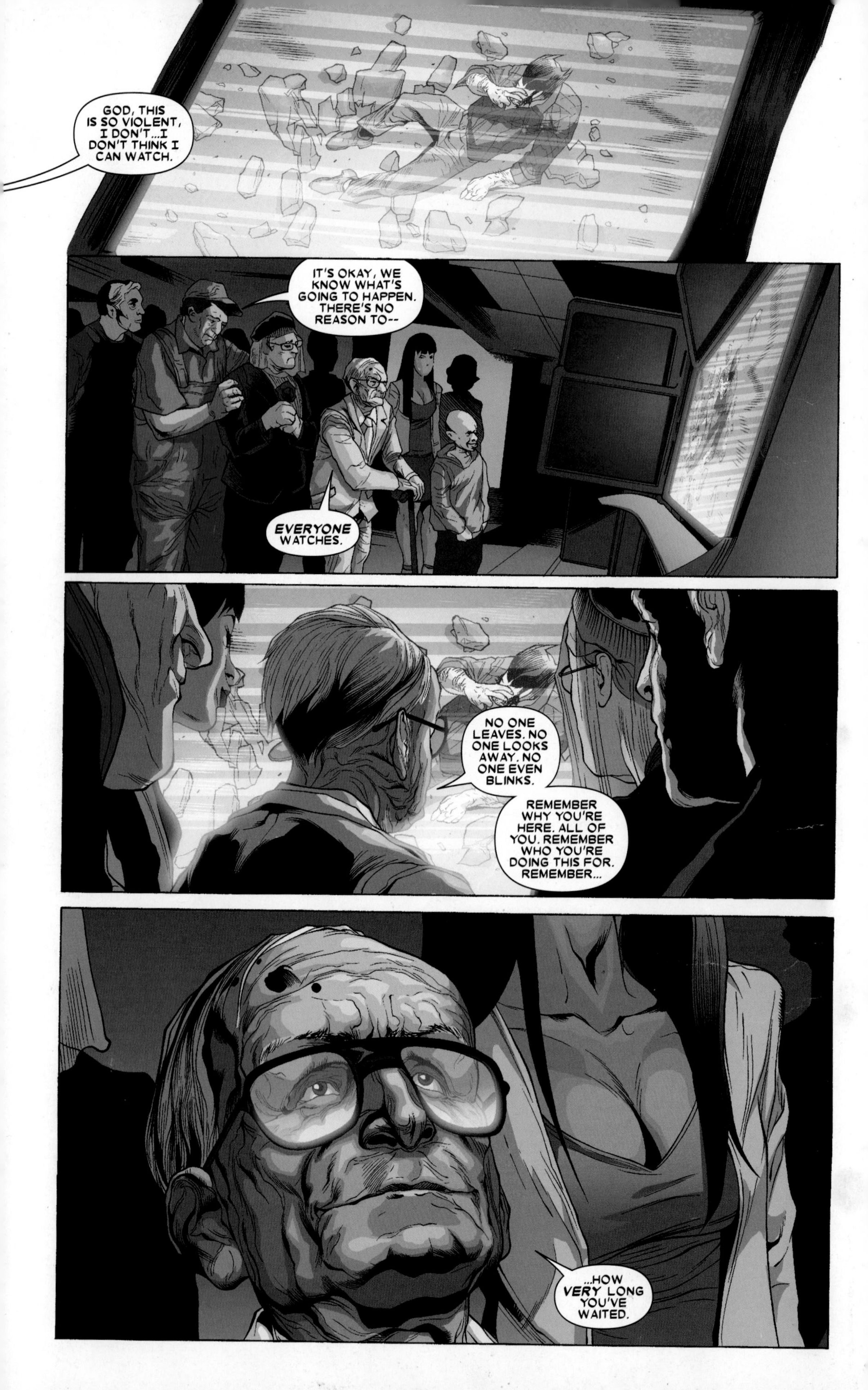
GOD, THIS IS SO VIOLENT, I DON'T...I DON'T THINK I CAN WATCH.
IT'S OKAY, WE KNOW WHAT'S GOING TO HAPPEN. THERE'S NO REASON TO--
EVERYONE WATCHES.
NO ONE LEAVES. NO ONE LOOKS AWAY. NO ONE EVEN BLINKS.
REMEMBER WHY YOU'RE HERE. ALL OF YOU. REMEMBER WHO YOU'RE DOING THIS FOR. REMEMBER...
...HOW VERY LONG YOU'VE WAITED.

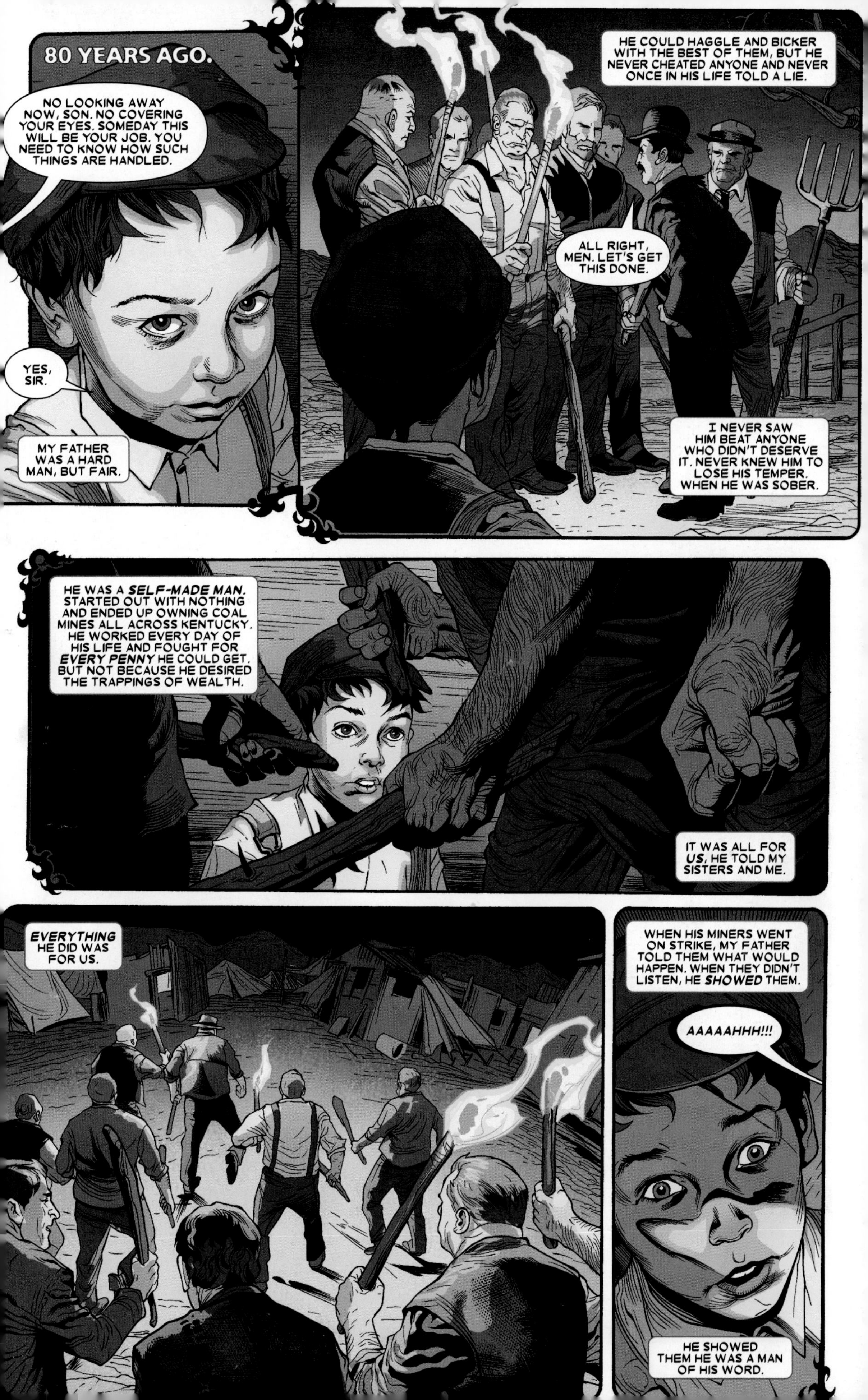

80 YEARS AGO.
NO LOOKING AWAY NOW, SON. NO COVERING YOUR EYES. SOMEDAY THIS WILL BE YOUR JOB. YOU NEED TO KNOW HOW SUCH THINGS ARE HANDLED.
YES, SIR.
MY FATHER WAS A HARD MAN, BUT FAIR.
HE COULD HAGGLE AND BICKER WITH THE BEST OF THEM, BUT HE NEVER CHEATED ANYONE AND NEVER ONCE IN HIS LIFE TOLD A LIE.
ALL RIGHT, MEN. LET'S GET THIS DONE.
I NEVER SAW HIM BEAT ANYONE WHO DIDN'T DESERVE IT. NEVER KNEW HIM TO LOSE HIS TEMPER. WHEN HE WAS SOBER.
HE WAS A *SELF-MADE MAN.* STARTED OUT WITH NOTHING AND ENDED UP OWNING COAL MINES ALL ACROSS KENTUCKY. HE WORKED EVERY DAY OF HIS LIFE AND FOUGHT FOR *EVERY PENNY* HE COULD GET. BUT NOT BECAUSE HE DESIRED THE TRAPPINGS OF WEALTH.
IT WAS ALL FOR *US*, HE TOLD MY SISTERS AND ME.
*EVERYTHING* HE DID WAS FOR US.
WHEN HIS MINERS WENT ON STRIKE, MY FATHER TOLD THEM WHAT WOULD HAPPEN. WHEN THEY DIDN'T LISTEN, HE *SHOWED* THEM.
*AAAAAHHH!!!*
HE SHOWED THEM HE WAS A MAN OF HIS WORD.

BUT THE STRIKE DIDN'T BREAK.

WE WILL NOT STARVE... IN A LAND OF PLENTY

PROSPERITY FOR ALL

ON STRIKE FOR LIVING WAGE

INSTEAD THE MINERS BROUGHT IN *SPEECHMAKERS* AND *UNION ORGANIZERS.* SOCIALIST RABBLE ROUSERS AND YANKEE LOUDMOUTHS AND SOME OLD WOMAN WHO CURSED WORSE THAN ANY MAN I'D EVER HEARD.

THEY TALKED OF BRINGING IN *GUNS.*

MY FATHER BROUGHT IN THE *PINKERTONS.*

THE UNION FOLK CALLED IT A MASSACRE.

BUT THE SPEECHES STOPPED. AND IT LOOKED LIKE THE MINERS WERE FINALLY READY TO GET BACK TO WORK. BUT THEN...

...THEY BROUGHT IN SOMEBODY NEW. SOME SPECIAL NEGOTIATOR FROM WAY UP NORTH. MY FATHER LAUGHED. ONLY...

...THIS WASN'T LIKE ANY NEGOTIATOR HE'D EVER SEEN.

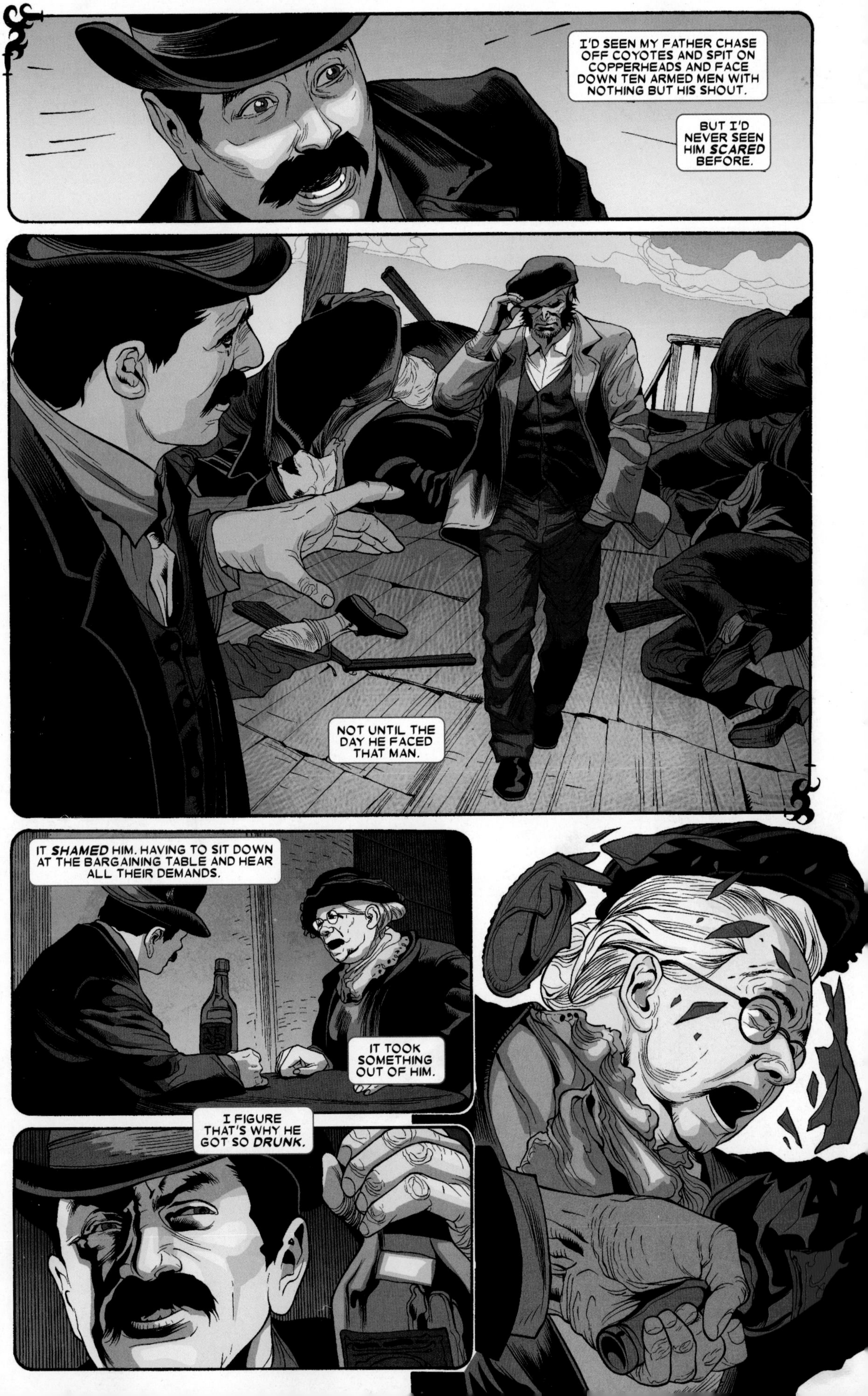
I'D SEEN MY FATHER CHASE OFF COYOTES AND SPIT ON COPPERHEADS AND FACE DOWN TEN ARMED MEN WITH NOTHING BUT HIS SHOUT.
BUT I'D NEVER SEEN HIM SCARED BEFORE.
NOT UNTIL THE DAY HE FACED THAT MAN.
IT SHAMED HIM. HAVING TO SIT DOWN AT THE BARGAINING TABLE AND HEAR ALL THEIR DEMANDS.
IT TOOK SOMETHING OUT OF HIM.
I FIGURE THAT'S WHY HE GOT SO DRUNK.

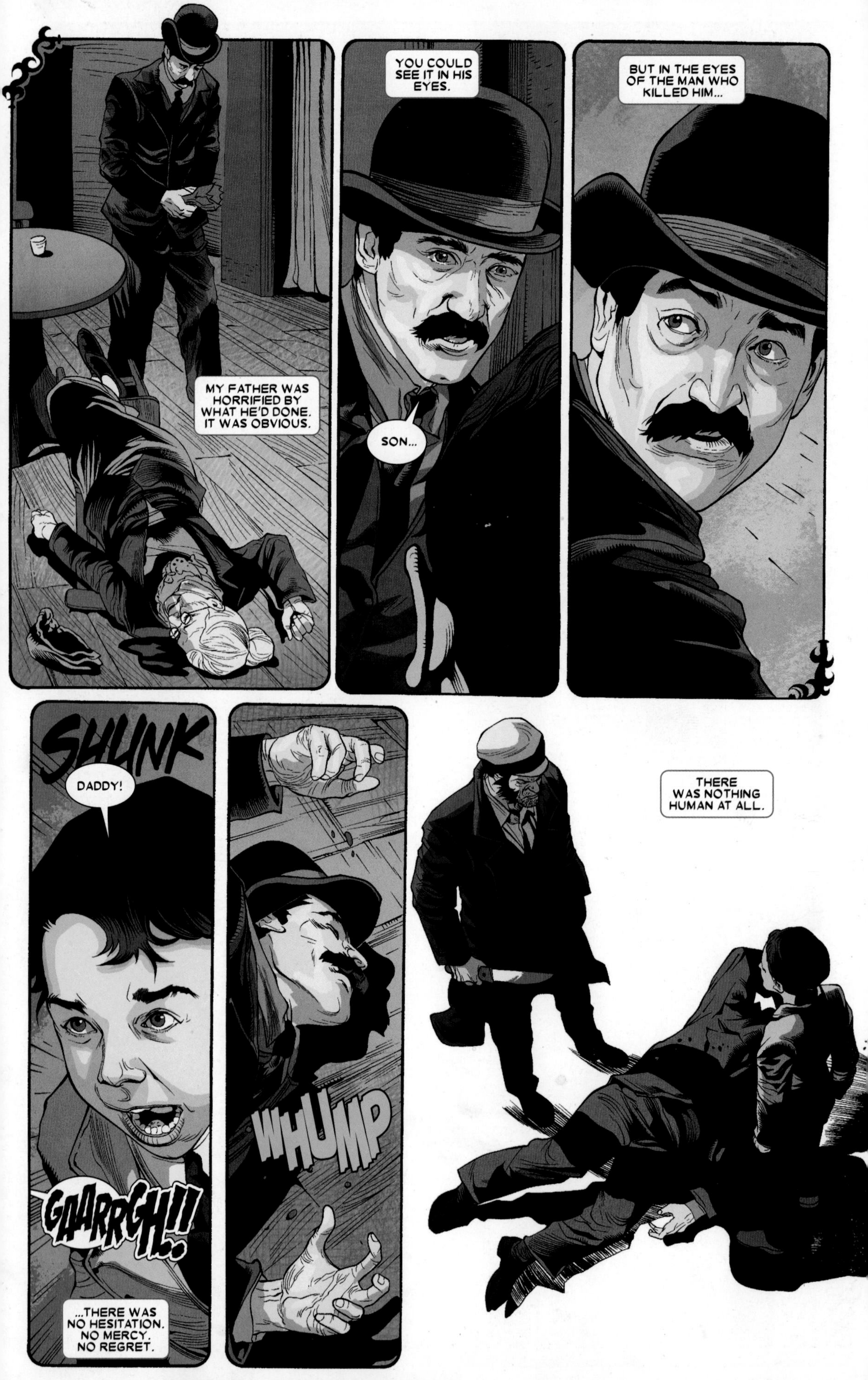
MY FATHER WAS HORRIFIED BY WHAT HE'D DONE. IT WAS OBVIOUS.
YOU COULD SEE IT IN HIS EYES.
SON...
BUT IN THE EYES OF THE MAN WHO KILLED HIM...
SHUNK
DADDY!
GAARRGH!!
...THERE WAS NO HESITATION. NO MERCY. NO REGRET.
WHUMP
THERE WAS NOTHING HUMAN AT ALL.

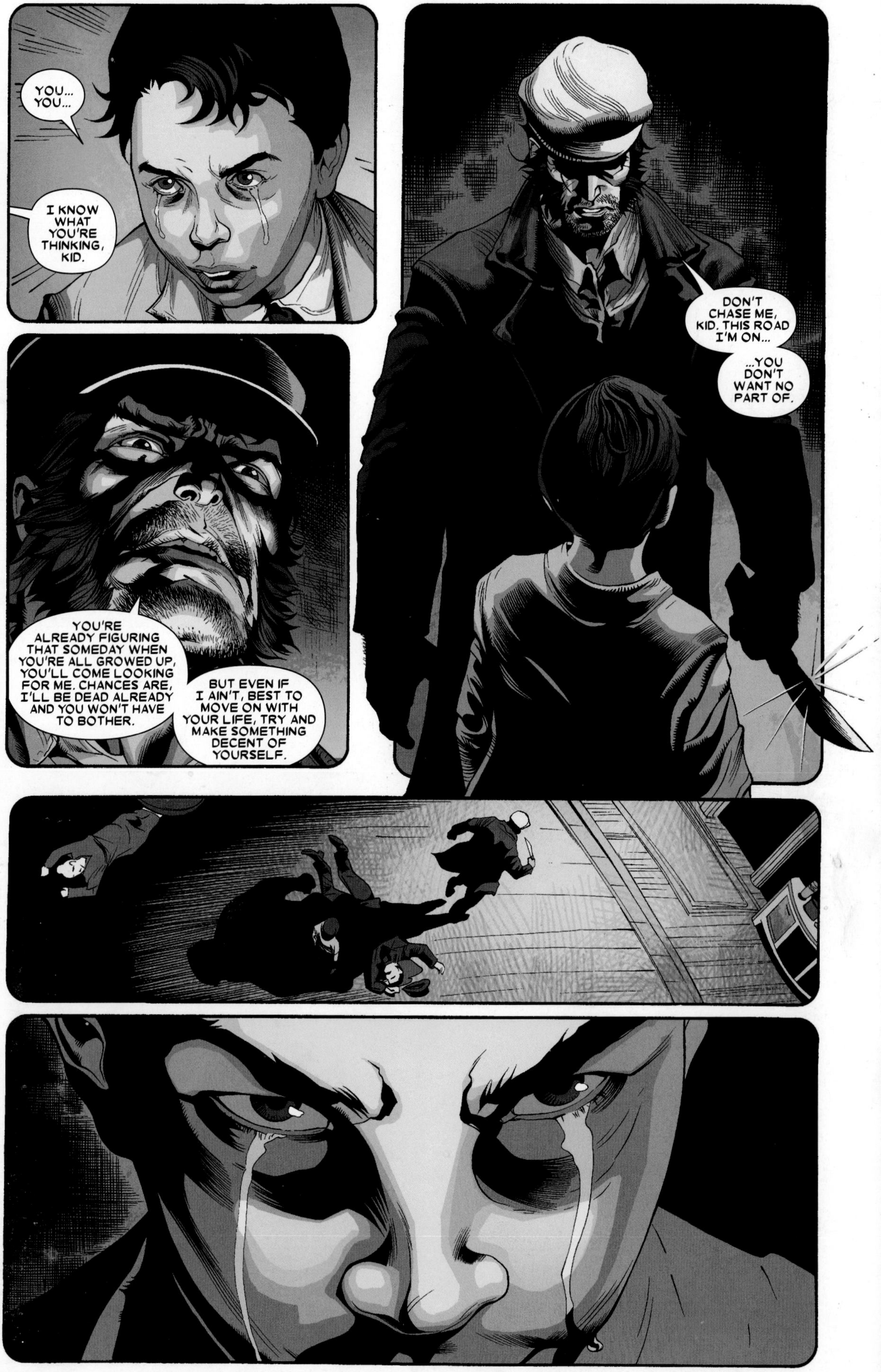
YOU... YOU...
I KNOW WHAT YOU'RE THINKING, KID.
DON'T CHASE ME, KID. THIS ROAD I'M ON...
...YOU DON'T WANT NO PART OF.
YOU'RE ALREADY FIGURING THAT SOMEDAY WHEN YOU'RE ALL GROWED UP, YOU'LL COME LOOKING FOR ME. CHANCES ARE, I'LL BE DEAD ALREADY AND YOU WON'T HAVE TO BOTHER.
BUT EVEN IF I AIN'T, BEST TO MOVE ON WITH YOUR LIFE, TRY AND MAKE SOMETHING DECENT OF YOURSELF.

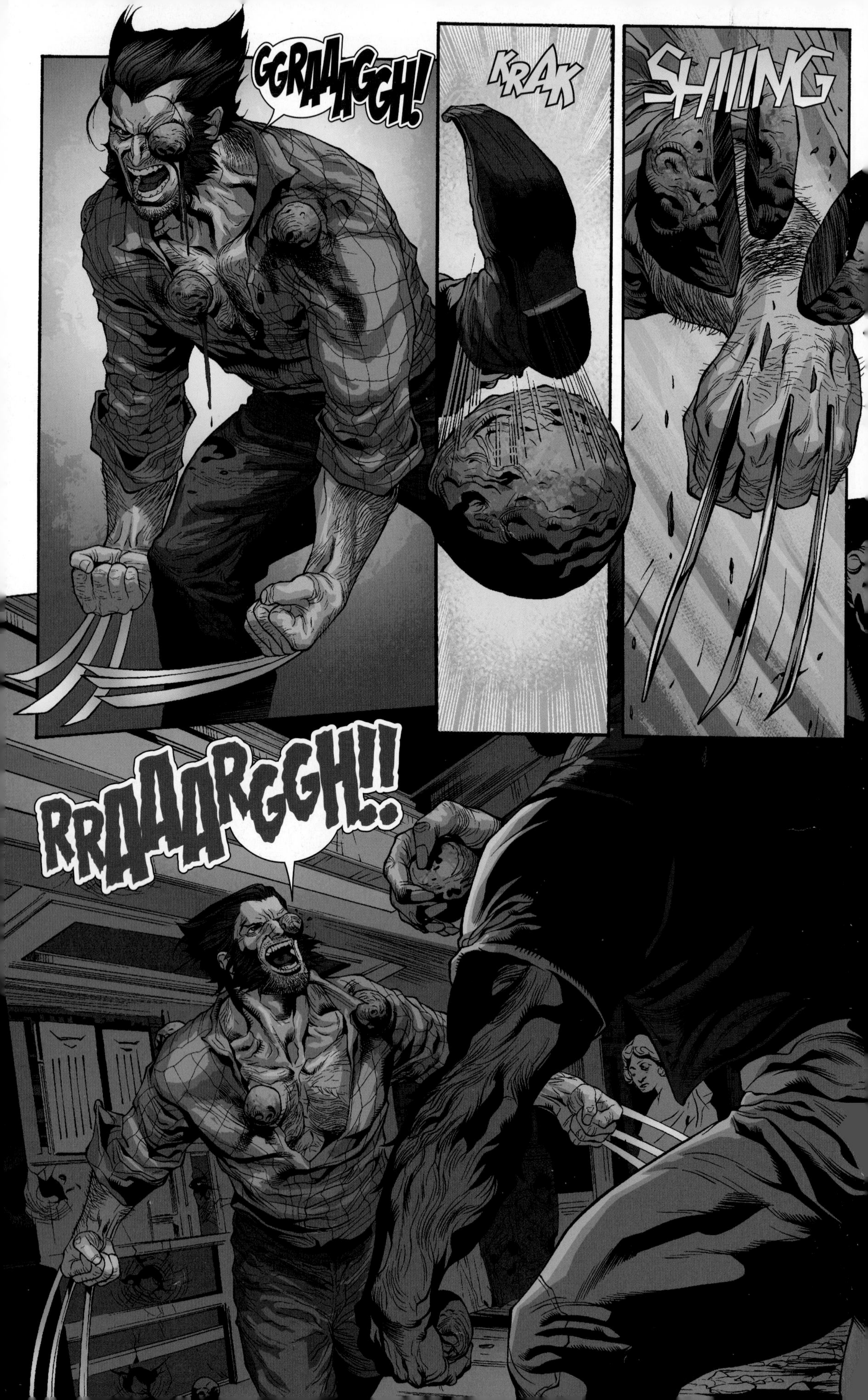
GGRAAAAGGH!
KRAK
SHIIING
RRAAARGGH!!

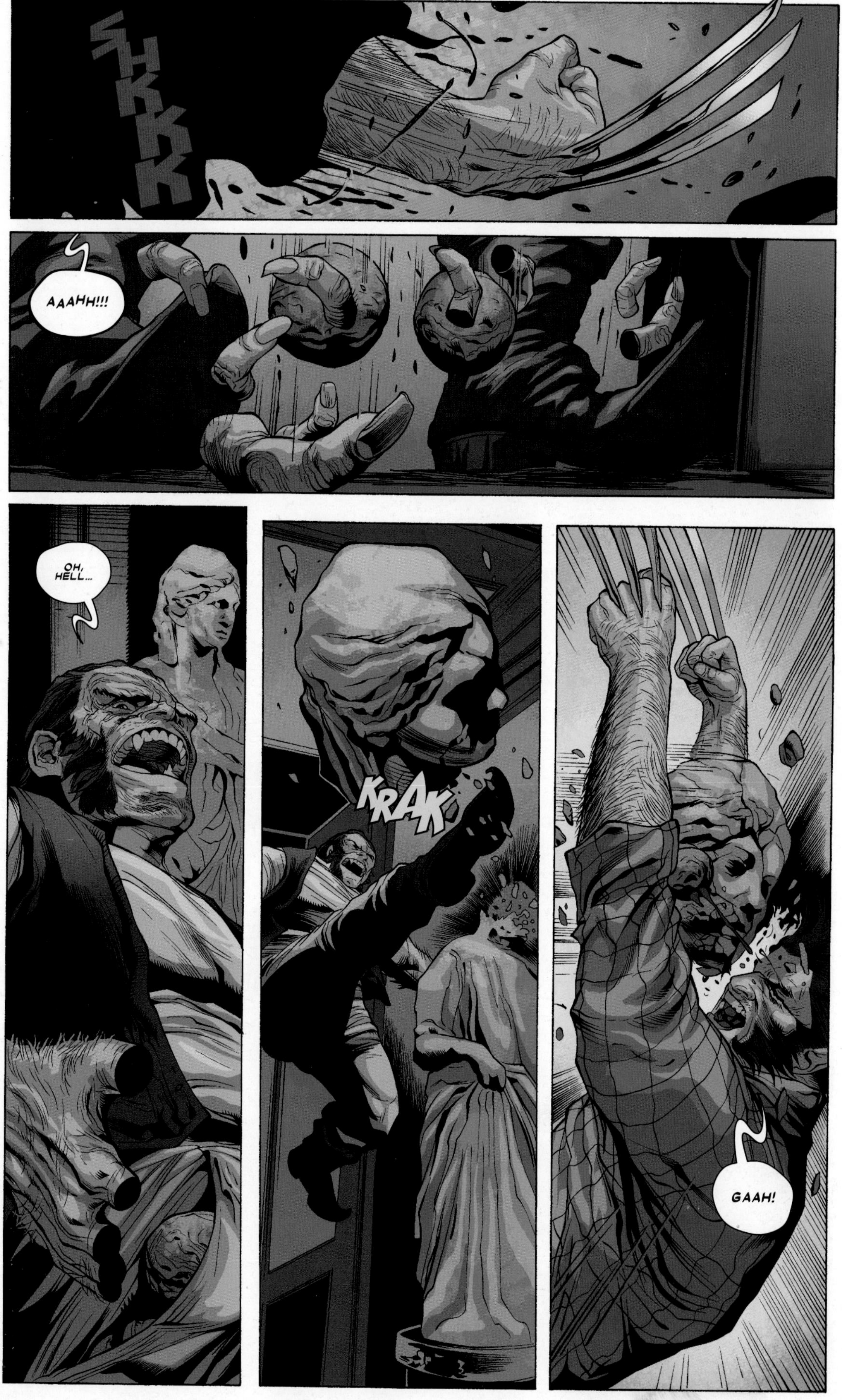
SHKKK
AAAHH!!!
OH, HELL...
KRAK
GAAH!

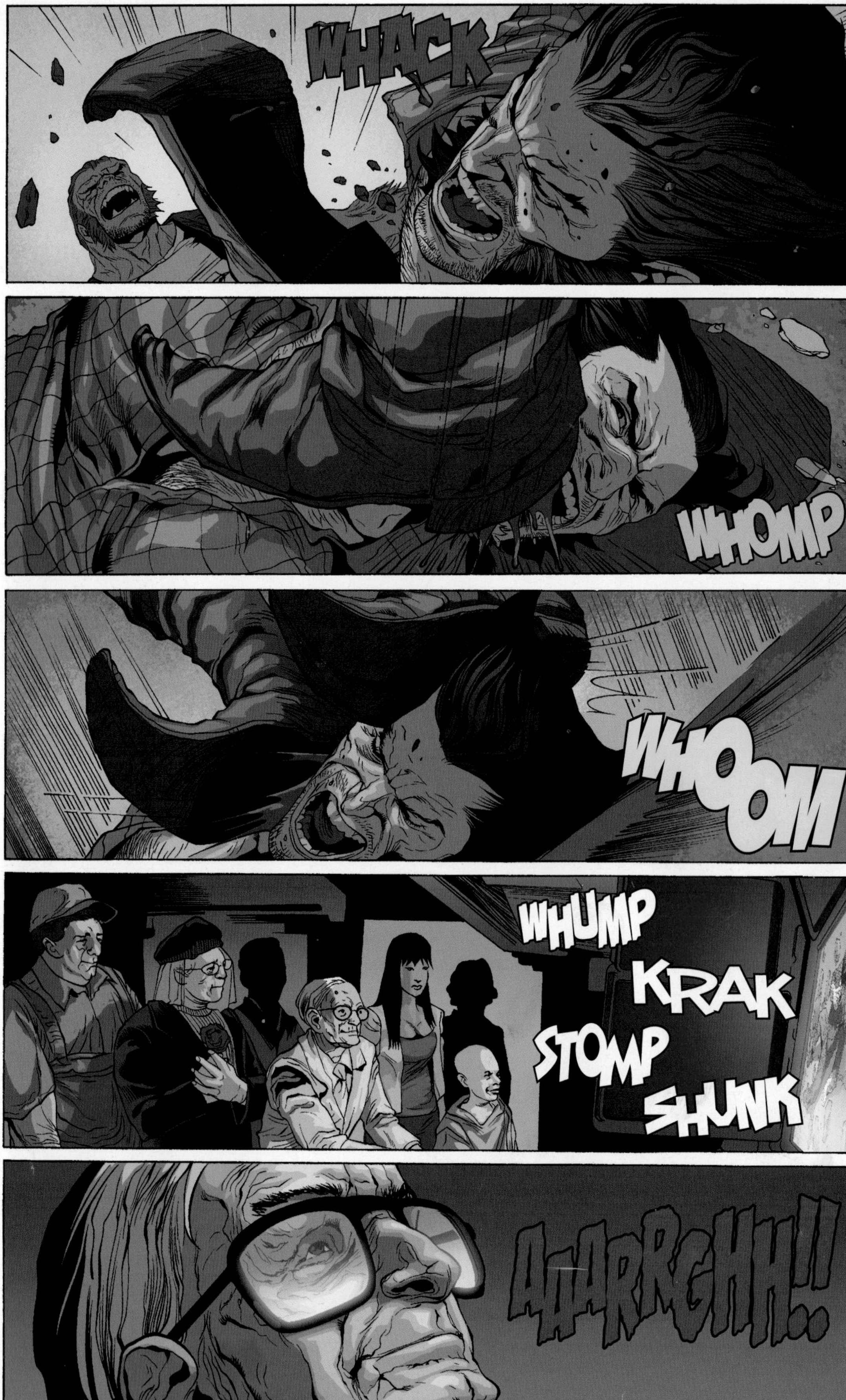
WHACK
WHOMP
WHOOOM
WHUMP
KRAK
STOMP
SHUNK
AAARRGHH!!

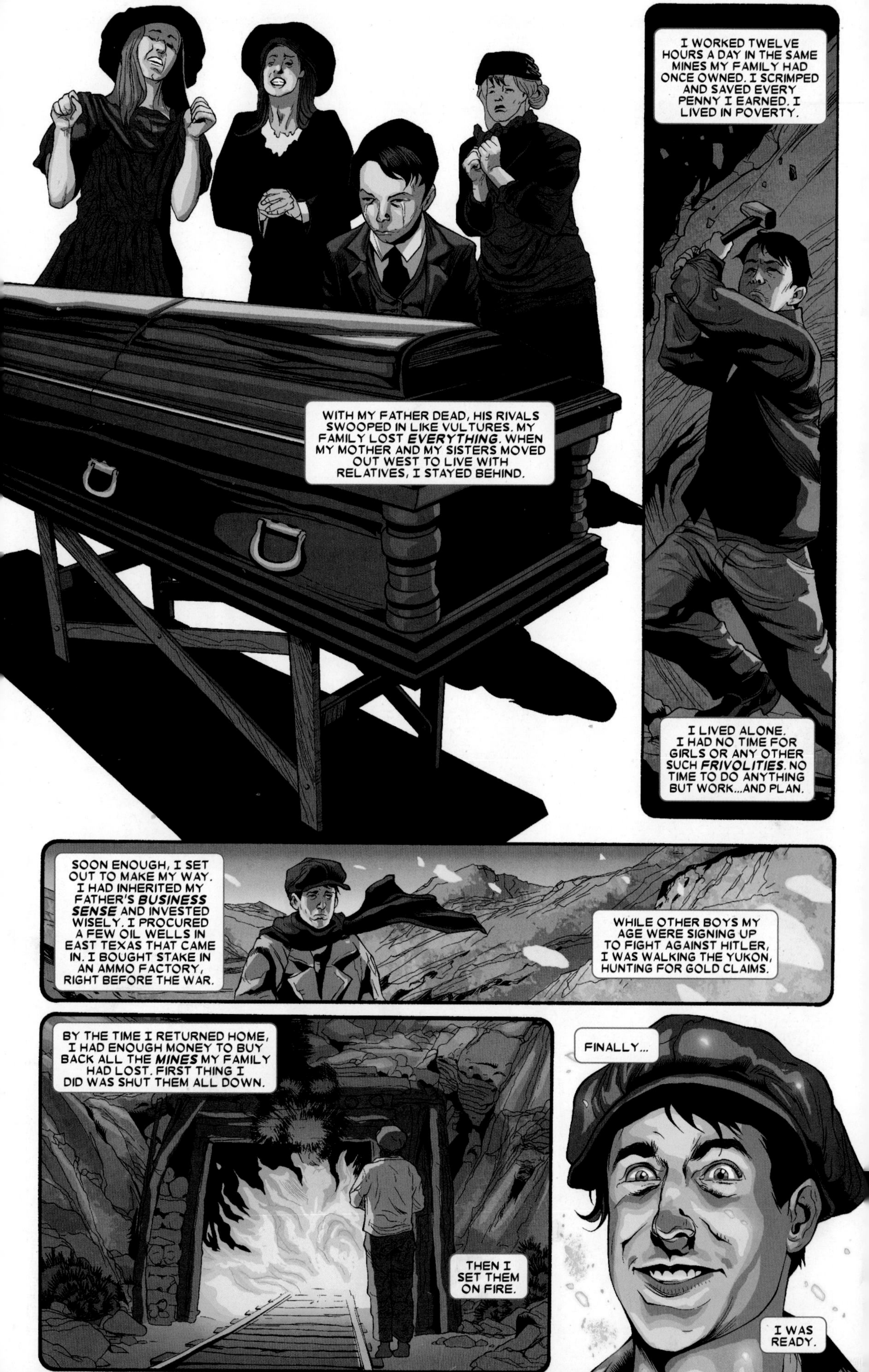
WITH MY FATHER DEAD, HIS RIVALS SWOOPED IN LIKE VULTURES. MY FAMILY LOST *EVERYTHING*. WHEN MY MOTHER AND MY SISTERS MOVED OUT WEST TO LIVE WITH RELATIVES, I STAYED BEHIND.
I WORKED TWELVE HOURS A DAY IN THE SAME MINES MY FAMILY HAD ONCE OWNED. I SCRIMPED AND SAVED EVERY PENNY I EARNED. I LIVED IN POVERTY.
I LIVED ALONE. I HAD NO TIME FOR GIRLS OR ANY OTHER SUCH *FRIVOLITIES*. NO TIME TO DO ANYTHING BUT WORK...AND PLAN.
SOON ENOUGH, I SET OUT TO MAKE MY WAY. I HAD INHERITED MY FATHER'S *BUSINESS SENSE* AND INVESTED WISELY. I PROCURED A FEW OIL WELLS IN EAST TEXAS THAT CAME IN. I BOUGHT STAKE IN AN AMMO FACTORY, RIGHT BEFORE THE WAR.
WHILE OTHER BOYS MY AGE WERE SIGNING UP TO FIGHT AGAINST HITLER, I WAS WALKING THE YUKON, HUNTING FOR GOLD CLAIMS.
BY THE TIME I RETURNED HOME, I HAD ENOUGH MONEY TO BUY BACK ALL THE *MINES* MY FAMILY HAD LOST. FIRST THING I DID WAS SHUT THEM ALL DOWN.
THEN I SET THEM ON FIRE.
FINALLY...
I WAS READY.

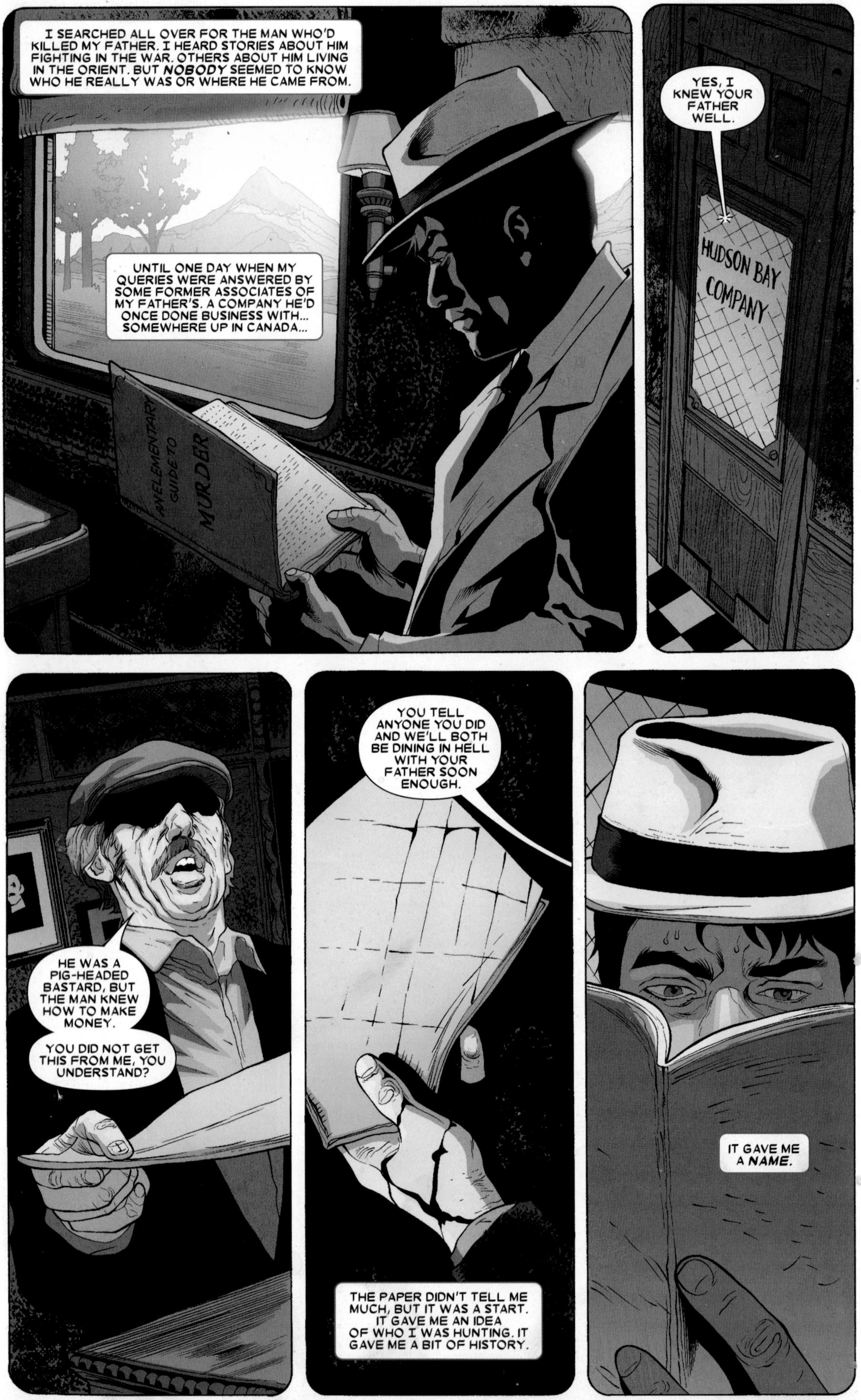
I SEARCHED ALL OVER FOR THE MAN WHO'D KILLED MY FATHER. I HEARD STORIES ABOUT HIM FIGHTING IN THE WAR. OTHERS ABOUT HIM LIVING IN THE ORIENT. BUT NOBODY SEEMED TO KNOW WHO HE REALLY WAS OR WHERE HE CAME FROM.
UNTIL ONE DAY WHEN MY QUERIES WERE ANSWERED BY SOME FORMER ASSOCIATES OF MY FATHER'S. A COMPANY HE'D ONCE DONE BUSINESS WITH... SOMEWHERE UP IN CANADA...
AN ELEMENTARY GUIDE TO MURDER
YES, I KNEW YOUR FATHER WELL.
HUDSON BAY COMPANY
HE WAS A PIG-HEADED BASTARD, BUT THE MAN KNEW HOW TO MAKE MONEY.
YOU DID NOT GET THIS FROM ME, YOU UNDERSTAND?
YOU TELL ANYONE YOU DID AND WE'LL BOTH BE DINING IN HELL WITH YOUR FATHER SOON ENOUGH.
THE PAPER DIDN'T TELL ME MUCH, BUT IT WAS A START. IT GAVE ME AN IDEA OF WHO I WAS HUNTING. IT GAVE ME A BIT OF HISTORY.
IT GAVE ME A NAME.

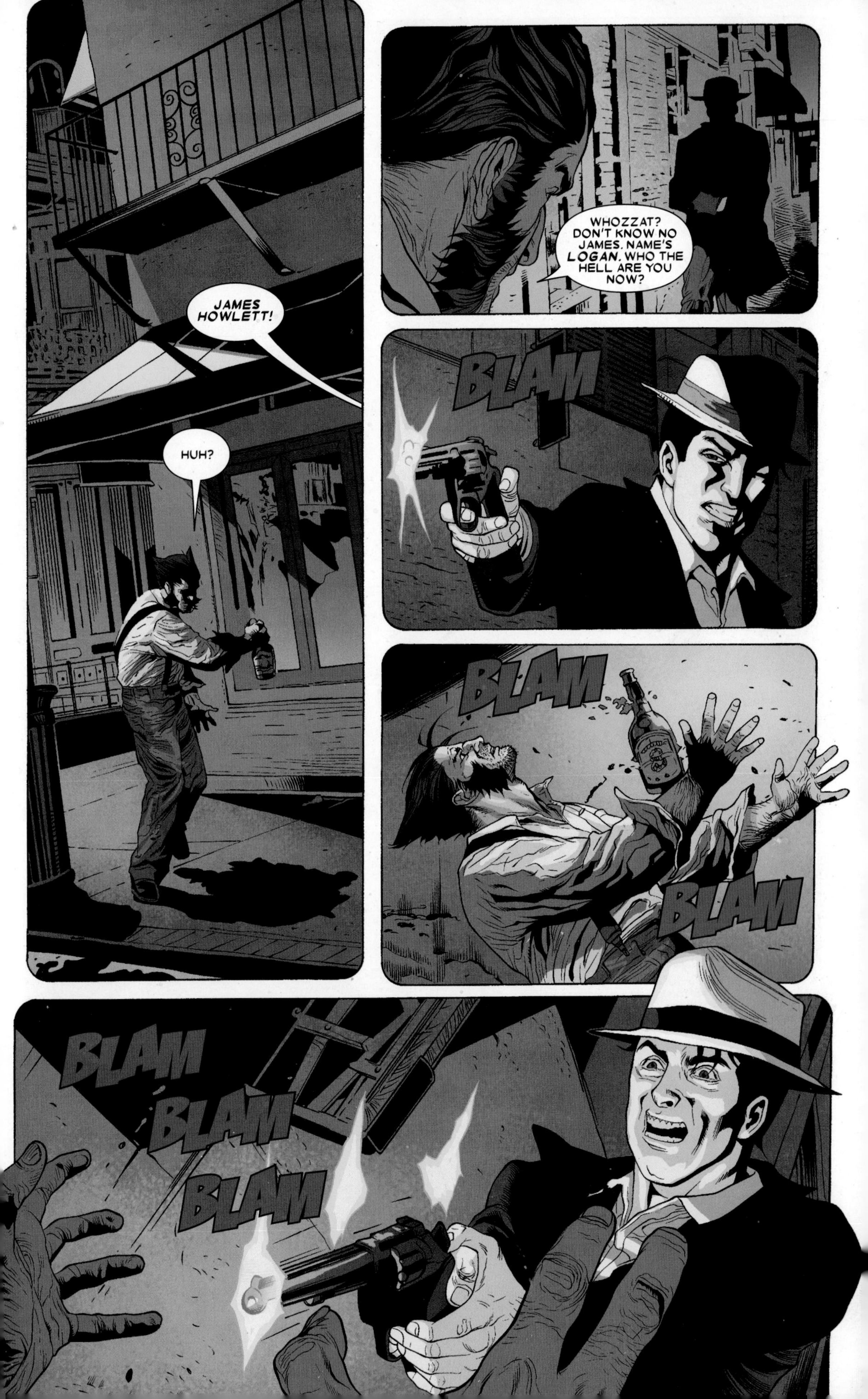
JAMES HOWLETT!
HUH?
WHOZZAT? DON'T KNOW NO JAMES. NAME'S LOGAN. WHO THE HELL ARE YOU NOW?
BLAM
BLAM
BLAM
BLAM
BLAM
BLAM

PTEWW

I DID IT, FATHER. YOU ARE AVENGED.

JUST LIKE THAT, I FELT A TREMENDOUS BURDEN LIFTED OFF MY SHOULDERS.

MY DEBT HAD BEEN PAID. NOW, AT LAST, I WAS FREE TO GO OUT AND BECOME MY *OWN MAN*. TO MARRY AND HAVE CHILDREN. TO RESTORE THE FAMILY NAME.

I FELT A SUDDEN RUSH OF EXCITEMENT. I FELT THE BEGINNINGS OF JOY. FOR THE FIRST TIME EVER, I FELT REAL HOPE. AND THEN...

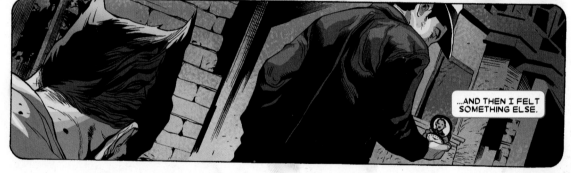

...AND THEN I FELT SOMETHING ELSE.

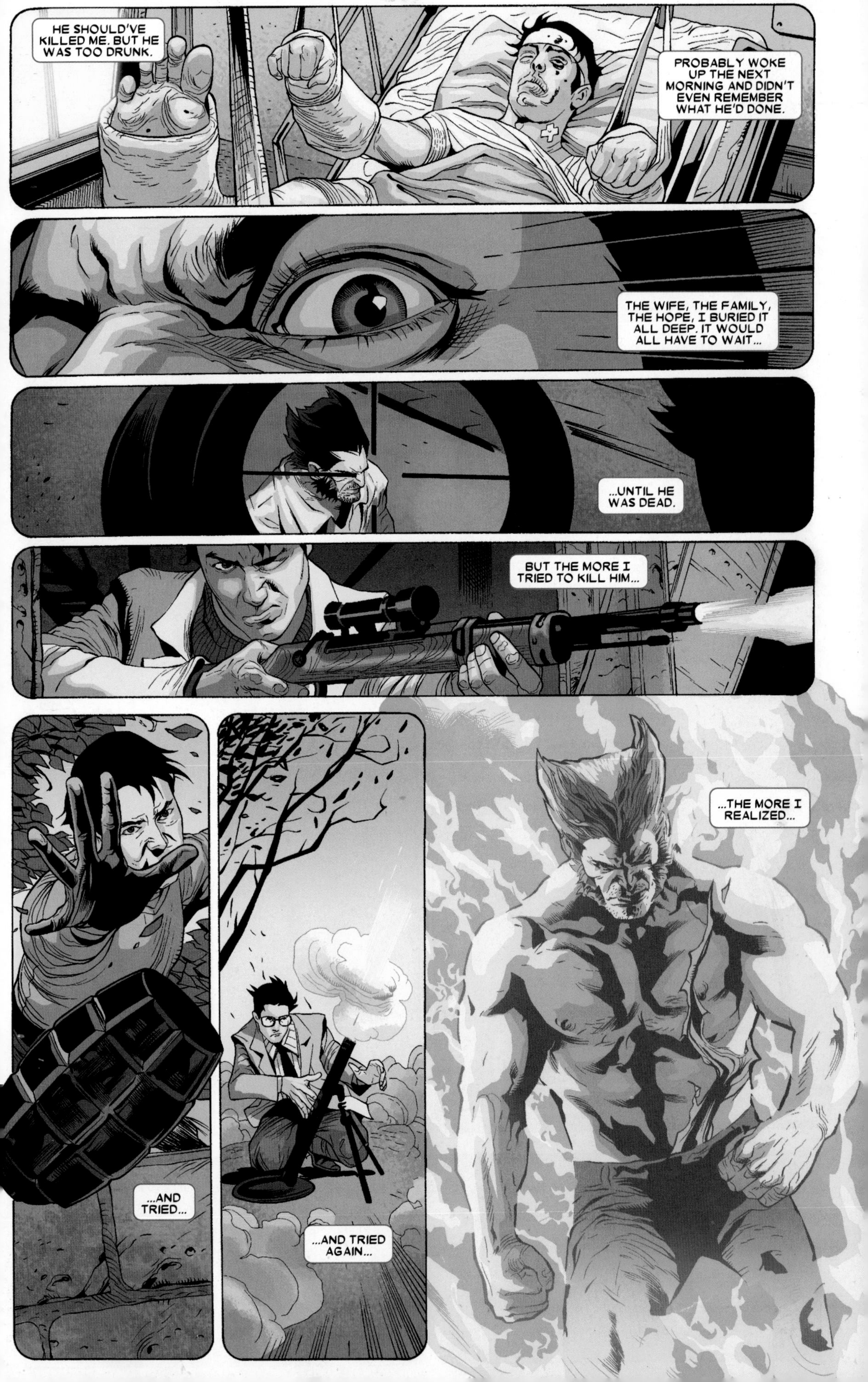
HE SHOULD'VE KILLED ME. BUT HE WAS TOO DRUNK.
PROBABLY WOKE UP THE NEXT MORNING AND DIDN'T EVEN REMEMBER WHAT HE'D DONE.
THE WIFE, THE FAMILY, THE HOPE, I BURIED IT ALL DEEP. IT WOULD ALL HAVE TO WAIT...
...UNTIL HE WAS DEAD.
BUT THE MORE I TRIED TO KILL HIM...
...AND TRIED...
...AND TRIED AGAIN...
...THE MORE I REALIZED...

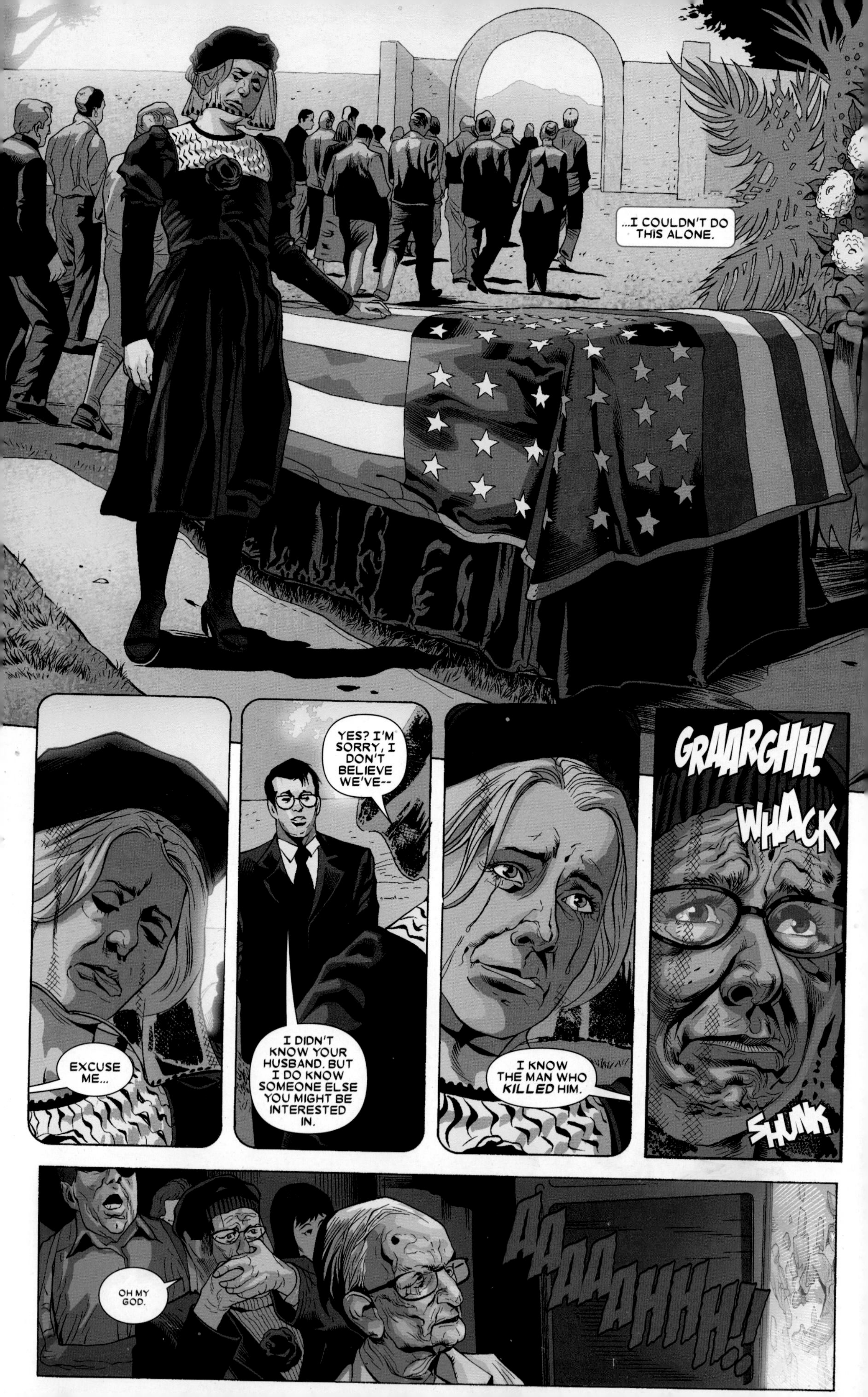

...I COULDN'T DO THIS ALONE.
EXCUSE ME...
YES? I'M SORRY, I DON'T BELIEVE WE'VE--
I DIDN'T KNOW YOUR HUSBAND, BUT I DO KNOW SOMEONE ELSE YOU MIGHT BE INTERESTED IN.
I KNOW THE MAN WHO *KILLED* HIM.
GRAARGHH!
WHACK
SHUNK
OH MY GOD.
AAAAAAHHHH!!

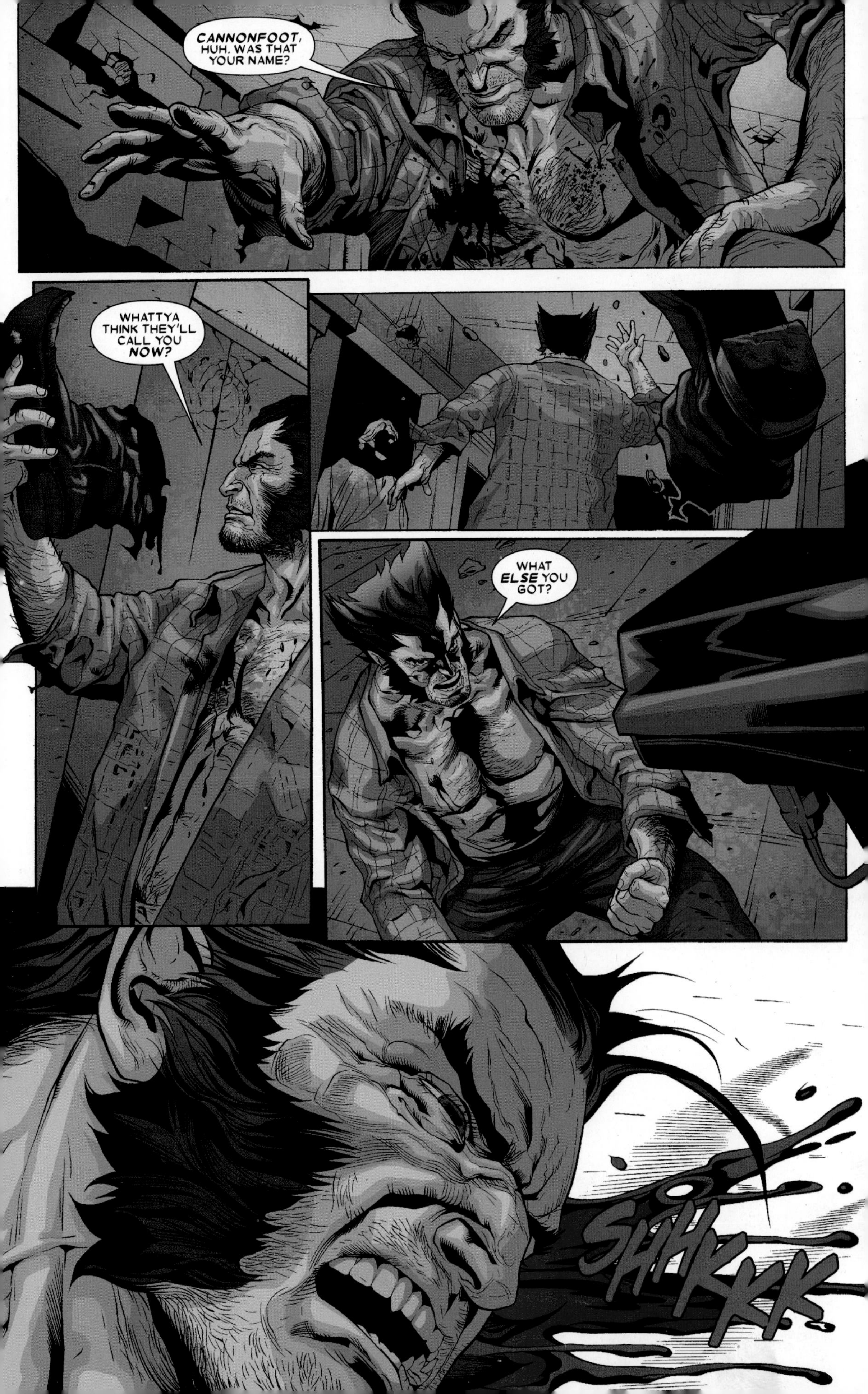
CANNONFOOT, HUH. WAS THAT YOUR NAME?
WHATTYA THINK THEY'LL CALL YOU NOW?
WHAT ELSE YOU GOT?
SHHKKK

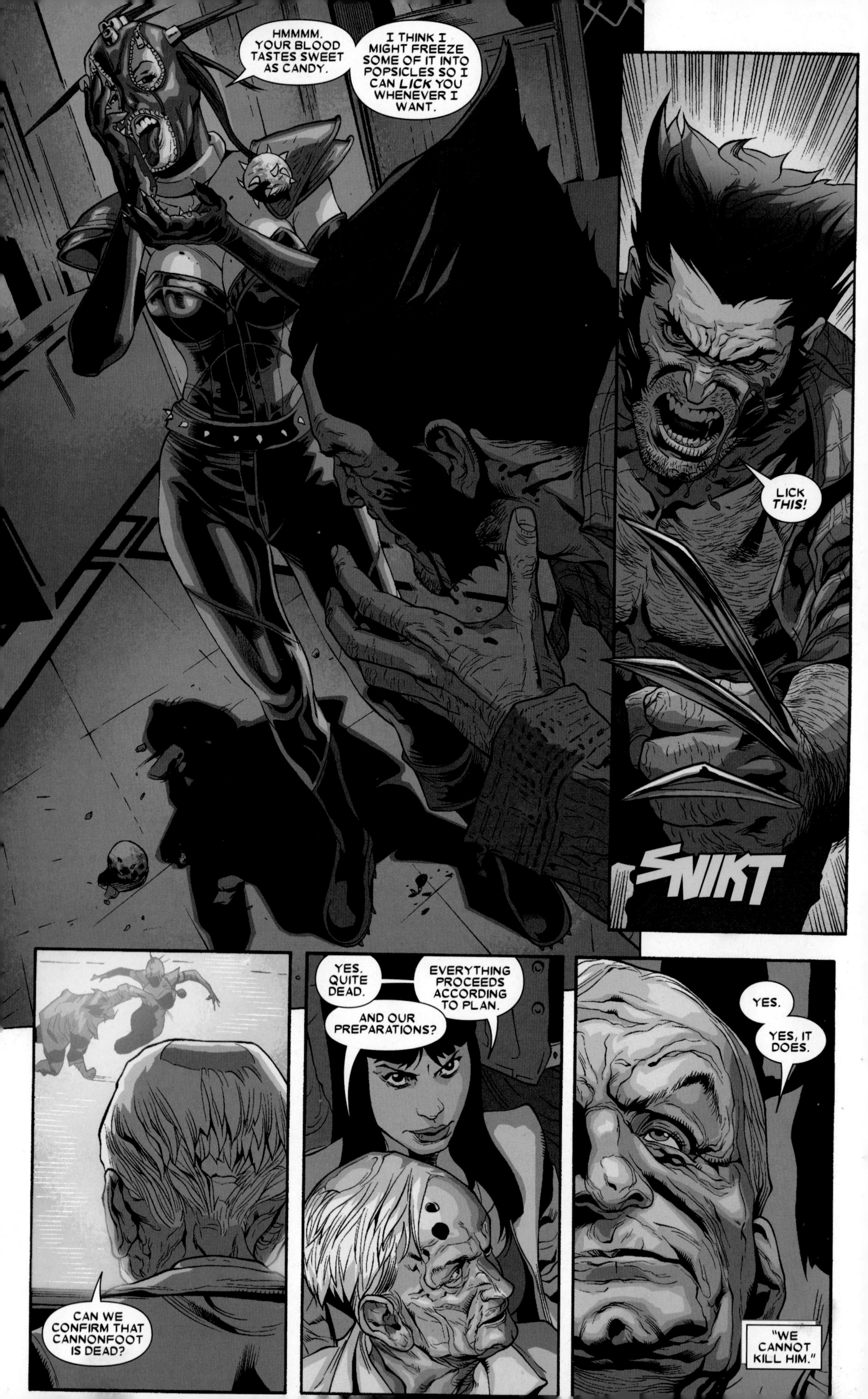
HMMMM. YOUR BLOOD TASTES SWEET AS CANDY.
I THINK I MIGHT FREEZE SOME OF IT INTO POPSICLES SO I CAN LICK YOU WHENEVER I WANT.
LICK THIS!
SNIKT
CAN WE CONFIRM THAT CANNONFOOT IS DEAD?
YES. QUITE DEAD.
AND OUR PREPARATIONS?
EVERYTHING PROCEEDS ACCORDING TO PLAN.
YES.
YES, IT DOES.
"WE CANNOT KILL HIM."

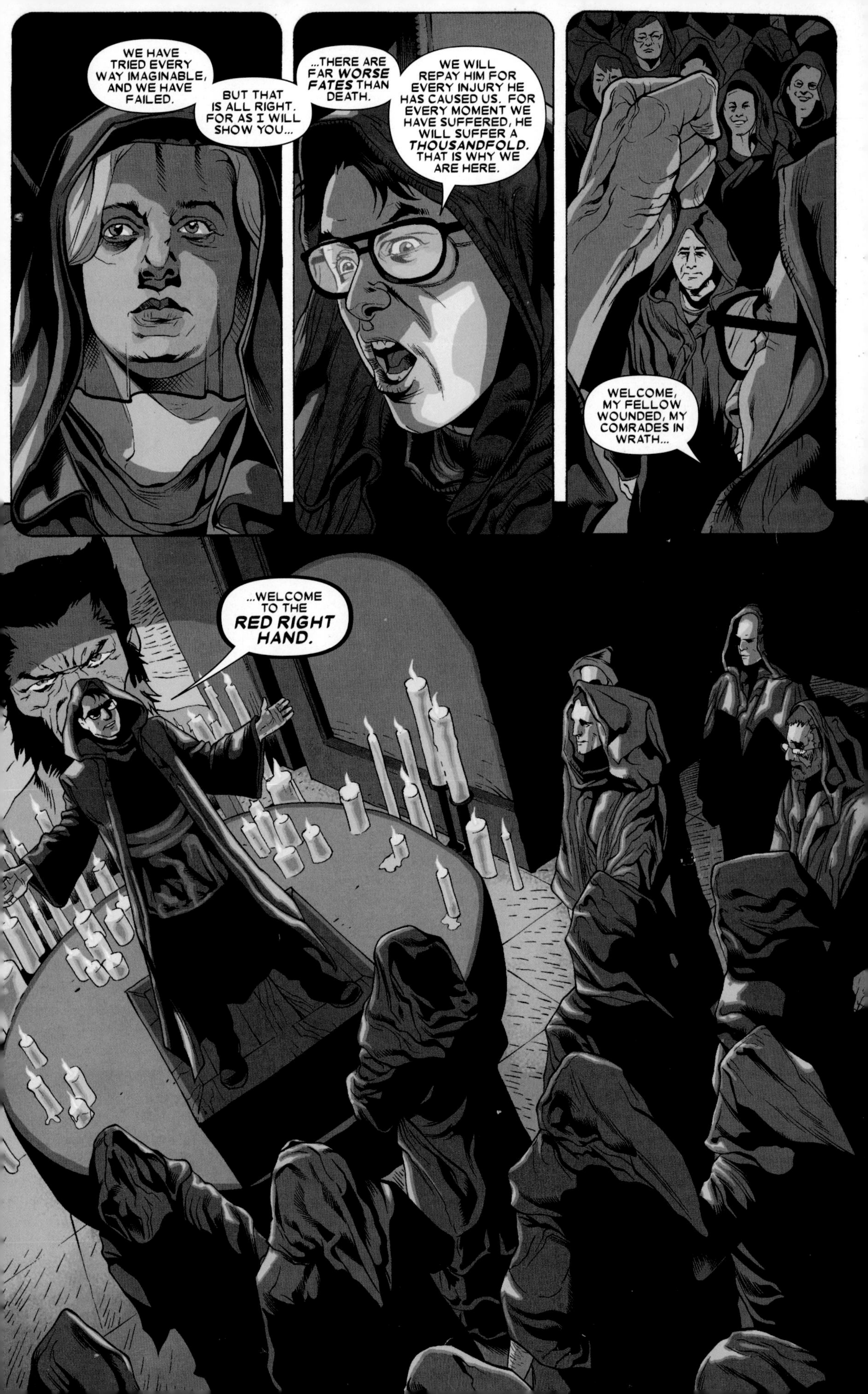
WE HAVE TRIED EVERY WAY IMAGINABLE, AND WE HAVE FAILED.
BUT THAT IS ALL RIGHT. FOR AS I WILL SHOW YOU...
...THERE ARE FAR WORSE FATES THAN DEATH.
WE WILL REPAY HIM FOR EVERY INJURY HE HAS CAUSED US. FOR EVERY MOMENT WE HAVE SUFFERED, HE WILL SUFFER A THOUSANDFOLD. THAT IS WHY WE ARE HERE.
WELCOME, MY FELLOW WOUNDED, MY COMRADES IN WRATH...
...WELCOME TO THE RED RIGHT HAND.

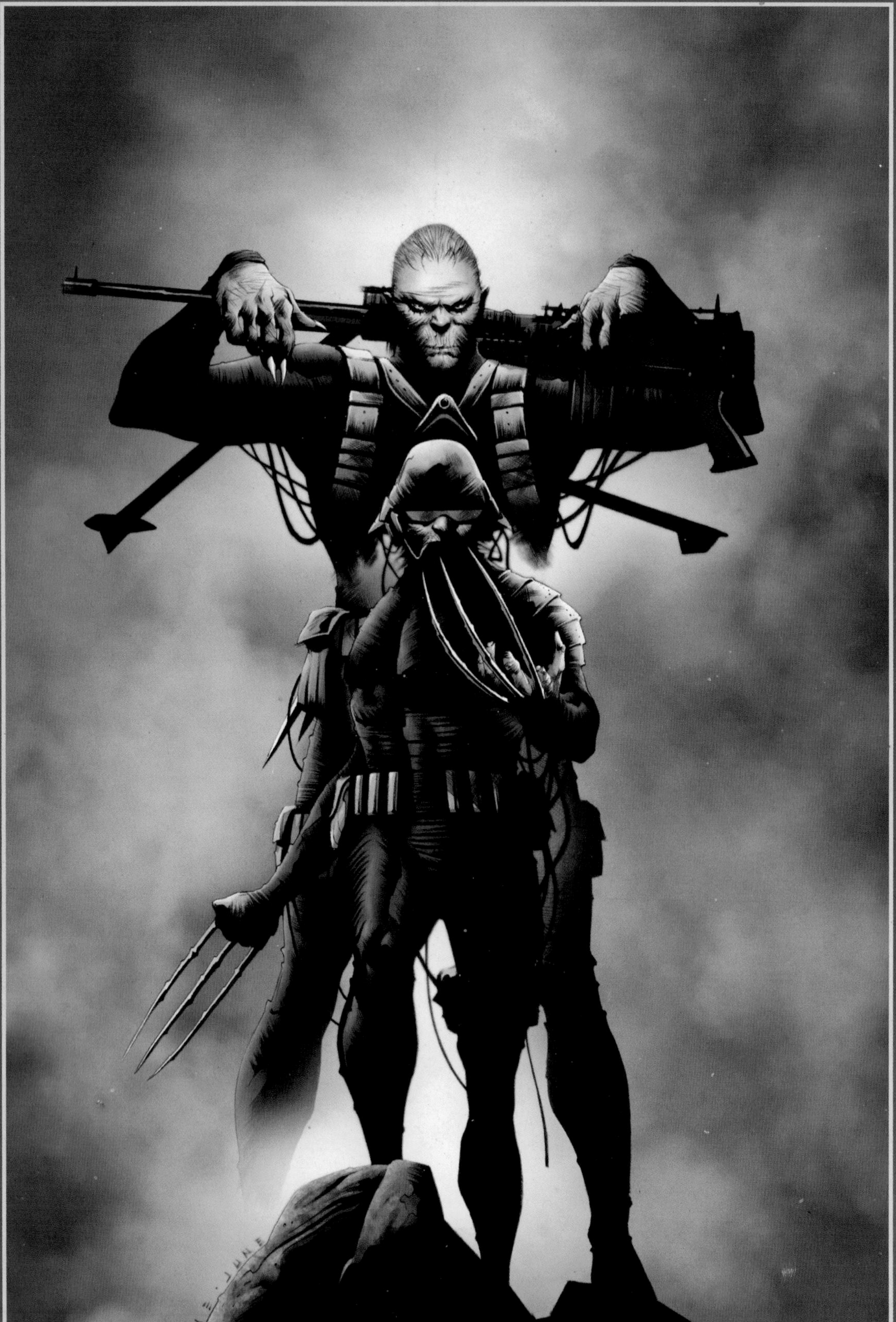

# 11

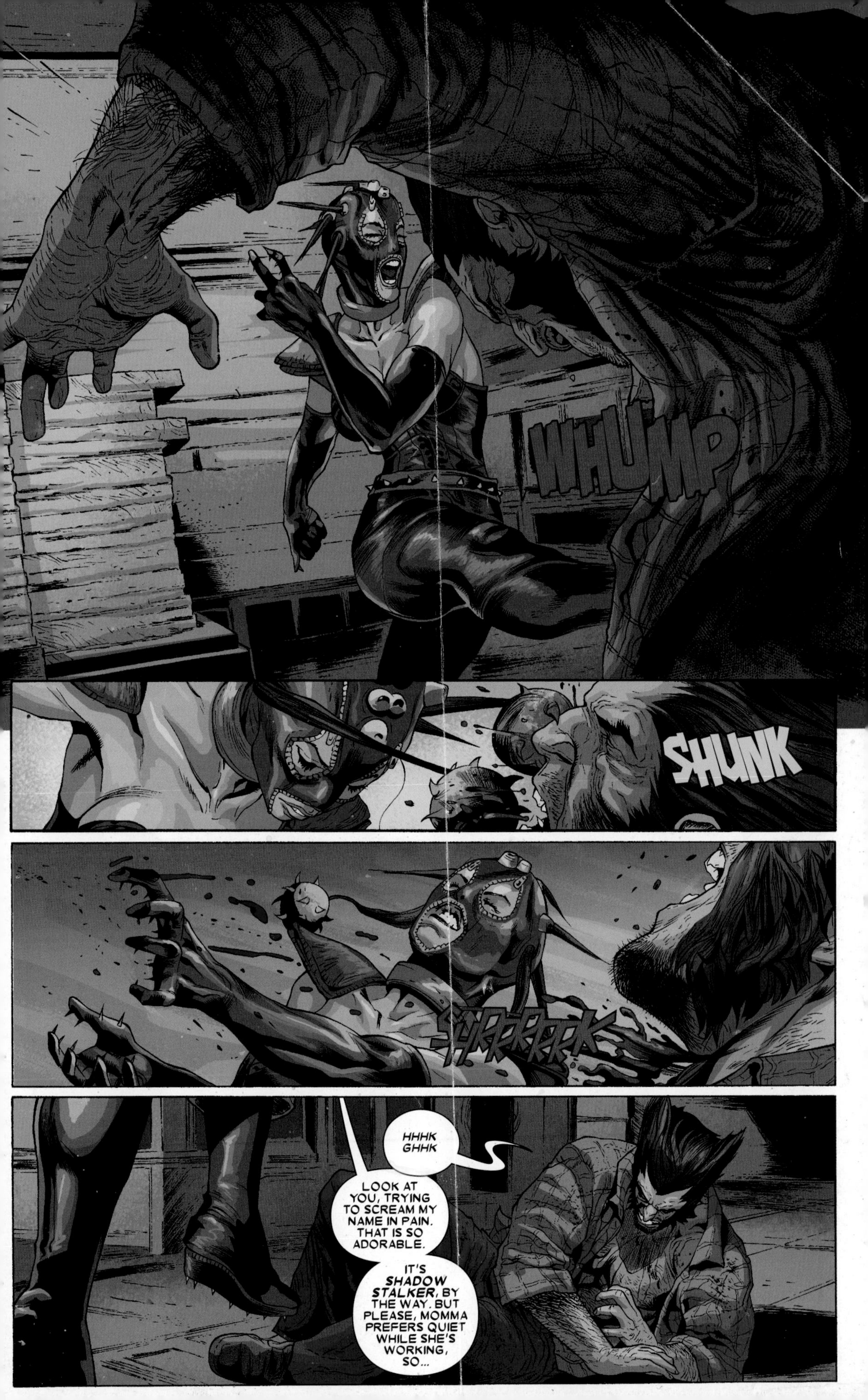
WHUMP
SHUNK
SHRRRRRK
HHHK GHHK
LOOK AT YOU, TRYING TO SCREAM MY NAME IN PAIN. THAT IS SO ADORABLE.
IT'S SHADOW STALKER, BY THE WAY. BUT PLEASE, MOMMA PREFERS QUIET WHILE SHE'S WORKING, SO...

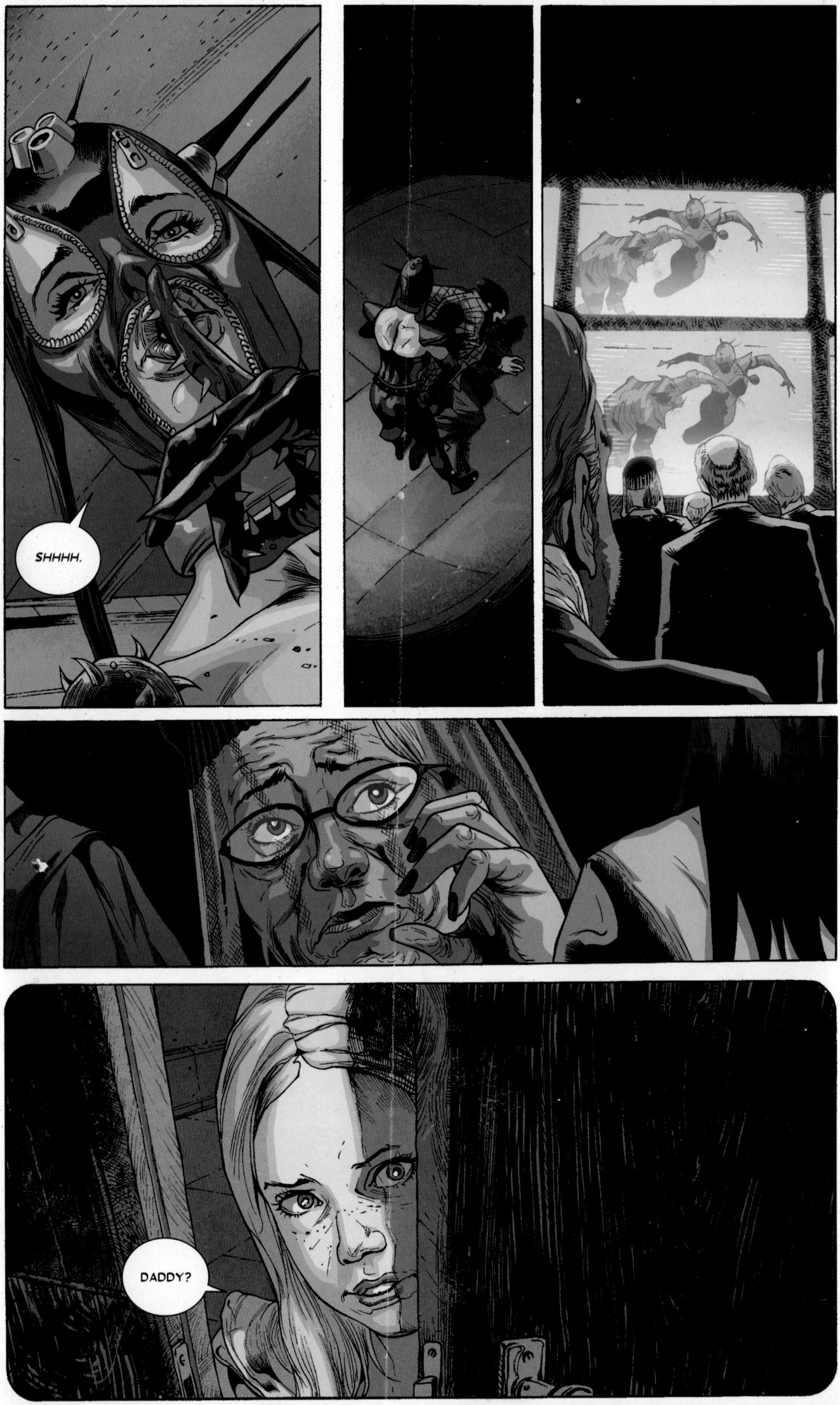
SHHHH.
DADDY?

AFTER MY MOTHER DIED, I WAS ALL MY FATHER HAD. WELL, ME...

DADDY, I'M HUNGRY.

...AND HIS WORK.

DADDY?

MY FATHER WAS A MAN OF GREAT IMPORTANCE. A HIGH-RANKING OFFICIAL WITH THE O.S.S. DURING THE WAR. HE SAID HE KNEW THINGS THAT FEW OTHER MEN IN THE WORLD WOULD EVER KNOW.

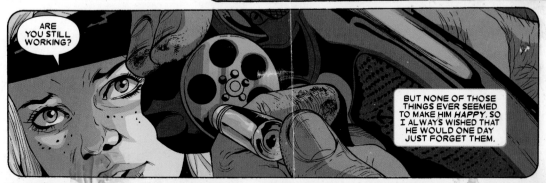

ARE YOU STILL WORKING?

BUT NONE OF THOSE THINGS EVER SEEMED TO MAKE HIM HAPPY. SO I ALWAYS WISHED THAT HE WOULD ONE DAY JUST FORGET THEM.

TELL YOU IN A MINUTE, SWEETHEART.

SOMETIMES HE DID, TOO.

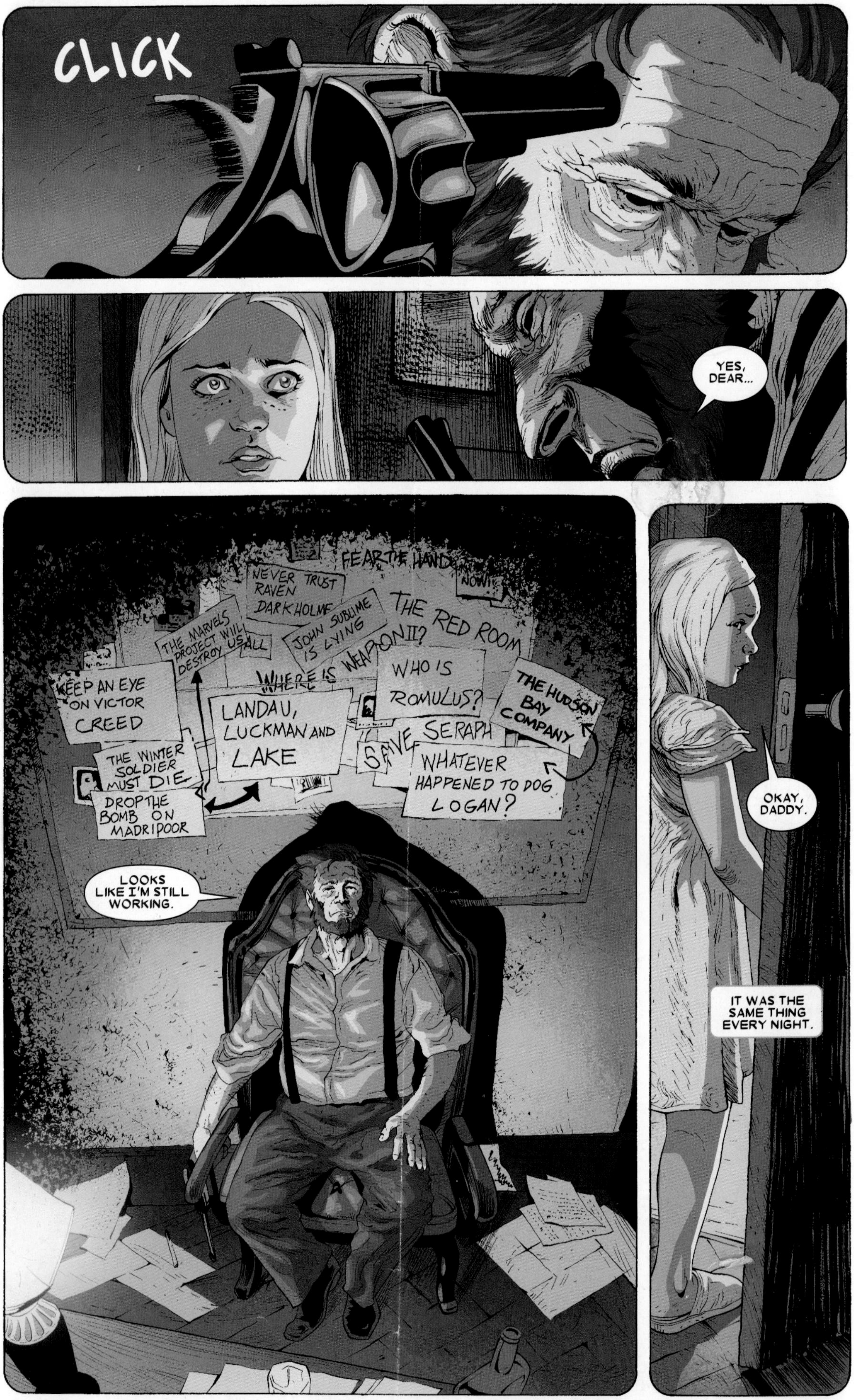
CLICK
YES, DEAR...
FEAR THE HAND
NEVER TRUST RAVEN DARKHOLME
THE RED ROOM
JOHN SUBLIME IS LYING
THE MARVELS PROJECT WILL DESTROY US ALL
WHERE IS WEAPON II?
WHO IS ROMULUS?
THE HUDSON BAY COMPANY
KEEP AN EYE ON VICTOR CREED
LANDAU, LUCKMAN AND LAKE
SAVE SERAPH
THE WINTER SOLDIER MUST DIE
WHATEVER HAPPENED TO DOG LOGAN?
DROP THE BOMB ON MADRIPOOR
LOOKS LIKE I'M STILL WORKING.
OKAY, DADDY.
IT WAS THE SAME THING EVERY NIGHT.

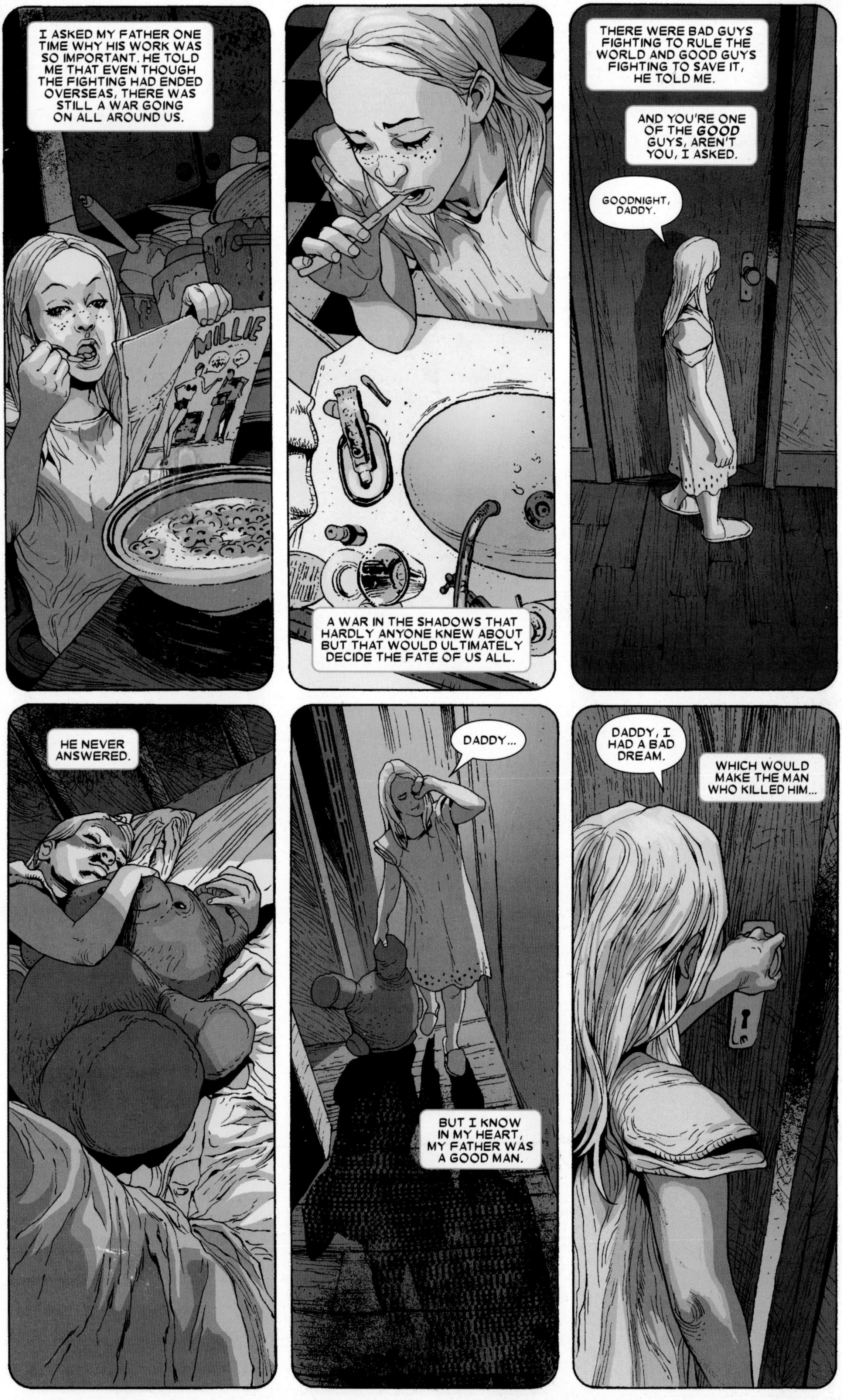
I ASKED MY FATHER ONE TIME WHY HIS WORK WAS SO IMPORTANT. HE TOLD ME THAT EVEN THOUGH THE FIGHTING HAD ENDED OVERSEAS, THERE WAS STILL A WAR GOING ON ALL AROUND US.
MILLIE
A WAR IN THE SHADOWS THAT HARDLY ANYONE KNEW ABOUT BUT THAT WOULD ULTIMATELY DECIDE THE FATE OF US ALL.
THERE WERE BAD GUYS FIGHTING TO RULE THE WORLD AND GOOD GUYS FIGHTING TO SAVE IT, HE TOLD ME.
AND YOU'RE ONE OF THE *GOOD* GUYS, AREN'T YOU, I ASKED.
GOODNIGHT, DADDY.
HE NEVER ANSWERED.
DADDY...
BUT I KNOW IN MY HEART, MY FATHER WAS A GOOD MAN.
DADDY, I HAD A BAD DREAM.
WHICH WOULD MAKE THE MAN WHO KILLED HIM...

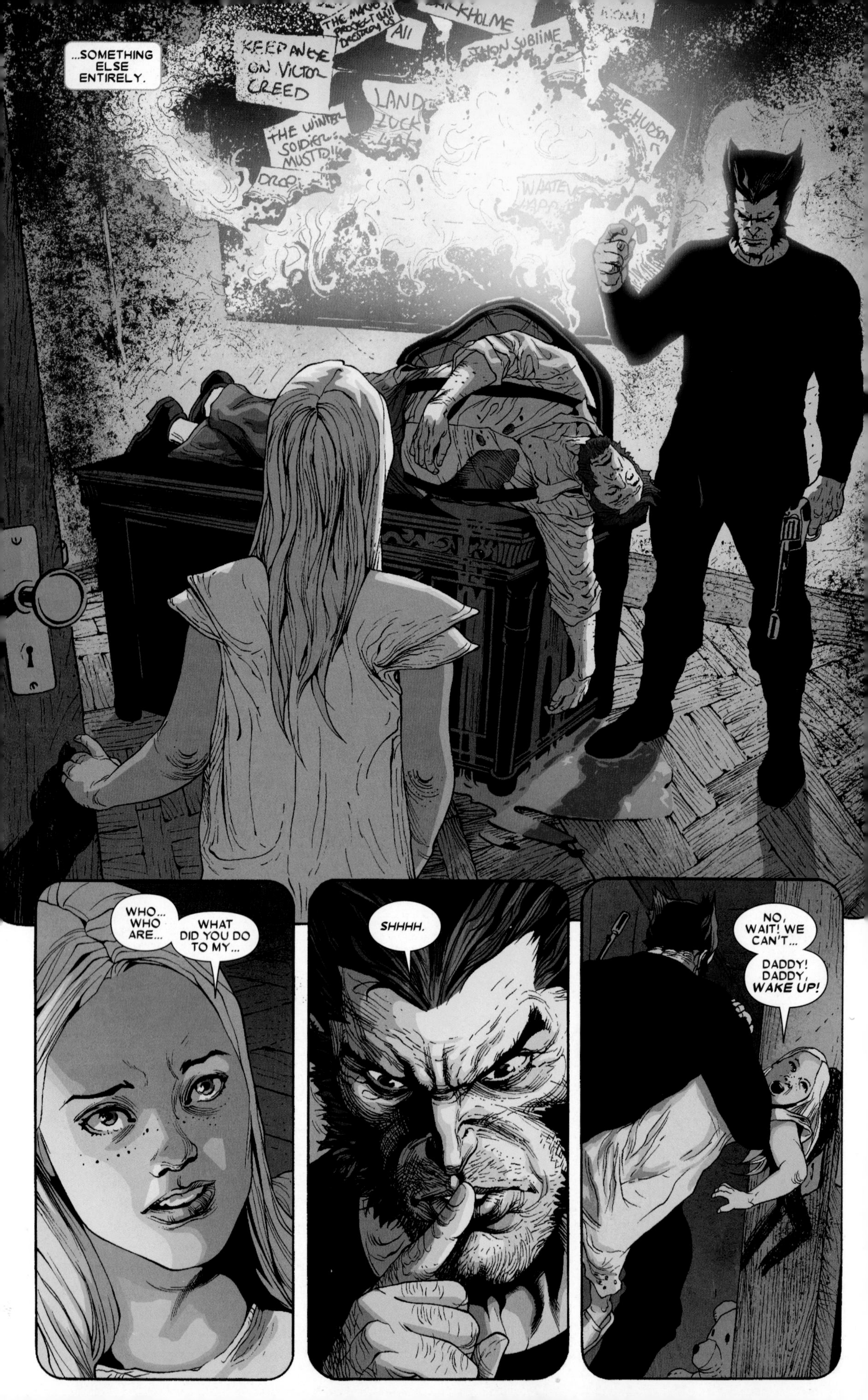
...SOMETHING ELSE ENTIRELY.
KEEP AN EYE ON VICTOR CREED
WHO... WHO ARE...
WHAT DID YOU DO TO MY...
SHHHH.
NO, WAIT! WE CAN'T...
DADDY! DADDY, WAKE UP!

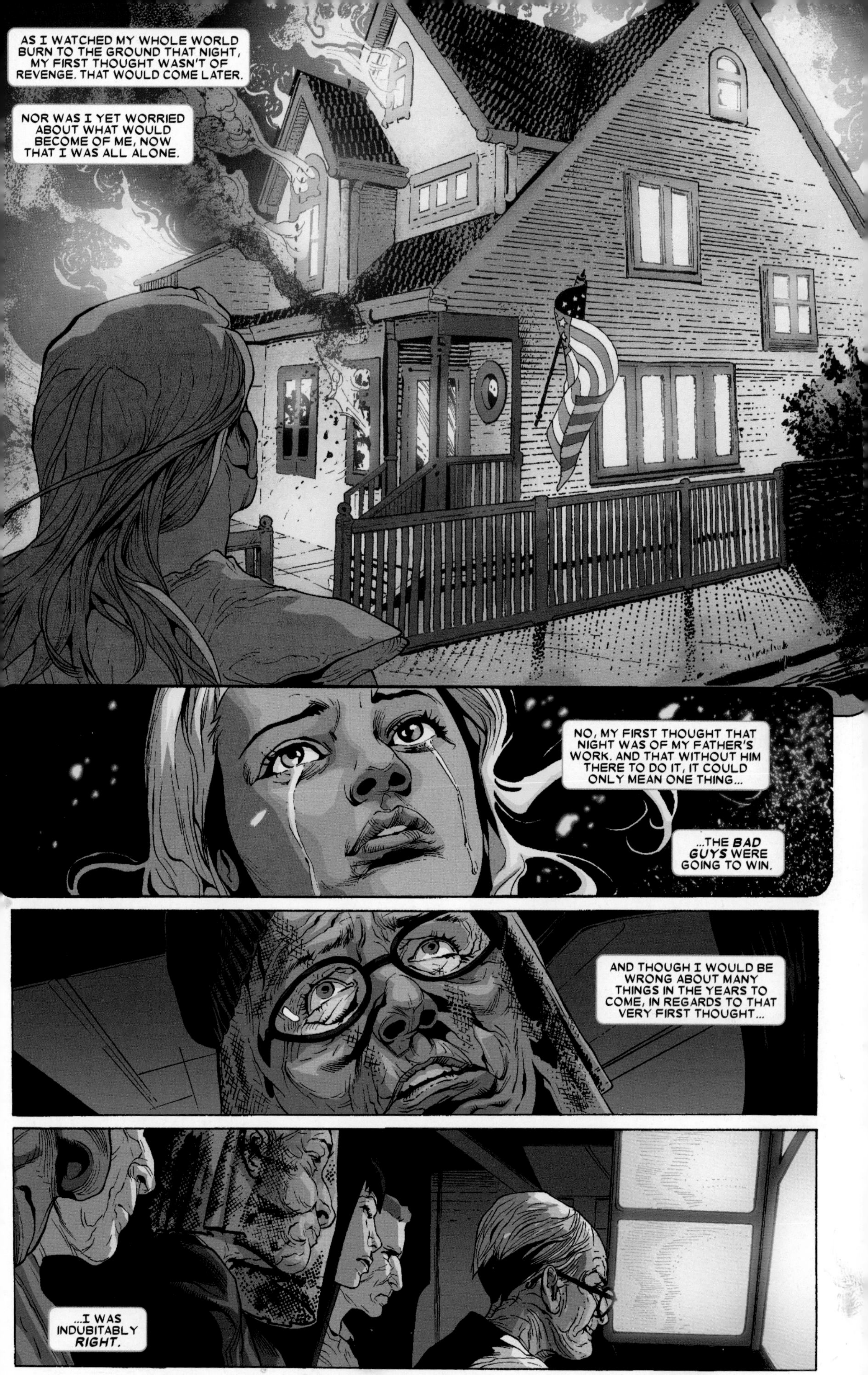
AS I WATCHED MY WHOLE WORLD BURN TO THE GROUND THAT NIGHT, MY FIRST THOUGHT WASN'T OF REVENGE. THAT WOULD COME LATER.
NOR WAS I YET WORRIED ABOUT WHAT WOULD BECOME OF ME, NOW THAT I WAS ALL ALONE.
NO, MY FIRST THOUGHT THAT NIGHT WAS OF MY FATHER'S WORK. AND THAT WITHOUT HIM THERE TO DO IT, IT COULD ONLY MEAN ONE THING...
...THE *BAD GUYS* WERE GOING TO WIN.
AND THOUGH I WOULD BE WRONG ABOUT MANY THINGS IN THE YEARS TO COME, IN REGARDS TO THAT VERY FIRST THOUGHT...
...I WAS INDUBITABLY *RIGHT*.

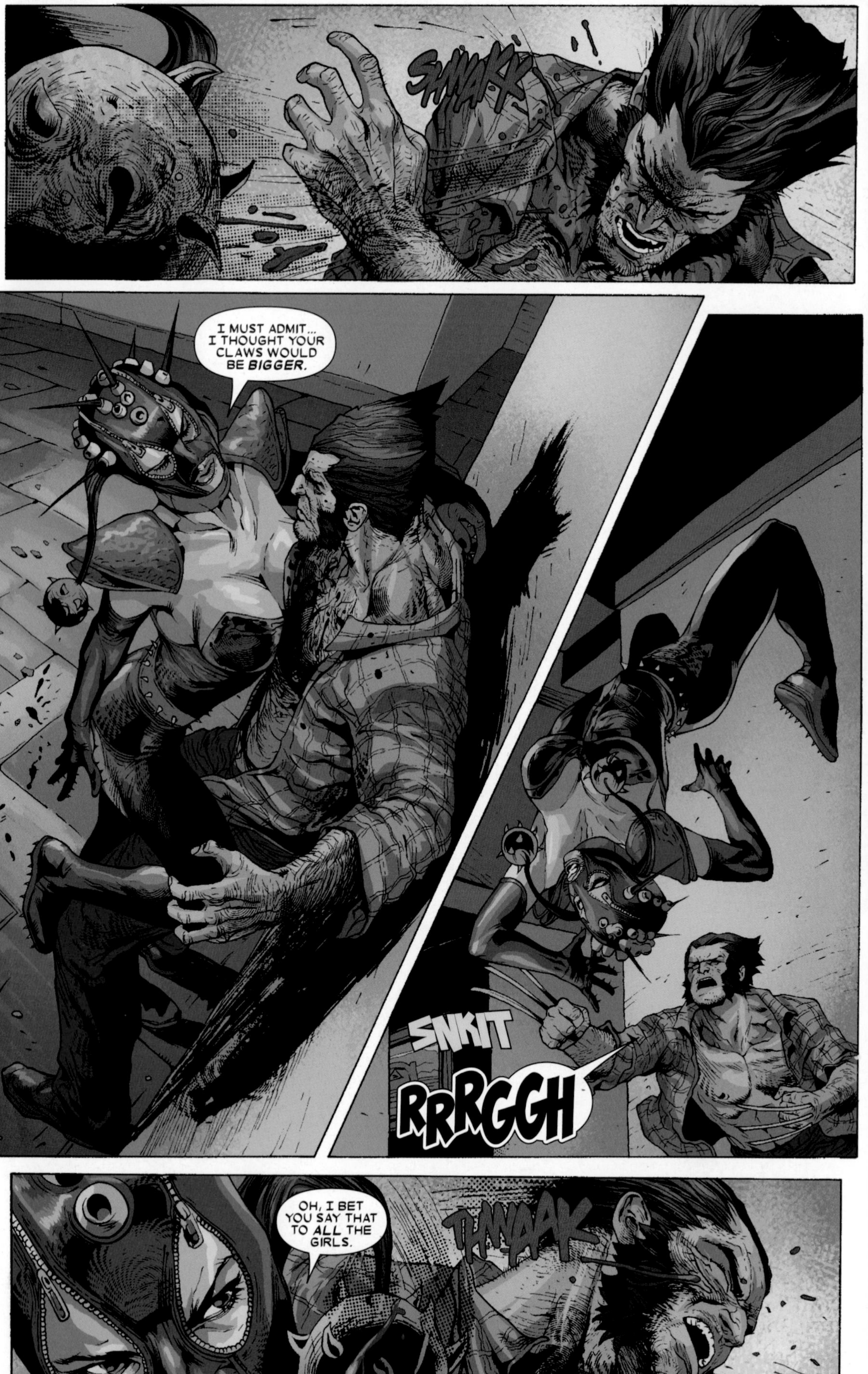
SNAKK
I MUST ADMIT... I THOUGHT YOUR CLAWS WOULD BE *BIGGER*.
SNKIT
RRRGGH
OH, I BET YOU SAY THAT TO *ALL* THE GIRLS.
THMAAK

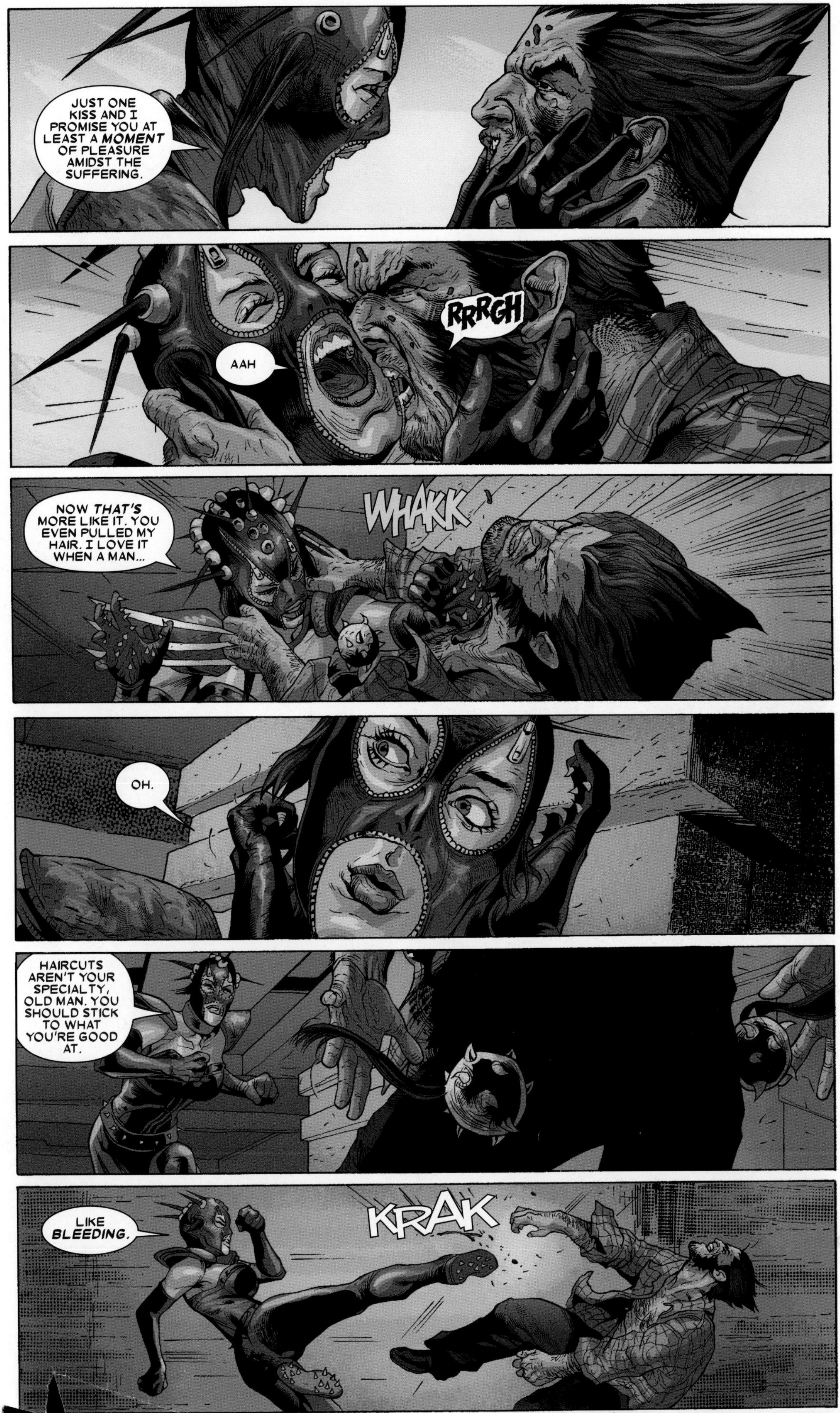
JUST ONE KISS AND I PROMISE YOU AT LEAST A MOMENT OF PLEASURE AMIDST THE SUFFERING.
RRRGH
AAH
NOW THAT'S MORE LIKE IT. YOU EVEN PULLED MY HAIR. I LOVE IT WHEN A MAN...
WHAKK
OH.
HAIRCUTS AREN'T YOUR SPECIALTY, OLD MAN. YOU SHOULD STICK TO WHAT YOU'RE GOOD AT.
LIKE BLEEDING.
KRAK

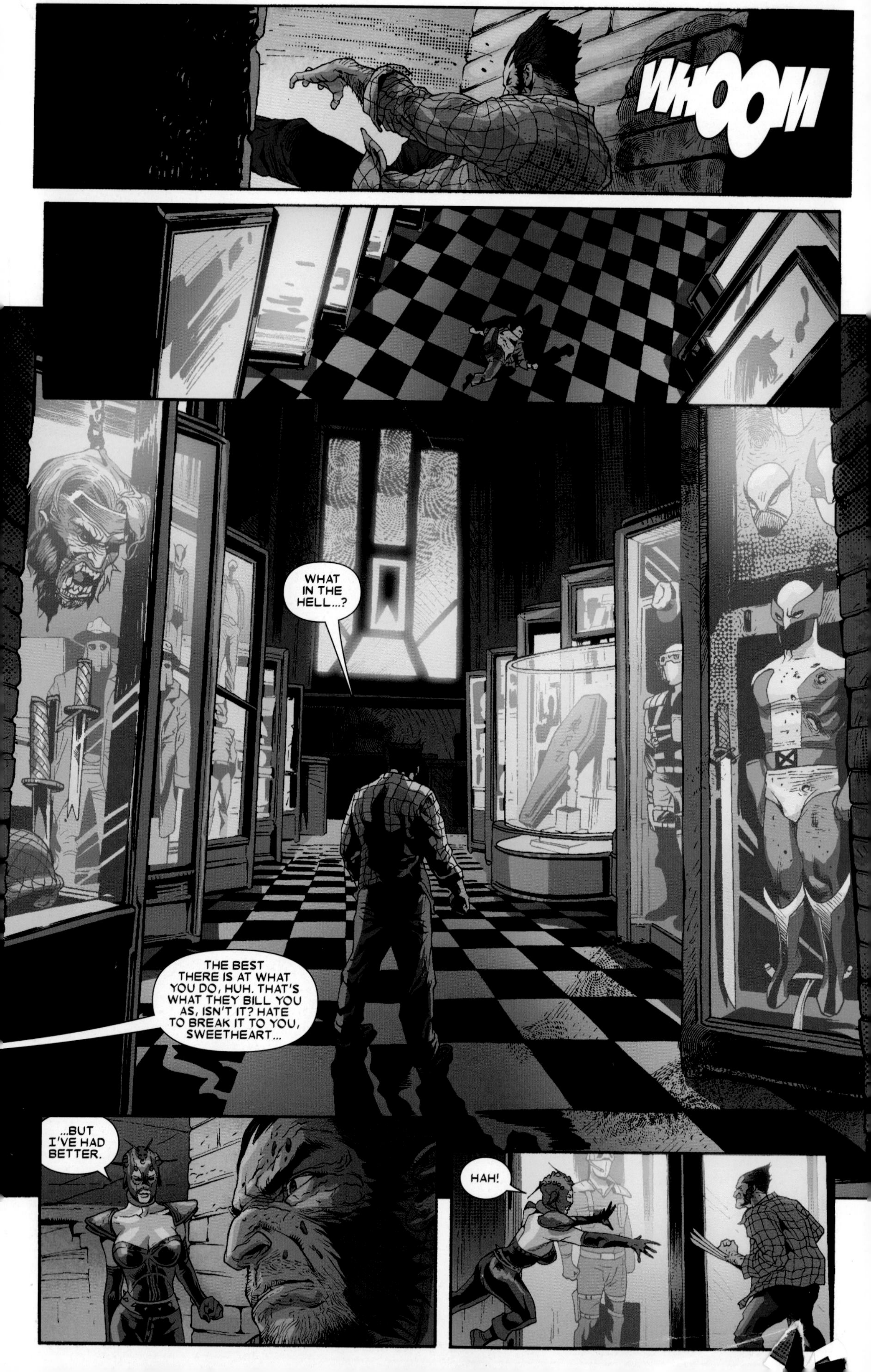
WHOOM
WHAT IN THE HELL...?
THE BEST THERE IS AT WHAT YOU DO, HUH. THAT'S WHAT THEY BILL YOU AS, ISN'T IT? HATE TO BREAK IT TO YOU, SWEETHEART...
...BUT I'VE HAD BETTER.
HAH!

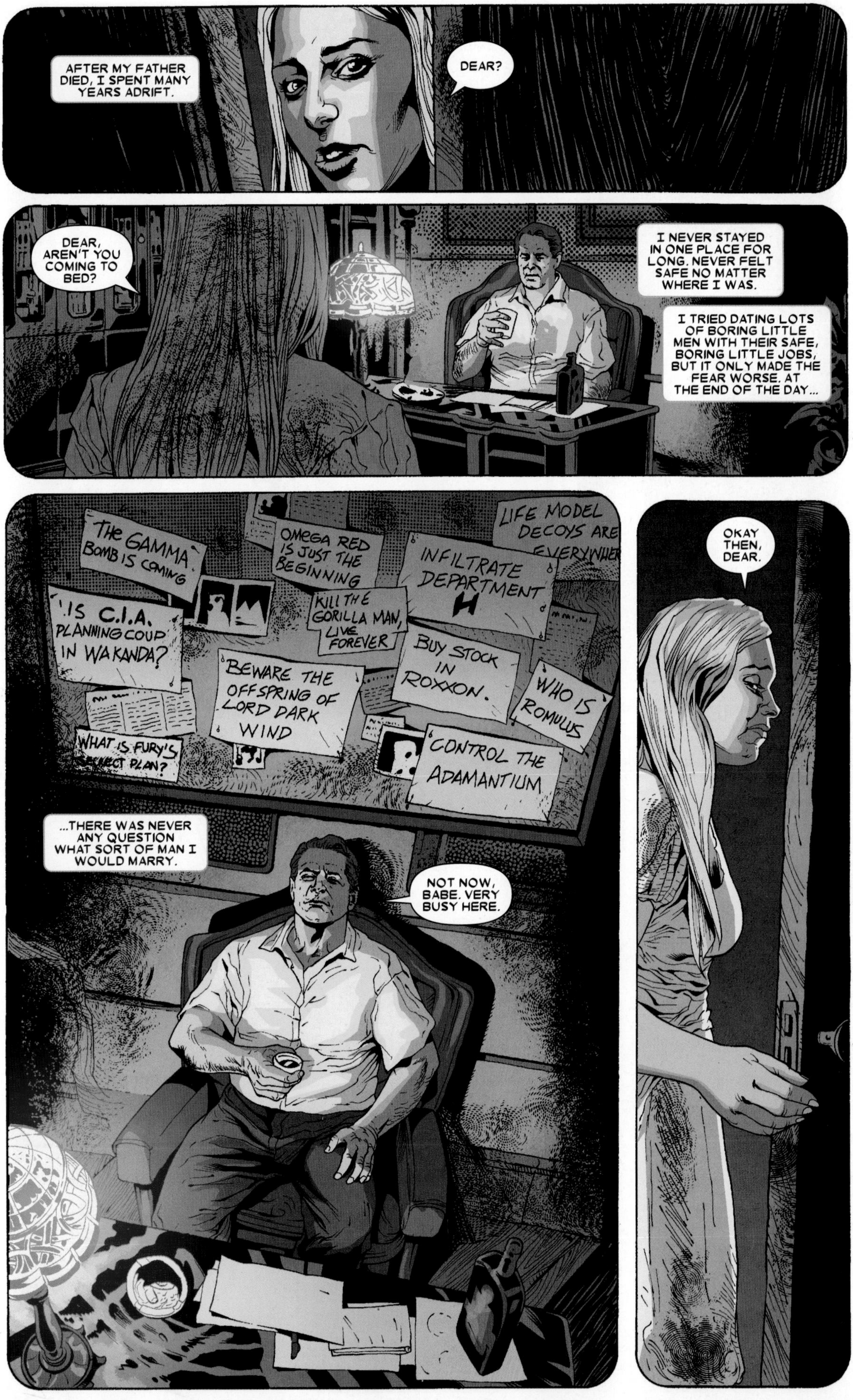
AFTER MY FATHER DIED, I SPENT MANY YEARS ADRIFT.
DEAR?
DEAR, AREN'T YOU COMING TO BED?
I NEVER STAYED IN ONE PLACE FOR LONG. NEVER FELT SAFE NO MATTER WHERE I WAS.
I TRIED DATING LOTS OF BORING LITTLE MEN WITH THEIR SAFE, BORING LITTLE JOBS, BUT IT ONLY MADE THE FEAR WORSE. AT THE END OF THE DAY...
THE GAMMA BOMB IS COMING
OMEGA RED IS JUST THE BEGINNING
LIFE MODEL DECOYS ARE EVERYWHER
INFILTRATE DEPARTMENT H
IS C.I.A. PLANNING COUP IN WAKANDA?
KILL THE GORILLA MAN, LIVE FOREVER
BUY STOCK IN ROXXON.
BEWARE THE OFFSPRING OF LORD DARK WIND
WHO IS ROMULUS
WHAT IS FURY'S SECRECT PLAN?
CONTROL THE ADAMANTIUM
...THERE WAS NEVER ANY QUESTION WHAT SORT OF MAN I WOULD MARRY.
NOT NOW, BABE. VERY BUSY HERE.
OKAY THEN, DEAR.

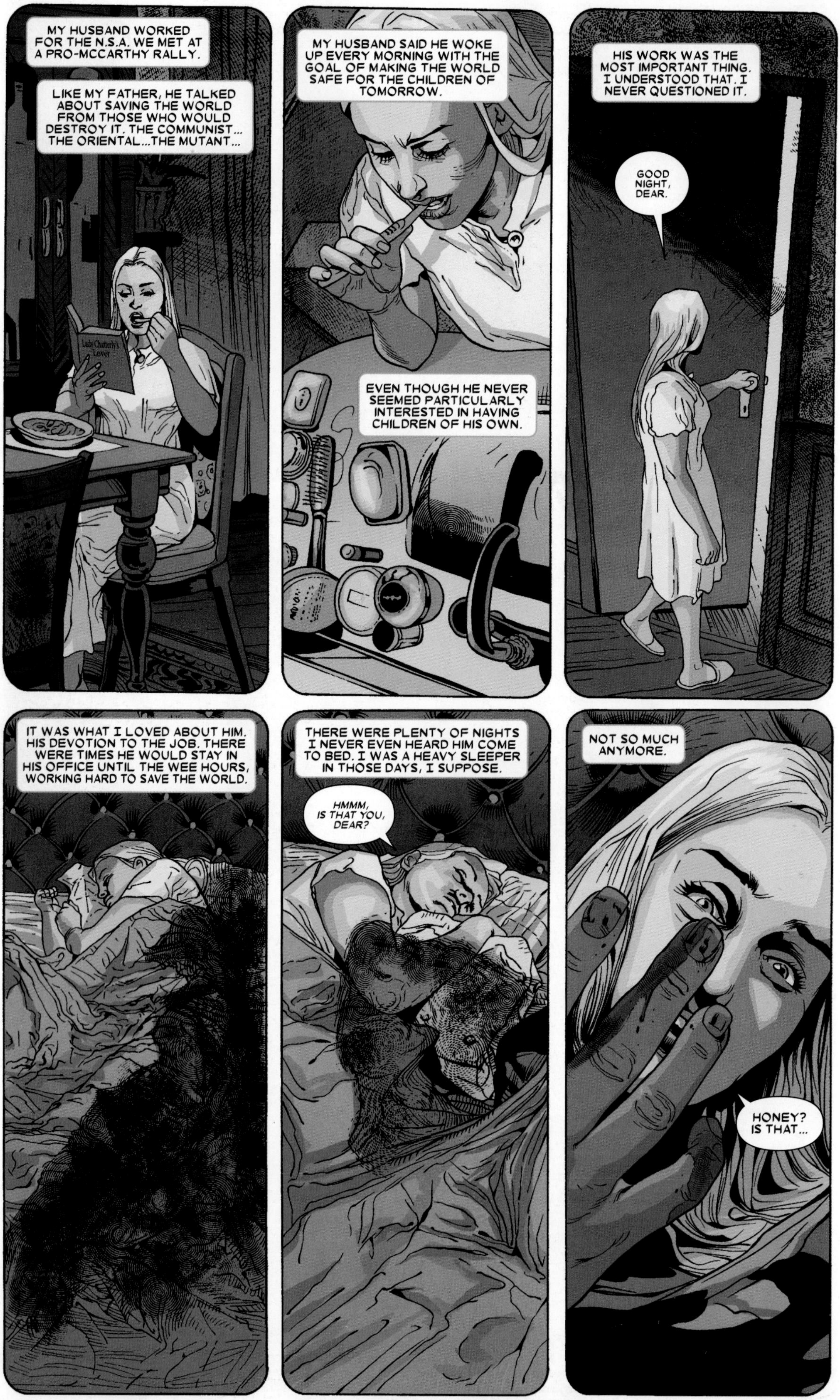
MY HUSBAND WORKED FOR THE N.S.A. WE MET AT A PRO-McCARTHY RALLY.
LIKE MY FATHER, HE TALKED ABOUT SAVING THE WORLD FROM THOSE WHO WOULD DESTROY IT. THE COMMUNIST... THE ORIENTAL...THE MUTANT...
Lady Chatterly's Lover
MY HUSBAND SAID HE WOKE UP EVERY MORNING WITH THE GOAL OF MAKING THE WORLD SAFE FOR THE CHILDREN OF TOMORROW.
EVEN THOUGH HE NEVER SEEMED PARTICULARLY INTERESTED IN HAVING CHILDREN OF HIS OWN.
HIS WORK WAS THE MOST IMPORTANT THING. I UNDERSTOOD THAT. I NEVER QUESTIONED IT.
GOOD NIGHT, DEAR.
IT WAS WHAT I LOVED ABOUT HIM. HIS DEVOTION TO THE JOB. THERE WERE TIMES HE WOULD STAY IN HIS OFFICE UNTIL THE WEE HOURS, WORKING HARD TO SAVE THE WORLD.
THERE WERE PLENTY OF NIGHTS I NEVER EVEN HEARD HIM COME TO BED. I WAS A HEAVY SLEEPER IN THOSE DAYS, I SUPPOSE.
HMMM, IS THAT YOU, DEAR?
NOT SO MUCH ANYMORE.
HONEY? IS THAT...

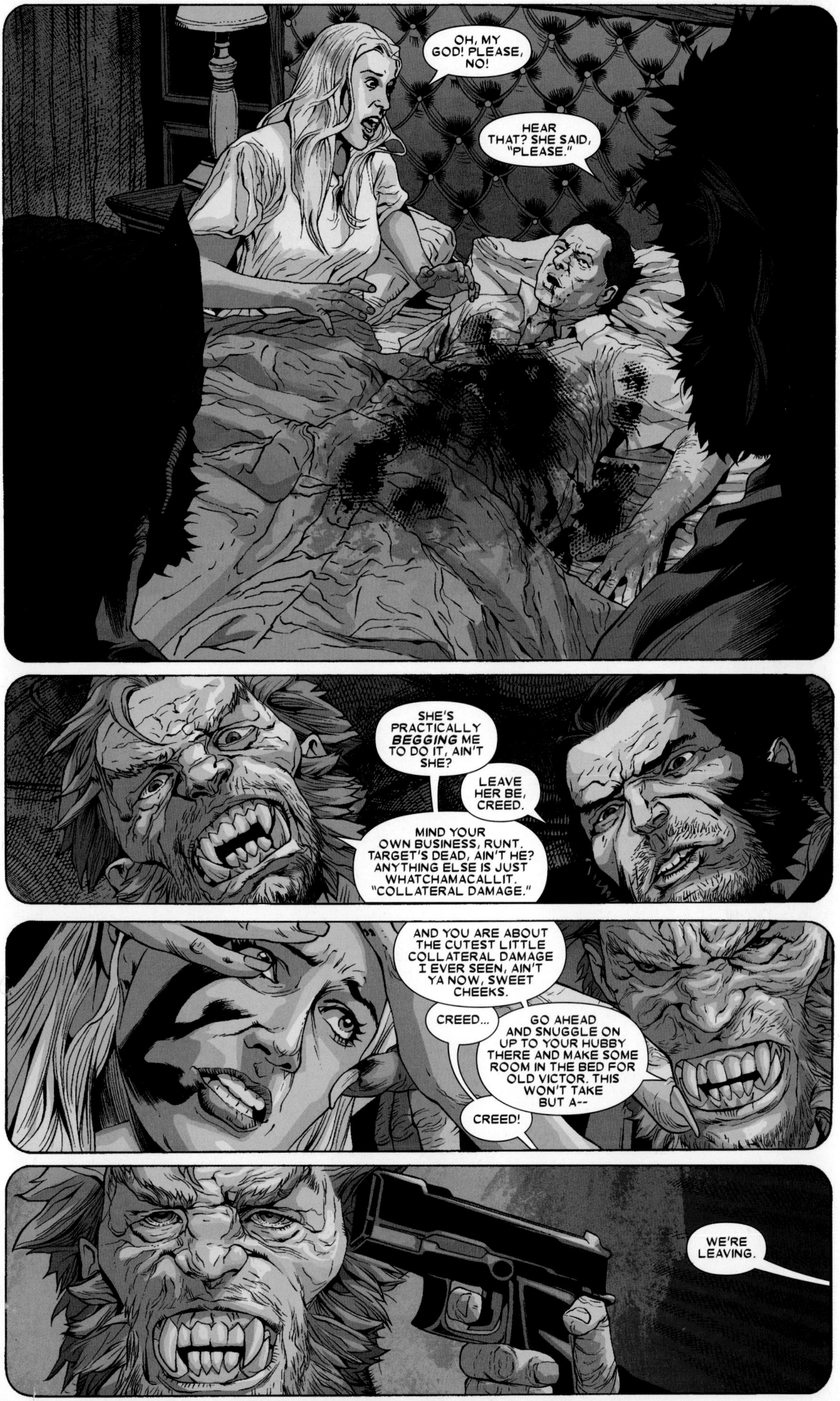
OH, MY GOD! PLEASE, NO!
HEAR THAT? SHE SAID, "PLEASE."
SHE'S PRACTICALLY *BEGGING* ME TO DO IT, AIN'T SHE?
LEAVE HER BE, CREED.
MIND YOUR OWN BUSINESS, RUNT. TARGET'S DEAD, AIN'T HE? ANYTHING ELSE IS JUST WHATCHAMACALLIT. "COLLATERAL DAMAGE."
AND YOU ARE ABOUT THE CUTEST LITTLE COLLATERAL DAMAGE I EVER SEEN, AIN'T YA NOW, SWEET CHEEKS.
CREED...
GO AHEAD AND SNUGGLE ON UP TO YOUR HUBBY THERE AND MAKE SOME ROOM IN THE BED FOR OLD VICTOR. THIS WON'T TAKE BUT A--
CREED!
WE'RE LEAVING.

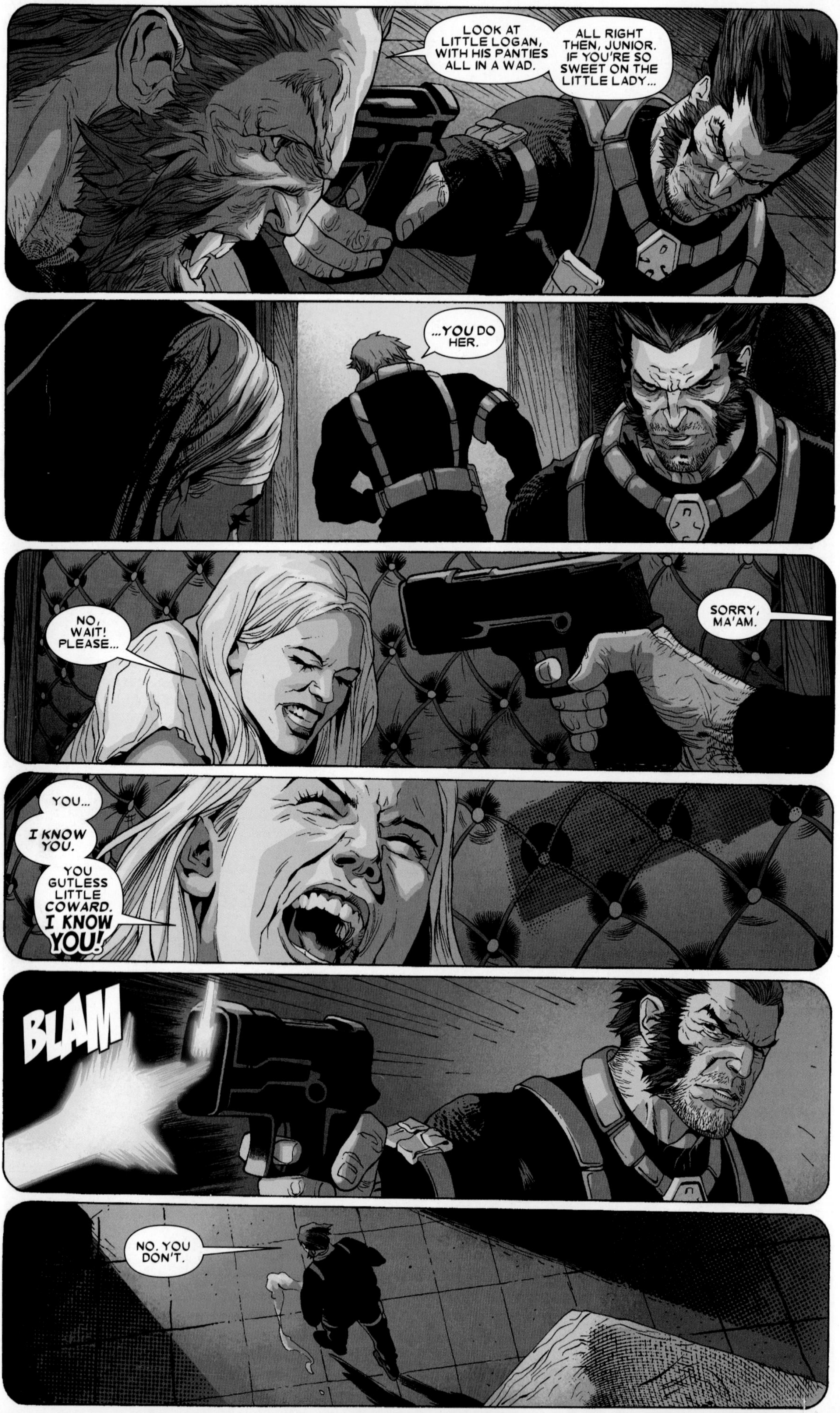
LOOK AT LITTLE LOGAN, WITH HIS PANTIES ALL IN A WAD.
ALL RIGHT THEN, JUNIOR. IF YOU'RE SO SWEET ON THE LITTLE LADY...
...YOU DO HER.
NO, WAIT! PLEASE...
SORRY, MA'AM.
YOU...
I KNOW YOU.
YOU GUTLESS LITTLE COWARD. I KNOW YOU!
BLAM
NO. YOU DON'T.

HE HAS MANY DIFFERENT NAMES.

LOGAN TO SOME. TO OTHERS, WEAPON X OR THE WOLVERINE.

HIS MOTHER NAMED HIM JAMES.

SOME HAVE CALLED HIM A MONSTER. AN INHUMAN BEAST.

OTHERS SAY HE'S A MINDLESS KILLING MACHINE, A WEAPON, WHO'S BEEN BRAINWASHED SO MANY TIMES HE DOESN'T EVEN KNOW WHO HE IS.

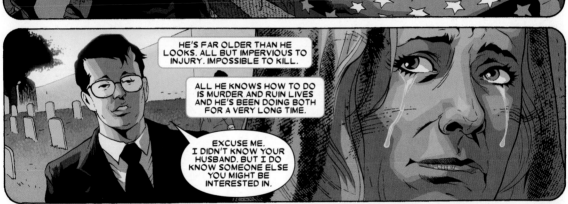

HE'S FAR OLDER THAN HE LOOKS. ALL BUT IMPERVIOUS TO INJURY. IMPOSSIBLE TO KILL.

ALL HE KNOWS HOW TO DO IS MURDER AND RUIN LIVES AND HE'S BEEN DOING BOTH FOR A VERY LONG TIME.

EXCUSE ME. I DIDN'T KNOW YOUR HUSBAND. BUT I DO KNOW SOMEONE ELSE YOU MIGHT BE INTERESTED IN.

HE IS THE FOULEST VILLAIN WHO EVER WALKED THE EARTH AND HE DESERVES EVERY OUNCE OF SUFFERING AND MISERY WE CAN EVER POSSIBLY BESTOW UPON HIM.

THAT'S WHAT I KNOW ABOUT THE MAN WHO KILLED MY FATHER AND KILLED MY HUSBAND.

THAT'S WHAT I LEARNED FROM THE *RED RIGHT HAND*.

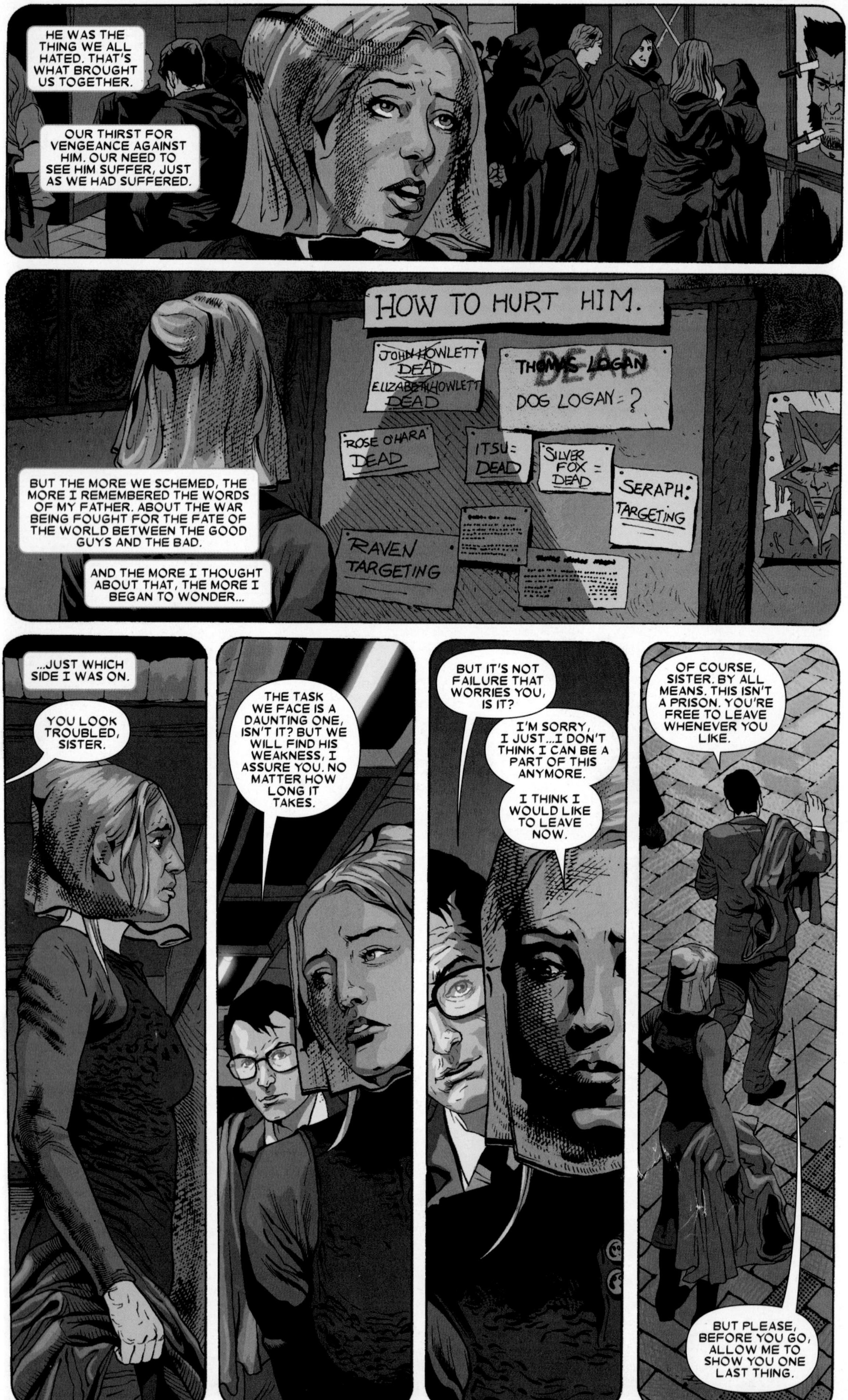
HE WAS THE THING WE ALL HATED. THAT'S WHAT BROUGHT US TOGETHER.
OUR THIRST FOR VENGEANCE AGAINST HIM. OUR NEED TO SEE HIM SUFFER, JUST AS WE HAD SUFFERED.
HOW TO HURT HIM.
JOHN HOWLETT DEAD
ELIZABETH HOWLETT DEAD
THOMAS LOGAN DEAD
DOG LOGAN = ?
ROSE O'HARA DEAD
ITSU = DEAD
SILVER FOX = DEAD
SERAPH: TARGETING
RAVEN TARGETING
BUT THE MORE WE SCHEMED, THE MORE I REMEMBERED THE WORDS OF MY FATHER. ABOUT THE WAR BEING FOUGHT FOR THE FATE OF THE WORLD BETWEEN THE GOOD GUYS AND THE BAD.
AND THE MORE I THOUGHT ABOUT THAT, THE MORE I BEGAN TO WONDER...
...JUST WHICH SIDE I WAS ON.
YOU LOOK TROUBLED, SISTER.
THE TASK WE FACE IS A DAUNTING ONE, ISN'T IT? BUT WE WILL FIND HIS WEAKNESS, I ASSURE YOU. NO MATTER HOW LONG IT TAKES.
BUT IT'S NOT FAILURE THAT WORRIES YOU, IS IT?
I'M SORRY, I JUST...I DON'T THINK I CAN BE A PART OF THIS ANYMORE.
I THINK I WOULD LIKE TO LEAVE NOW.
OF COURSE, SISTER. BY ALL MEANS. THIS ISN'T A PRISON. YOU'RE FREE TO LEAVE WHENEVER YOU LIKE.
BUT PLEASE, BEFORE YOU GO, ALLOW ME TO SHOW YOU ONE LAST THING.

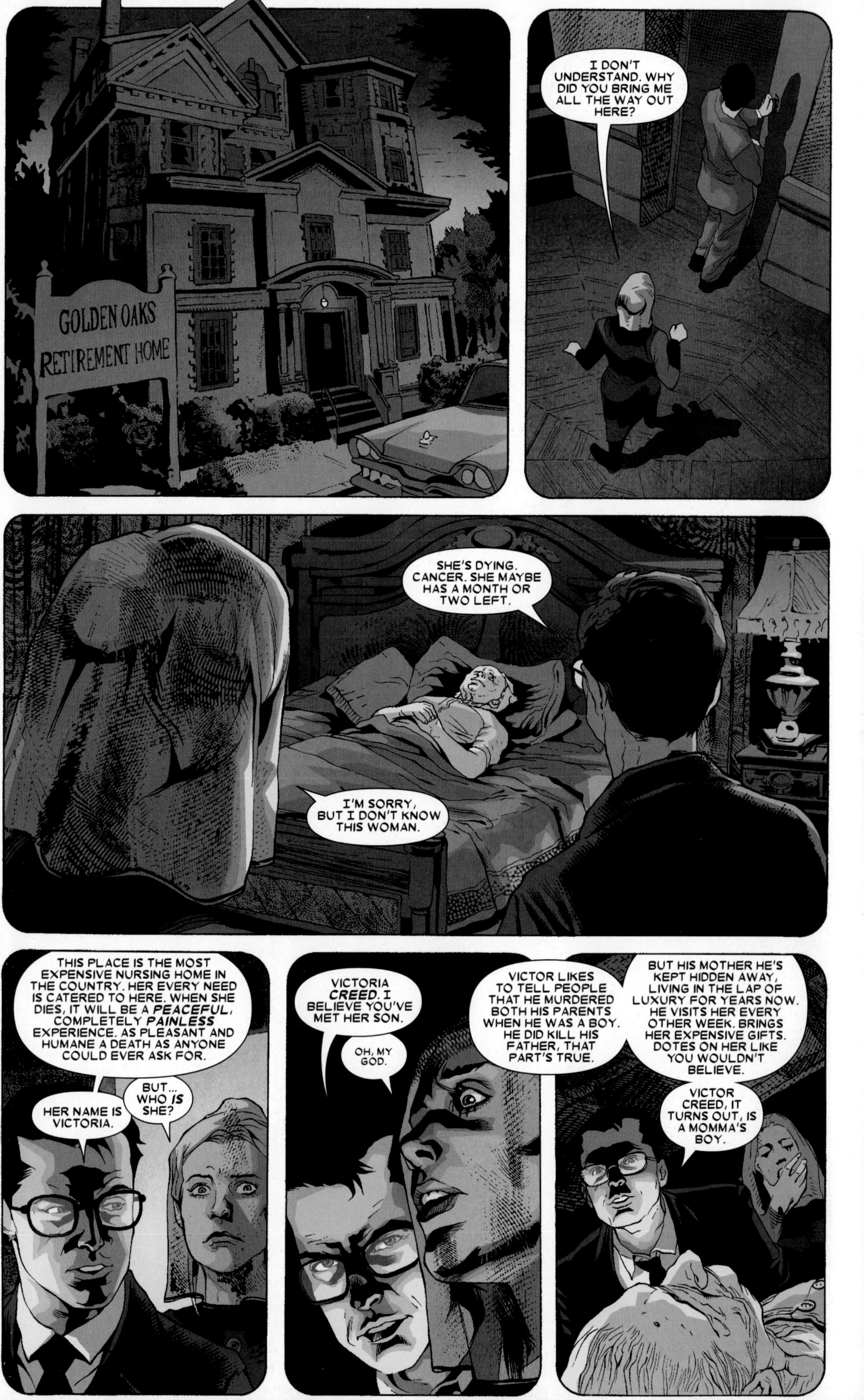
GOLDEN OAKS
RETIREMENT HOME
I DON'T UNDERSTAND. WHY DID YOU BRING ME ALL THE WAY OUT HERE?
SHE'S DYING. CANCER. SHE MAYBE HAS A MONTH OR TWO LEFT.
I'M SORRY, BUT I DON'T KNOW THIS WOMAN.
THIS PLACE IS THE MOST EXPENSIVE NURSING HOME IN THE COUNTRY. HER EVERY NEED IS CATERED TO HERE. WHEN SHE DIES, IT WILL BE A *PEACEFUL*, COMPLETELY *PAINLESS* EXPERIENCE. AS PLEASANT AND HUMANE A DEATH AS ANYONE COULD EVER ASK FOR.
BUT... WHO *IS* SHE?
HER NAME IS VICTORIA.
VICTORIA *CREED*. I BELIEVE YOU'VE MET HER SON.
OH, MY GOD.
VICTOR LIKES TO TELL PEOPLE THAT HE MURDERED BOTH HIS PARENTS WHEN HE WAS A BOY. HE DID KILL HIS FATHER, THAT PART'S TRUE.
BUT HIS MOTHER HE'S KEPT HIDDEN AWAY, LIVING IN THE LAP OF LUXURY FOR YEARS NOW. HE VISITS HER EVERY OTHER WEEK. BRINGS HER EXPENSIVE GIFTS. DOTES ON HER LIKE YOU WOULDN'T BELIEVE.
VICTOR CREED, IT TURNS OUT, IS A MOMMA'S BOY.

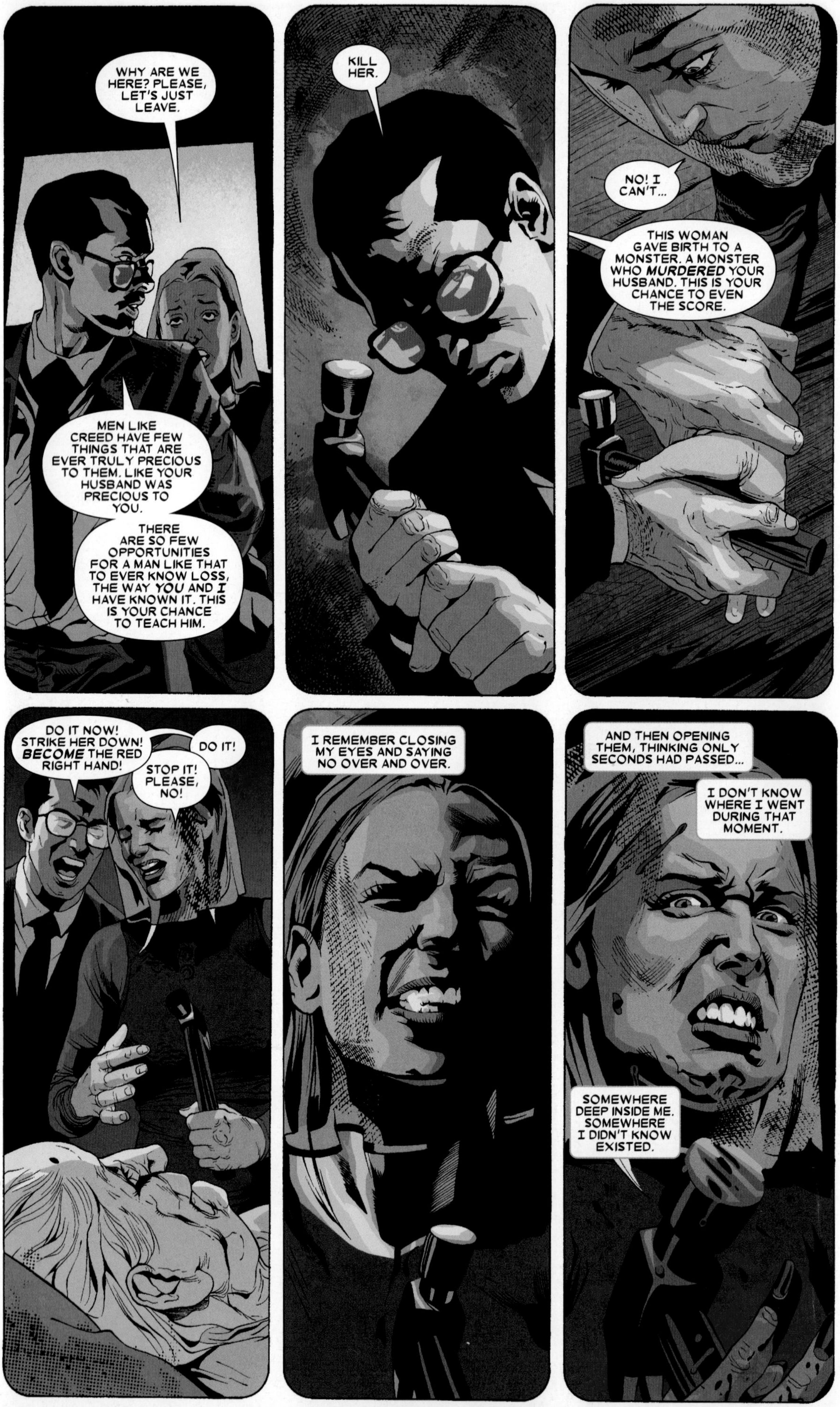
WHY ARE WE HERE? PLEASE, LET'S JUST LEAVE.
MEN LIKE CREED HAVE FEW THINGS THAT ARE EVER TRULY PRECIOUS TO THEM. LIKE YOUR HUSBAND WAS PRECIOUS TO YOU.
THERE ARE SO FEW OPPORTUNITIES FOR A MAN LIKE THAT TO EVER KNOW LOSS, THE WAY *YOU* AND *I* HAVE KNOWN IT. THIS IS YOUR CHANCE TO TEACH HIM.
KILL HER.
NO! I CAN'T...
THIS WOMAN GAVE BIRTH TO A MONSTER. A MONSTER WHO *MURDERED* YOUR HUSBAND. THIS IS YOUR CHANCE TO EVEN THE SCORE.
DO IT NOW! STRIKE HER DOWN! *BECOME* THE RED RIGHT HAND!
DO IT!
STOP IT! PLEASE, NO!
I REMEMBER CLOSING MY EYES AND SAYING NO OVER AND OVER.
AND THEN OPENING THEM, THINKING ONLY SECONDS HAD PASSED...
I DON'T KNOW WHERE I WENT DURING THAT MOMENT.
SOMEWHERE DEEP INSIDE ME. SOMEWHERE I DIDN'T KNOW EXISTED.

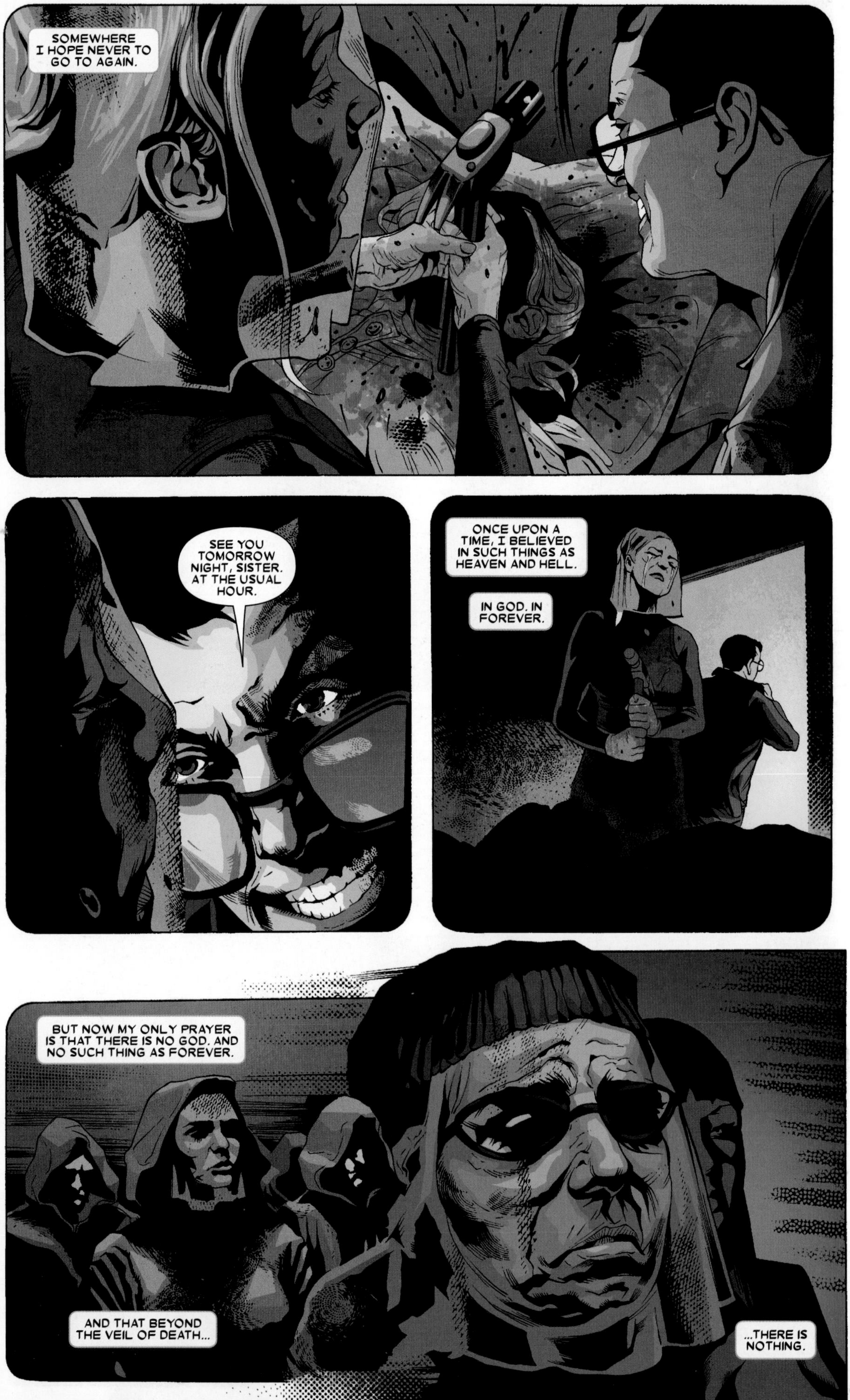
SOMEWHERE I HOPE NEVER TO GO TO AGAIN.
SEE YOU TOMORROW NIGHT, SISTER. AT THE USUAL HOUR.
ONCE UPON A TIME, I BELIEVED IN SUCH THINGS AS HEAVEN AND HELL.
IN GOD. IN FOREVER.
BUT NOW MY ONLY PRAYER IS THAT THERE IS NO GOD. AND NO SUCH THING AS FOREVER.
AND THAT BEYOND THE VEIL OF DEATH...
...THERE IS NOTHING.

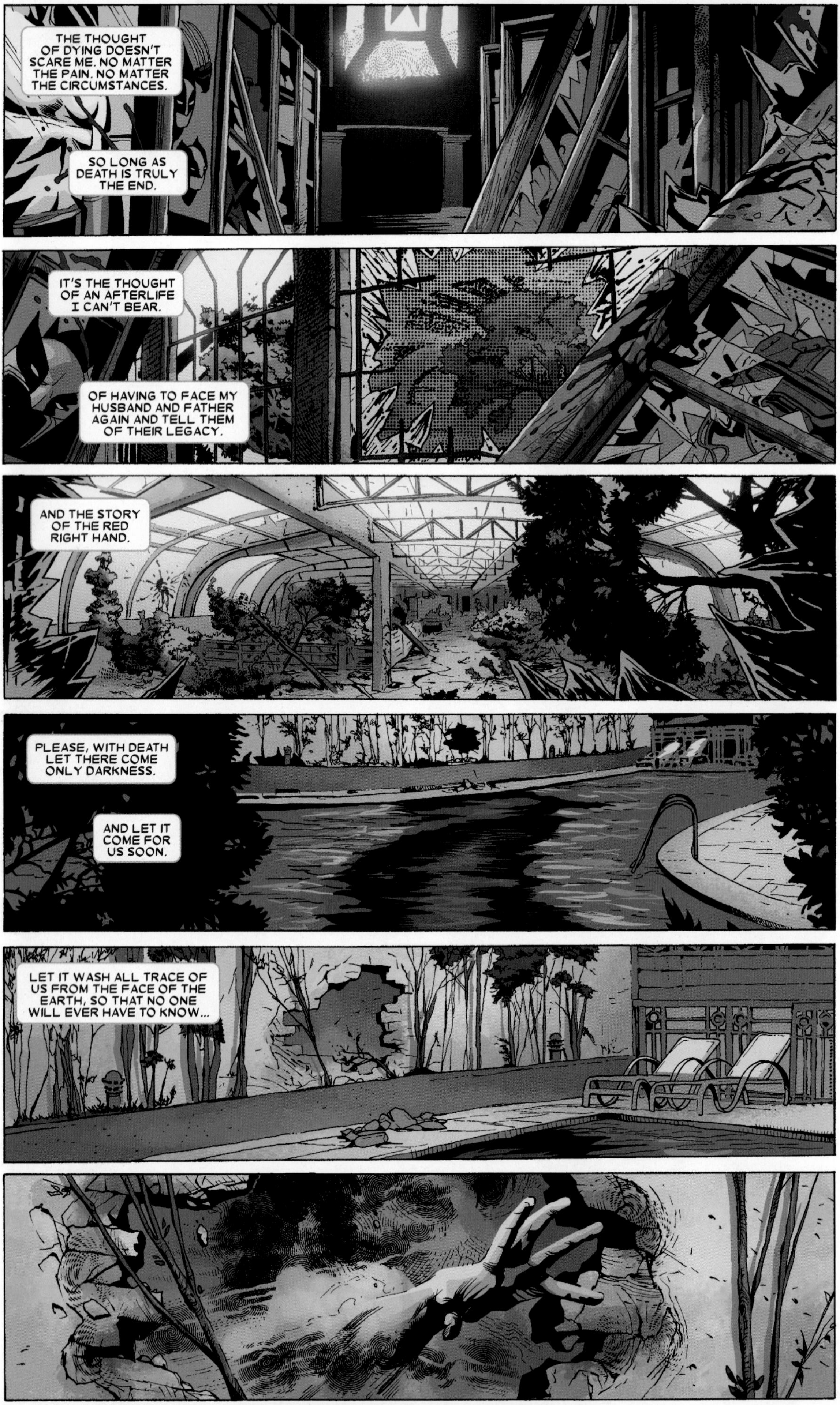
THE THOUGHT OF DYING DOESN'T SCARE ME. NO MATTER THE PAIN. NO MATTER THE CIRCUMSTANCES.
SO LONG AS DEATH IS TRULY THE END.
IT'S THE THOUGHT OF AN AFTERLIFE I CAN'T BEAR.
OF HAVING TO FACE MY HUSBAND AND FATHER AGAIN AND TELL THEM OF THEIR LEGACY.
AND THE STORY OF THE RED RIGHT HAND.
PLEASE, WITH DEATH LET THERE COME ONLY DARKNESS.
AND LET IT COME FOR US SOON.
LET IT WASH ALL TRACE OF US FROM THE FACE OF THE EARTH, SO THAT NO ONE WILL EVER HAVE TO KNOW...

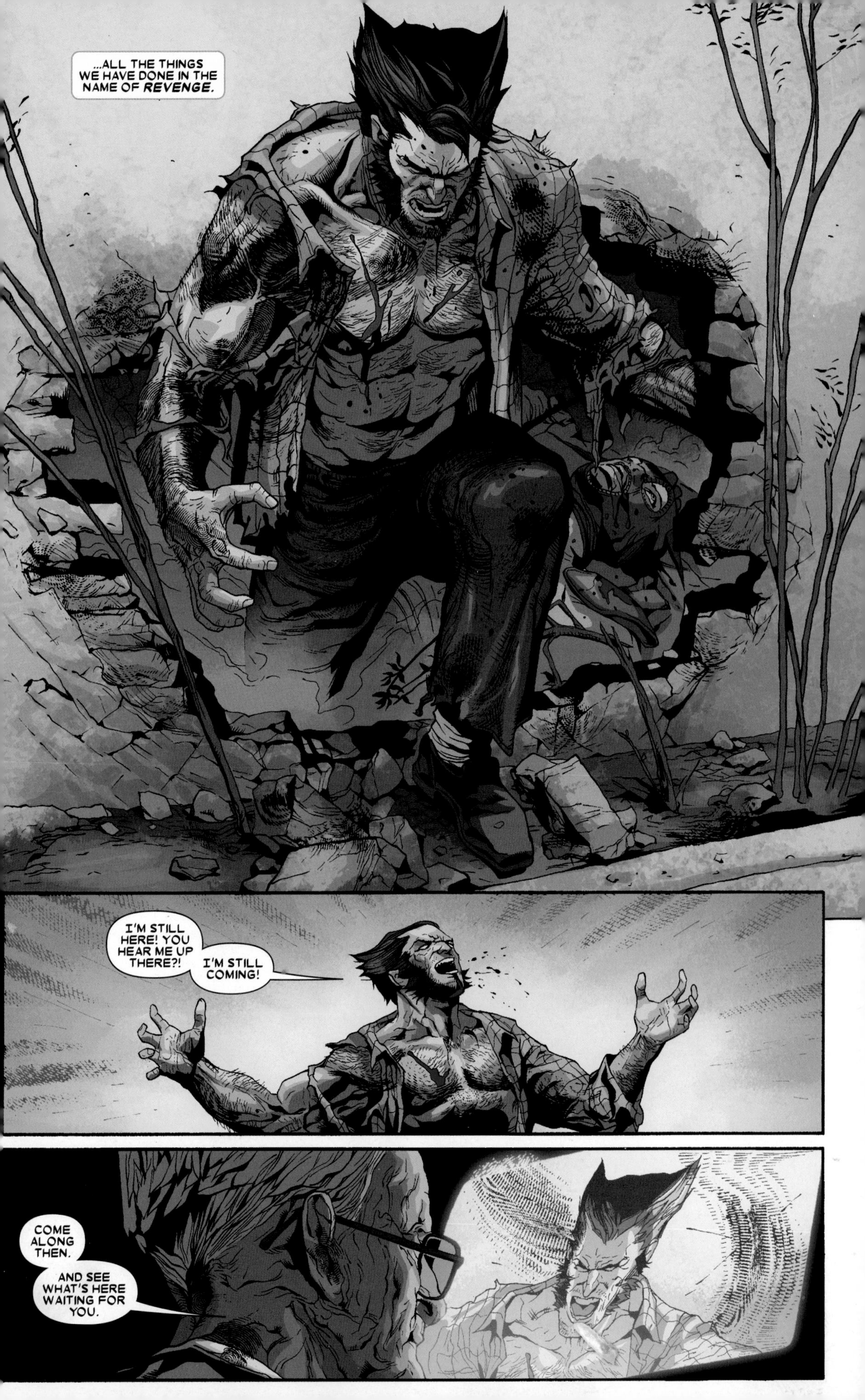
...ALL THE THINGS WE HAVE DONE IN THE NAME OF *REVENGE.*
I'M STILL HERE! YOU HEAR ME UP THERE?!
I'M STILL COMING!
COME ALONG THEN.
AND SEE WHAT'S HERE WAITING FOR YOU.

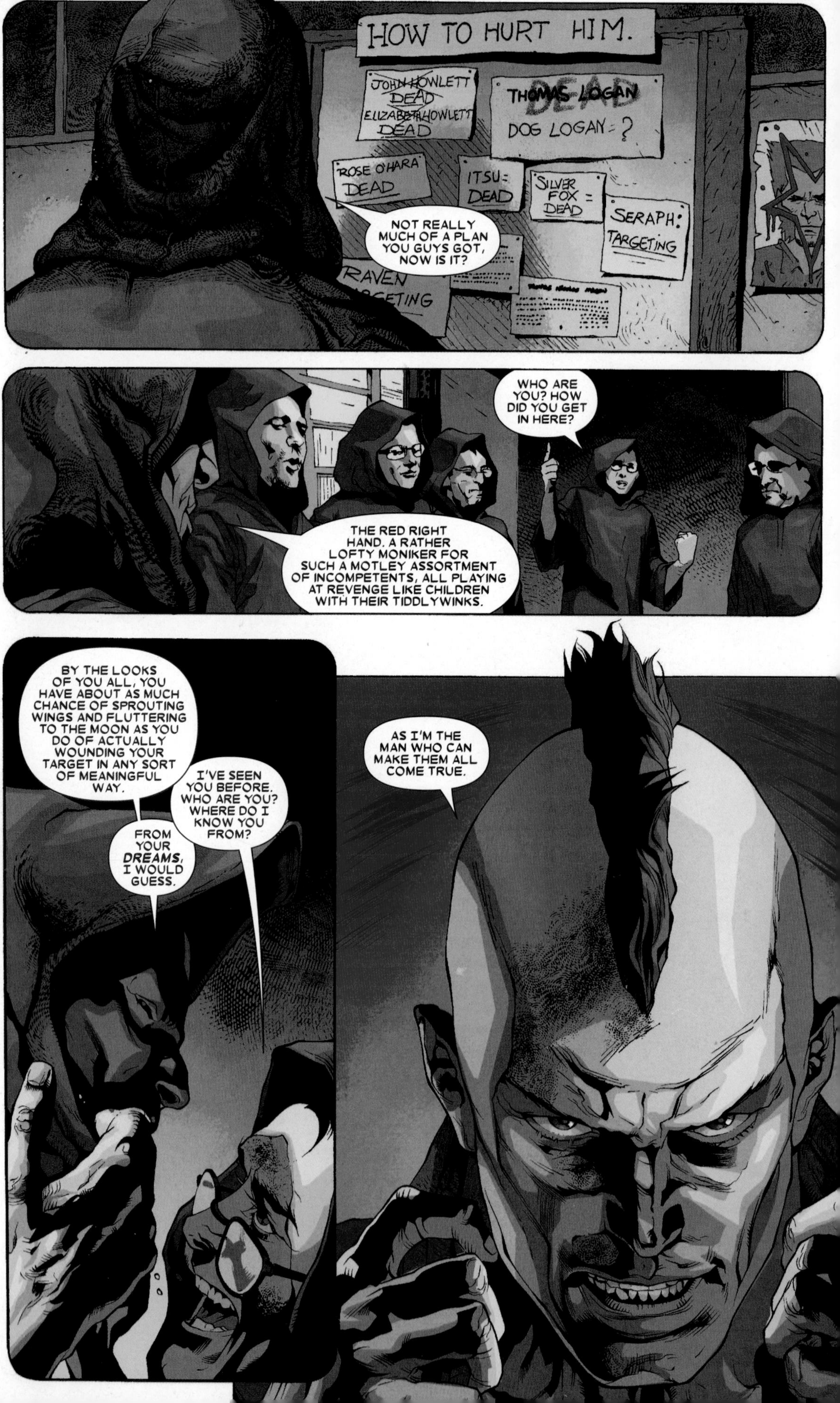

HOW TO HURT HIM.
JOHN HOWLETT DEAD
ELIZABETH HOWLETT DEAD
THOMAS LOGAN DEAD
DOG LOGAN = ?
ROSE O'HARA DEAD
ITSU = DEAD
SILVER FOX = DEAD
SERAPH: TARGETING
RAVEN TARGETING
NOT REALLY MUCH OF A PLAN YOU GUYS GOT, NOW IS IT?
WHO ARE YOU? HOW DID YOU GET IN HERE?
THE RED RIGHT HAND. A RATHER LOFTY MONIKER FOR SUCH A MOTLEY ASSORTMENT OF INCOMPETENTS, ALL PLAYING AT REVENGE LIKE CHILDREN WITH THEIR TIDDLYWINKS.
BY THE LOOKS OF YOU ALL, YOU HAVE ABOUT AS MUCH CHANCE OF SPROUTING WINGS AND FLUTTERING TO THE MOON AS YOU DO OF ACTUALLY WOUNDING YOUR TARGET IN ANY SORT OF MEANINGFUL WAY.
I'VE SEEN YOU BEFORE. WHO ARE YOU? WHERE DO I KNOW YOU FROM?
FROM YOUR DREAMS, I WOULD GUESS.
AS I'M THE MAN WHO CAN MAKE THEM ALL COME TRUE.

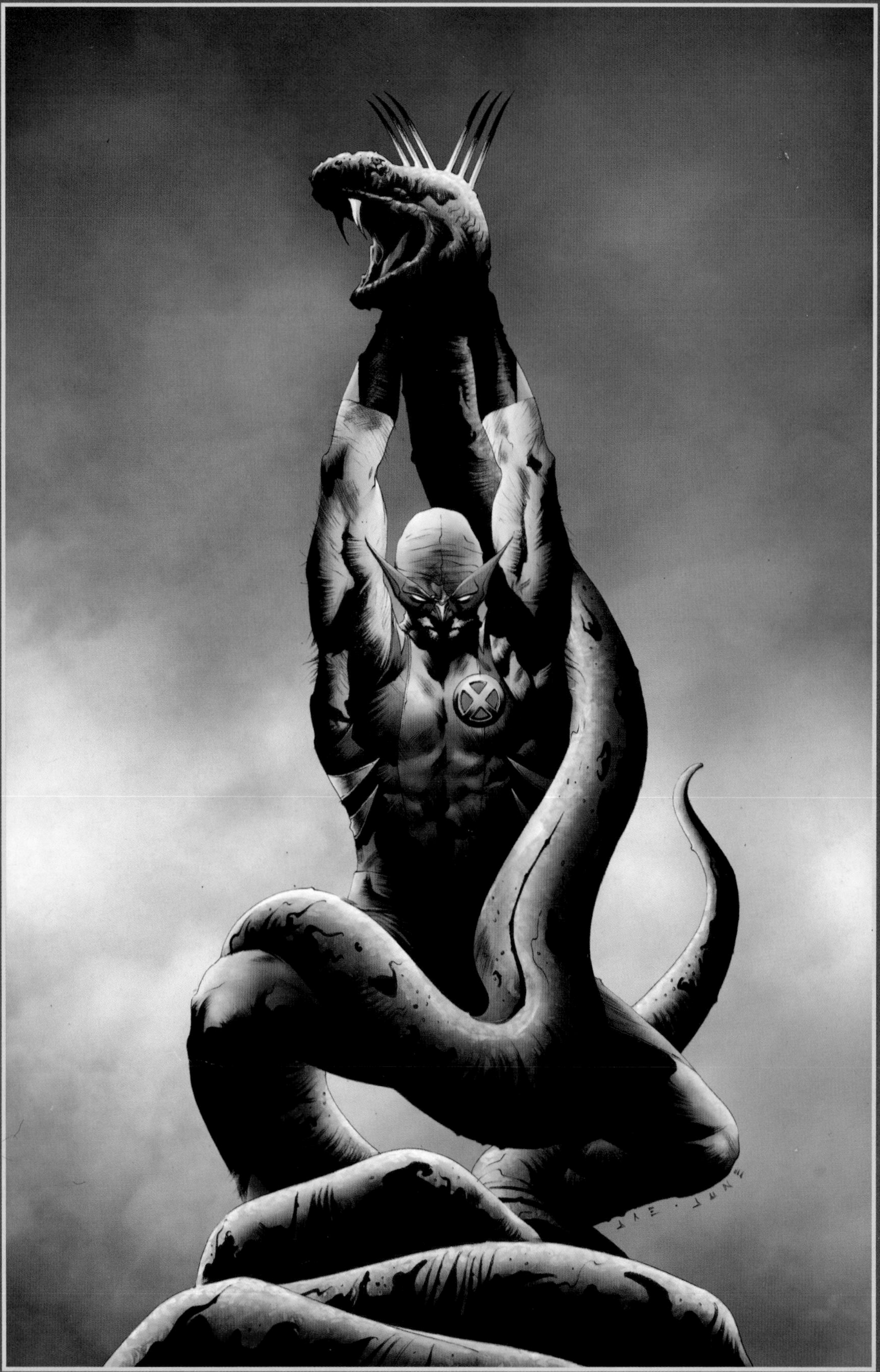

12

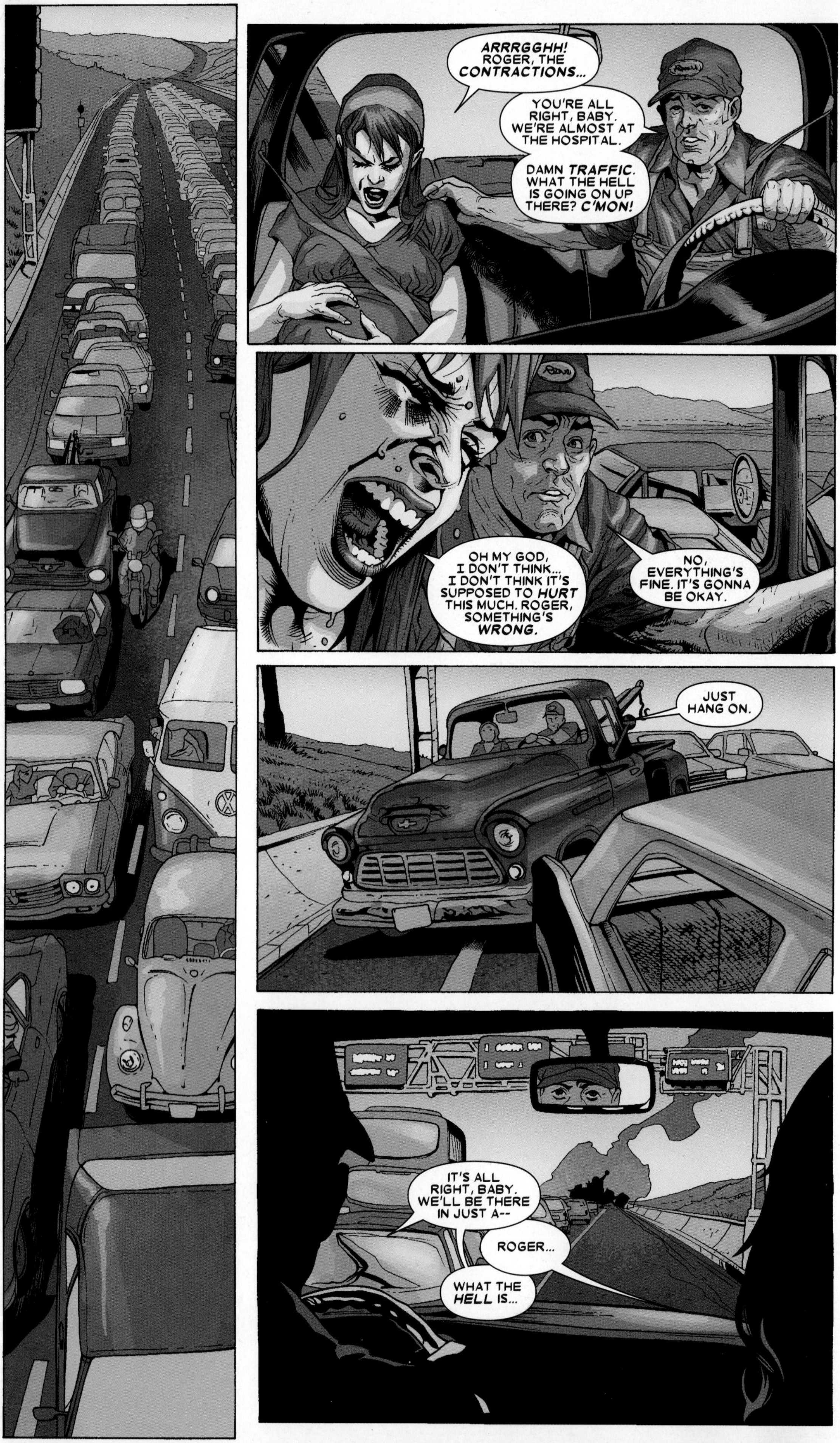
ARRRGGHH! ROGER, THE CONTRACTIONS...
YOU'RE ALL RIGHT, BABY. WE'RE ALMOST AT THE HOSPITAL.
DAMN TRAFFIC. WHAT THE HELL IS GOING ON UP THERE? C'MON!
OH MY GOD, I DON'T THINK... I DON'T THINK IT'S SUPPOSED TO HURT THIS MUCH. ROGER, SOMETHING'S WRONG.
NO, EVERYTHING'S FINE. IT'S GONNA BE OKAY.
JUST HANG ON.
IT'S ALL RIGHT, BABY. WE'LL BE THERE IN JUST A--
ROGER...
WHAT THE HELL IS...

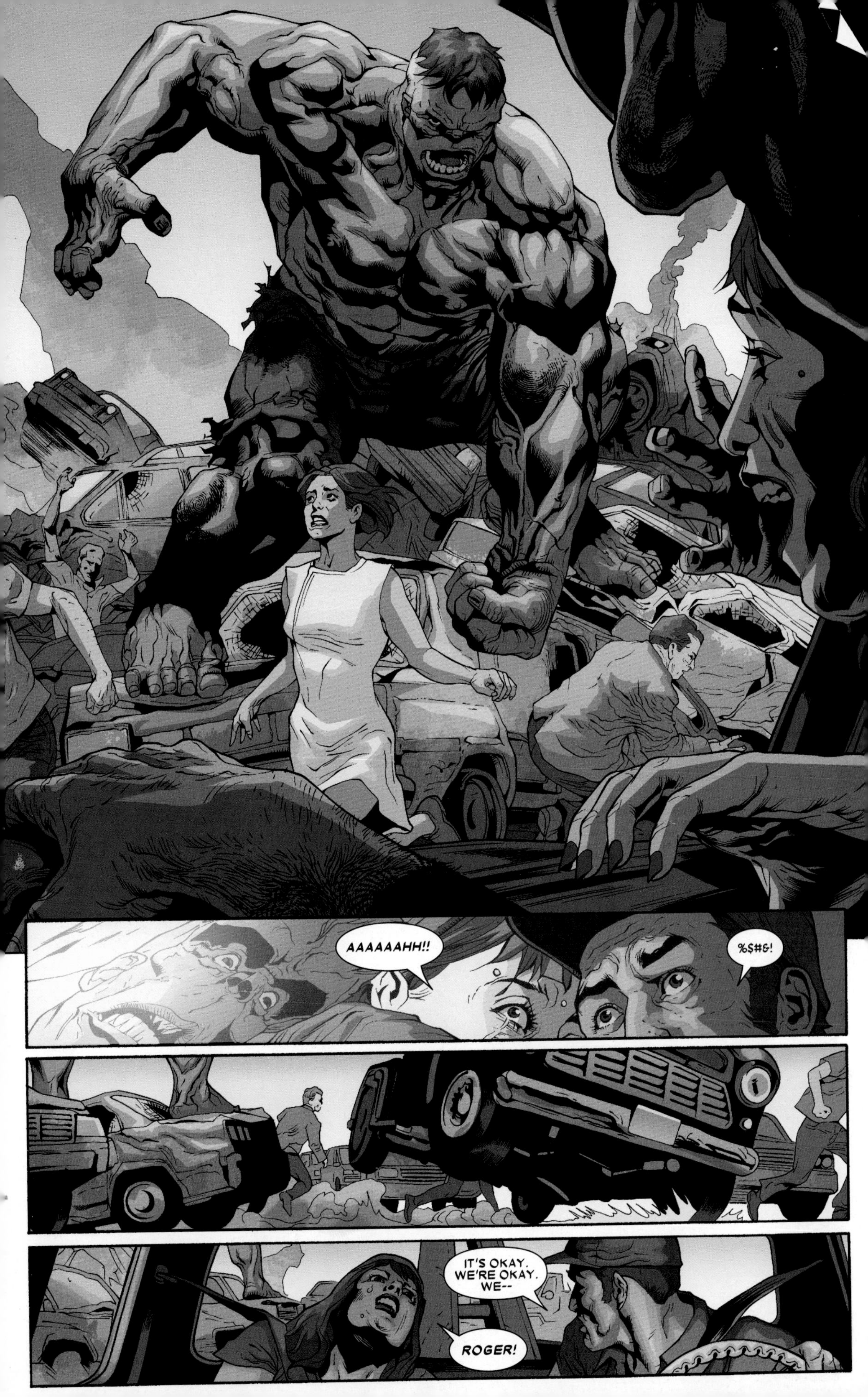
AAAAAAHH!!
%$#&!
IT'S OKAY. WE'RE OKAY. WE--
ROGER!

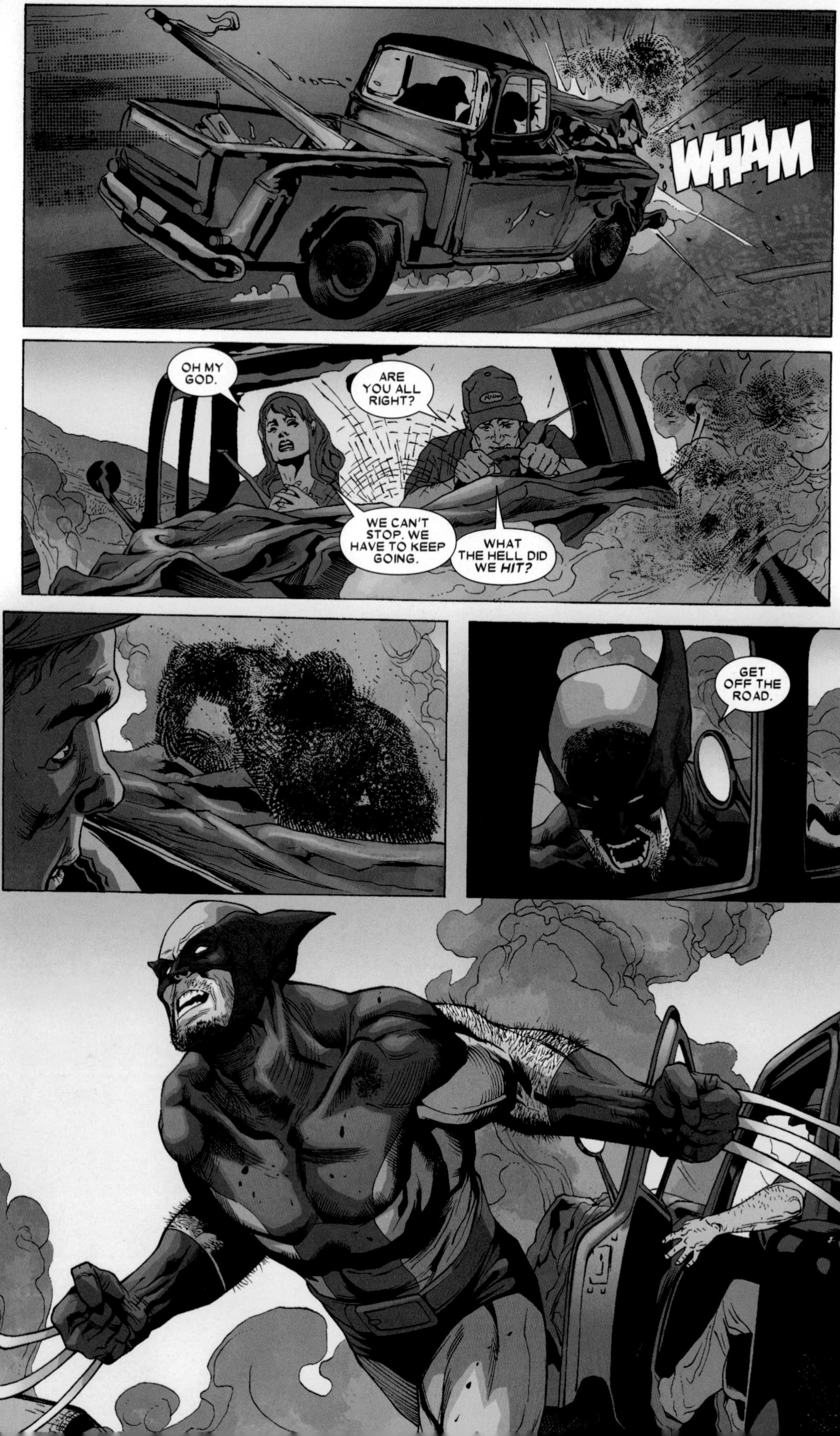
WHAM
OH MY GOD.
ARE YOU ALL RIGHT?
WE CAN'T STOP. WE HAVE TO KEEP GOING.
WHAT THE HELL DID WE HIT?
GET OFF THE ROAD.

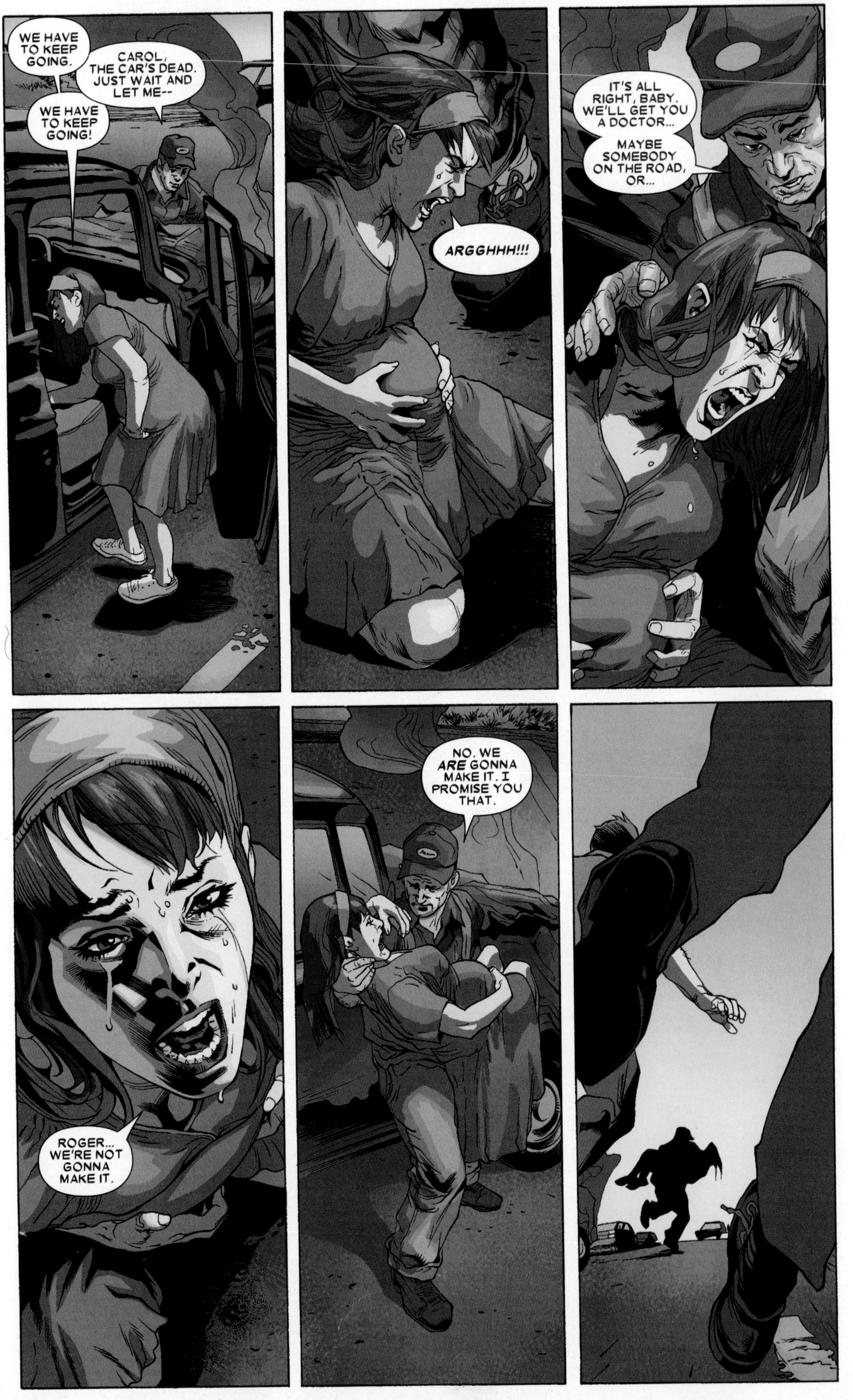
WE HAVE TO KEEP GOING.
CAROL, THE CAR'S DEAD. JUST WAIT AND LET ME--
WE HAVE TO KEEP GOING!
ARGGHHH!!!
IT'S ALL RIGHT, BABY. WE'LL GET YOU A DOCTOR...
MAYBE SOMEBODY ON THE ROAD, OR...
ROGER... WE'RE NOT GONNA MAKE IT.
NO. WE ARE GONNA MAKE IT. I PROMISE YOU THAT.

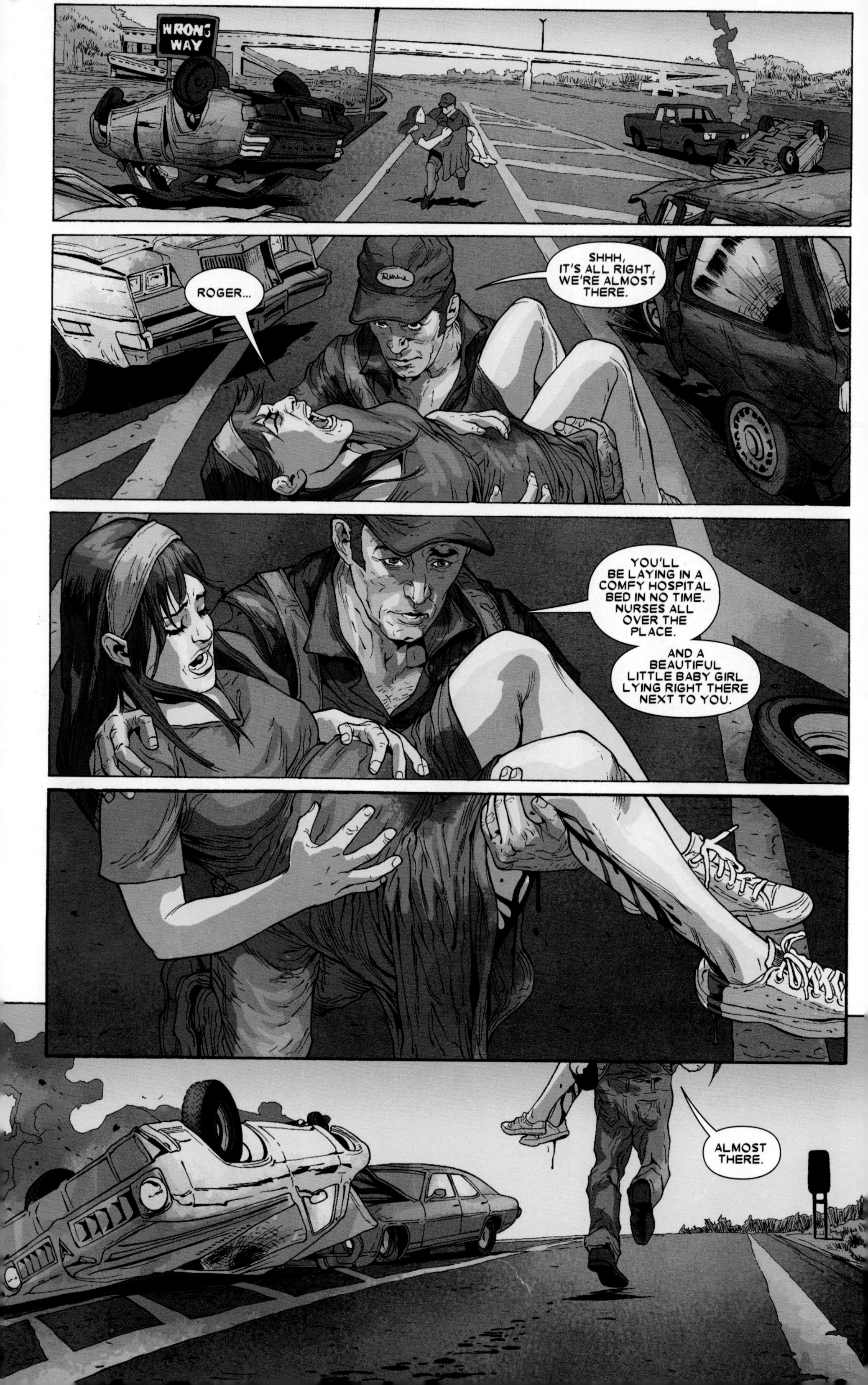
WRONG WAY
ROGER...
SHHH, IT'S ALL RIGHT, WE'RE ALMOST THERE.
YOU'LL BE LAYING IN A COMFY HOSPITAL BED IN NO TIME. NURSES ALL OVER THE PLACE.
AND A BEAUTIFUL LITTLE BABY GIRL LYING RIGHT THERE NEXT TO YOU.
ALMOST THERE.

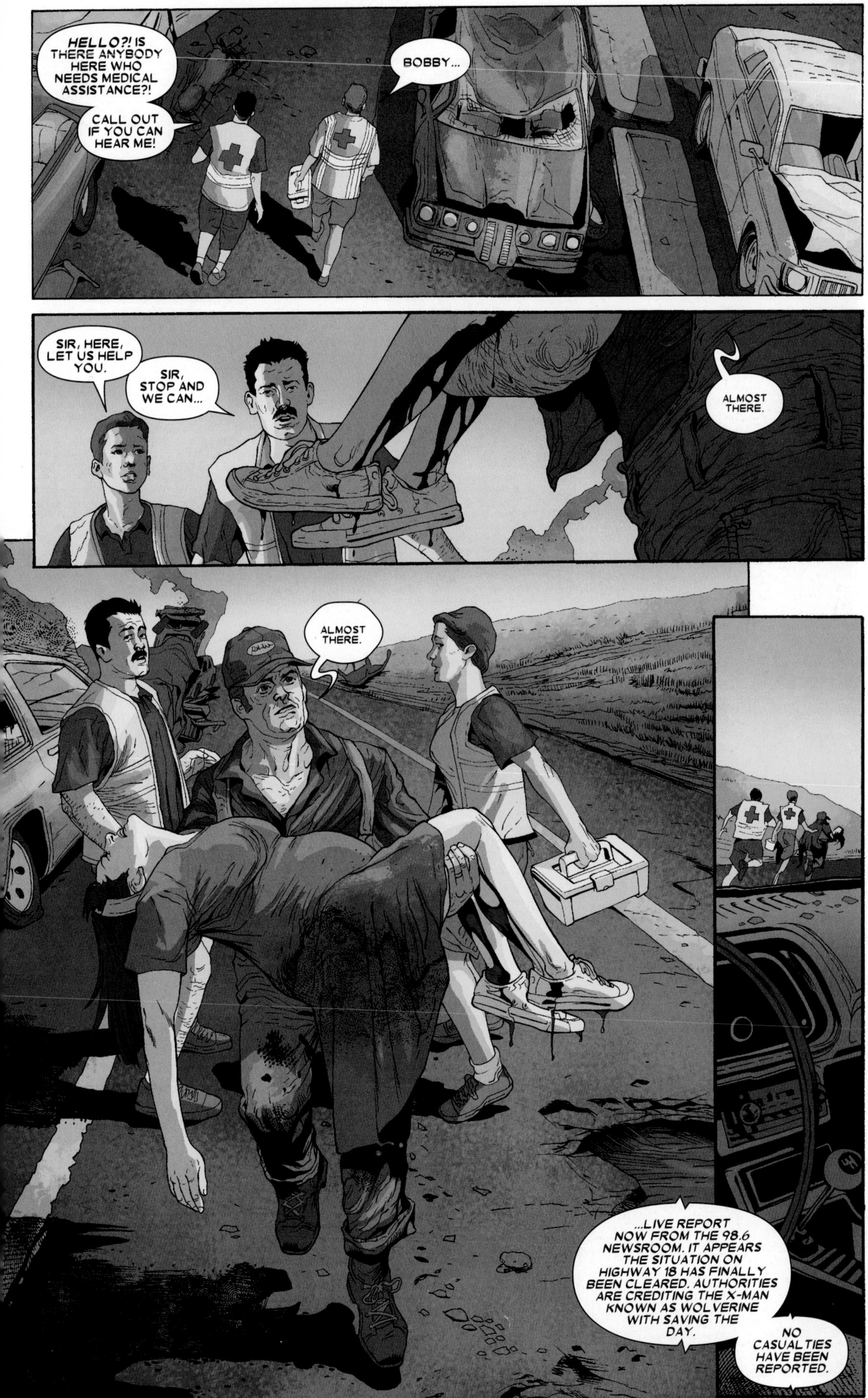
HELLO?! IS THERE ANYBODY HERE WHO NEEDS MEDICAL ASSISTANCE?!
CALL OUT IF YOU CAN HEAR ME!
BOBBY...
SIR, HERE, LET US HELP YOU.
SIR, STOP AND WE CAN...
ALMOST THERE.
ALMOST THERE.
...LIVE REPORT NOW FROM THE 98.6 NEWSROOM. IT APPEARS THE SITUATION ON HIGHWAY 18 HAS FINALLY BEEN CLEARED. AUTHORITIES ARE CREDITING THE X-MAN KNOWN AS WOLVERINE WITH SAVING THE DAY.
NO CASUALTIES HAVE BEEN REPORTED.

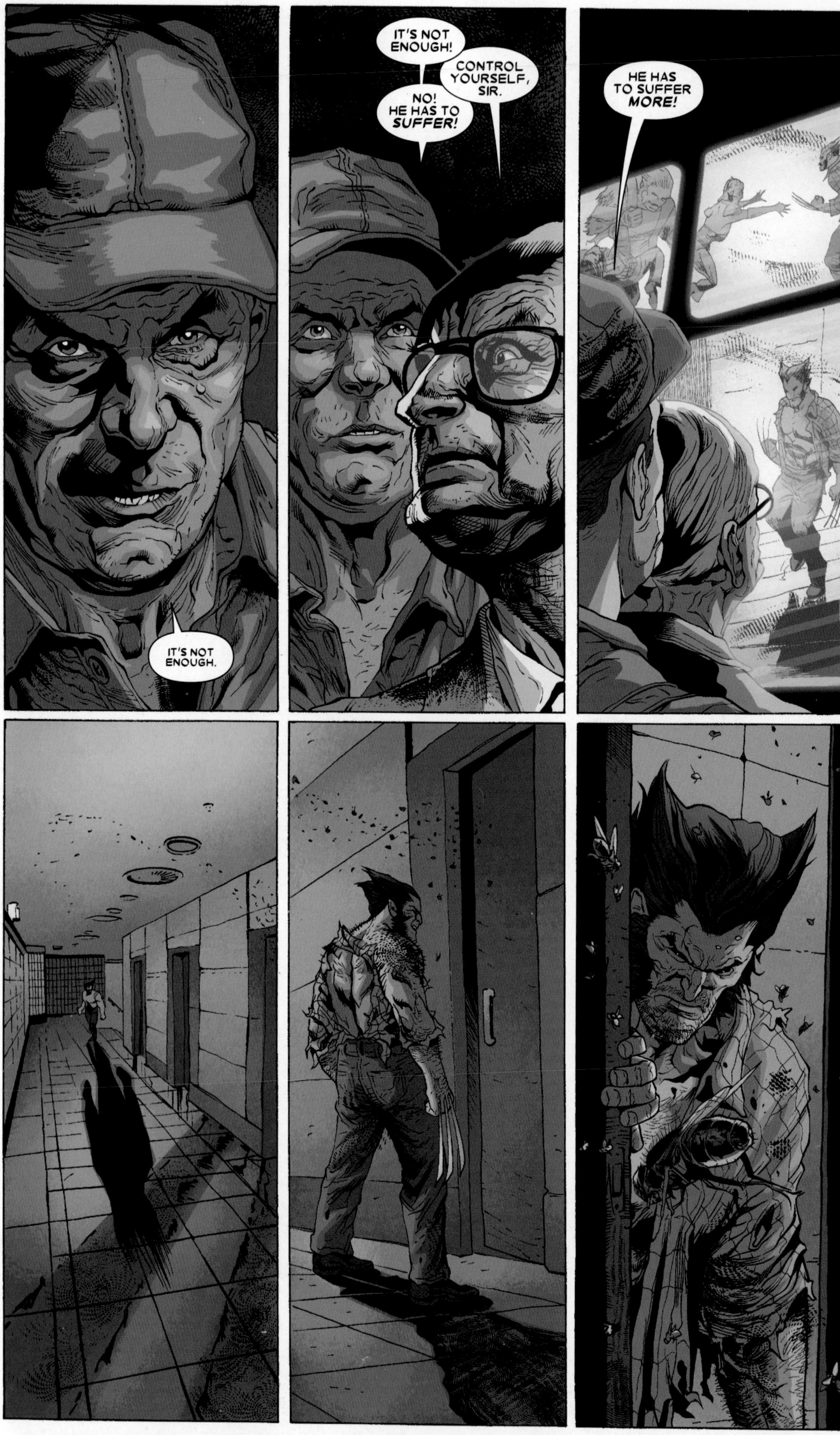
IT'S NOT ENOUGH.
IT'S NOT ENOUGH!
NO! HE HAS TO SUFFER!
CONTROL YOURSELF, SIR.
HE HAS TO SUFFER MORE!

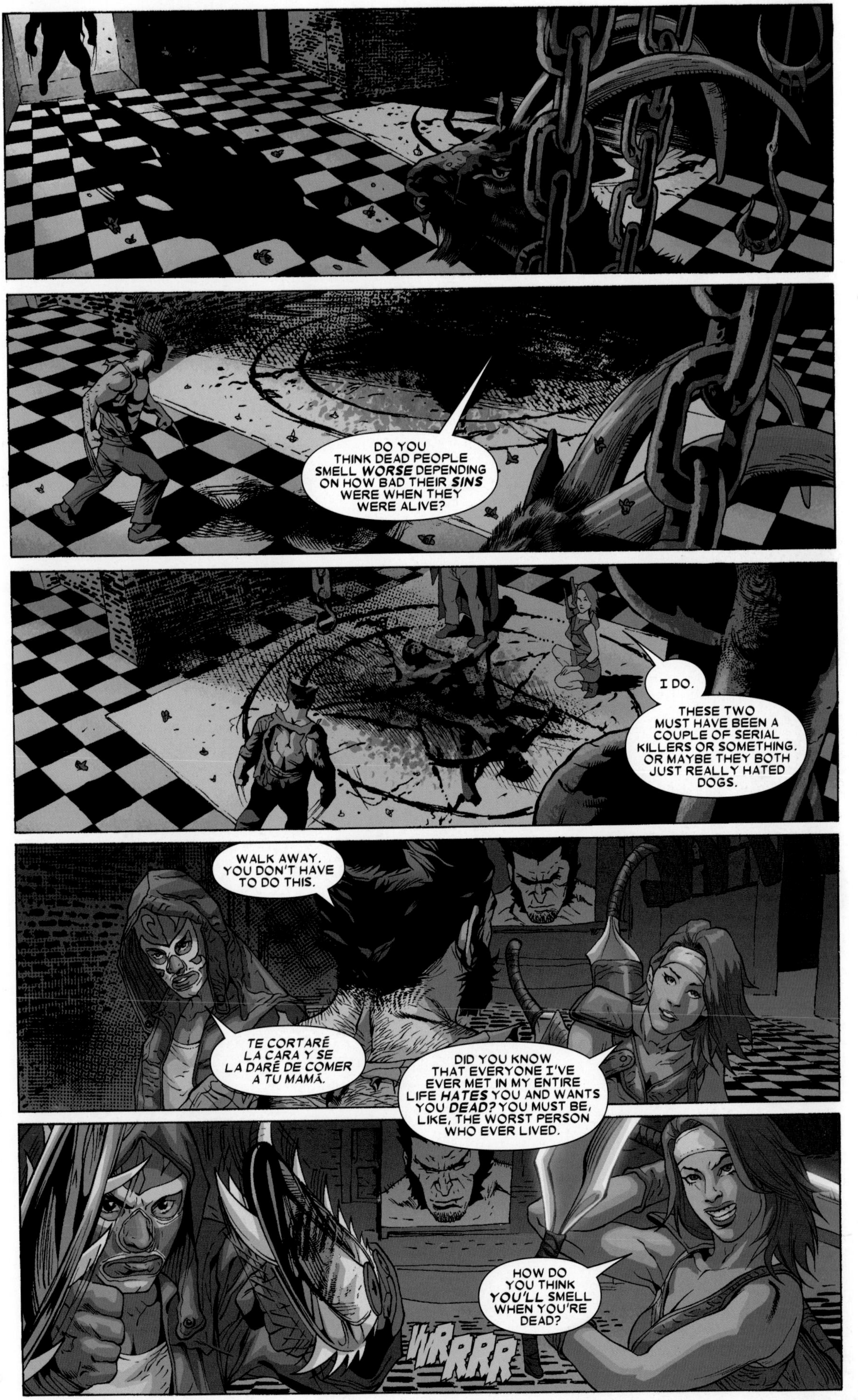
DO YOU THINK DEAD PEOPLE SMELL WORSE DEPENDING ON HOW BAD THEIR SINS WERE WHEN THEY WERE ALIVE?
I DO.
THESE TWO MUST HAVE BEEN A COUPLE OF SERIAL KILLERS OR SOMETHING. OR MAYBE THEY BOTH JUST REALLY HATED DOGS.
WALK AWAY. YOU DON'T HAVE TO DO THIS.
TE CORTARÉ LA CARA Y SE LA DARÉ DE COMER A TU MAMÁ.
DID YOU KNOW THAT EVERYONE I'VE EVER MET IN MY ENTIRE LIFE HATES YOU AND WANTS YOU DEAD? YOU MUST BE, LIKE, THE WORST PERSON WHO EVER LIVED.
HOW DO YOU THINK YOU'LL SMELL WHEN YOU'RE DEAD?
WRRRR

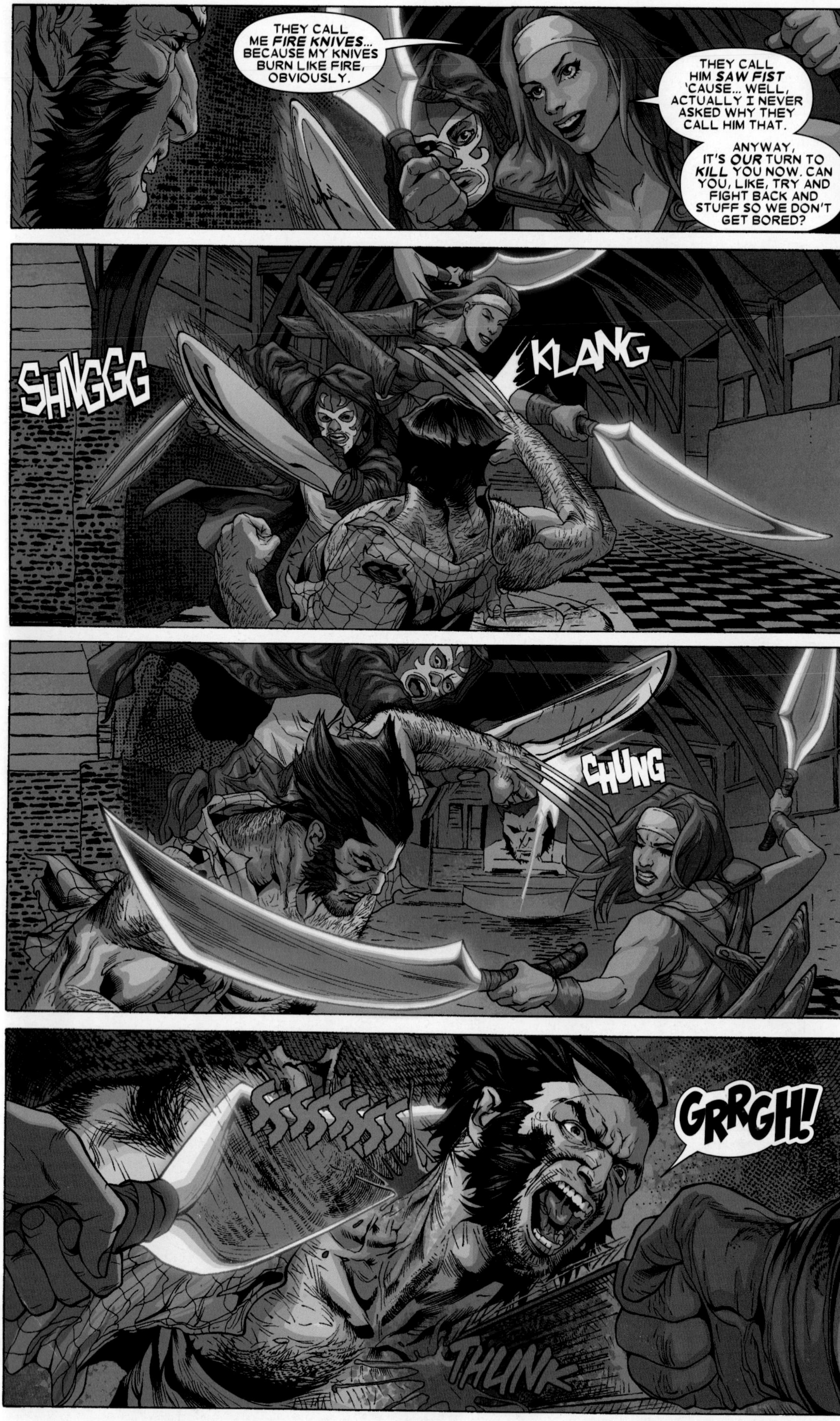
THEY CALL ME FIRE KNIVES... BECAUSE MY KNIVES BURN LIKE FIRE, OBVIOUSLY.
THEY CALL HIM SAW FIST 'CAUSE... WELL, ACTUALLY I NEVER ASKED WHY THEY CALL HIM THAT.
ANYWAY, IT'S OUR TURN TO KILL YOU NOW. CAN YOU, LIKE, TRY AND FIGHT BACK AND STUFF SO WE DON'T GET BORED?
SHNGGG
KLANG
CHUNG
GRRGH!
THUNK

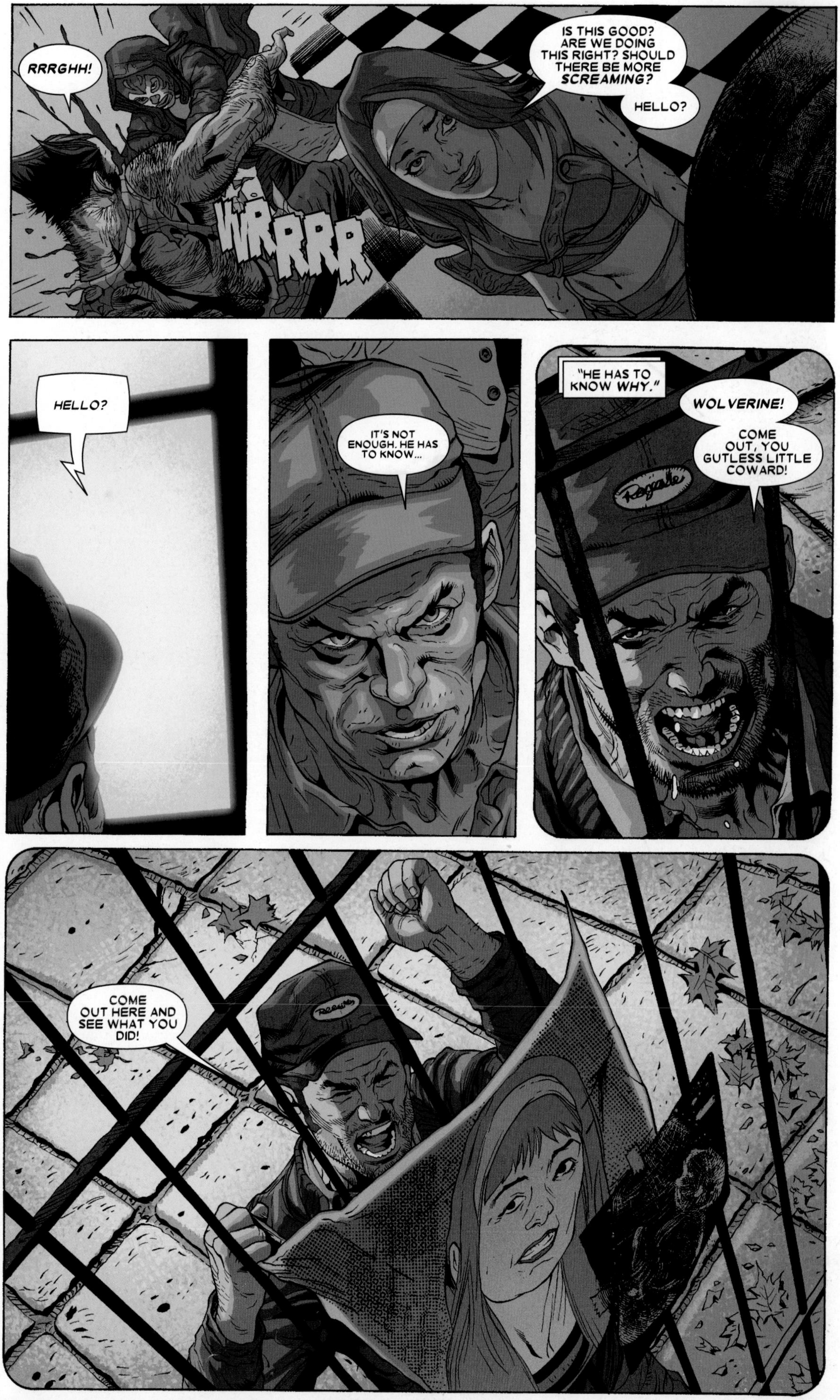
RRRGHH!
IS THIS GOOD? ARE WE DOING THIS RIGHT? SHOULD THERE BE MORE SCREAMING?
HELLO?
WRRRR
HELLO?
IT'S NOT ENOUGH. HE HAS TO KNOW...
"HE HAS TO KNOW WHY."
WOLVERINE!
COME OUT, YOU GUTLESS LITTLE COWARD!
COME OUT HERE AND SEE WHAT YOU DID!

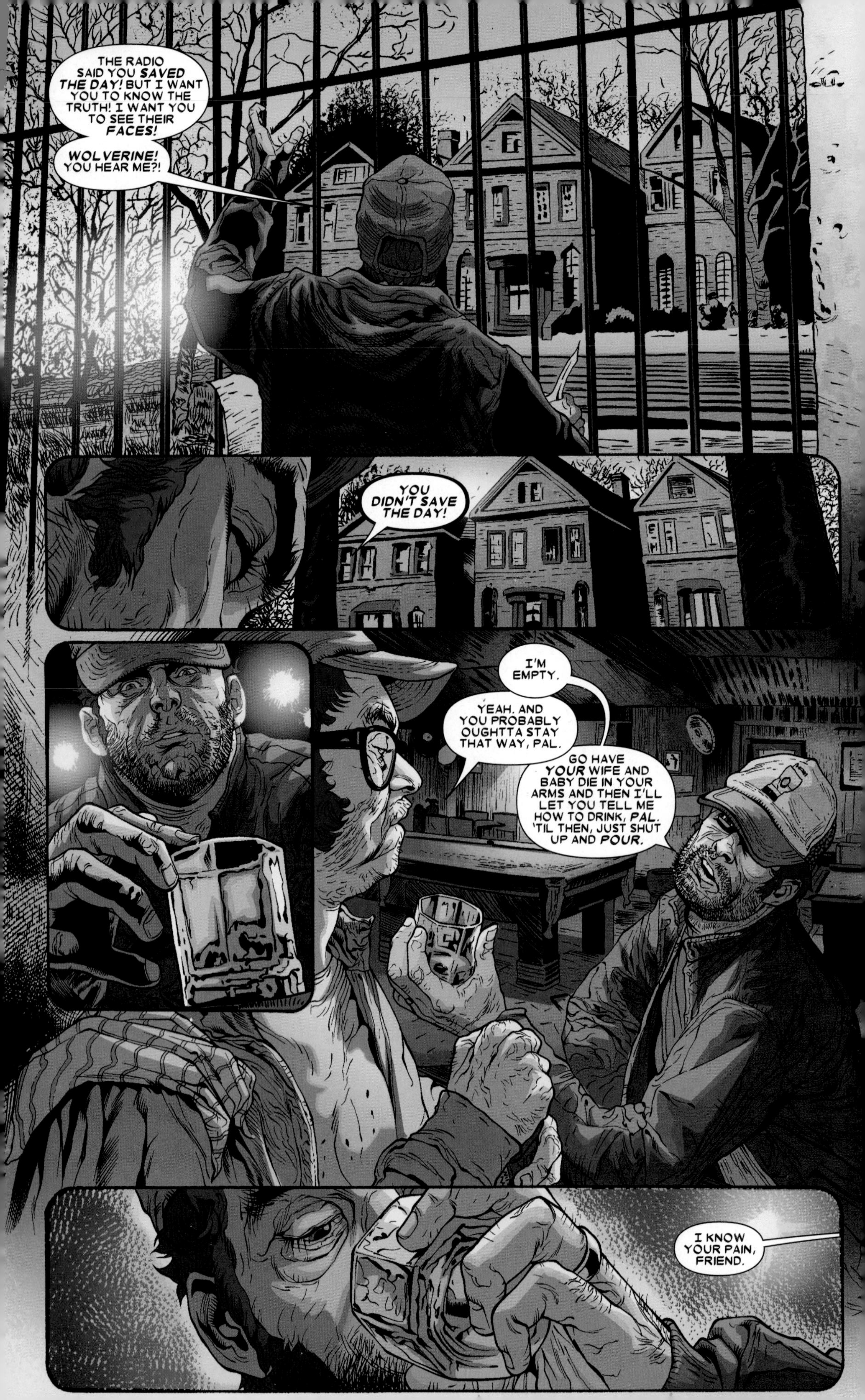
THE RADIO SAID YOU SAVED THE DAY! BUT I WANT YOU TO KNOW THE TRUTH! I WANT YOU TO SEE THEIR FACES!
WOLVERINE! YOU HEAR ME?!
YOU DIDN'T SAVE THE DAY!
I'M EMPTY.
YEAH. AND YOU PROBABLY OUGHTTA STAY THAT WAY, PAL.
GO HAVE YOUR WIFE AND BABY DIE IN YOUR ARMS AND THEN I'LL LET YOU TELL ME HOW TO DRINK, PAL. 'TIL THEN, JUST SHUT UP AND POUR.
I KNOW YOUR PAIN, FRIEND.

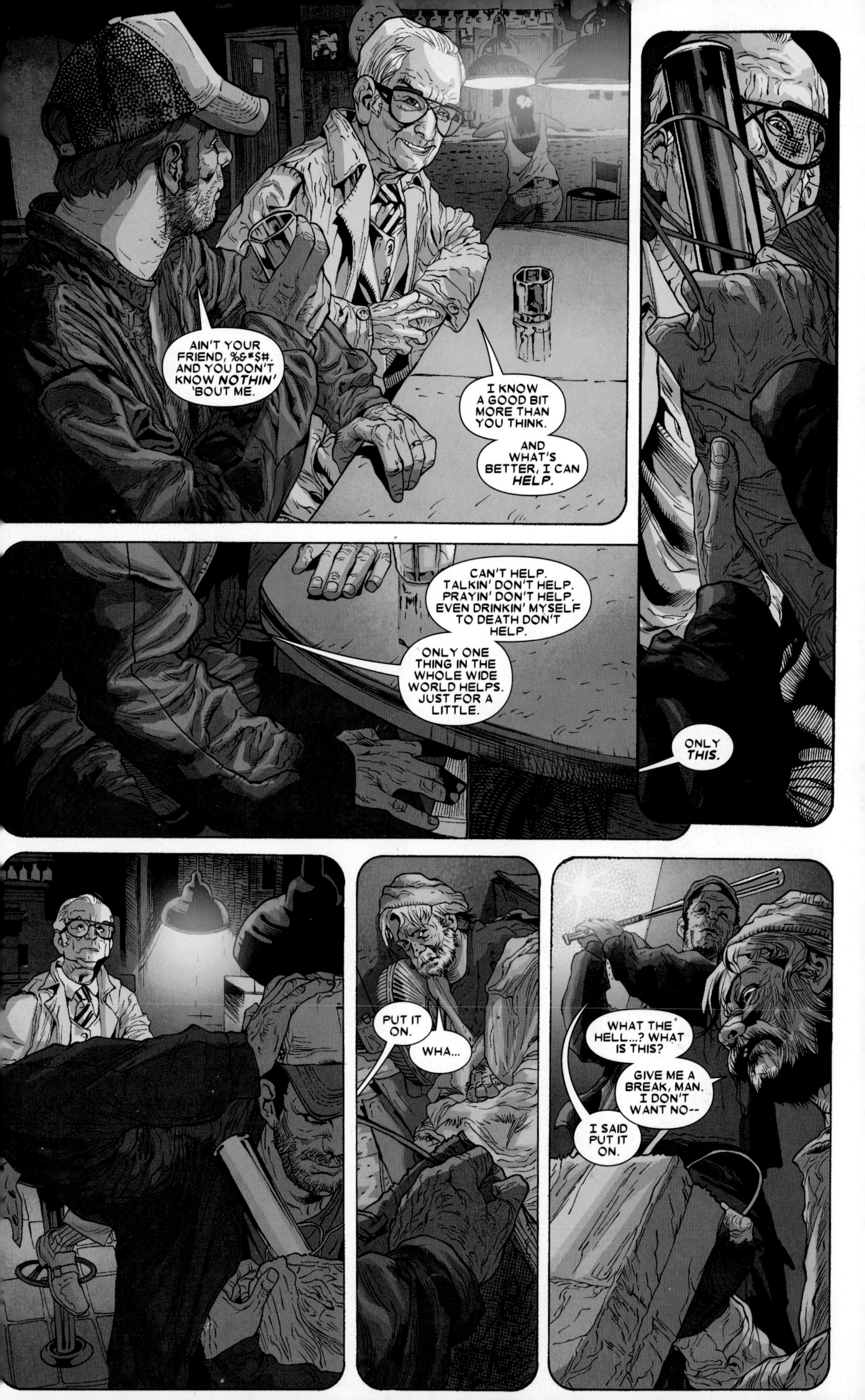
AIN'T YOUR FRIEND, %&*$#. AND YOU DON'T KNOW NOTHIN' 'BOUT ME.
I KNOW A GOOD BIT MORE THAN YOU THINK.
AND WHAT'S BETTER, I CAN HELP.
CAN'T HELP. TALKIN' DON'T HELP. PRAYIN' DON'T HELP. EVEN DRINKIN' MYSELF TO DEATH DON'T HELP.
ONLY ONE THING IN THE WHOLE WIDE WORLD HELPS. JUST FOR A LITTLE.
ONLY THIS.
PUT IT ON.
WHA...
WHAT THE HELL...? WHAT IS THIS?
GIVE ME A BREAK, MAN. I DON'T WANT NO--
I SAID PUT IT ON.

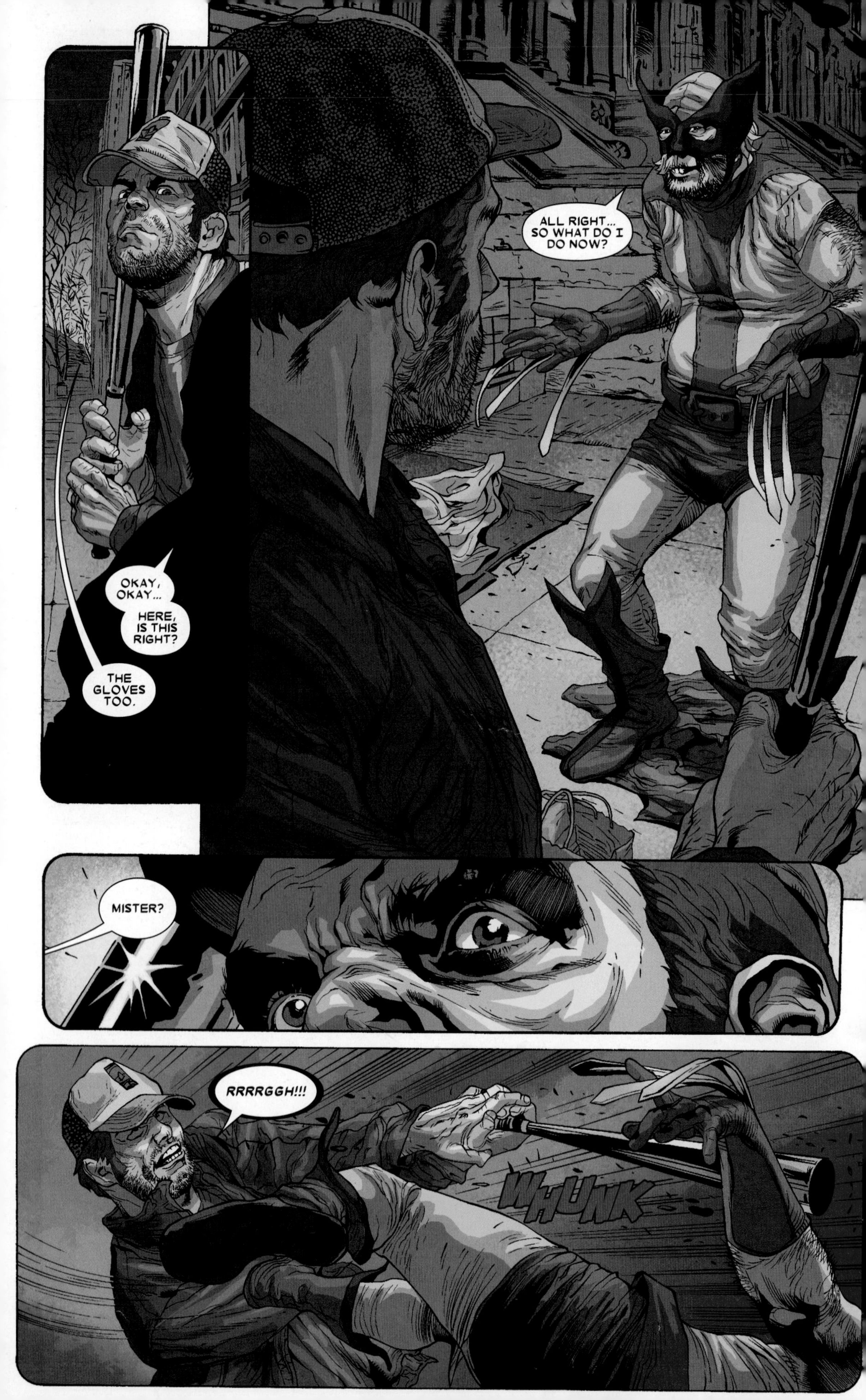
ALL RIGHT... SO WHAT DO I DO NOW?
OKAY, OKAY...
HERE, IS THIS RIGHT?
THE GLOVES TOO.
MISTER?
RRRRGGH!!!
WHUNK

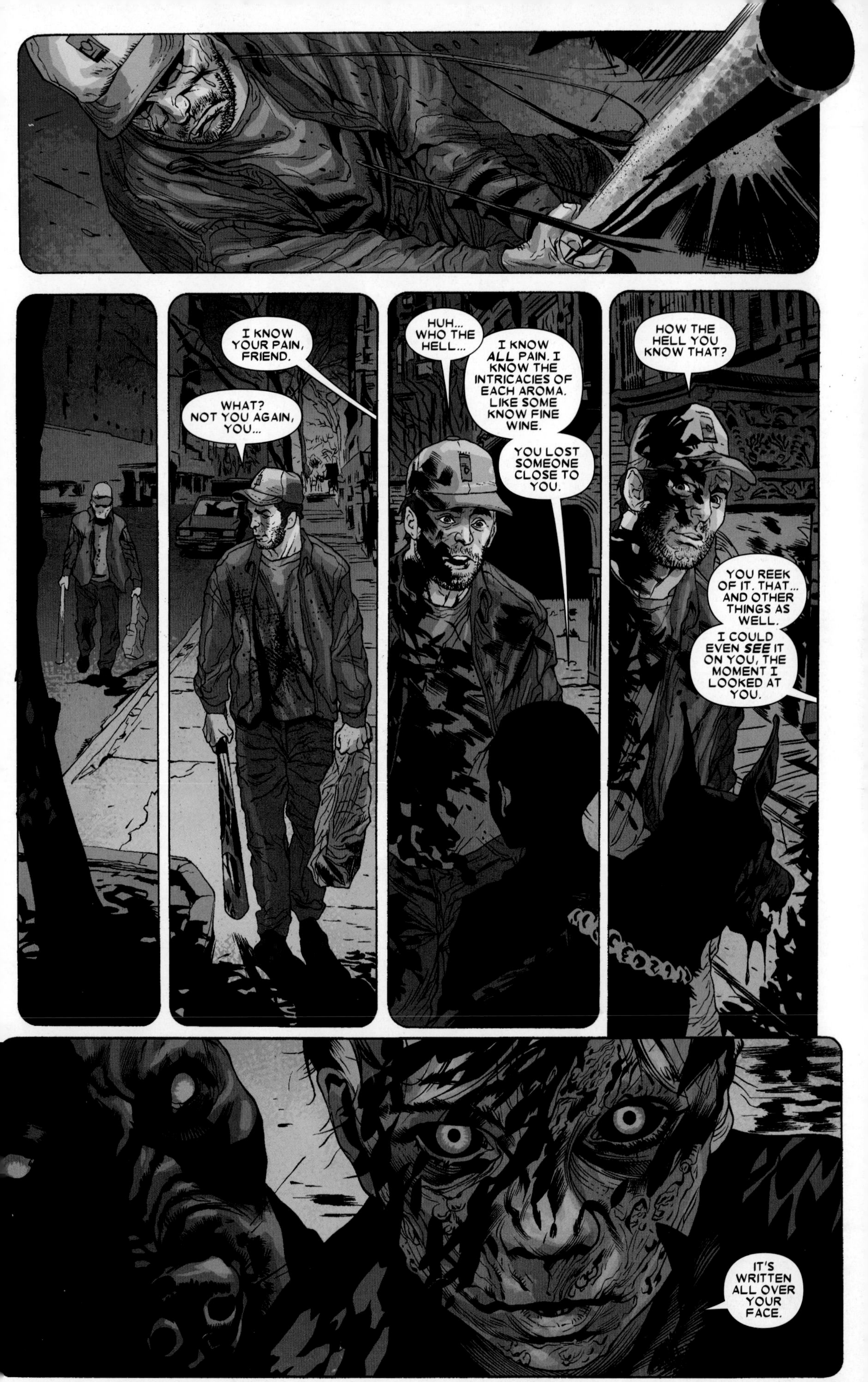
I KNOW YOUR PAIN, FRIEND.
WHAT? NOT YOU AGAIN, YOU...
HUH... WHO THE HELL...
I KNOW ALL PAIN. I KNOW THE INTRICACIES OF EACH AROMA. LIKE SOME KNOW FINE WINE.
YOU LOST SOMEONE CLOSE TO YOU.
HOW THE HELL YOU KNOW THAT?
YOU REEK OF IT. THAT... AND OTHER THINGS AS WELL.
I COULD EVEN SEE IT ON YOU, THE MOMENT I LOOKED AT YOU.
IT'S WRITTEN ALL OVER YOUR FACE.

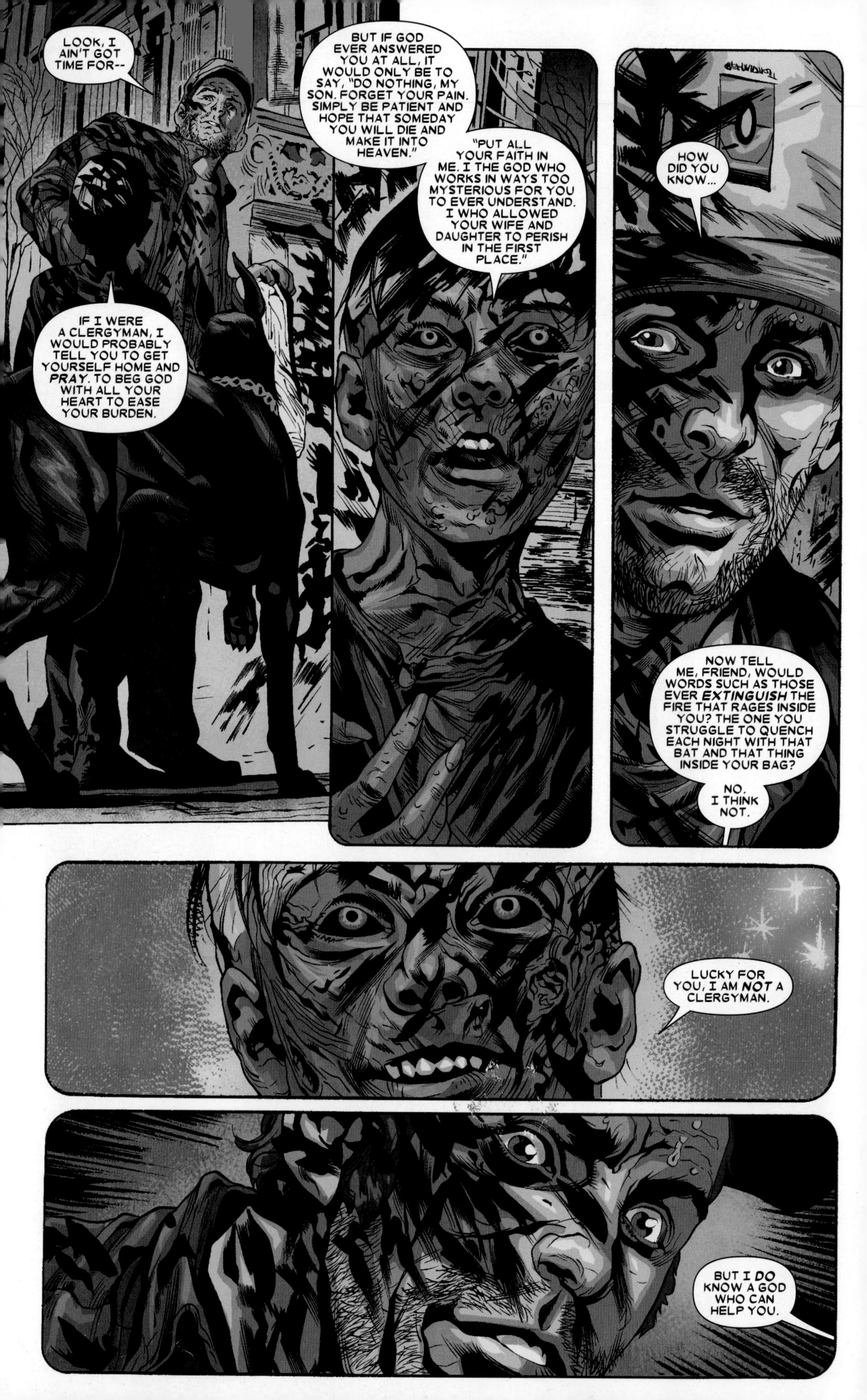
LOOK, I AIN'T GOT TIME FOR--
IF I WERE A CLERGYMAN, I WOULD PROBABLY TELL YOU TO GET YOURSELF HOME AND PRAY. TO BEG GOD WITH ALL YOUR HEART TO EASE YOUR BURDEN.
BUT IF GOD EVER ANSWERED YOU AT ALL, IT WOULD ONLY BE TO SAY, "DO NOTHING, MY SON. FORGET YOUR PAIN. SIMPLY BE PATIENT AND HOPE THAT SOMEDAY YOU WILL DIE AND MAKE IT INTO HEAVEN."
"PUT ALL YOUR FAITH IN ME. I THE GOD WHO WORKS IN WAYS TOO MYSTERIOUS FOR YOU TO EVER UNDERSTAND. I WHO ALLOWED YOUR WIFE AND DAUGHTER TO PERISH IN THE FIRST PLACE."
HOW DID YOU KNOW...
NOW TELL ME, FRIEND, WOULD WORDS SUCH AS THOSE EVER EXTINGUISH THE FIRE THAT RAGES INSIDE YOU? THE ONE YOU STRUGGLE TO QUENCH EACH NIGHT WITH THAT BAT AND THAT THING INSIDE YOUR BAG?
NO. I THINK NOT.
LUCKY FOR YOU, I AM NOT A CLERGYMAN.
BUT I DO KNOW A GOD WHO CAN HELP YOU.

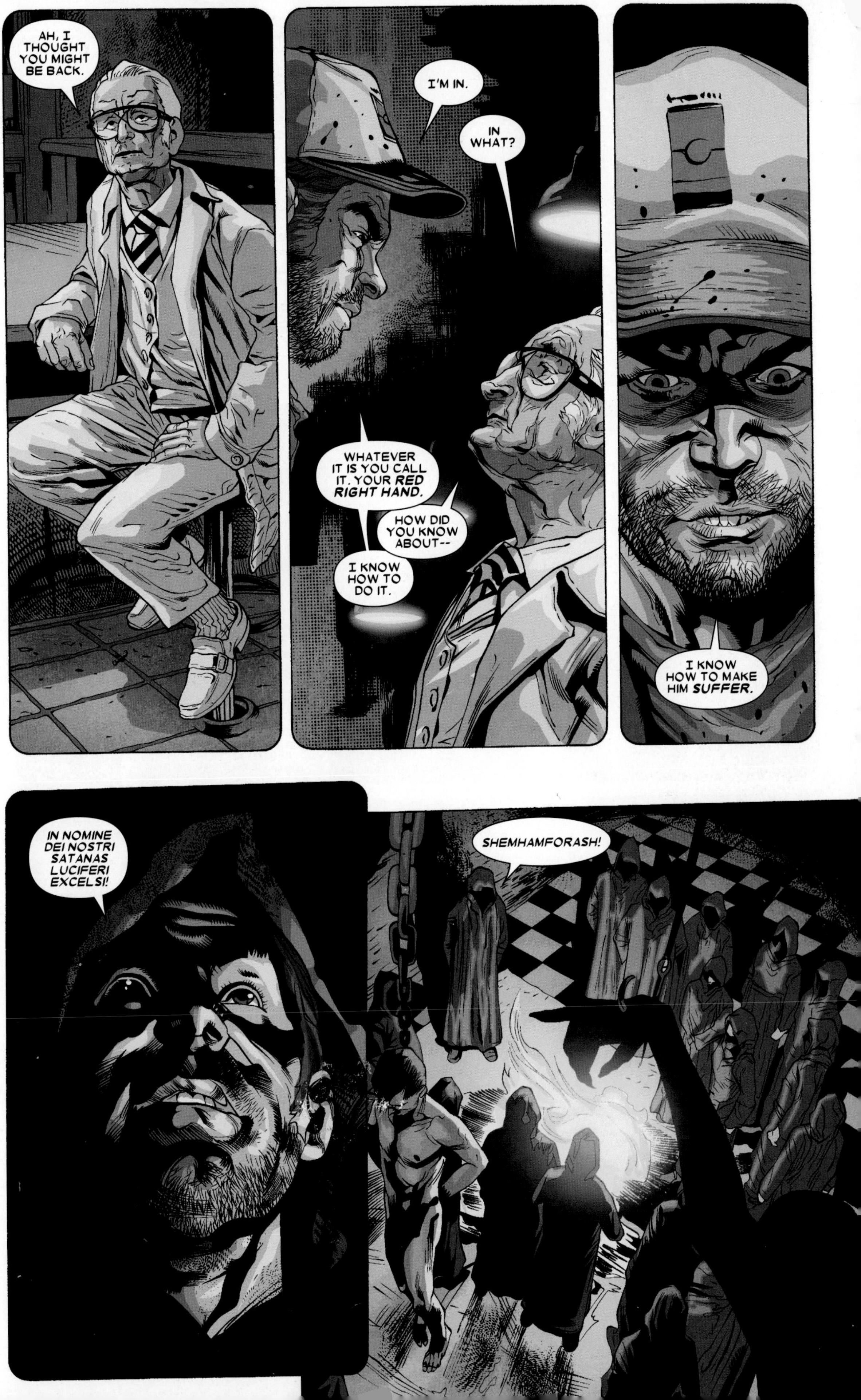
AH, I THOUGHT YOU MIGHT BE BACK.
I'M IN.
IN WHAT?
WHATEVER IT IS YOU CALL IT. YOUR RED RIGHT HAND.
HOW DID YOU KNOW ABOUT--
I KNOW HOW TO DO IT.
I KNOW HOW TO MAKE HIM SUFFER.
IN NOMINE DEI NOSTRI SATANAS LUCIFERI EXCELSI!
SHEMHAMFORASH!

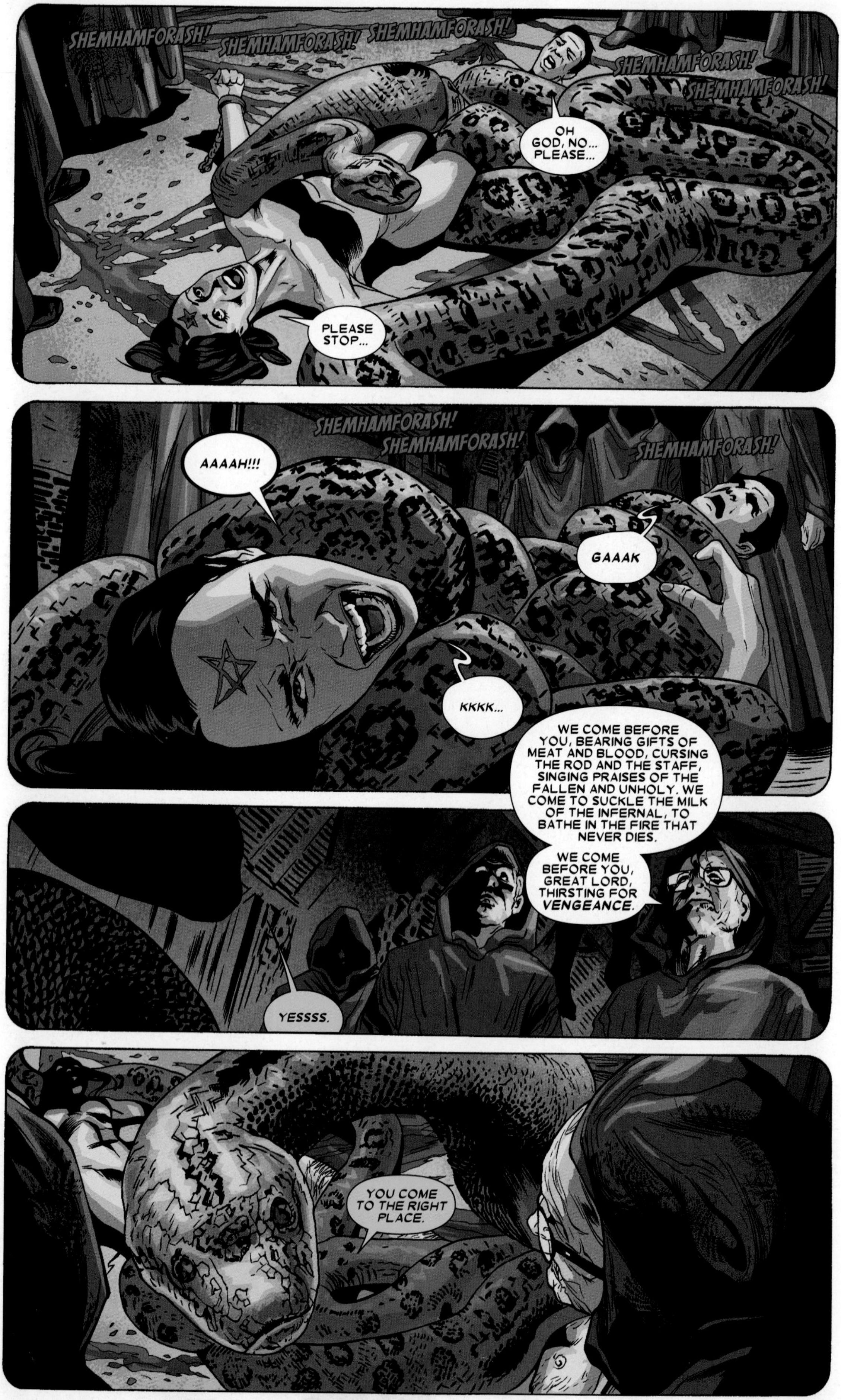
SHEMHAMFORASH! SHEMHAMFORASH! SHEMHAMFORASH!
SHEMHAMFORASH! SHEMHAMFORASH!
OH GOD, NO... PLEASE...
PLEASE STOP...
SHEMHAMFORASH! SHEMHAMFORASH!
SHEMHAMFORASH!
AAAAH!!!
GAAAK
KKKK...
WE COME BEFORE YOU, BEARING GIFTS OF MEAT AND BLOOD, CURSING THE ROD AND THE STAFF, SINGING PRAISES OF THE FALLEN AND UNHOLY. WE COME TO SUCKLE THE MILK OF THE INFERNAL, TO BATHE IN THE FIRE THAT NEVER DIES.
WE COME BEFORE YOU, GREAT LORD, THIRSTING FOR VENGEANCE.
YESSSS.
YOU COME TO THE RIGHT PLACE.

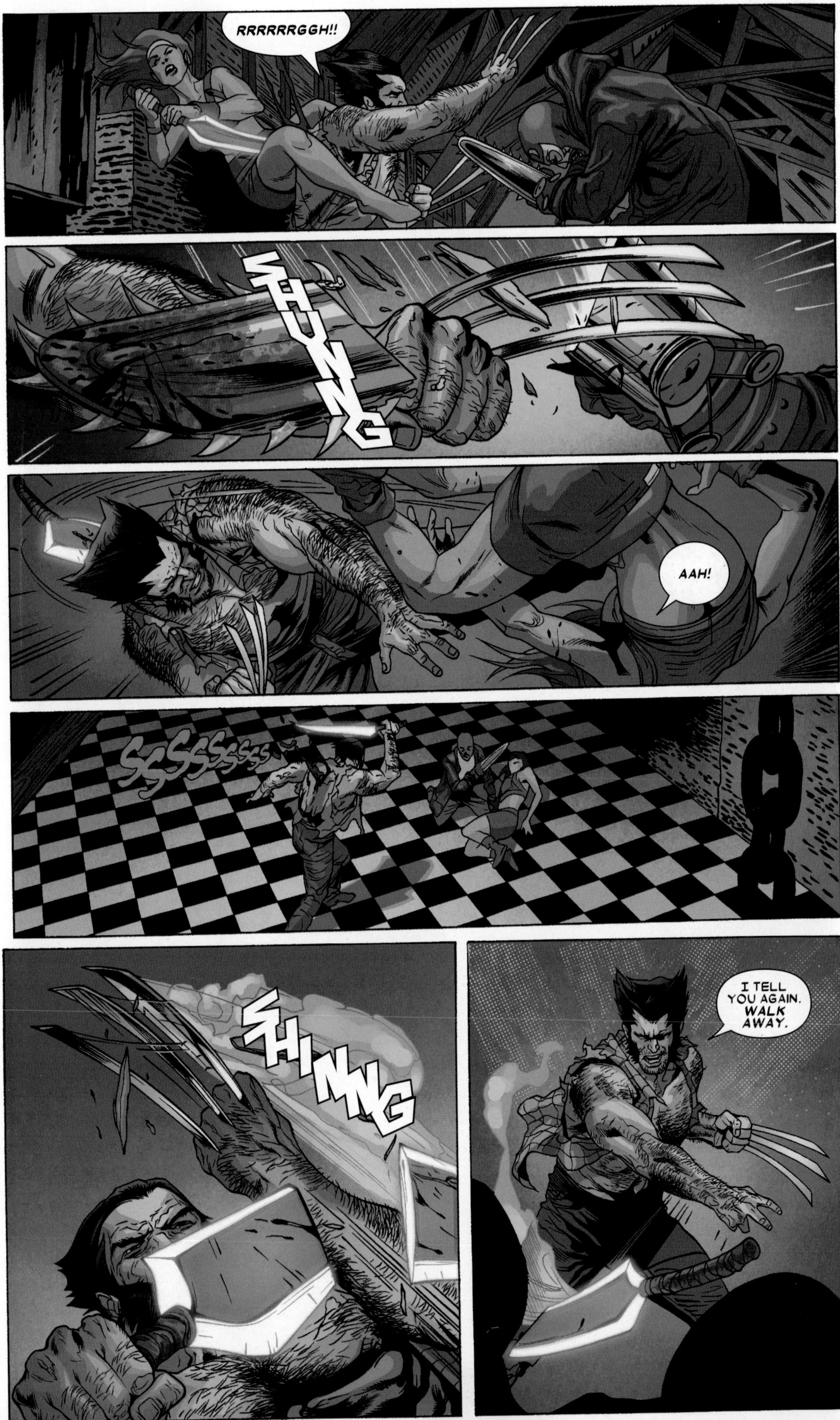
RRRRRRGGH!!
SHUNNG
AAH!
SSSSSSSSS
SHINNNG
I TELL YOU AGAIN. WALK AWAY.

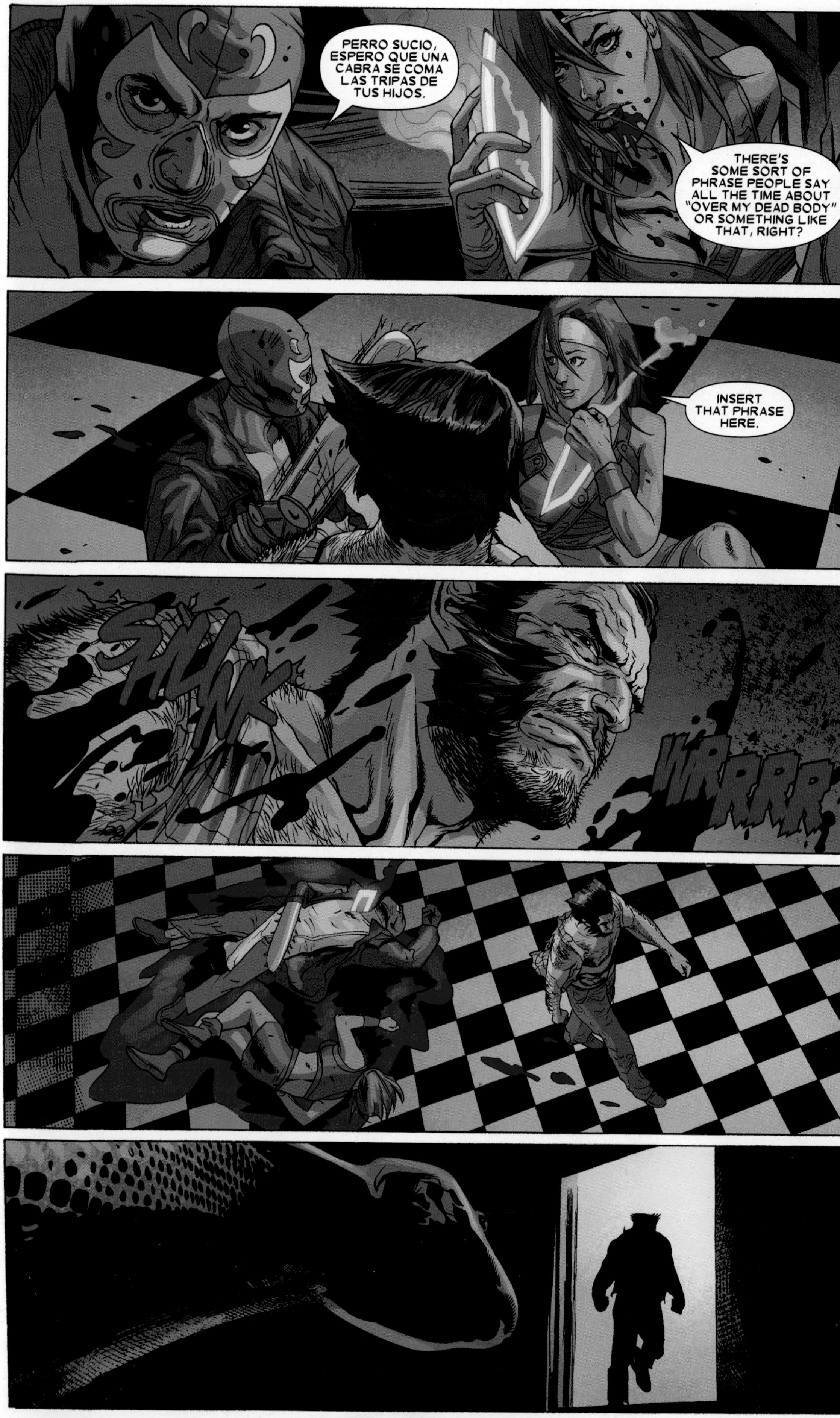
PERRO SUCIO, ESPERO QUE UNA CABRA SE COMA LAS TRIPAS DE TUS HIJOS.
THERE'S SOME SORT OF PHRASE PEOPLE SAY ALL THE TIME ABOUT "OVER MY DEAD BODY" OR SOMETHING LIKE THAT, RIGHT?
INSERT THAT PHRASE HERE.
SHUNK
VRRRR

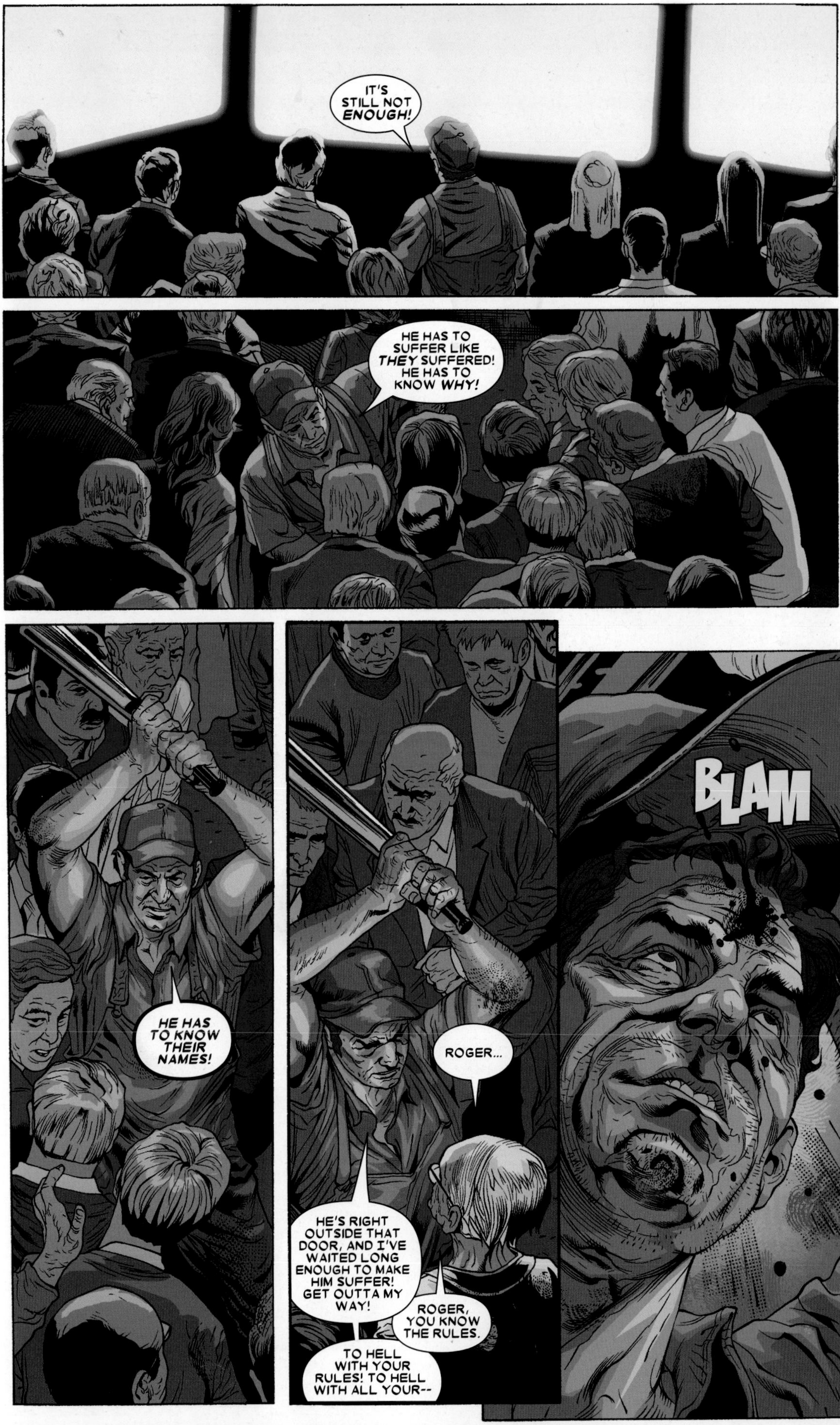
IT'S STILL NOT ENOUGH!
HE HAS TO SUFFER LIKE THEY SUFFERED! HE HAS TO KNOW WHY!
HE HAS TO KNOW THEIR NAMES!
ROGER...
HE'S RIGHT OUTSIDE THAT DOOR, AND I'VE WAITED LONG ENOUGH TO MAKE HIM SUFFER! GET OUTTA MY WAY!
ROGER, YOU KNOW THE RULES.
TO HELL WITH YOUR RULES! TO HELL WITH ALL YOUR--
BLAM

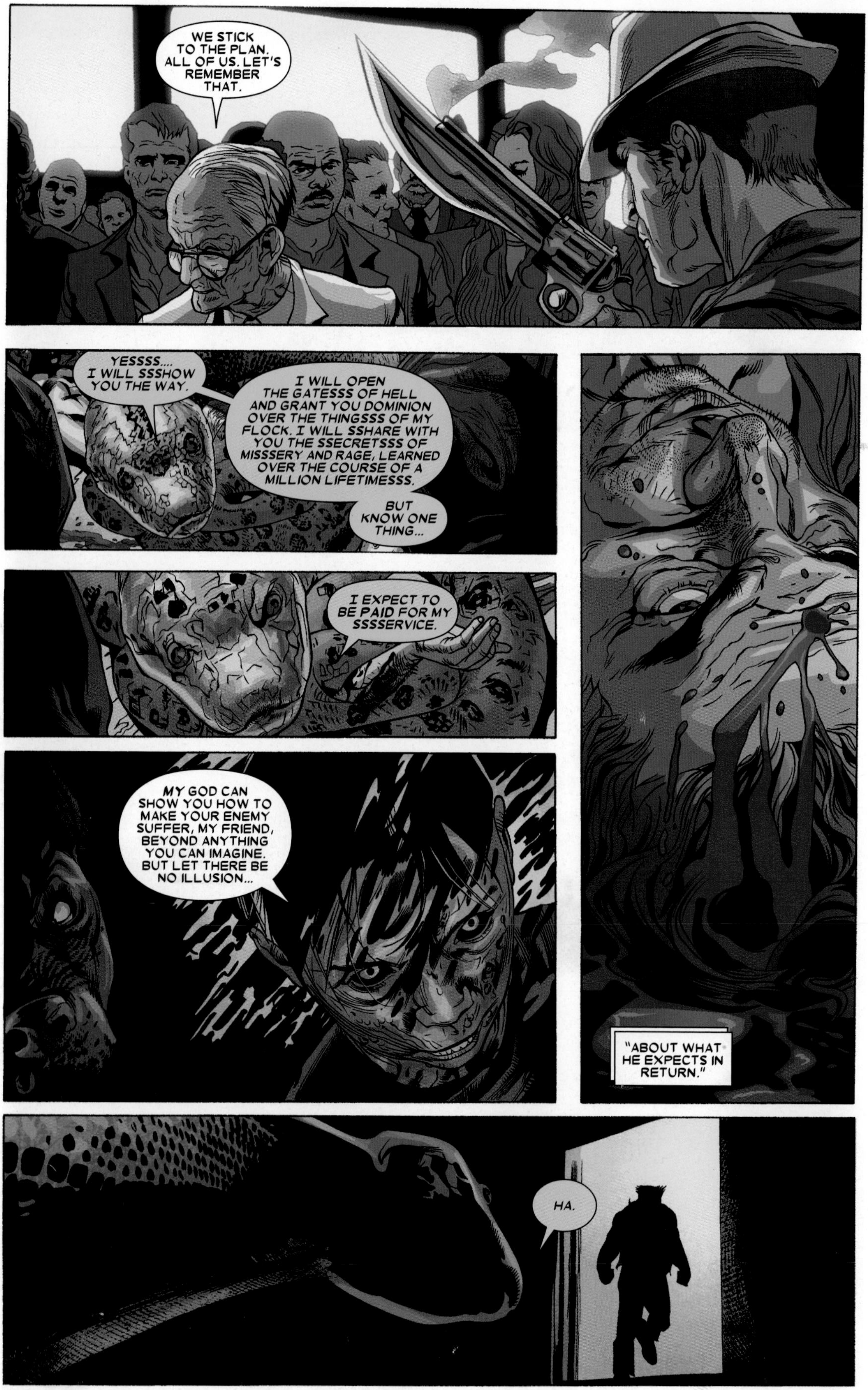
WE STICK TO THE PLAN. ALL OF US. LET'S REMEMBER THAT.
YESSSS.... I WILL SSSHOW YOU THE WAY.
I WILL OPEN THE GATESSS OF HELL AND GRANT YOU DOMINION OVER THE THINGSSS OF MY FLOCK. I WILL SSHARE WITH YOU THE SSECRETSSS OF MISSSERY AND RAGE, LEARNED OVER THE COURSE OF A MILLION LIFETIMESSS.
BUT KNOW ONE THING...
I EXPECT TO BE PAID FOR MY SSSSERVICE.
MY GOD CAN SHOW YOU HOW TO MAKE YOUR ENEMY SUFFER, MY FRIEND, BEYOND ANYTHING YOU CAN IMAGINE. BUT LET THERE BE NO ILLUSION...
"ABOUT WHAT HE EXPECTS IN RETURN."
HA.

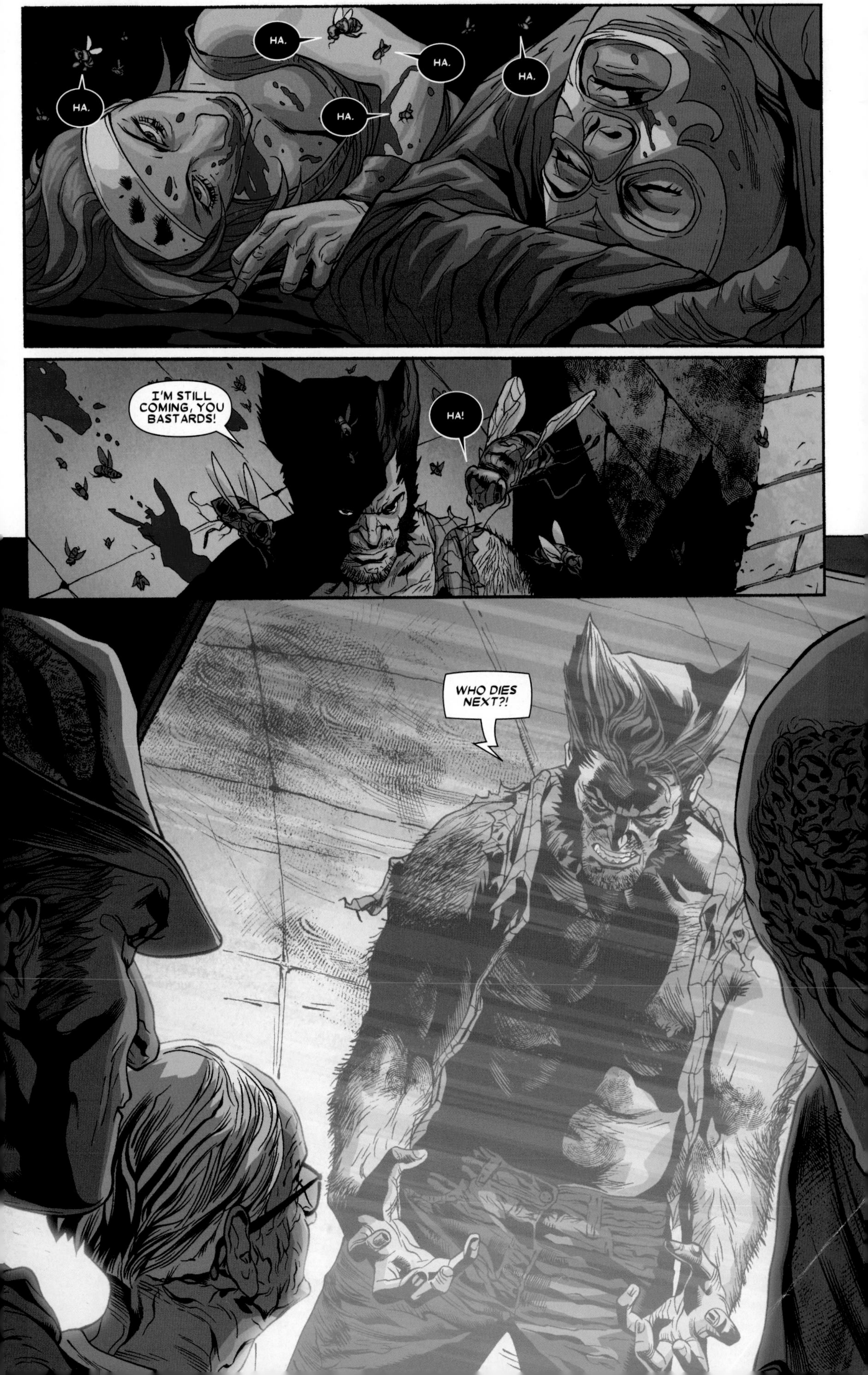
HA.
HA.
HA.
HA.
HA.
I'M STILL COMING, YOU BASTARDS!
HA!
WHO DIES NEXT?!

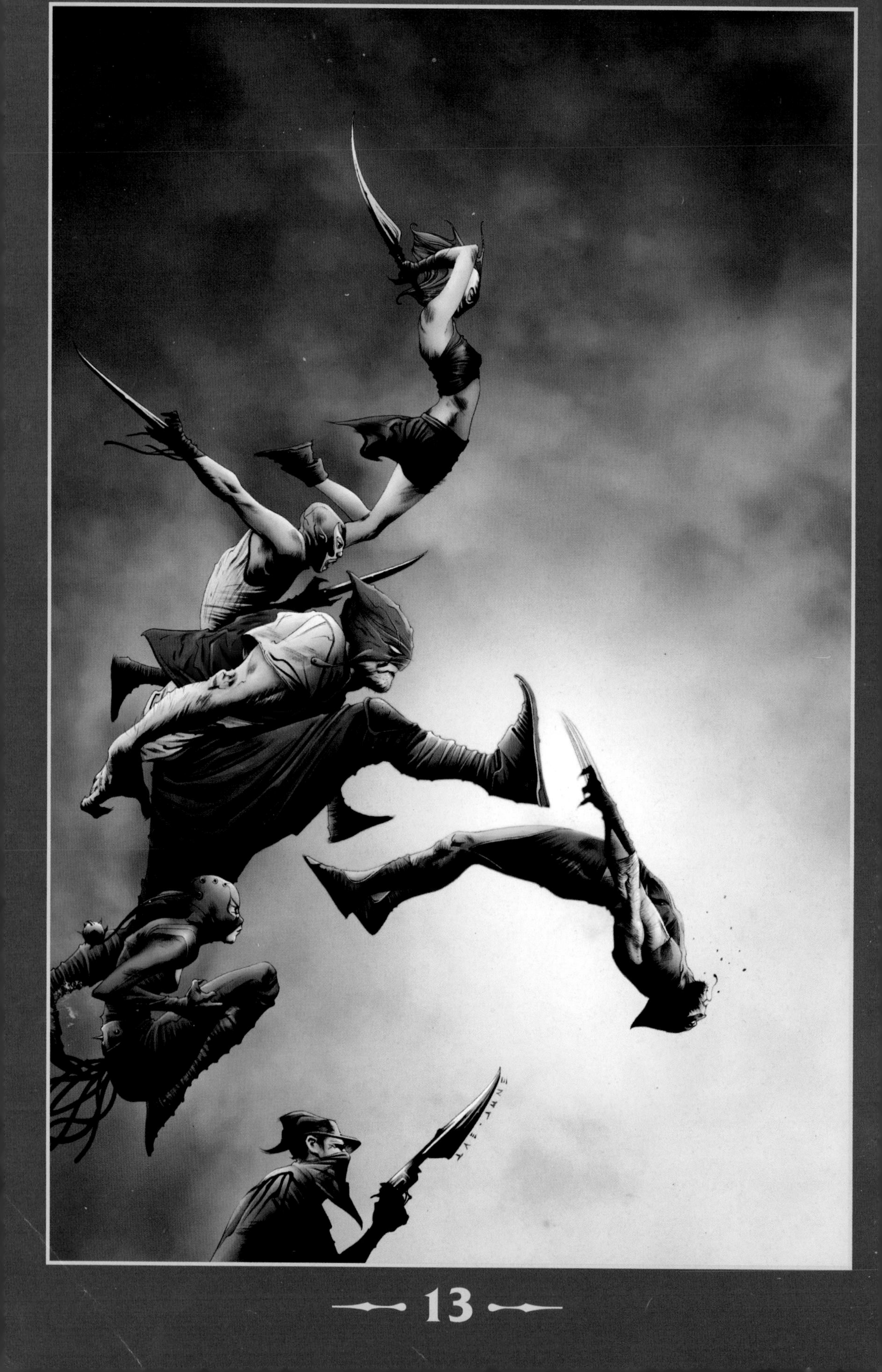

13

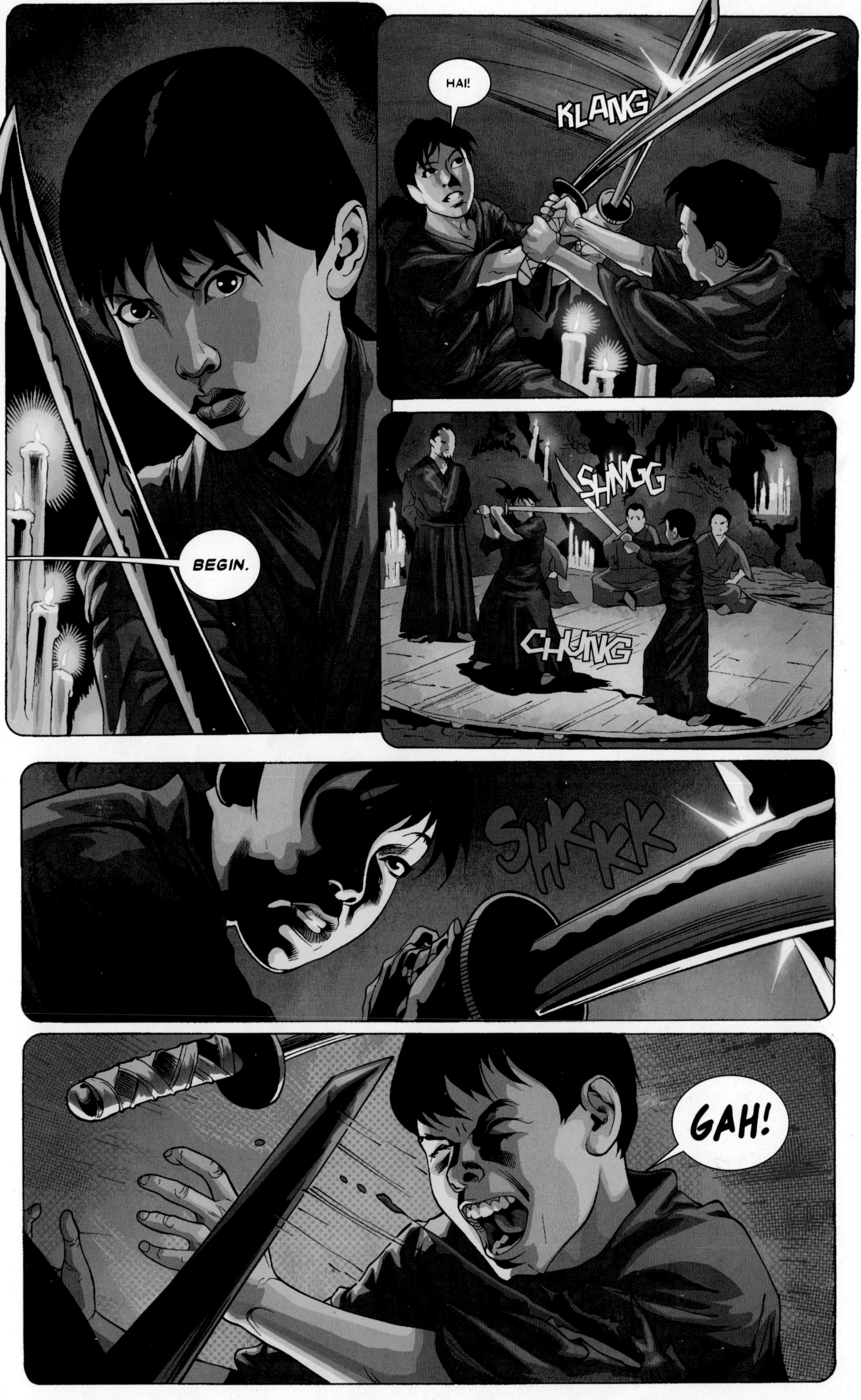
BEGIN.
HAI!
KLANG
SHNGG
CHUNG
SHKKK
GAH!

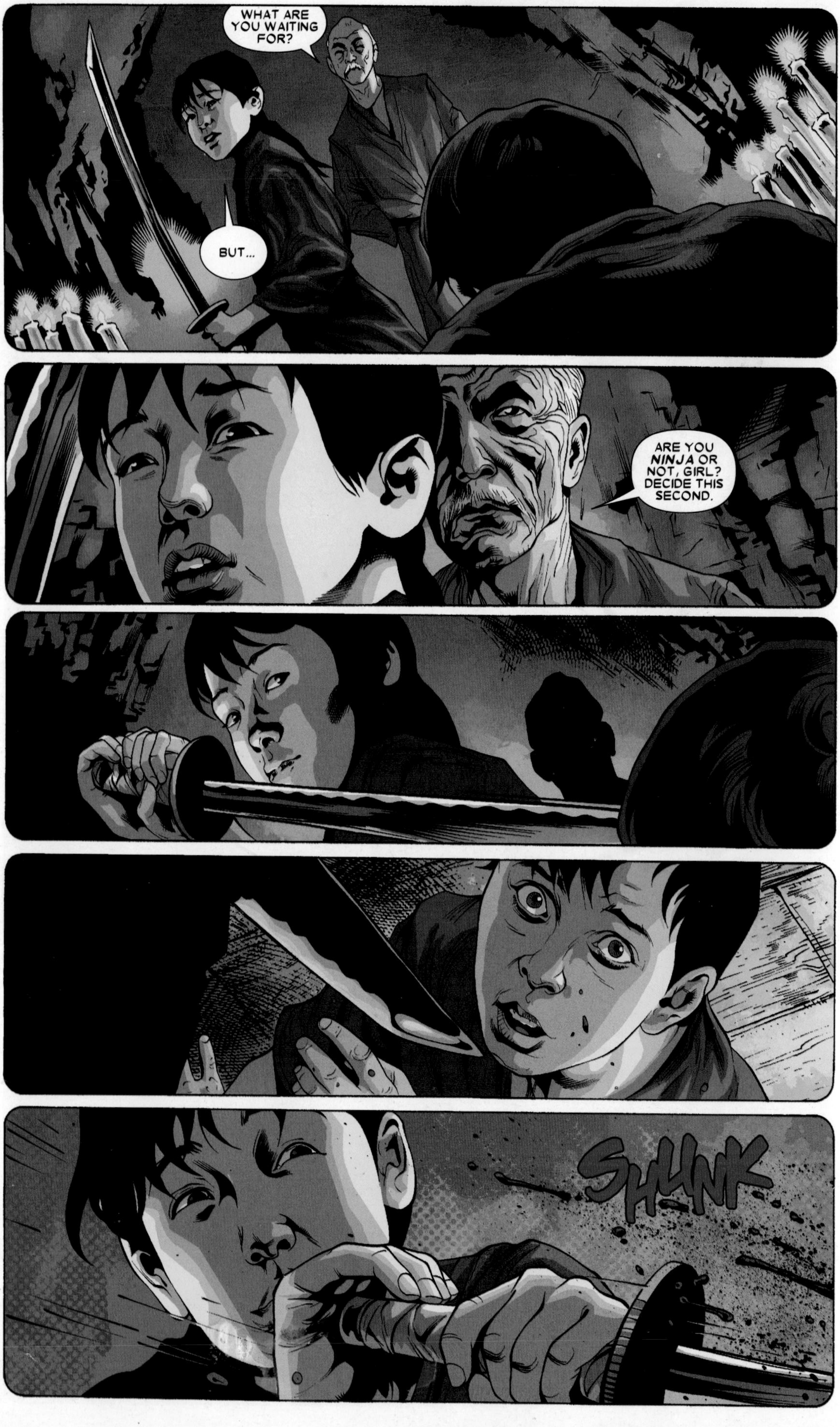
WHAT ARE YOU WAITING FOR?
BUT...
ARE YOU *NINJA* OR NOT, GIRL? DECIDE THIS SECOND.
SHUNK

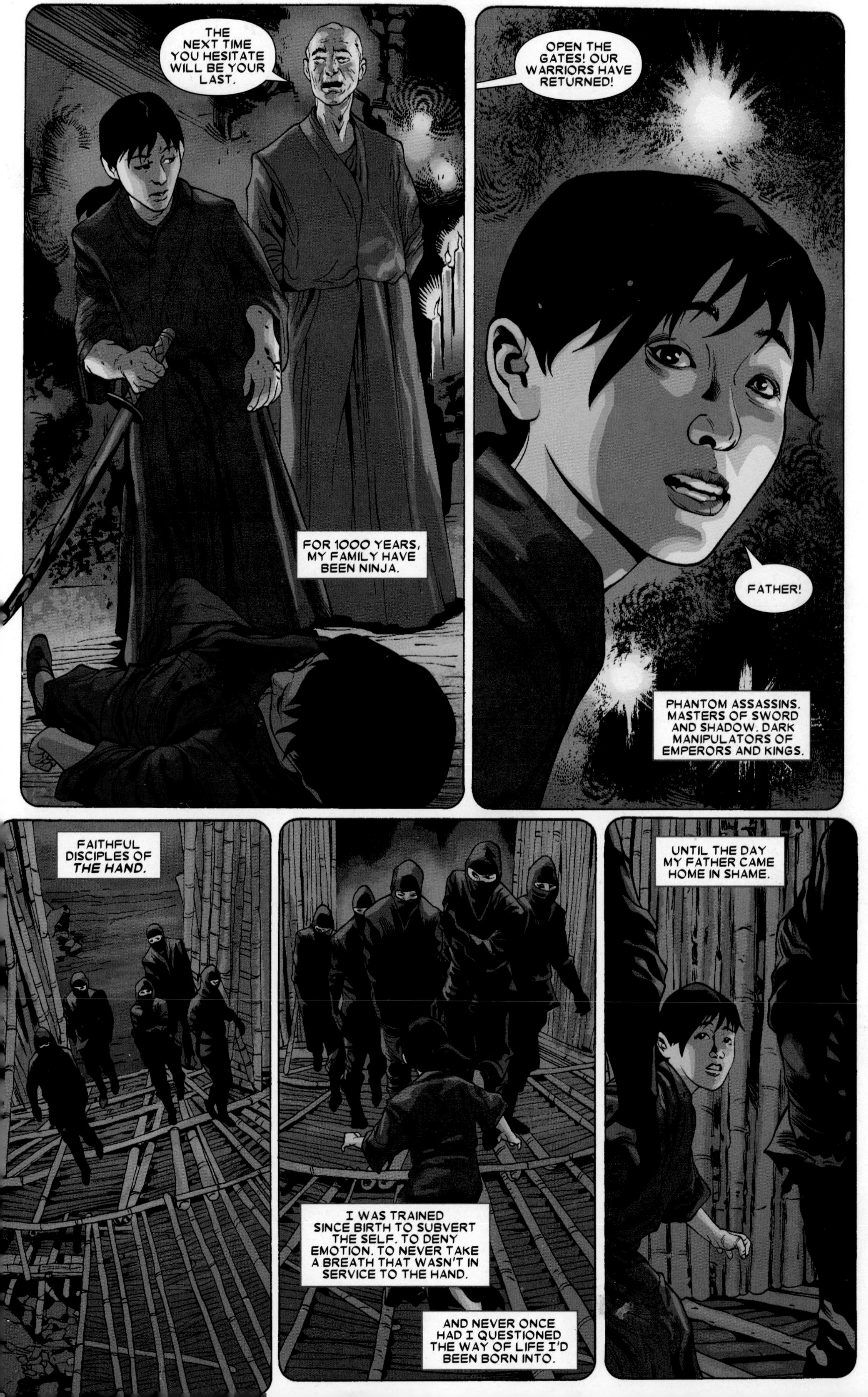
THE NEXT TIME YOU HESITATE WILL BE YOUR LAST.
FOR 1000 YEARS, MY FAMILY HAVE BEEN NINJA.
OPEN THE GATES! OUR WARRIORS HAVE RETURNED!
FATHER!
PHANTOM ASSASSINS. MASTERS OF SWORD AND SHADOW. DARK MANIPULATORS OF EMPERORS AND KINGS.
FAITHFUL DISCIPLES OF *THE HAND.*
I WAS TRAINED SINCE BIRTH TO SUBVERT THE SELF. TO DENY EMOTION. TO NEVER TAKE A BREATH THAT WASN'T IN SERVICE TO THE HAND.
AND NEVER ONCE HAD I QUESTIONED THE WAY OF LIFE I'D BEEN BORN INTO.
UNTIL THE DAY MY FATHER CAME HOME IN SHAME.

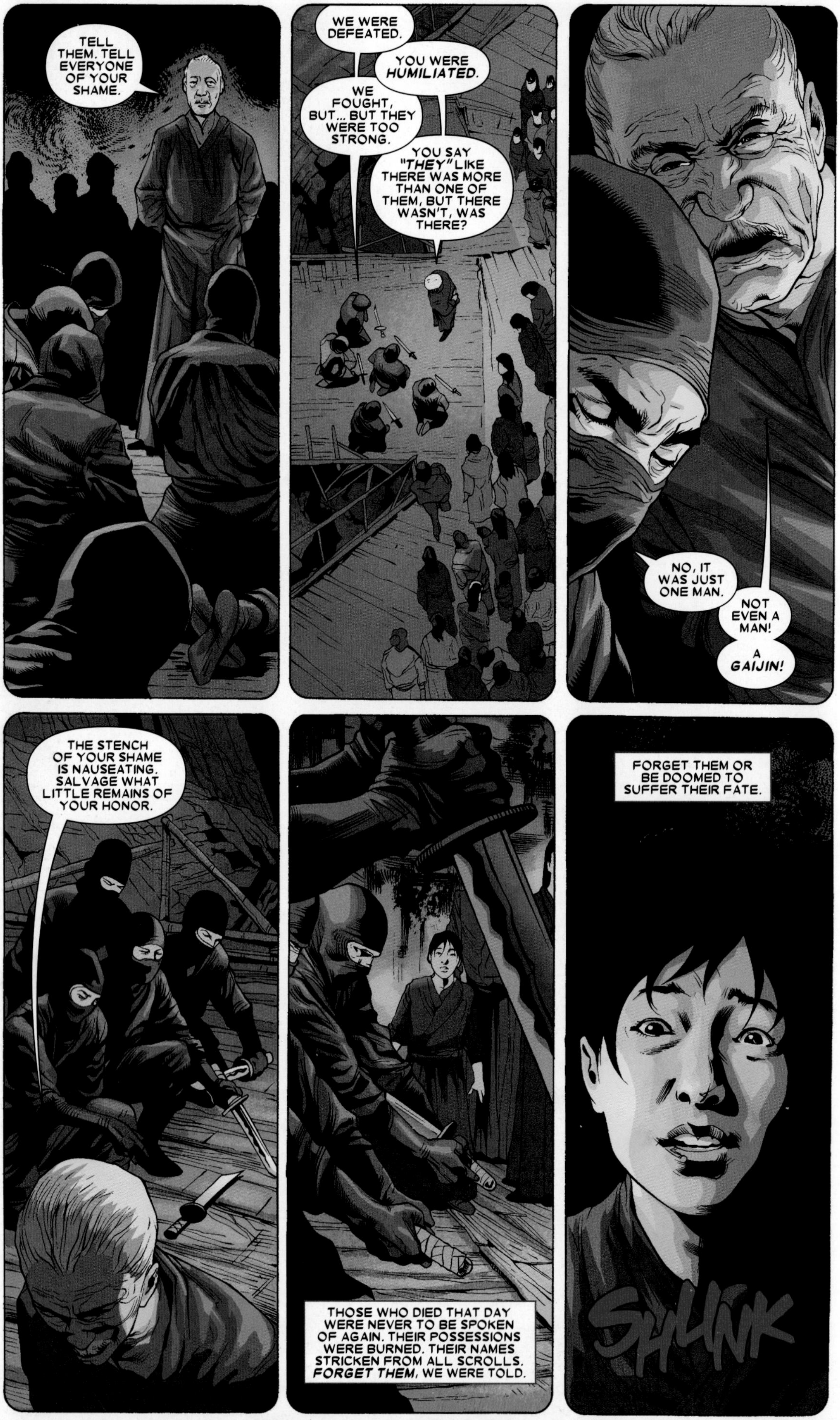
TELL THEM. TELL EVERYONE OF YOUR SHAME.
WE WERE DEFEATED.
YOU WERE HUMILIATED.
WE FOUGHT, BUT... BUT THEY WERE TOO STRONG.
YOU SAY "THEY" LIKE THERE WAS MORE THAN ONE OF THEM, BUT THERE WASN'T, WAS THERE?
NO, IT WAS JUST ONE MAN.
NOT EVEN A MAN!
A GAIJIN!
THE STENCH OF YOUR SHAME IS NAUSEATING. SALVAGE WHAT LITTLE REMAINS OF YOUR HONOR.
THOSE WHO DIED THAT DAY WERE NEVER TO BE SPOKEN OF AGAIN. THEIR POSSESSIONS WERE BURNED. THEIR NAMES STRICKEN FROM ALL SCROLLS. FORGET THEM, WE WERE TOLD.
FORGET THEM OR BE DOOMED TO SUFFER THEIR FATE.
SHUNK

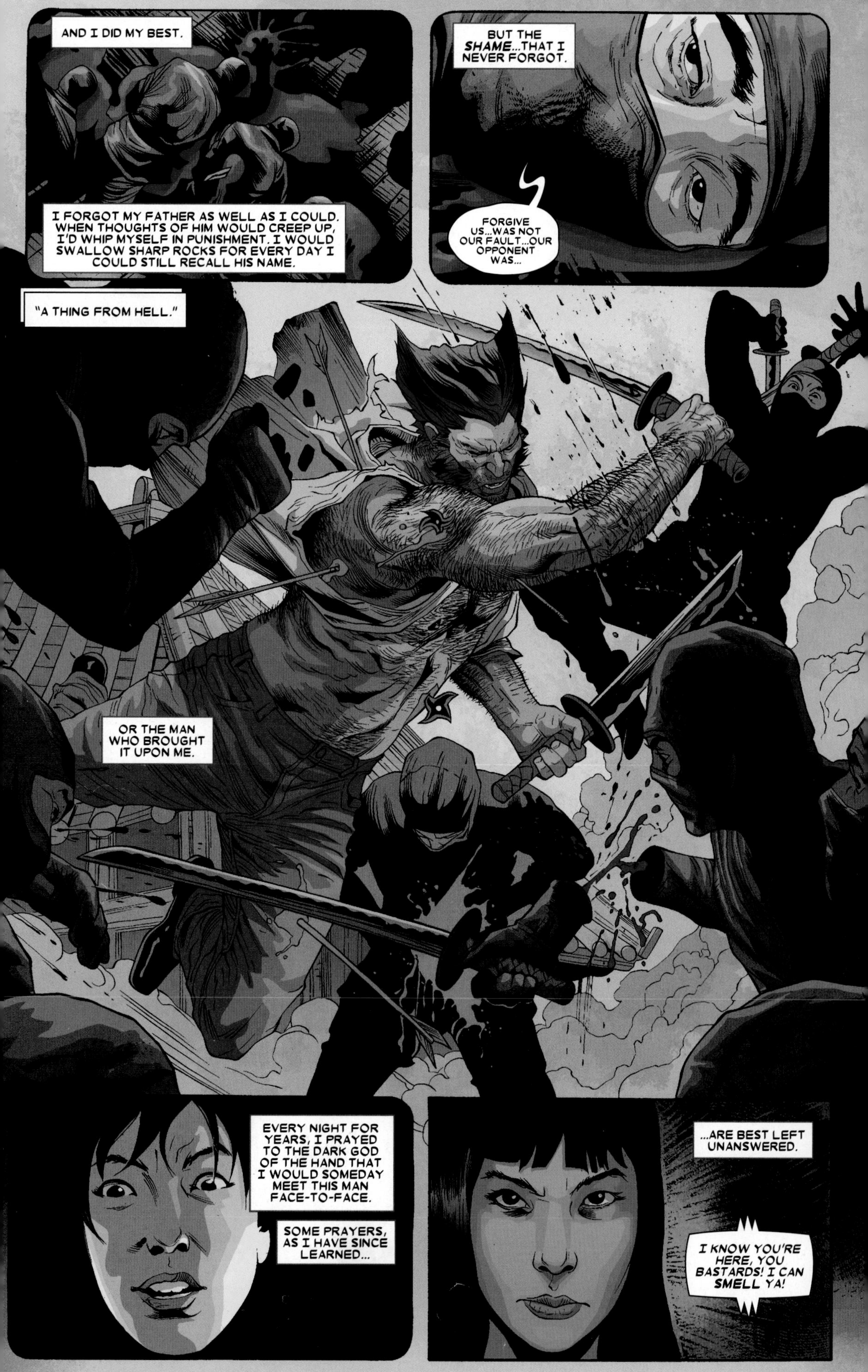
AND I DID MY BEST.
I FORGOT MY FATHER AS WELL AS I COULD. WHEN THOUGHTS OF HIM WOULD CREEP UP, I'D WHIP MYSELF IN PUNISHMENT. I WOULD SWALLOW SHARP ROCKS FOR EVERY DAY I COULD STILL RECALL HIS NAME.
BUT THE SHAME...THAT I NEVER FORGOT.
FORGIVE US...WAS NOT OUR FAULT...OUR OPPONENT WAS...
"A THING FROM HELL."
OR THE MAN WHO BROUGHT IT UPON ME.
EVERY NIGHT FOR YEARS, I PRAYED TO THE DARK GOD OF THE HAND THAT I WOULD SOMEDAY MEET THIS MAN FACE-TO-FACE.
SOME PRAYERS, AS I HAVE SINCE LEARNED...
...ARE BEST LEFT UNANSWERED.
I KNOW YOU'RE HERE, YOU BASTARDS! I CAN SMELL YA!

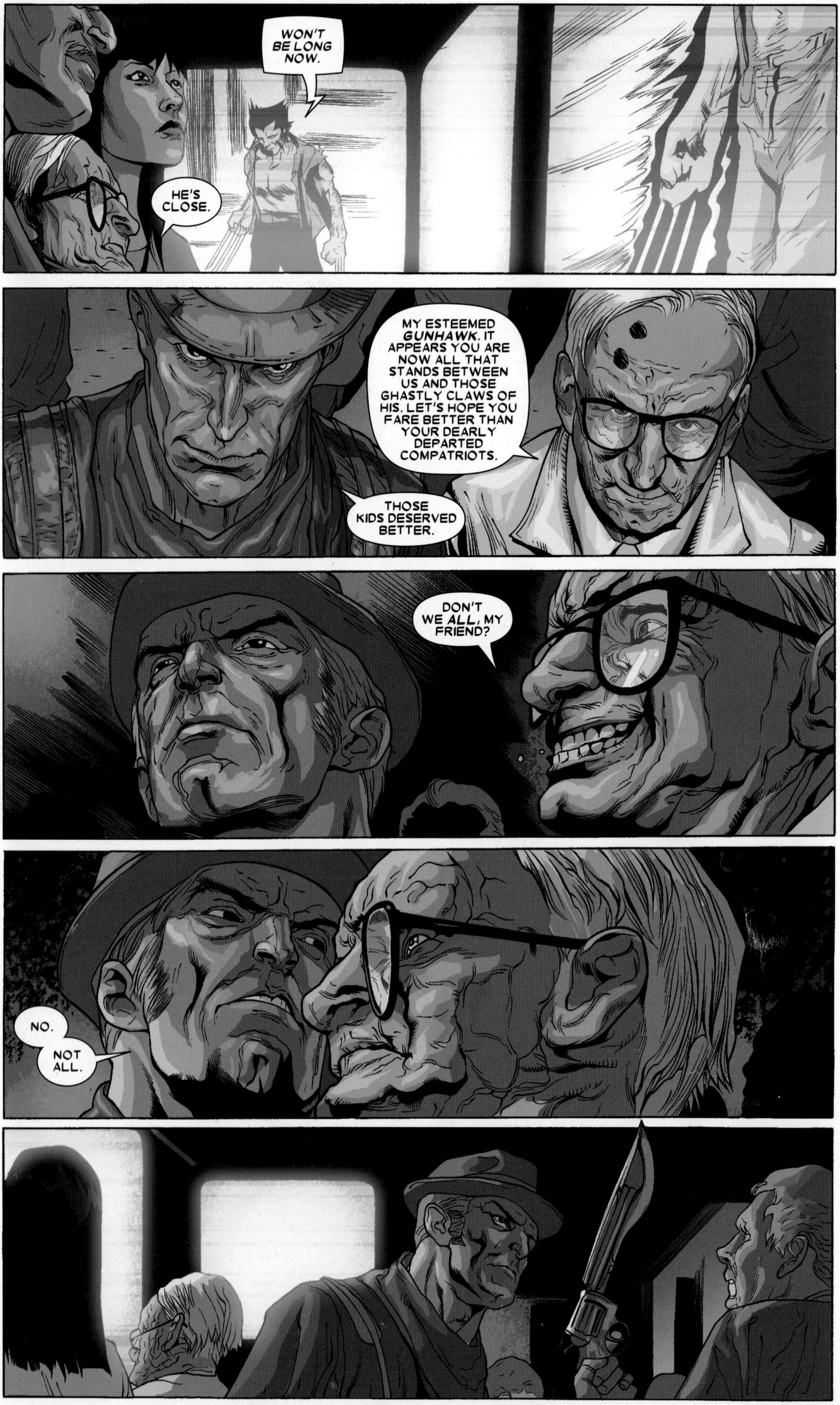
WON'T BE LONG NOW.
HE'S CLOSE.
MY ESTEEMED *GUNHAWK*. IT APPEARS YOU ARE NOW ALL THAT STANDS BETWEEN US AND THOSE GHASTLY CLAWS OF HIS. LET'S HOPE YOU FARE BETTER THAN YOUR DEARLY DEPARTED COMPATRIOTS.
THOSE KIDS DESERVED BETTER.
DON'T WE *ALL*, MY FRIEND?
NO.
NOT ALL.

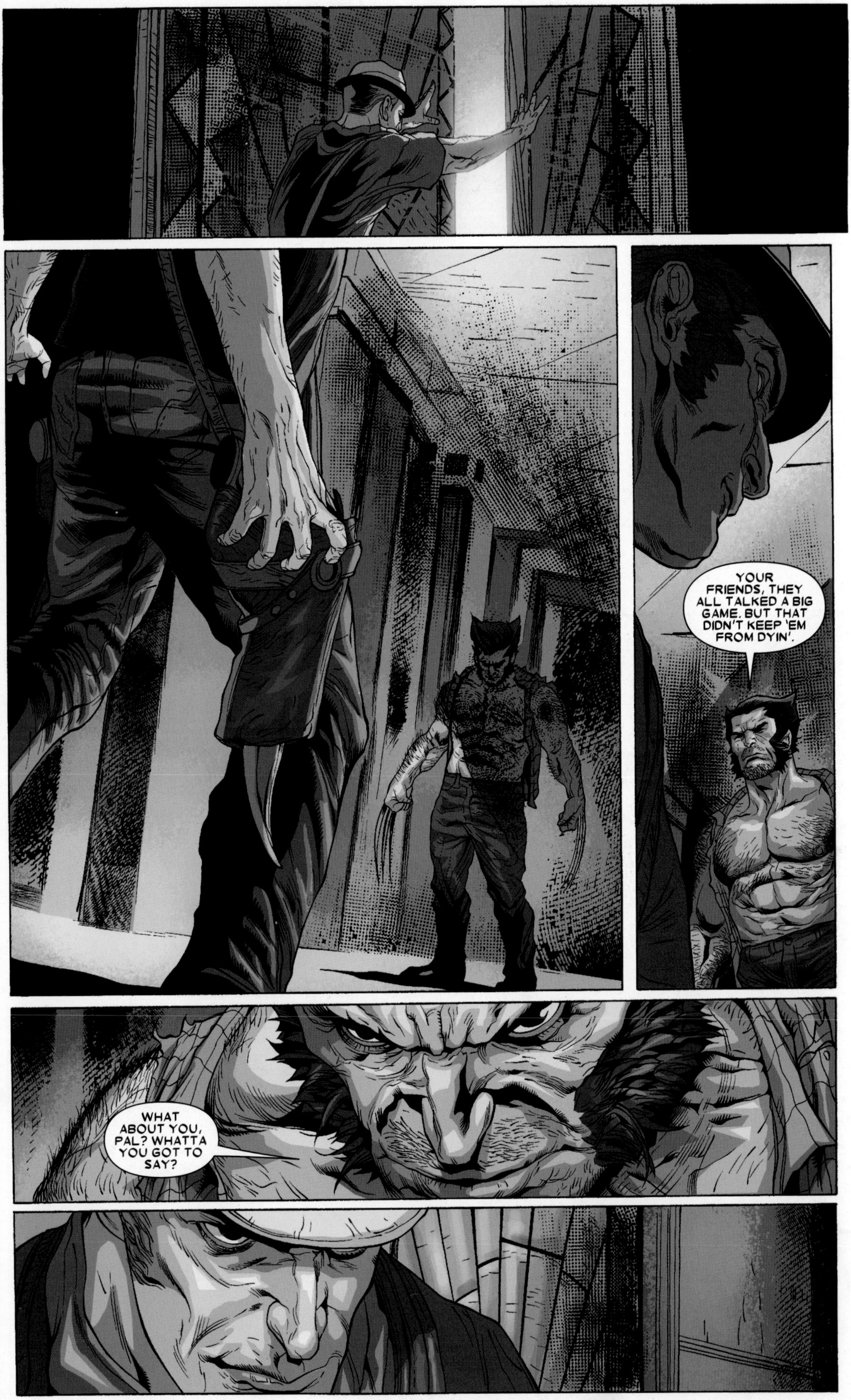
YOUR FRIENDS, THEY ALL TALKED A BIG GAME. BUT THAT DIDN'T KEEP 'EM FROM DYIN'.
WHAT ABOUT YOU, PAL? WHATTA YOU GOT TO SAY?

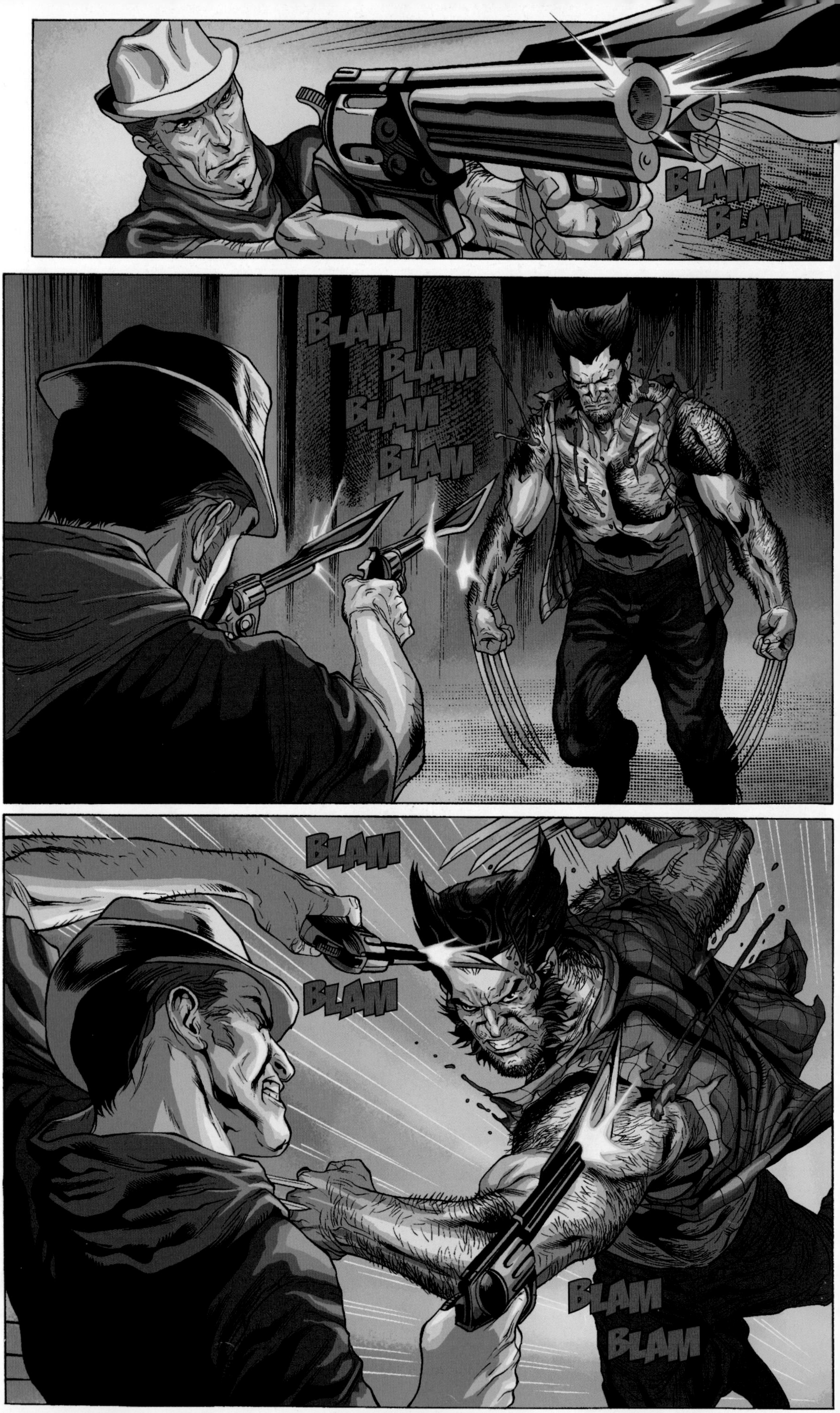
BLAM
BLAM
BLAM
BLAM
BLAM
BLAM
BLAM
BLAM
BLAM
BLAM

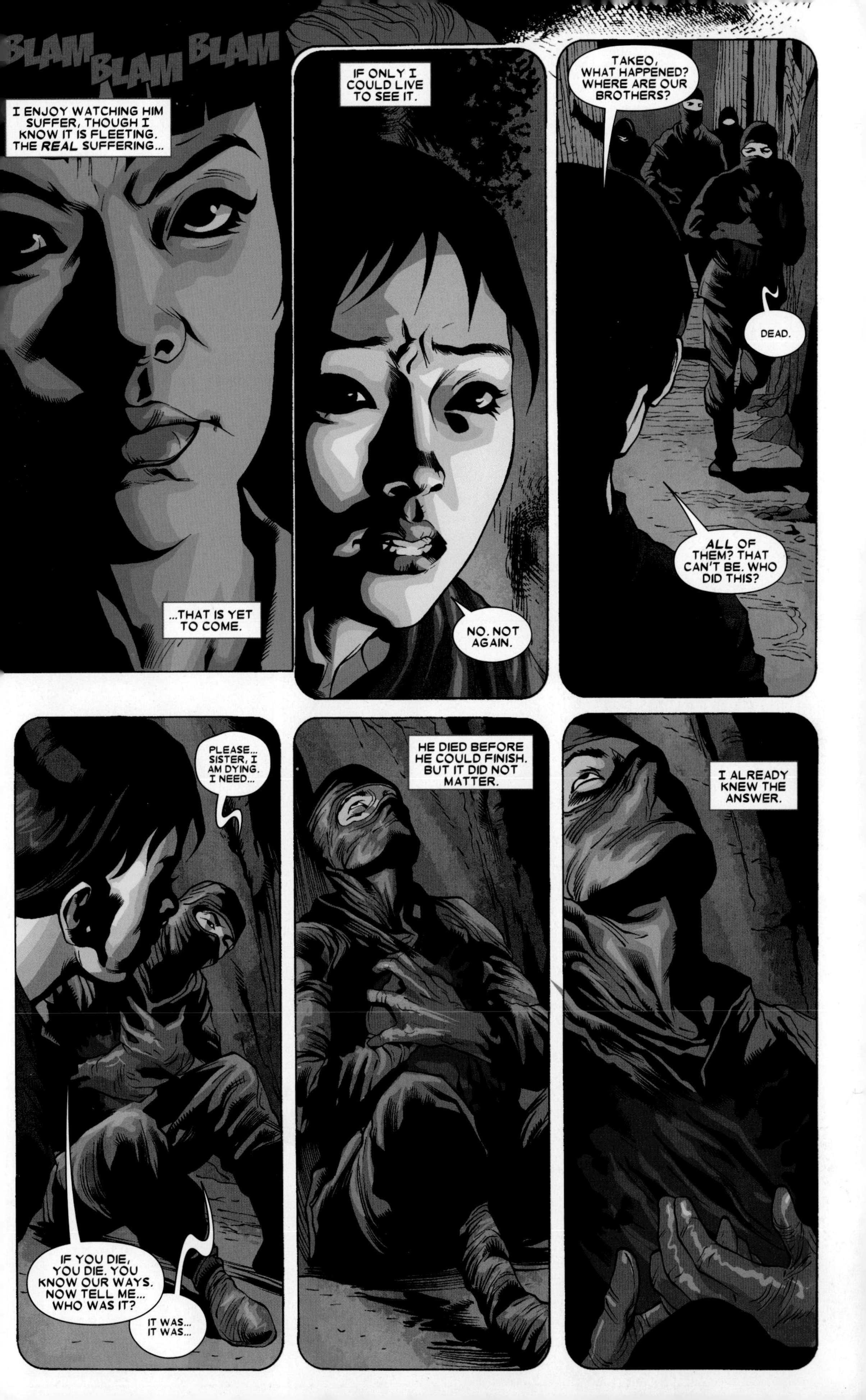
BLAM BLAM BLAM
I ENJOY WATCHING HIM SUFFER, THOUGH I KNOW IT IS FLEETING. THE REAL SUFFERING...
...THAT IS YET TO COME.
IF ONLY I COULD LIVE TO SEE IT.
NO. NOT AGAIN.
TAKEO, WHAT HAPPENED? WHERE ARE OUR BROTHERS?
DEAD.
ALL OF THEM? THAT CAN'T BE. WHO DID THIS?
PLEASE... SISTER, I AM DYING. I NEED...
IF YOU DIE, YOU DIE. YOU KNOW OUR WAYS. NOW TELL ME... WHO WAS IT?
IT WAS... IT WAS...
HE DIED BEFORE HE COULD FINISH. BUT IT DID NOT MATTER.
I ALREADY KNEW THE ANSWER.

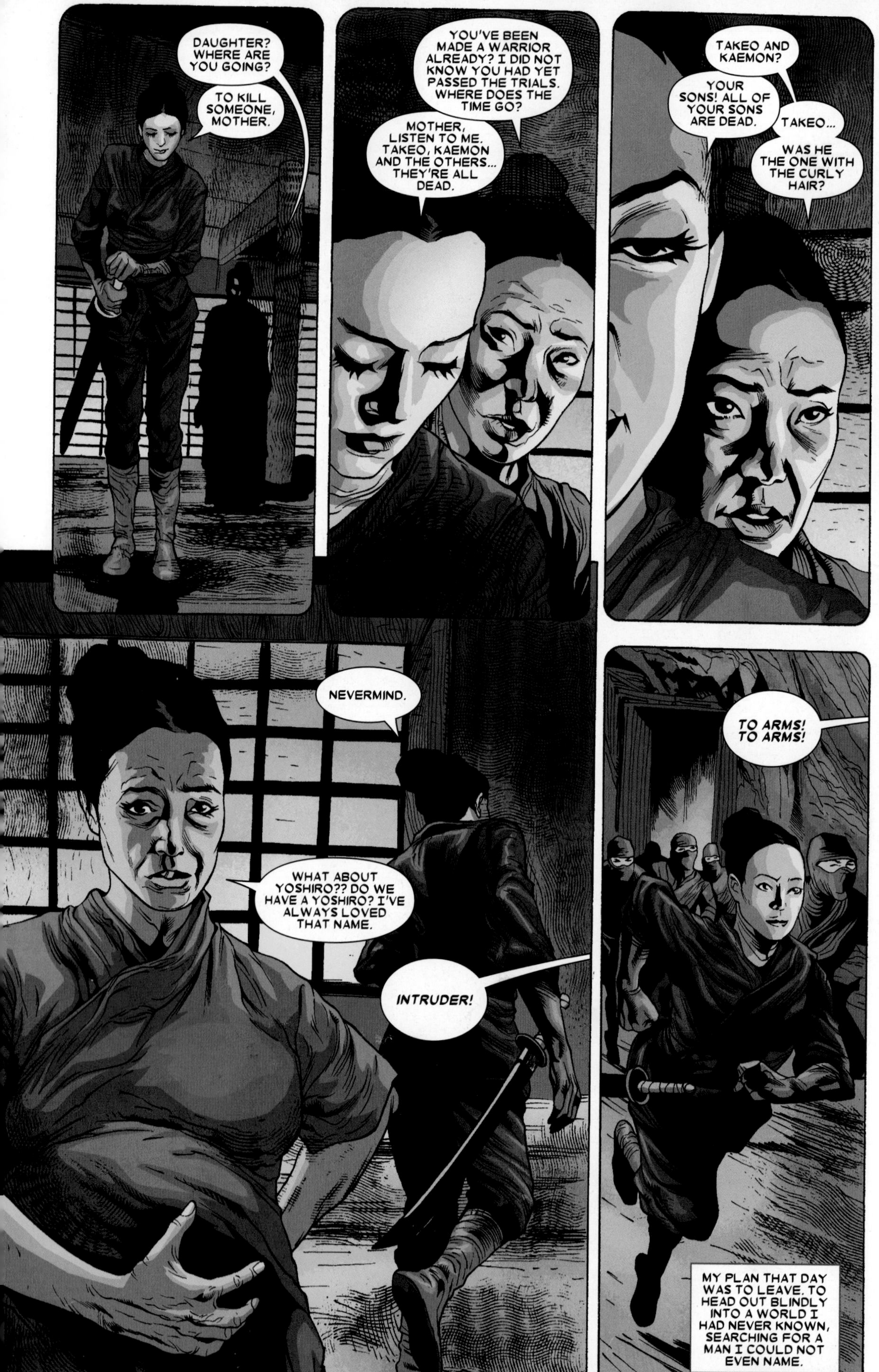
DAUGHTER? WHERE ARE YOU GOING?
TO KILL SOMEONE, MOTHER.
YOU'VE BEEN MADE A WARRIOR ALREADY? I DID NOT KNOW YOU HAD YET PASSED THE TRIALS. WHERE DOES THE TIME GO?
MOTHER, LISTEN TO ME. TAKEO, KAEMON AND THE OTHERS... THEY'RE ALL DEAD.
TAKEO AND KAEMON?
YOUR SONS! ALL OF YOUR SONS ARE DEAD.
TAKEO...
WAS HE THE ONE WITH THE CURLY HAIR?
NEVERMIND.
WHAT ABOUT YOSHIRO?? DO WE HAVE A YOSHIRO? I'VE ALWAYS LOVED THAT NAME.
INTRUDER!
TO ARMS! TO ARMS!
MY PLAN THAT DAY WAS TO LEAVE. TO HEAD OUT BLINDLY INTO A WORLD I HAD NEVER KNOWN, SEARCHING FOR A MAN I COULD NOT EVEN NAME.

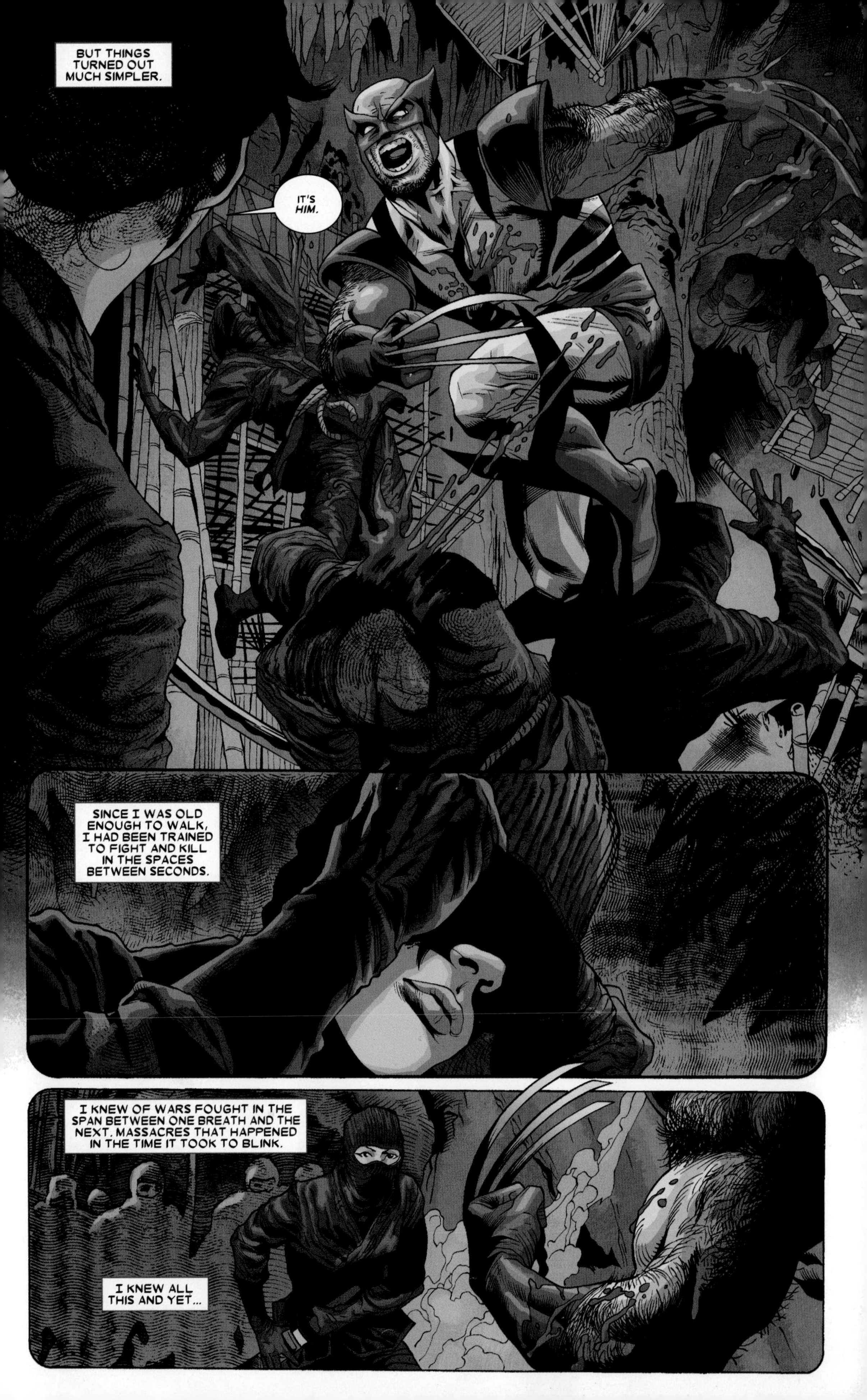
BUT THINGS TURNED OUT MUCH SIMPLER.
IT'S HIM.
SINCE I WAS OLD ENOUGH TO WALK, I HAD BEEN TRAINED TO FIGHT AND KILL IN THE SPACES BETWEEN SECONDS.
I KNEW OF WARS FOUGHT IN THE SPAN BETWEEN ONE BREATH AND THE NEXT. MASSACRES THAT HAPPENED IN THE TIME IT TOOK TO BLINK.
I KNEW ALL THIS AND YET...

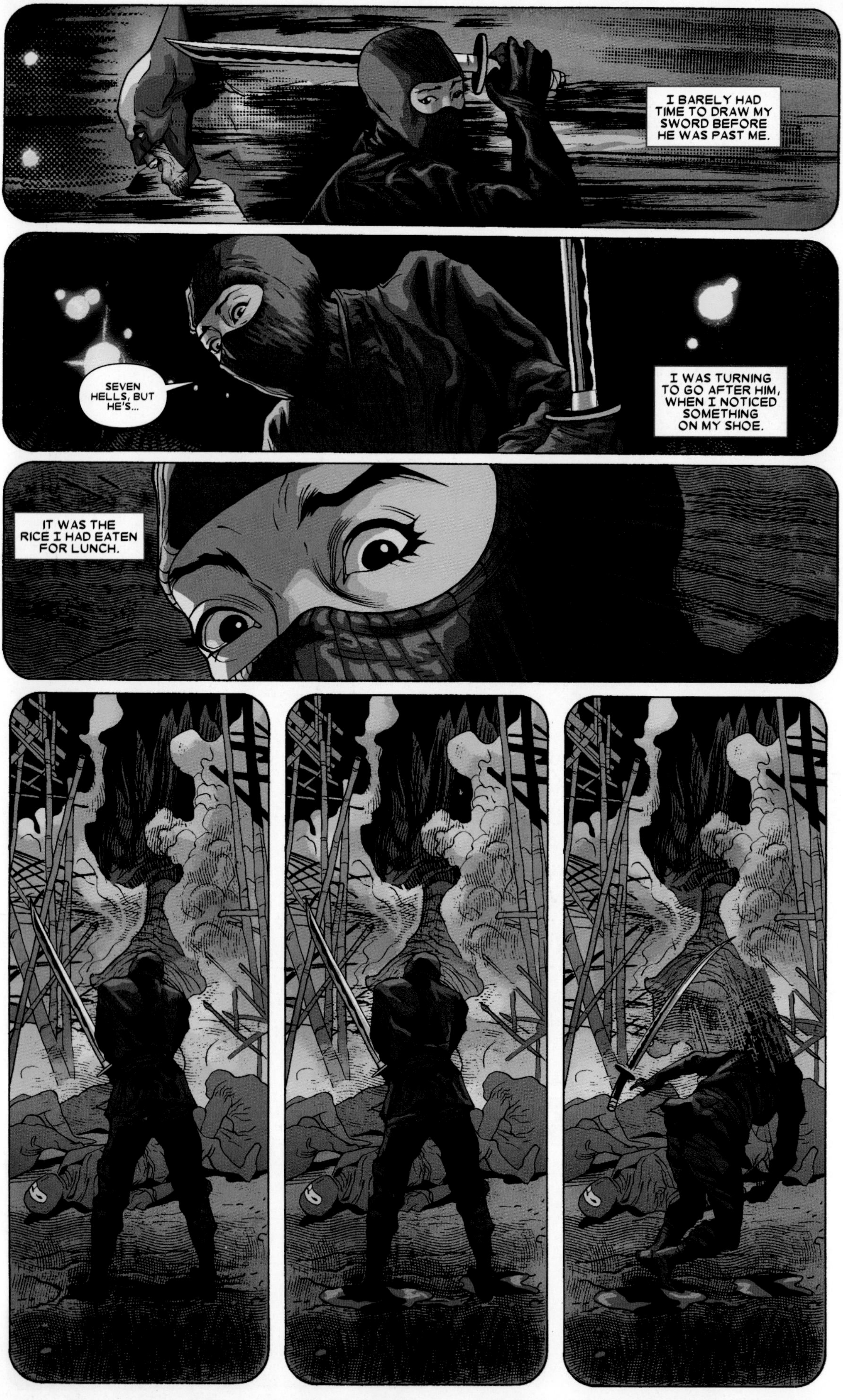
I BARELY HAD TIME TO DRAW MY SWORD BEFORE HE WAS PAST ME.
SEVEN HELLS, BUT HE'S...
I WAS TURNING TO GO AFTER HIM, WHEN I NOTICED SOMETHING ON MY SHOE.
IT WAS THE RICE I HAD EATEN FOR LUNCH.

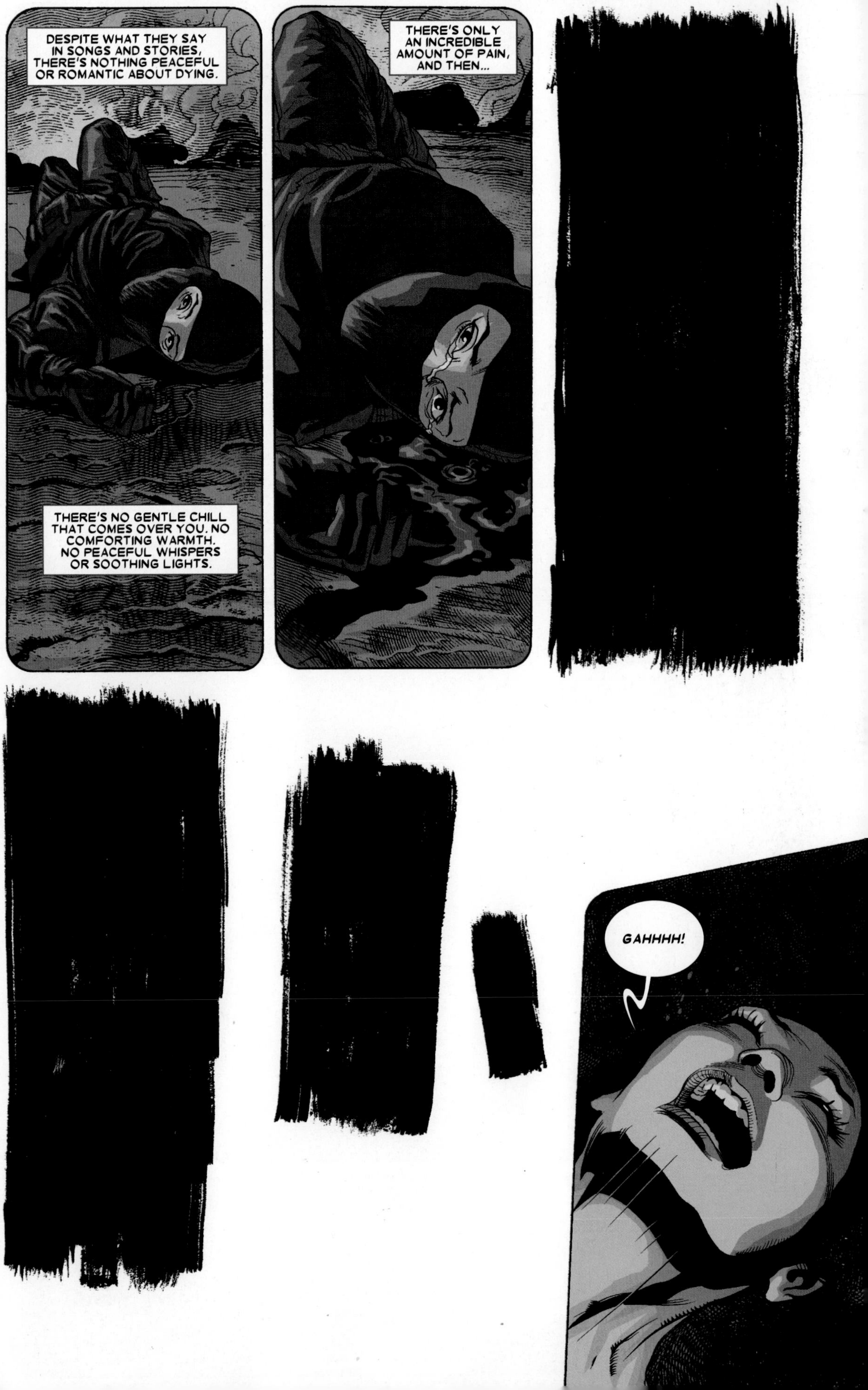
DESPITE WHAT THEY SAY IN SONGS AND STORIES, THERE'S NOTHING PEACEFUL OR ROMANTIC ABOUT DYING.
THERE'S NO GENTLE CHILL THAT COMES OVER YOU. NO COMFORTING WARMTH. NO PEACEFUL WHISPERS OR SOOTHING LIGHTS.
THERE'S ONLY AN INCREDIBLE AMOUNT OF PAIN, AND THEN...
GAHHHH!

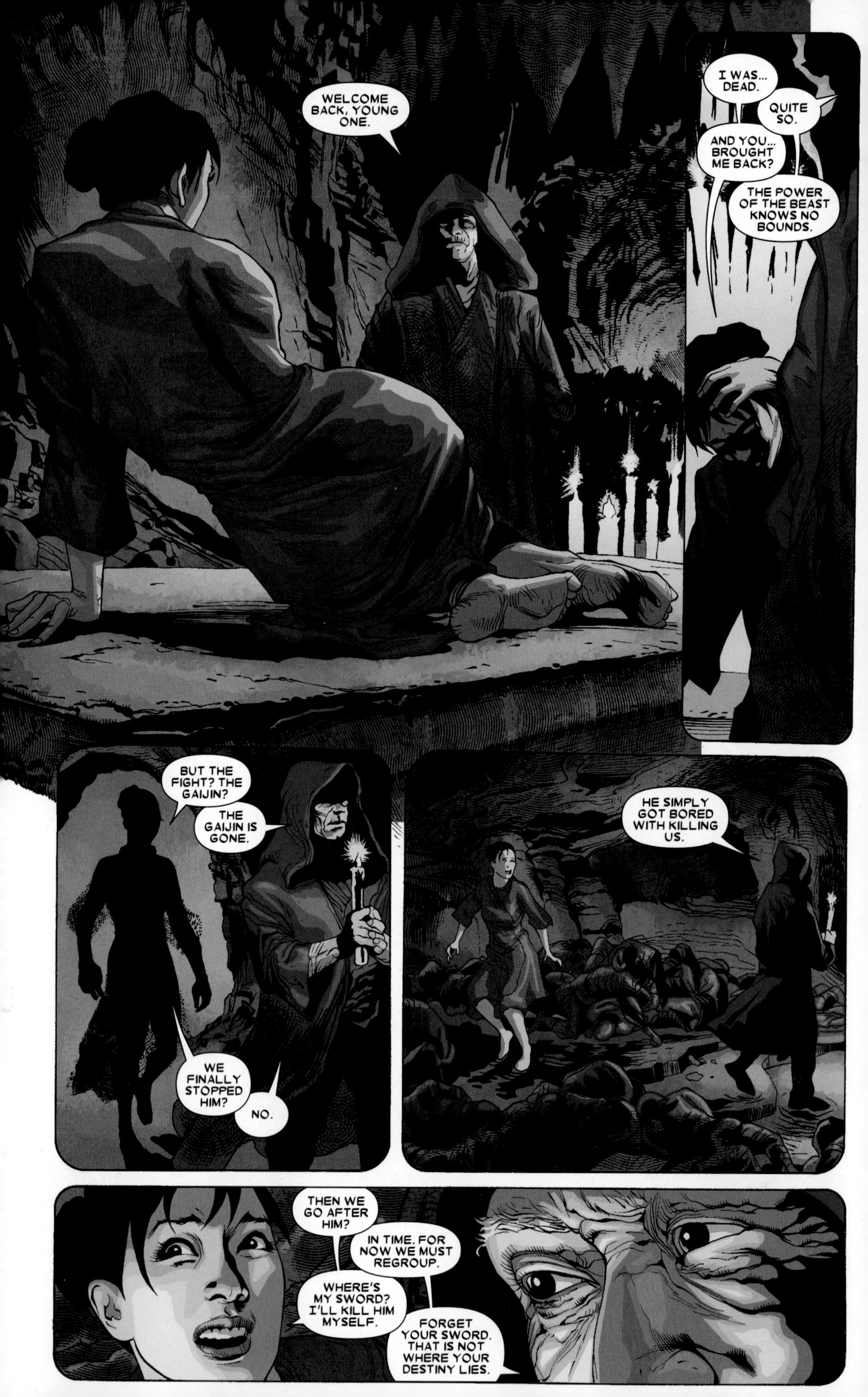
WELCOME BACK, YOUNG ONE.
I WAS... DEAD.
QUITE SO.
AND YOU... BROUGHT ME BACK?
THE POWER OF THE BEAST KNOWS NO BOUNDS.
BUT THE FIGHT? THE GAIJIN?
THE GAIJIN IS GONE.
WE FINALLY STOPPED HIM?
NO.
HE SIMPLY GOT BORED WITH KILLING US.
THEN WE GO AFTER HIM?
IN TIME. FOR NOW WE MUST REGROUP.
WHERE'S MY SWORD? I'LL KILL HIM MYSELF.
FORGET YOUR SWORD. THAT IS NOT WHERE YOUR DESTINY LIES.

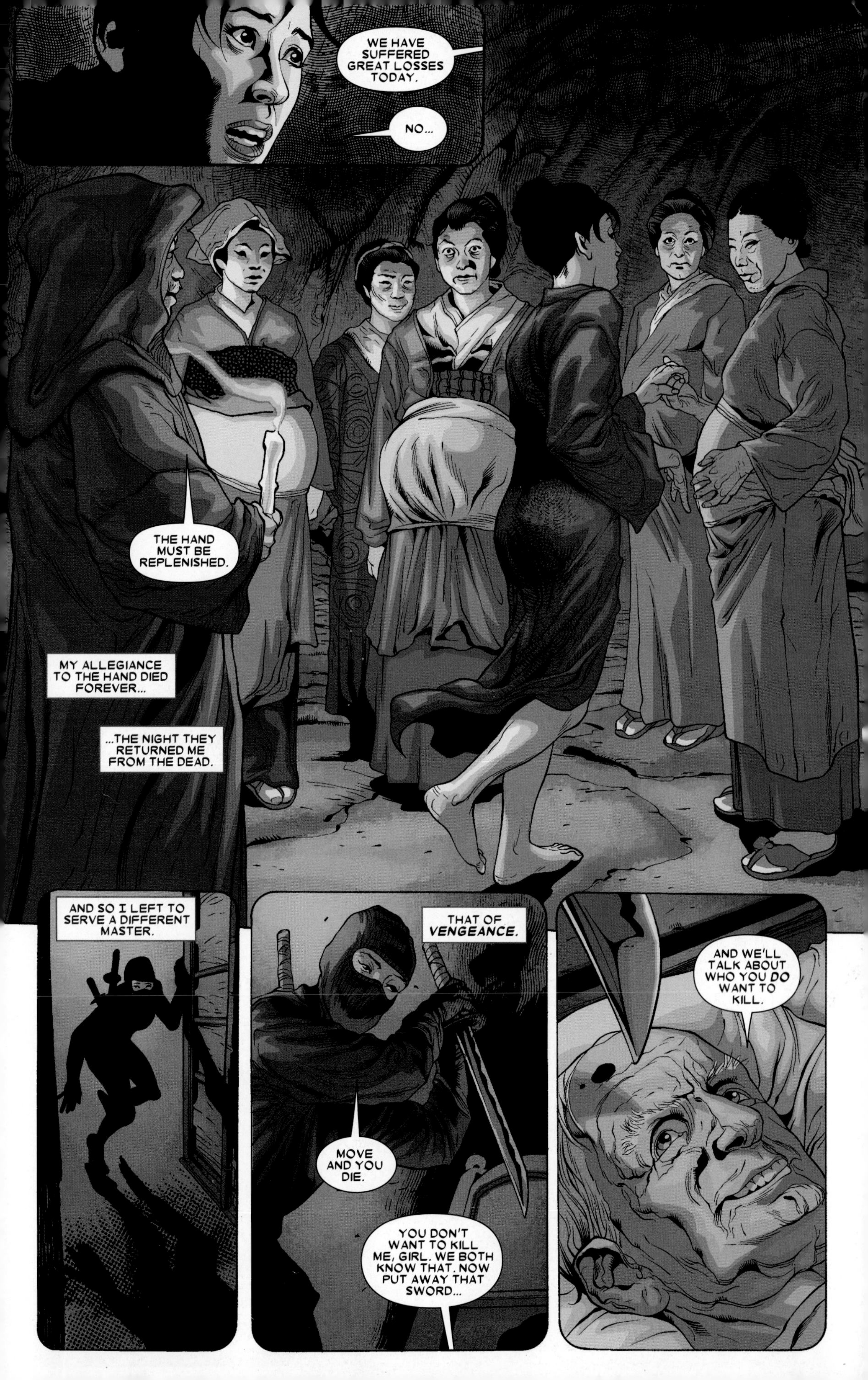
WE HAVE SUFFERED GREAT LOSSES TODAY.
NO...
THE HAND MUST BE REPLENISHED.
MY ALLEGIANCE TO THE HAND DIED FOREVER...
...THE NIGHT THEY RETURNED ME FROM THE DEAD.
AND SO I LEFT TO SERVE A DIFFERENT MASTER.
THAT OF *VENGEANCE.*
MOVE AND YOU DIE.
YOU DON'T WANT TO KILL ME, GIRL. WE BOTH KNOW THAT. NOW PUT AWAY THAT SWORD...
AND WE'LL TALK ABOUT WHO YOU *DO* WANT TO KILL.

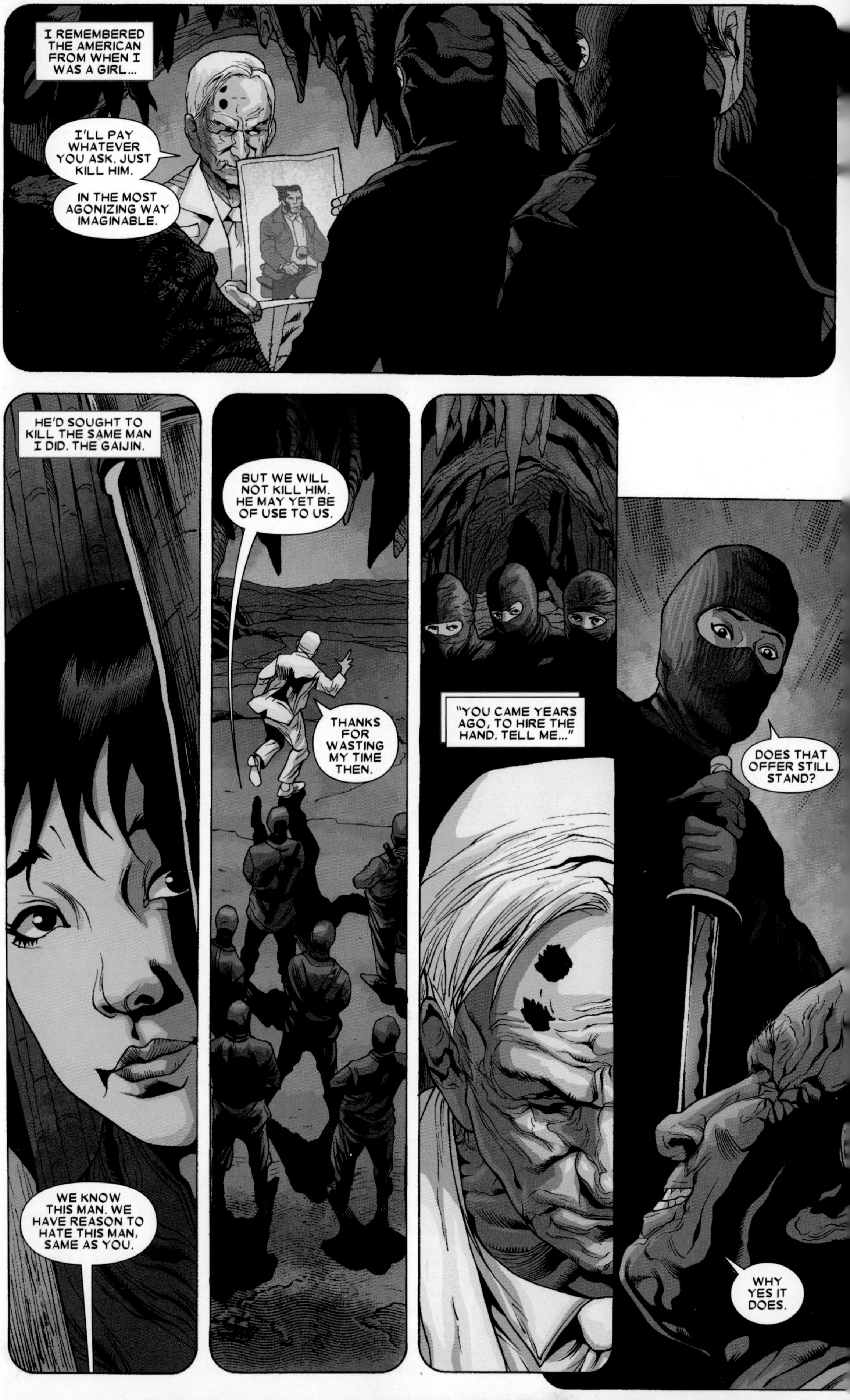
I REMEMBERED THE AMERICAN FROM WHEN I WAS A GIRL...
I'LL PAY WHATEVER YOU ASK. JUST KILL HIM.
IN THE MOST AGONIZING WAY IMAGINABLE.
HE'D SOUGHT TO KILL THE SAME MAN I DID. THE GAIJIN.
WE KNOW THIS MAN. WE HAVE REASON TO HATE THIS MAN, SAME AS YOU.
BUT WE WILL NOT KILL HIM. HE MAY YET BE OF USE TO US.
THANKS FOR WASTING MY TIME THEN.
"YOU CAME YEARS AGO, TO HIRE THE HAND. TELL ME..."
DOES THAT OFFER STILL STAND?
WHY YES IT DOES.

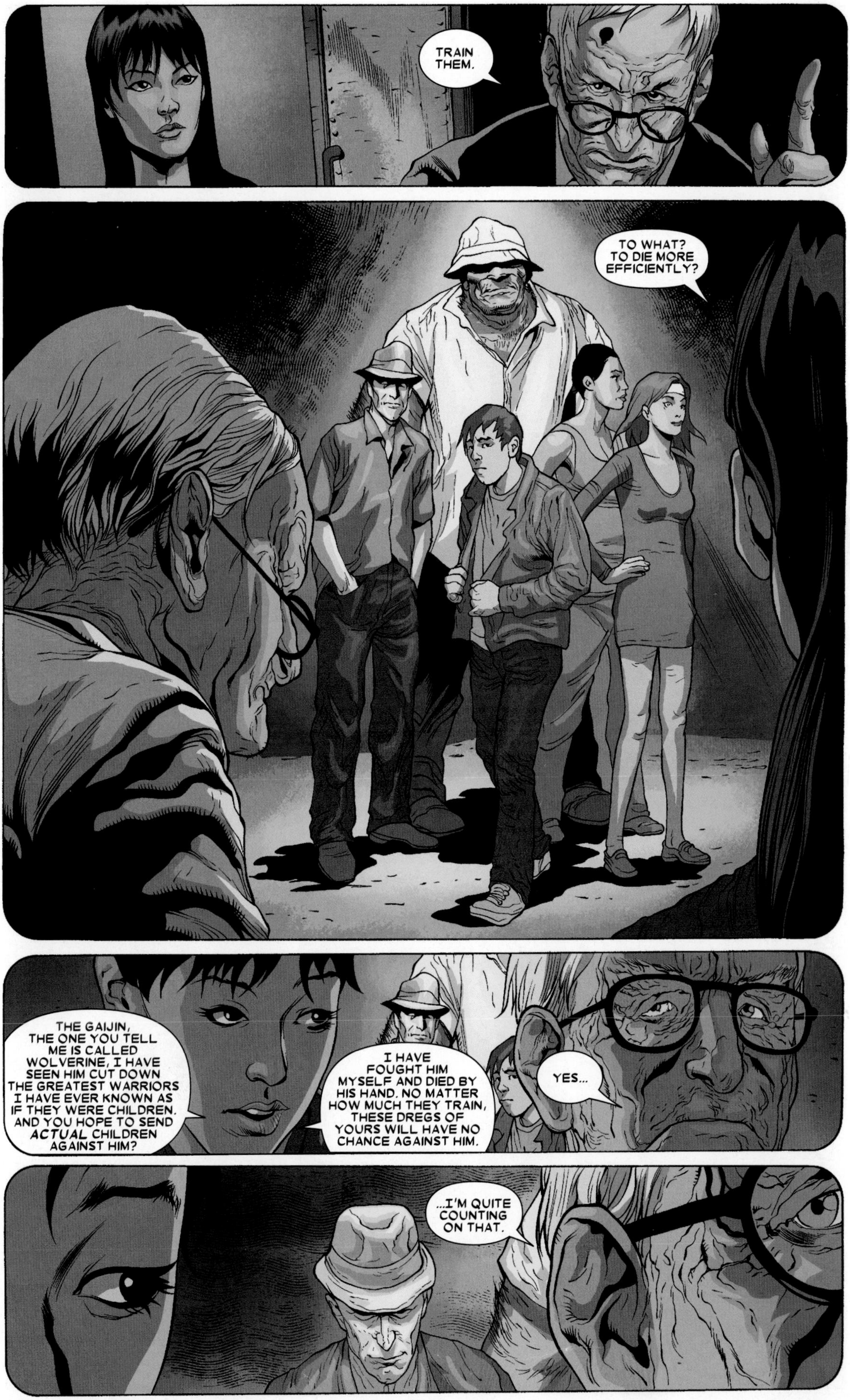
TRAIN THEM.
TO WHAT? TO DIE MORE EFFICIENTLY?
THE GAIJIN, THE ONE YOU TELL ME IS CALLED WOLVERINE, I HAVE SEEN HIM CUT DOWN THE GREATEST WARRIORS I HAVE EVER KNOWN AS IF THEY WERE CHILDREN. AND YOU HOPE TO SEND ACTUAL CHILDREN AGAINST HIM?
I HAVE FOUGHT HIM MYSELF AND DIED BY HIS HAND. NO MATTER HOW MUCH THEY TRAIN, THESE DREGS OF YOURS WILL HAVE NO CHANCE AGAINST HIM.
YES...
...I'M QUITE COUNTING ON THAT.

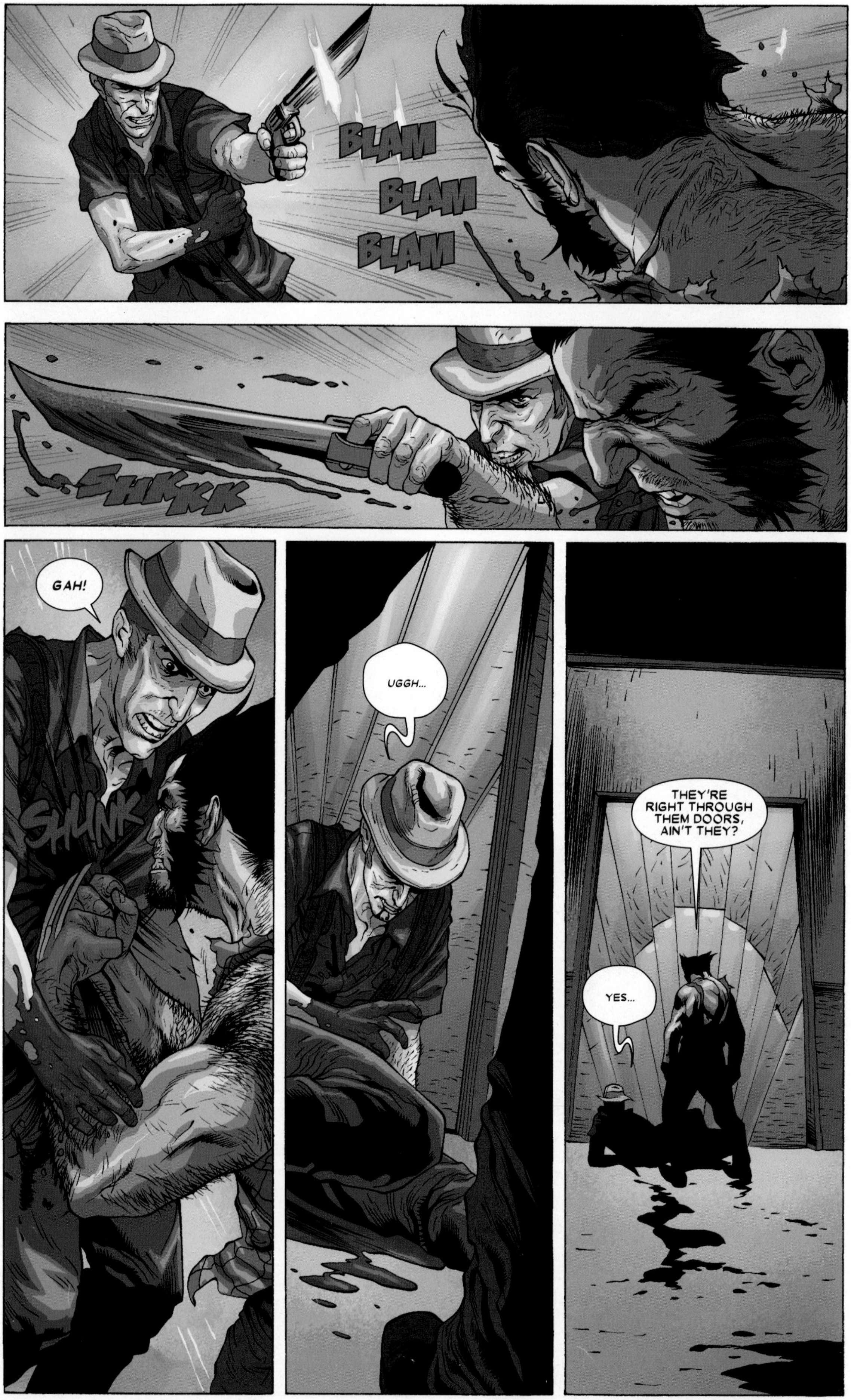
BLAM
BLAM
BLAM
SHKKK
GAH!
SHUNK
UGGH...
THEY'RE RIGHT THROUGH THEM DOORS, AIN'T THEY?
YES...

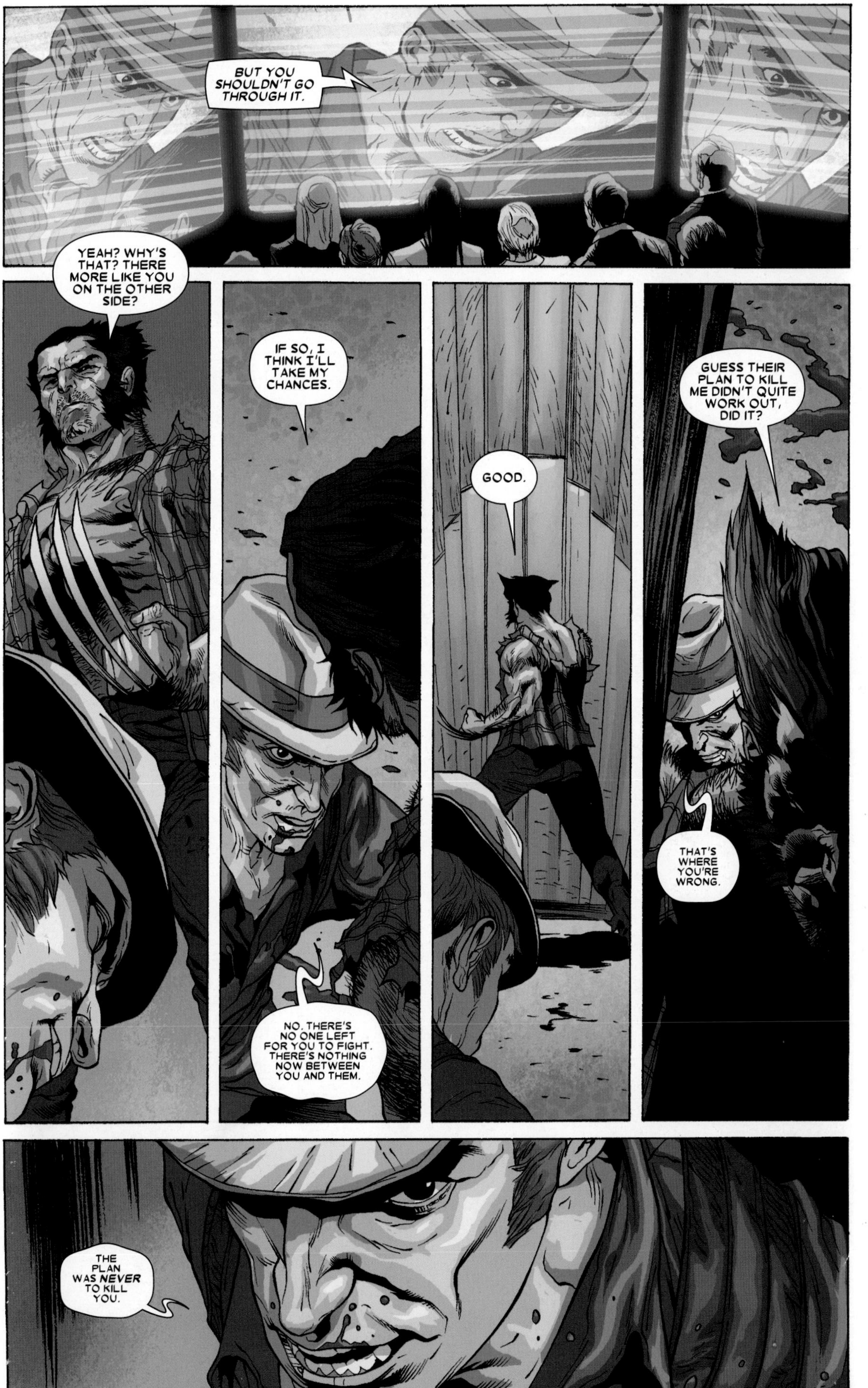
BUT YOU SHOULDN'T GO THROUGH IT.
YEAH? WHY'S THAT? THERE MORE LIKE YOU ON THE OTHER SIDE?
IF SO, I THINK I'LL TAKE MY CHANCES.
NO. THERE'S NO ONE LEFT FOR YOU TO FIGHT. THERE'S NOTHING NOW BETWEEN YOU AND THEM.
GOOD.
GUESS THEIR PLAN TO KILL ME DIDN'T QUITE WORK OUT, DID IT?
THAT'S WHERE YOU'RE WRONG.
THE PLAN WAS *NEVER* TO KILL YOU.

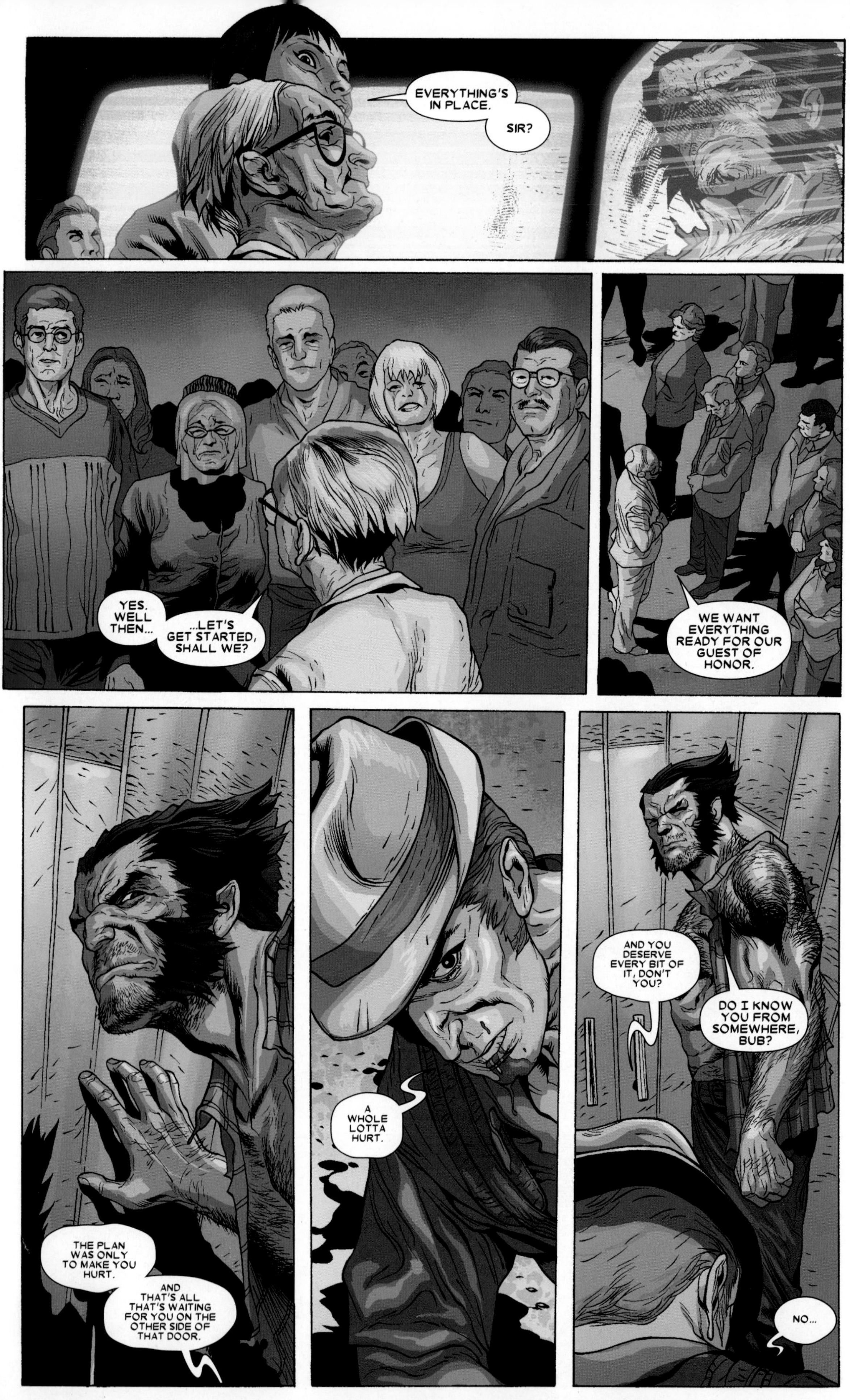
EVERYTHING'S IN PLACE.
SIR?
YES. WELL THEN...
...LET'S GET STARTED, SHALL WE?
WE WANT EVERYTHING READY FOR OUR GUEST OF HONOR.
THE PLAN WAS ONLY TO MAKE YOU HURT.
AND THAT'S ALL THAT'S WAITING FOR YOU ON THE OTHER SIDE OF THAT DOOR.
A WHOLE LOTTA HURT.
AND YOU DESERVE EVERY BIT OF IT, DON'T YOU?
DO I KNOW YOU FROM SOMEWHERE, BUB?
NO...

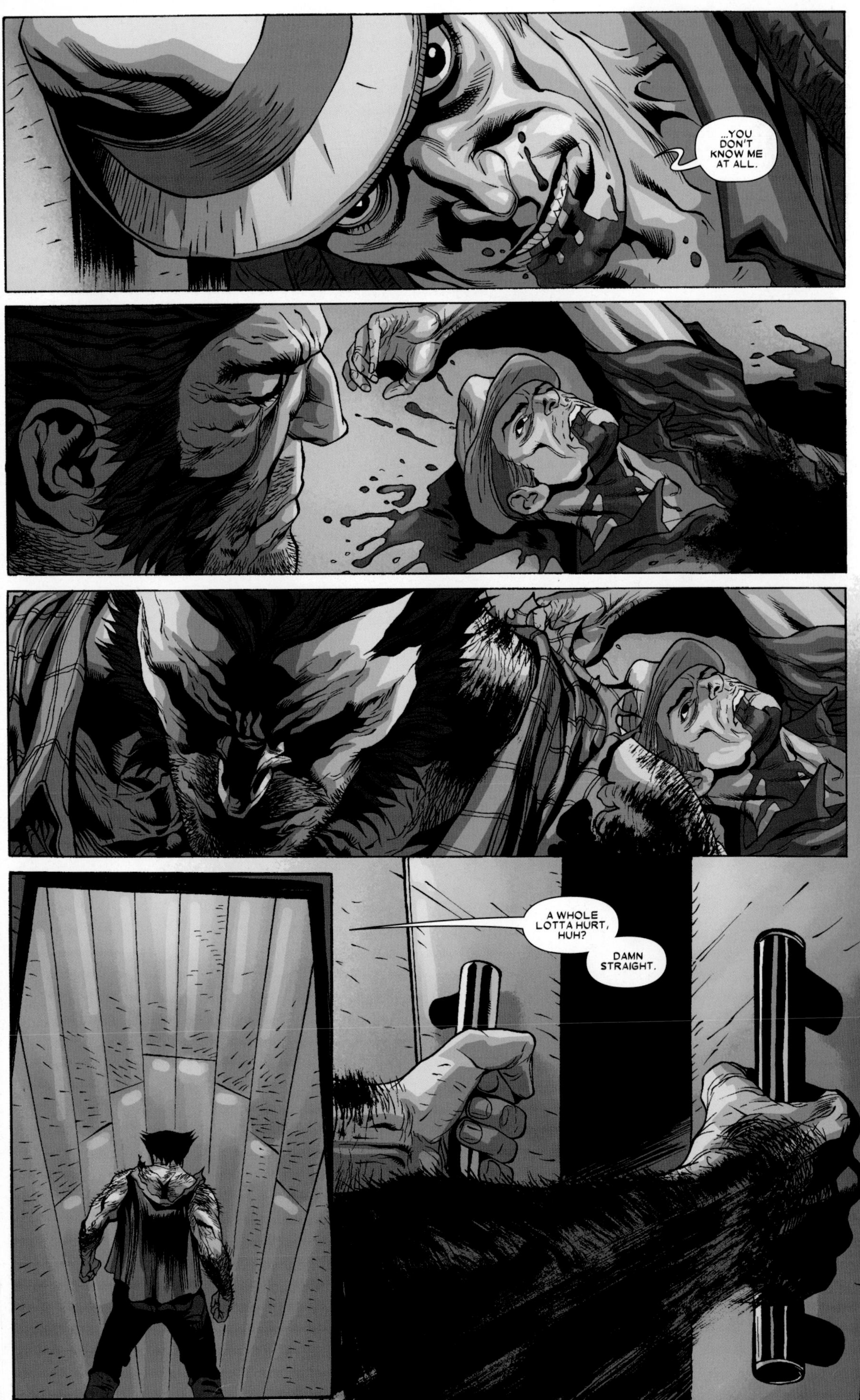
...YOU DON'T KNOW ME AT ALL.
A WHOLE LOTTA HURT, HUH?
DAMN STRAIGHT.

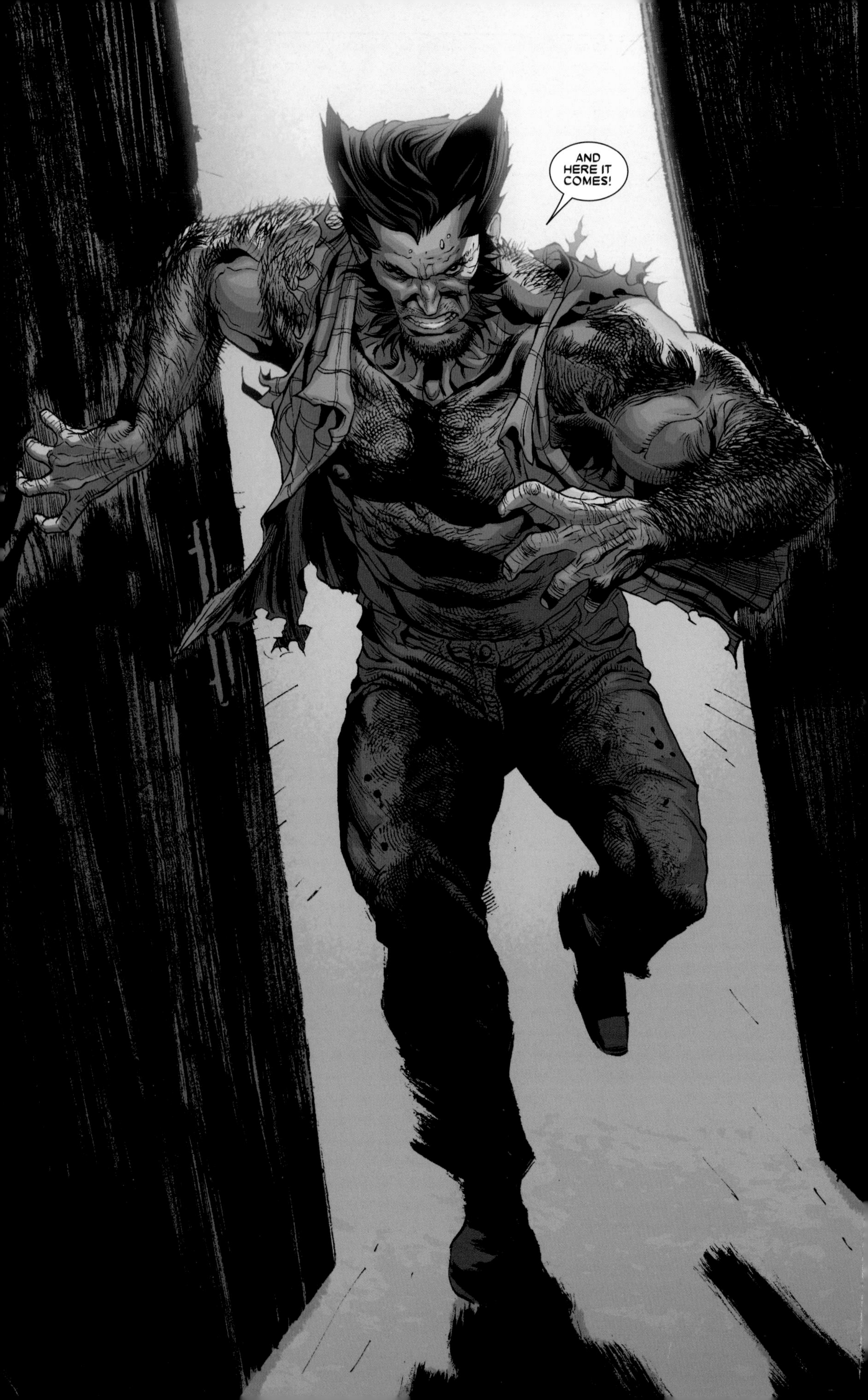
AND HERE IT COMES!

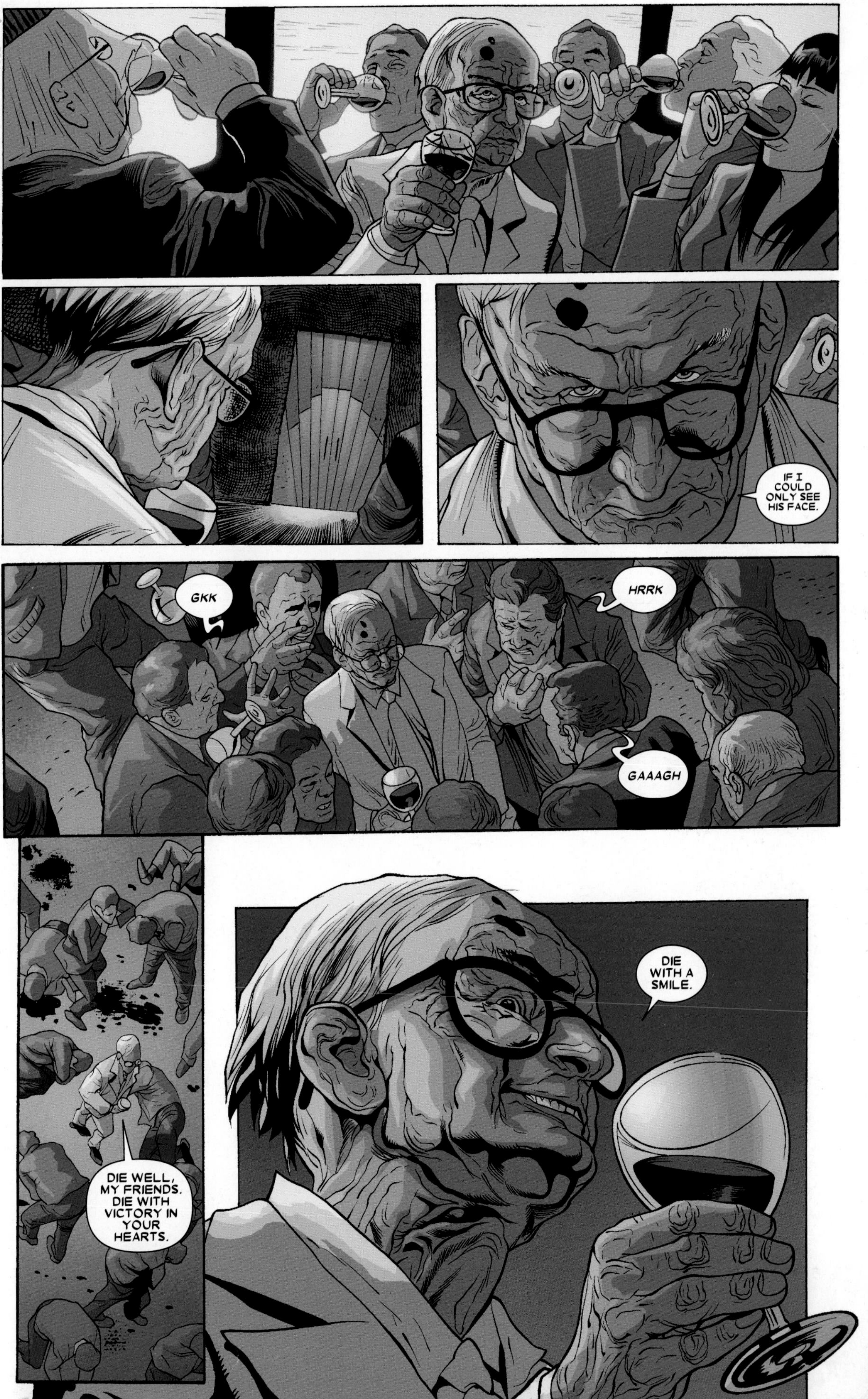
IF I COULD ONLY SEE HIS FACE.
GKK
HRRK
GAAAGH
DIE WELL, MY FRIENDS. DIE WITH VICTORY IN YOUR HEARTS.
DIE WITH A SMILE.

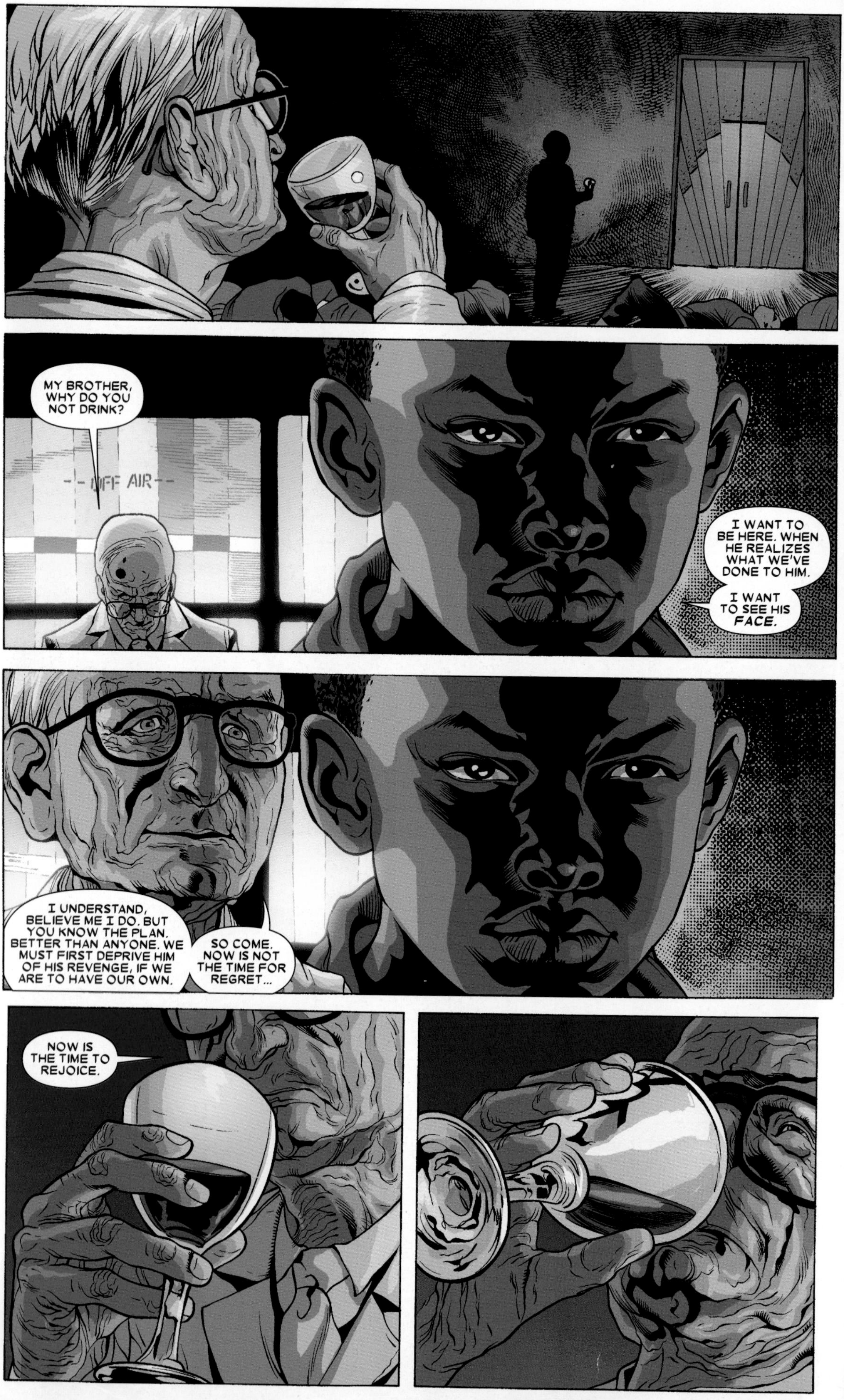

MY BROTHER, WHY DO YOU NOT DRINK?
--OFF AIR--
I WANT TO BE HERE. WHEN HE REALIZES WHAT WE'VE DONE TO HIM.
I WANT TO SEE HIS *FACE.*
I UNDERSTAND, BELIEVE ME I DO. BUT YOU KNOW THE PLAN. BETTER THAN ANYONE. WE MUST FIRST DEPRIVE HIM OF HIS REVENGE, IF WE ARE TO HAVE OUR OWN.
SO COME. NOW IS NOT THE TIME FOR REGRET...
NOW IS THE TIME TO REJOICE.

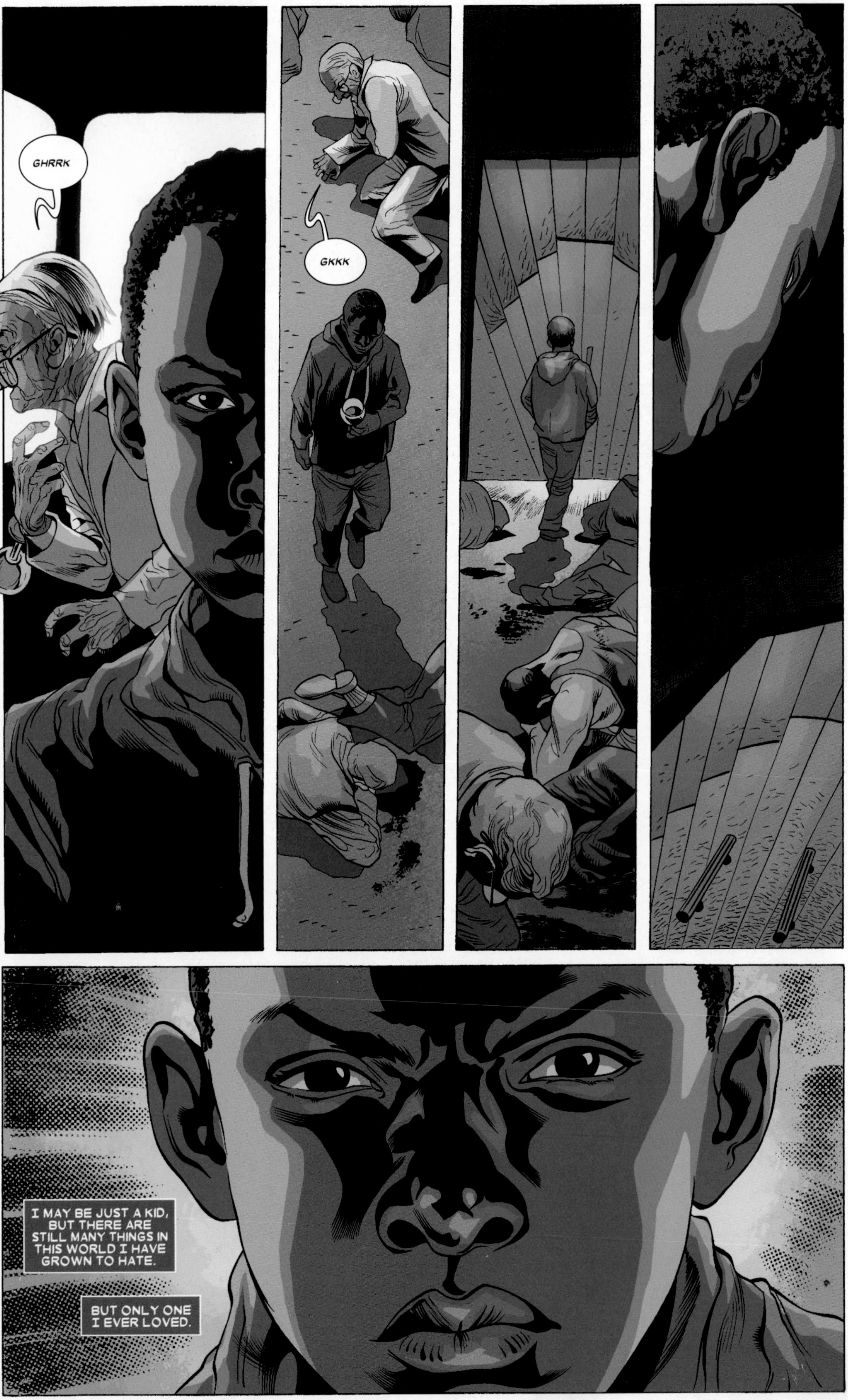
GHRRK
GKKK
I MAY BE JUST A KID, BUT THERE ARE STILL MANY THINGS IN THIS WORLD I HAVE GROWN TO HATE.
BUT ONLY ONE I EVER LOVED.

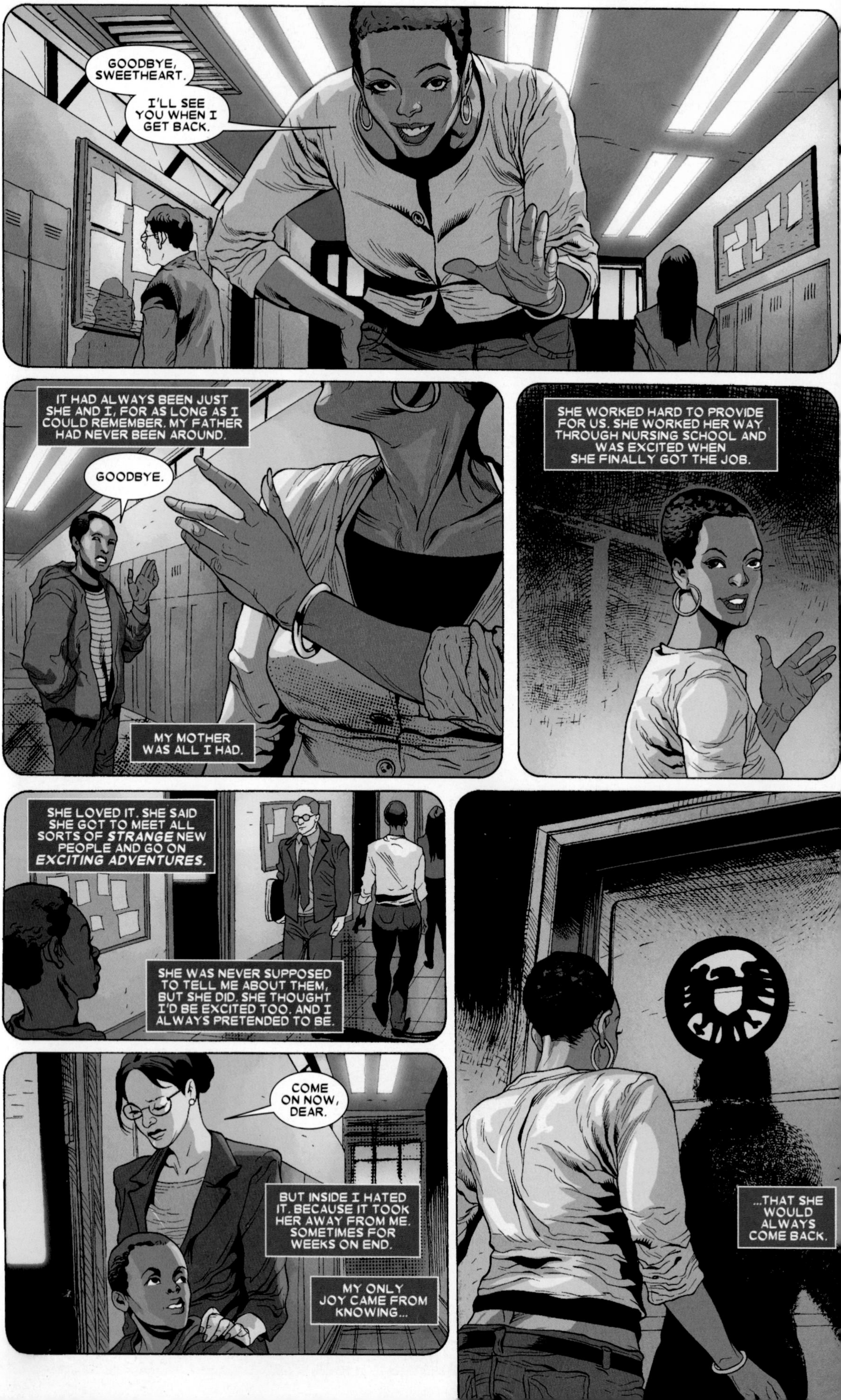
GOODBYE, SWEETHEART.
I'LL SEE YOU WHEN I GET BACK.
IT HAD ALWAYS BEEN JUST SHE AND I, FOR AS LONG AS I COULD REMEMBER. MY FATHER HAD NEVER BEEN AROUND.
GOODBYE.
MY MOTHER WAS ALL I HAD.
SHE WORKED HARD TO PROVIDE FOR US. SHE WORKED HER WAY THROUGH NURSING SCHOOL AND WAS EXCITED WHEN SHE FINALLY GOT THE JOB.
SHE LOVED IT. SHE SAID SHE GOT TO MEET ALL SORTS OF *STRANGE* NEW PEOPLE AND GO ON *EXCITING ADVENTURES*.
SHE WAS NEVER SUPPOSED TO TELL ME ABOUT THEM, BUT SHE DID. SHE THOUGHT I'D BE EXCITED TOO. AND I ALWAYS PRETENDED TO BE.
COME ON NOW, DEAR.
BUT INSIDE I HATED IT. BECAUSE IT TOOK HER AWAY FROM ME. SOMETIMES FOR WEEKS ON END.
MY ONLY JOY CAME FROM KNOWING...
...THAT SHE WOULD ALWAYS COME BACK.

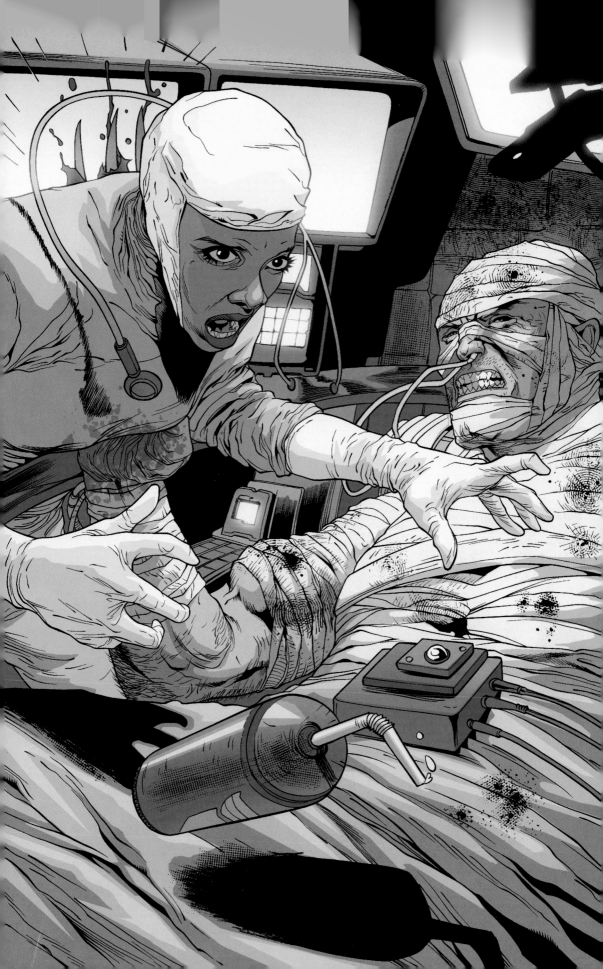

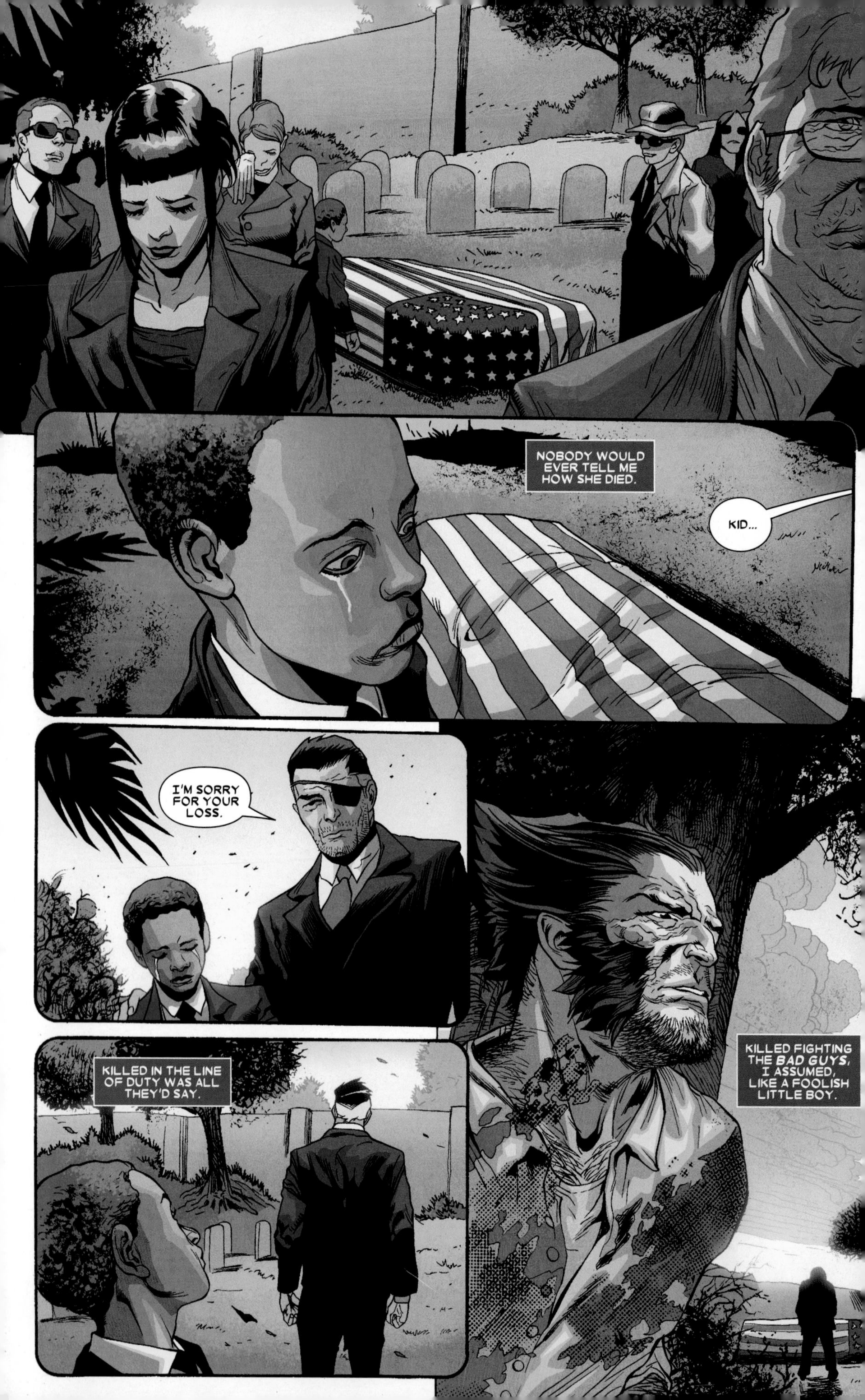
NOBODY WOULD EVER TELL ME HOW SHE DIED.
KID...
I'M SORRY FOR YOUR LOSS.
KILLED IN THE LINE OF DUTY WAS ALL THEY'D SAY.
KILLED FIGHTING THE *BAD GUYS,* I ASSUMED, LIKE A FOOLISH LITTLE BOY.

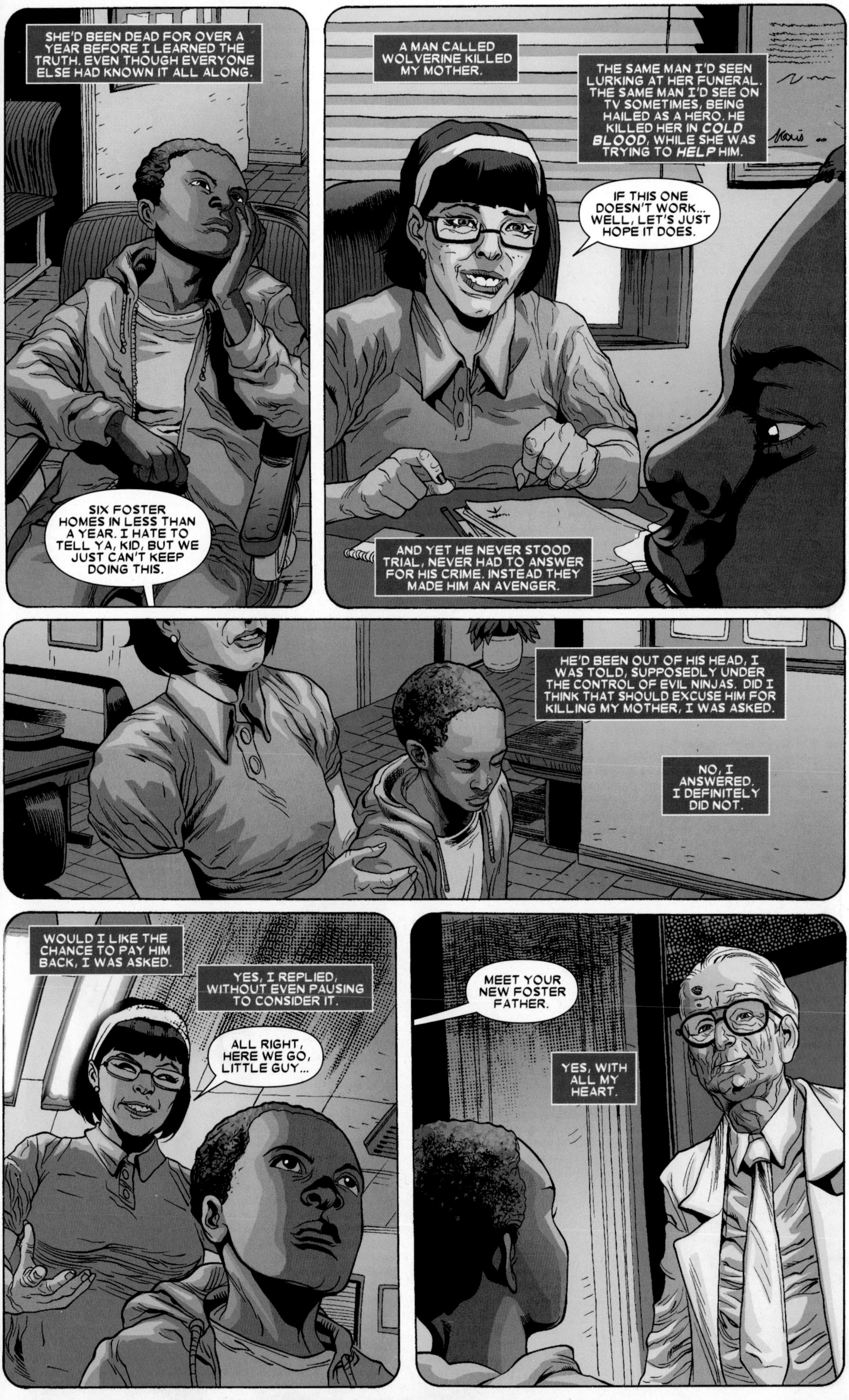
SHE'D BEEN DEAD FOR OVER A YEAR BEFORE I LEARNED THE TRUTH. EVEN THOUGH EVERYONE ELSE HAD KNOWN IT ALL ALONG.
SIX FOSTER HOMES IN LESS THAN A YEAR. I HATE TO TELL YA, KID, BUT WE JUST CAN'T KEEP DOING THIS.
A MAN CALLED WOLVERINE KILLED MY MOTHER.
THE SAME MAN I'D SEEN LURKING AT HER FUNERAL. THE SAME MAN I'D SEE ON TV SOMETIMES, BEING HAILED AS A HERO. HE KILLED HER IN COLD BLOOD, WHILE SHE WAS TRYING TO HELP HIM.
IF THIS ONE DOESN'T WORK... WELL, LET'S JUST HOPE IT DOES.
AND YET HE NEVER STOOD TRIAL, NEVER HAD TO ANSWER FOR HIS CRIME. INSTEAD THEY MADE HIM AN AVENGER.
HE'D BEEN OUT OF HIS HEAD, I WAS TOLD, SUPPOSEDLY UNDER THE CONTROL OF EVIL NINJAS. DID I THINK THAT SHOULD EXCUSE HIM FOR KILLING MY MOTHER, I WAS ASKED.
NO, I ANSWERED. I DEFINITELY DID NOT.
WOULD I LIKE THE CHANCE TO PAY HIM BACK, I WAS ASKED.
YES, I REPLIED, WITHOUT EVEN PAUSING TO CONSIDER IT.
ALL RIGHT, HERE WE GO, LITTLE GUY...
MEET YOUR NEW FOSTER FATHER.
YES, WITH ALL MY HEART.

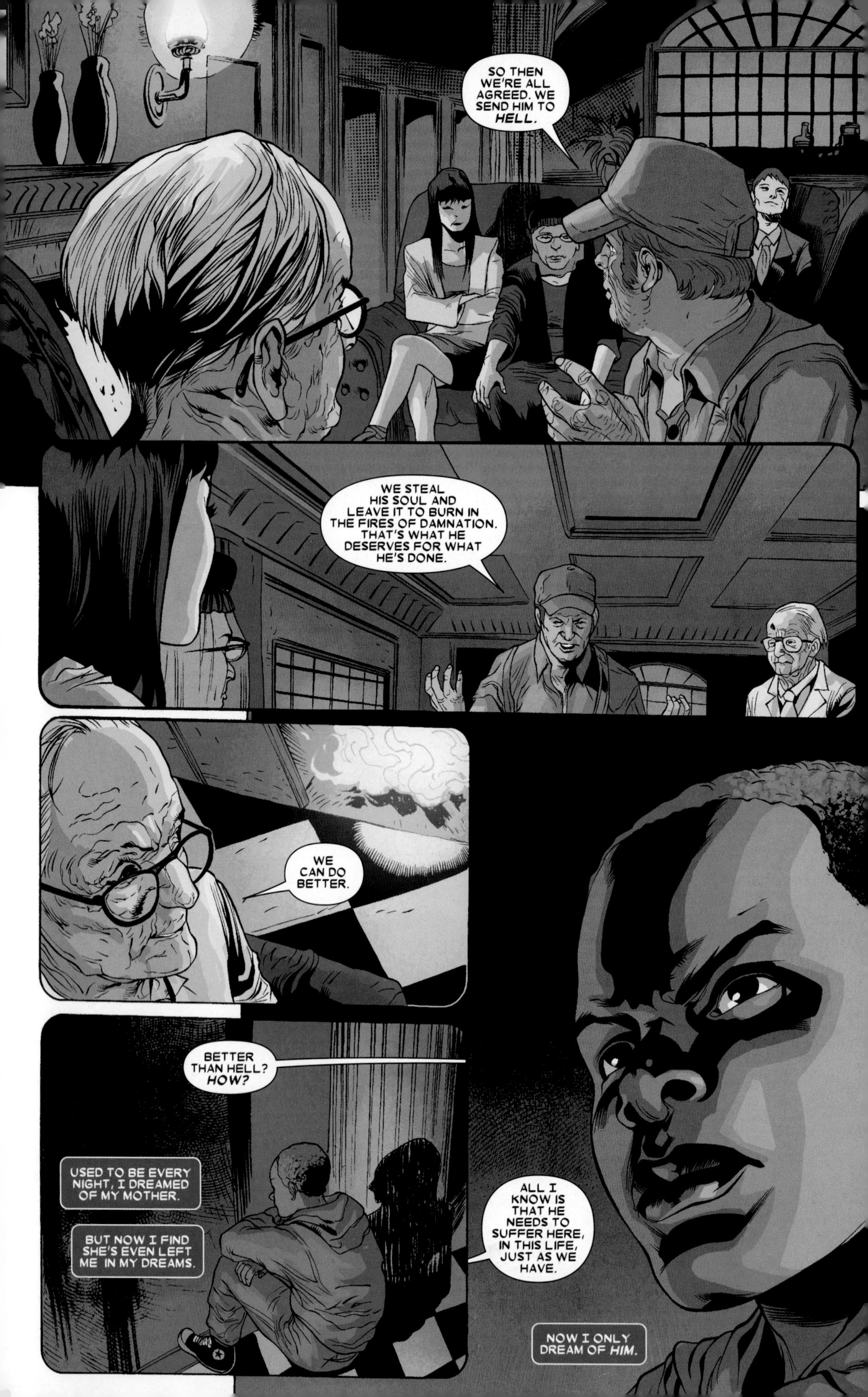
SO THEN WE'RE ALL AGREED. WE SEND HIM TO *HELL.*
WE STEAL HIS SOUL AND LEAVE IT TO BURN IN THE FIRES OF DAMNATION. THAT'S WHAT HE DESERVES FOR WHAT HE'S DONE.
WE CAN DO BETTER.
BETTER THAN HELL? *HOW?*
USED TO BE EVERY NIGHT, I DREAMED OF MY MOTHER.
BUT NOW I FIND SHE'S EVEN LEFT ME IN MY DREAMS.
ALL I KNOW IS THAT HE NEEDS TO SUFFER HERE, IN THIS LIFE, JUST AS WE HAVE.
NOW I ONLY DREAM OF *HIM.*

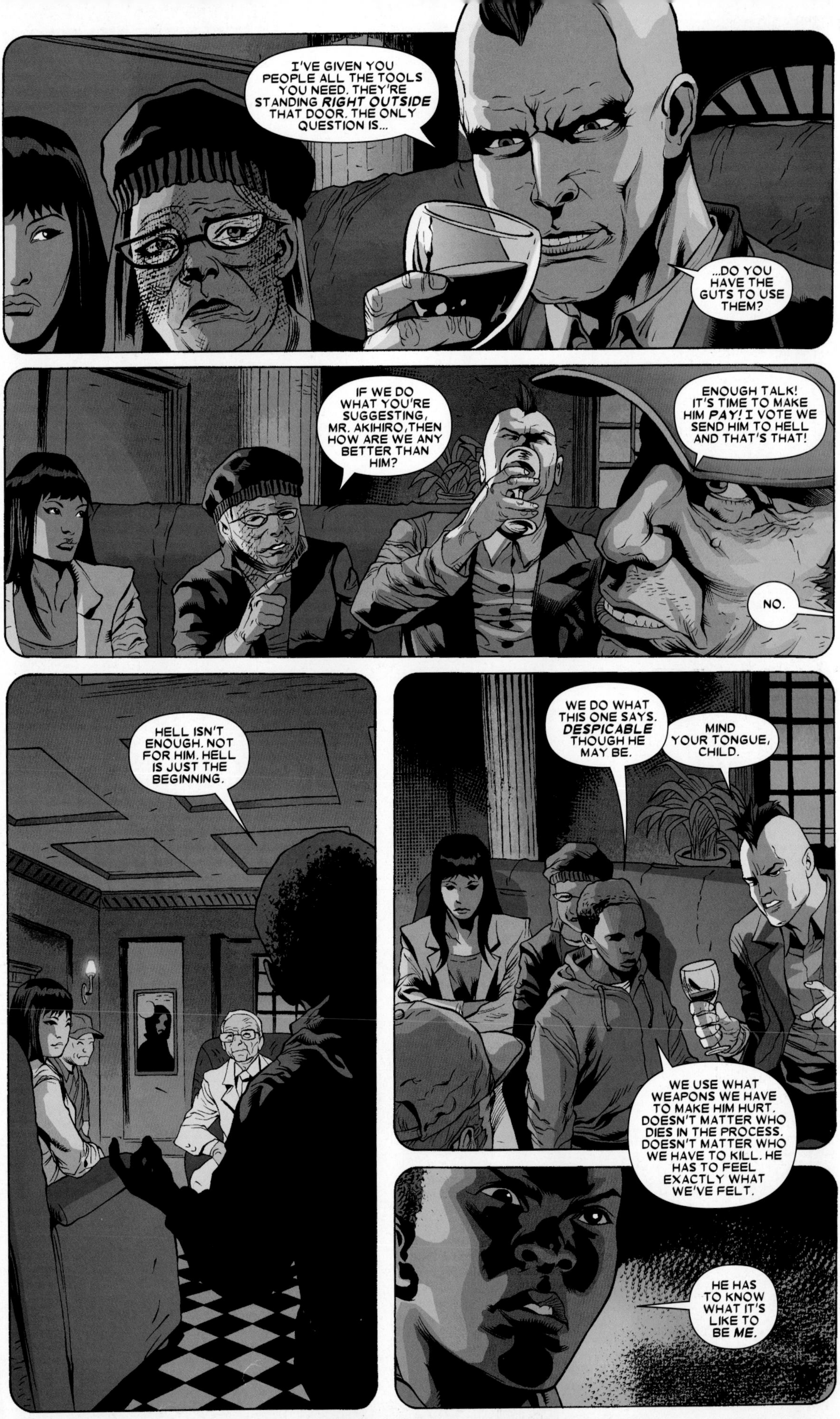
I'VE GIVEN YOU PEOPLE ALL THE TOOLS YOU NEED. THEY'RE STANDING RIGHT OUTSIDE THAT DOOR. THE ONLY QUESTION IS...
...DO YOU HAVE THE GUTS TO USE THEM?
IF WE DO WHAT YOU'RE SUGGESTING, MR. AKIHIRO, THEN HOW ARE WE ANY BETTER THAN HIM?
ENOUGH TALK! IT'S TIME TO MAKE HIM PAY! I VOTE WE SEND HIM TO HELL AND THAT'S THAT!
NO.
HELL ISN'T ENOUGH. NOT FOR HIM. HELL IS JUST THE BEGINNING.
WE DO WHAT THIS ONE SAYS. DESPICABLE THOUGH HE MAY BE.
MIND YOUR TONGUE, CHILD.
WE USE WHAT WEAPONS WE HAVE TO MAKE HIM HURT. DOESN'T MATTER WHO DIES IN THE PROCESS. DOESN'T MATTER WHO WE HAVE TO KILL. HE HAS TO FEEL EXACTLY WHAT WE'VE FELT.
HE HAS TO KNOW WHAT IT'S LIKE TO BE ME.

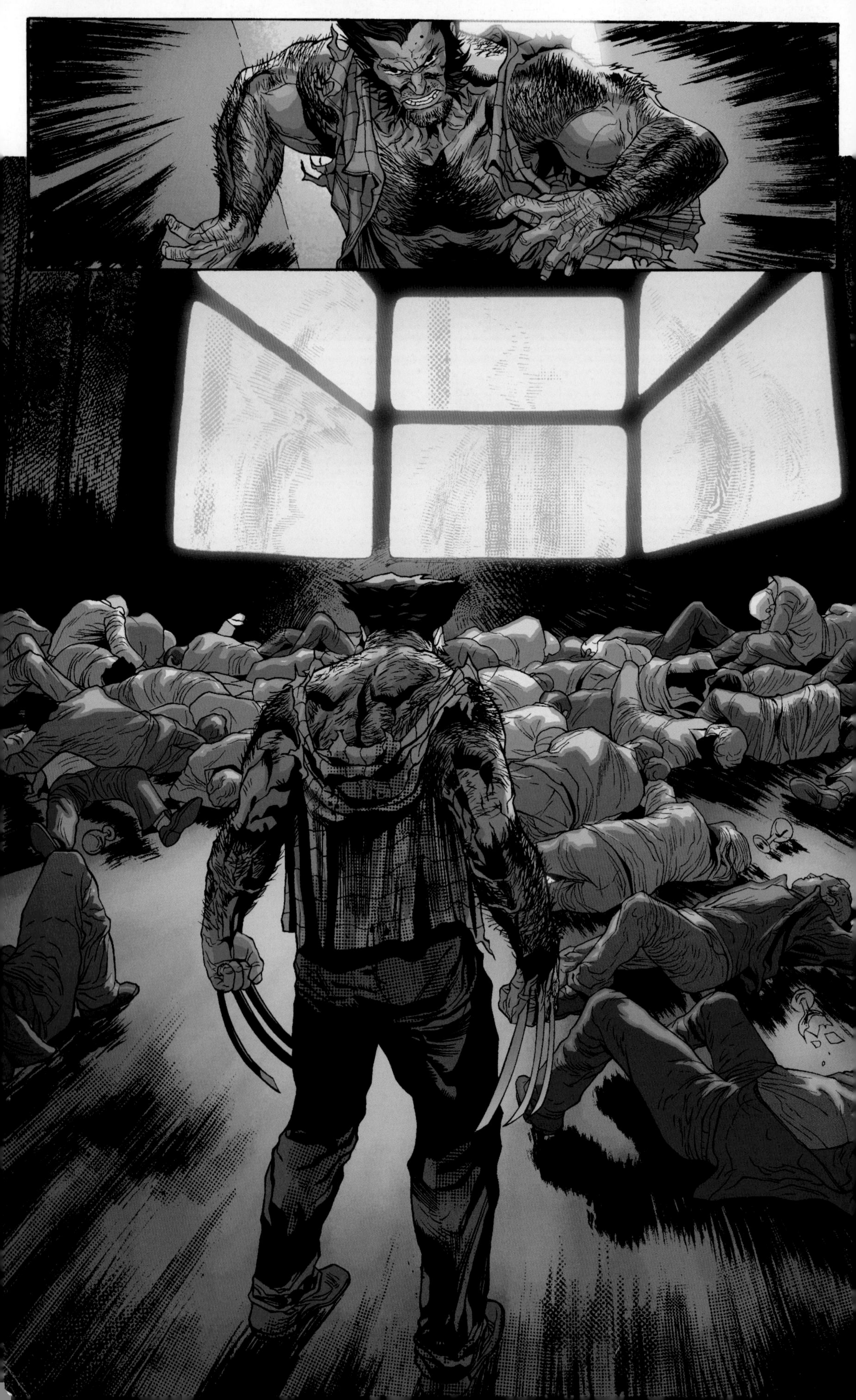

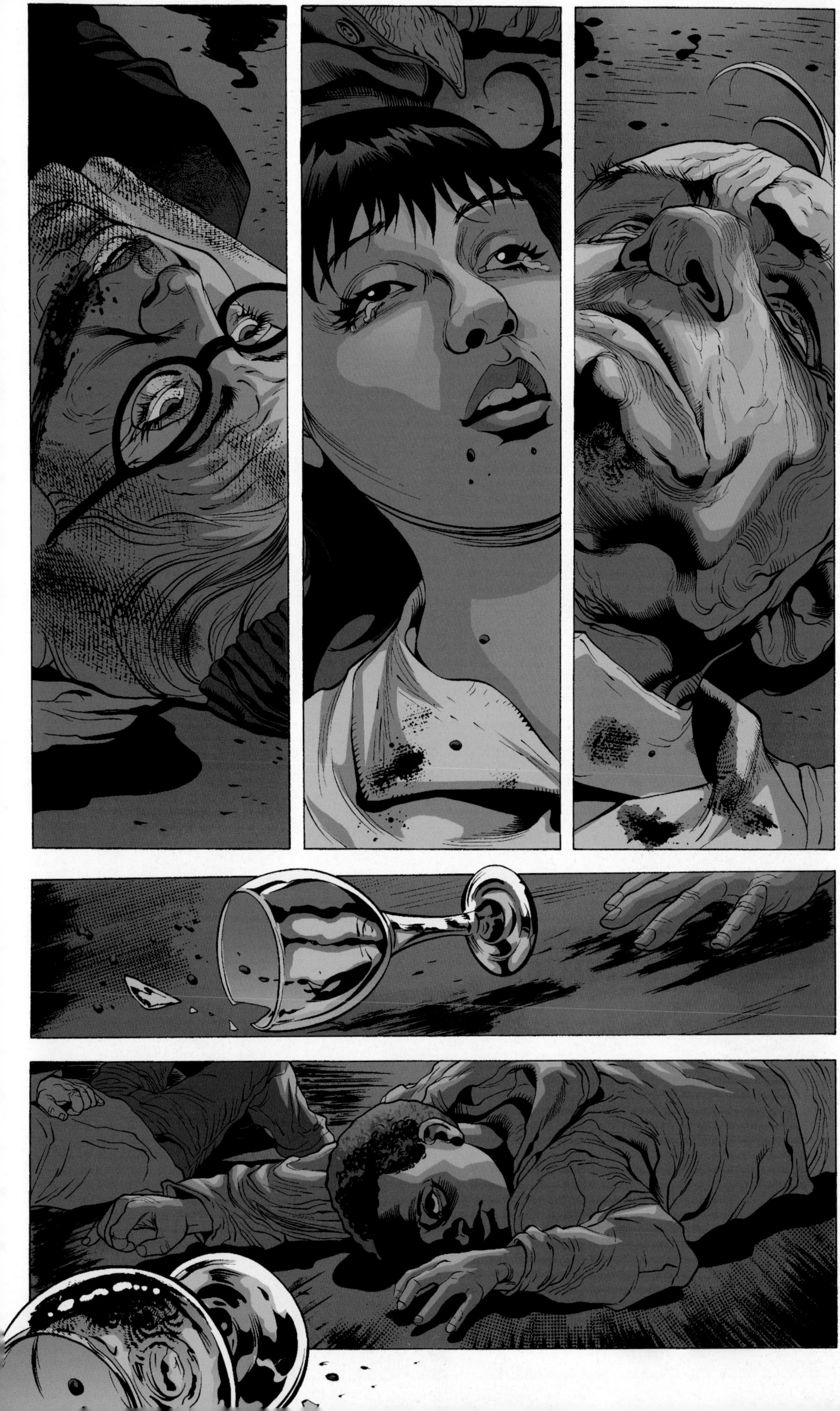

SUCH A DAMN WASTE.

HOPE YOU FOLKS ENJOY HELL AS MUCH AS I DID.

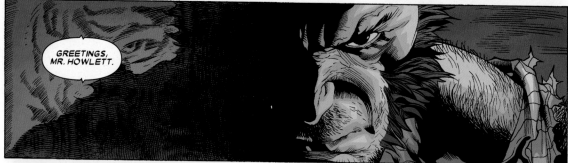

GREETINGS, MR. HOWLETT.

IF YOU'RE SEEING THIS MESSAGE, THAT MEANS THAT WE ARE DEAD.

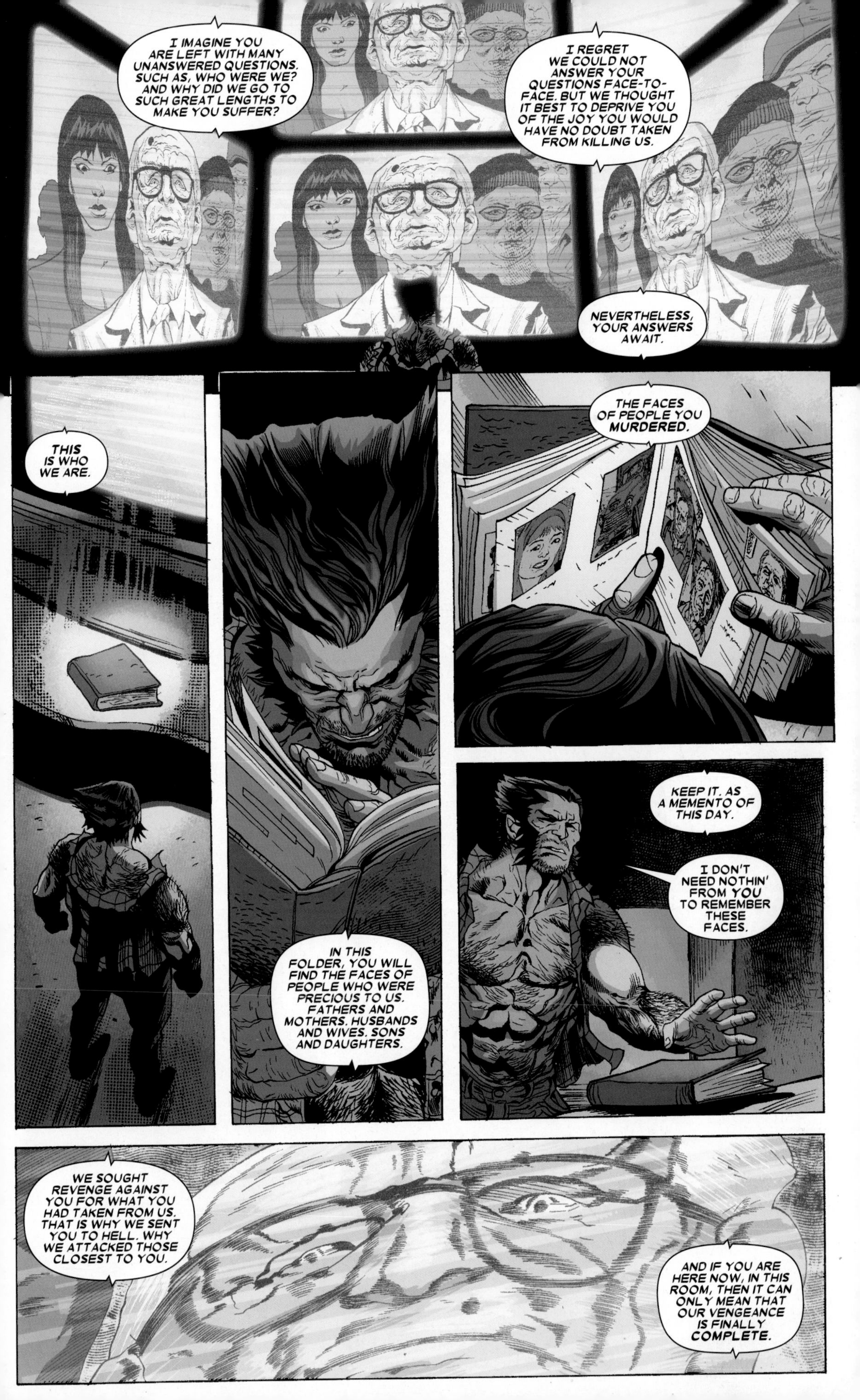
I IMAGINE YOU ARE LEFT WITH MANY UNANSWERED QUESTIONS. SUCH AS, WHO WERE WE? AND WHY DID WE GO TO SUCH GREAT LENGTHS TO MAKE YOU SUFFER?
I REGRET WE COULD NOT ANSWER YOUR QUESTIONS FACE-TO-FACE. BUT WE THOUGHT IT BEST TO DEPRIVE YOU OF THE JOY YOU WOULD HAVE NO DOUBT TAKEN FROM KILLING US.
NEVERTHELESS, YOUR ANSWERS AWAIT.
THIS IS WHO WE ARE.
IN THIS FOLDER, YOU WILL FIND THE FACES OF PEOPLE WHO WERE PRECIOUS TO US. FATHERS AND MOTHERS. HUSBANDS AND WIVES. SONS AND DAUGHTERS.
THE FACES OF PEOPLE YOU MURDERED.
KEEP IT. AS A MEMENTO OF THIS DAY.
I DON'T NEED NOTHIN' FROM YOU TO REMEMBER THESE FACES.
WE SOUGHT REVENGE AGAINST YOU FOR WHAT YOU HAD TAKEN FROM US. THAT IS WHY WE SENT YOU TO HELL. WHY WE ATTACKED THOSE CLOSEST TO YOU.
AND IF YOU ARE HERE NOW, IN THIS ROOM, THEN IT CAN ONLY MEAN THAT OUR VENGEANCE IS FINALLY COMPLETE.

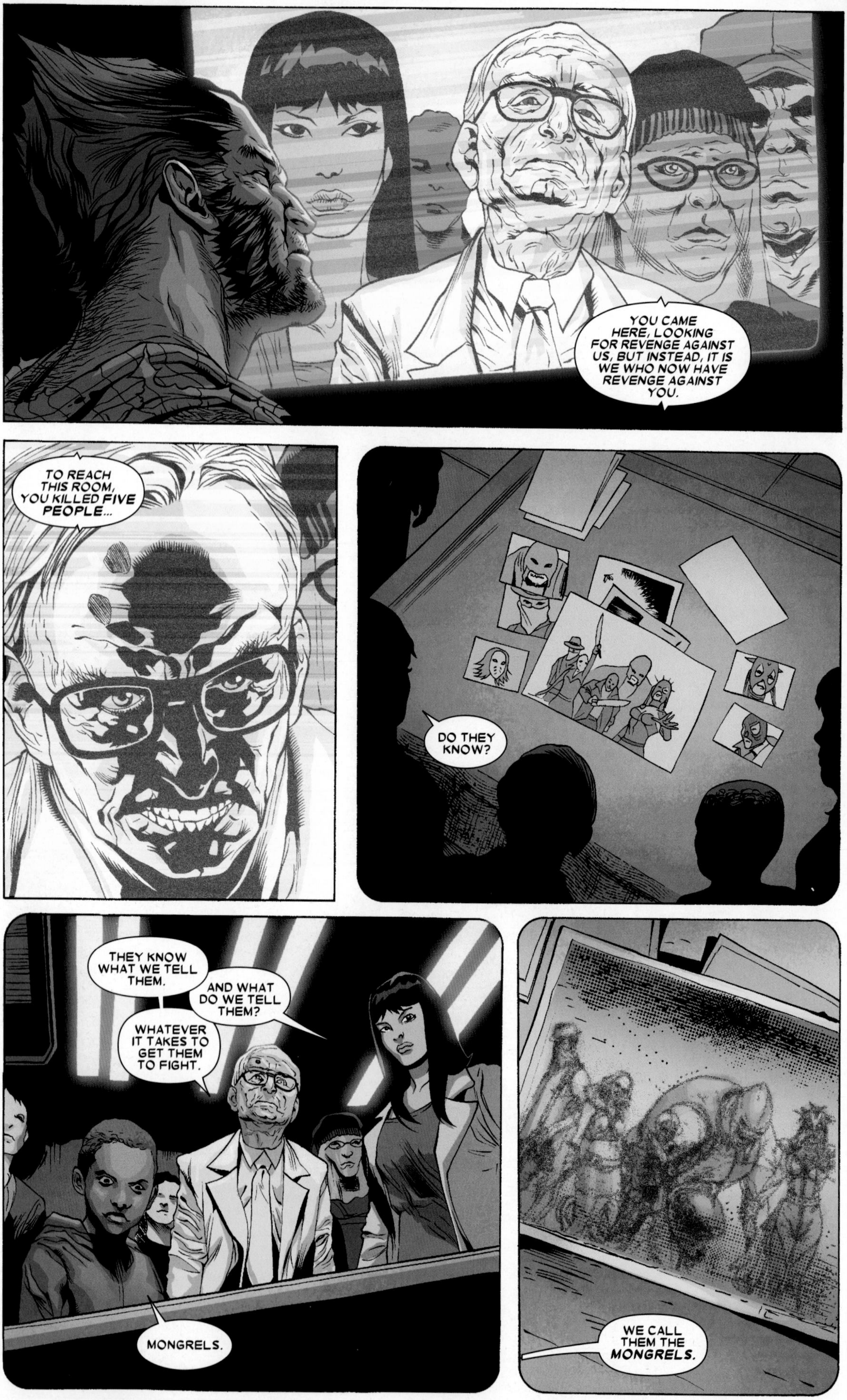

YOU CAME HERE, LOOKING FOR REVENGE AGAINST US, BUT INSTEAD, IT IS WE WHO NOW HAVE REVENGE AGAINST YOU.
TO REACH THIS ROOM, YOU KILLED FIVE PEOPLE...
DO THEY KNOW?
THEY KNOW WHAT WE TELL THEM.
AND WHAT DO WE TELL THEM?
WHATEVER IT TAKES TO GET THEM TO FIGHT.
MONGRELS.
WE CALL THEM THE MONGRELS.

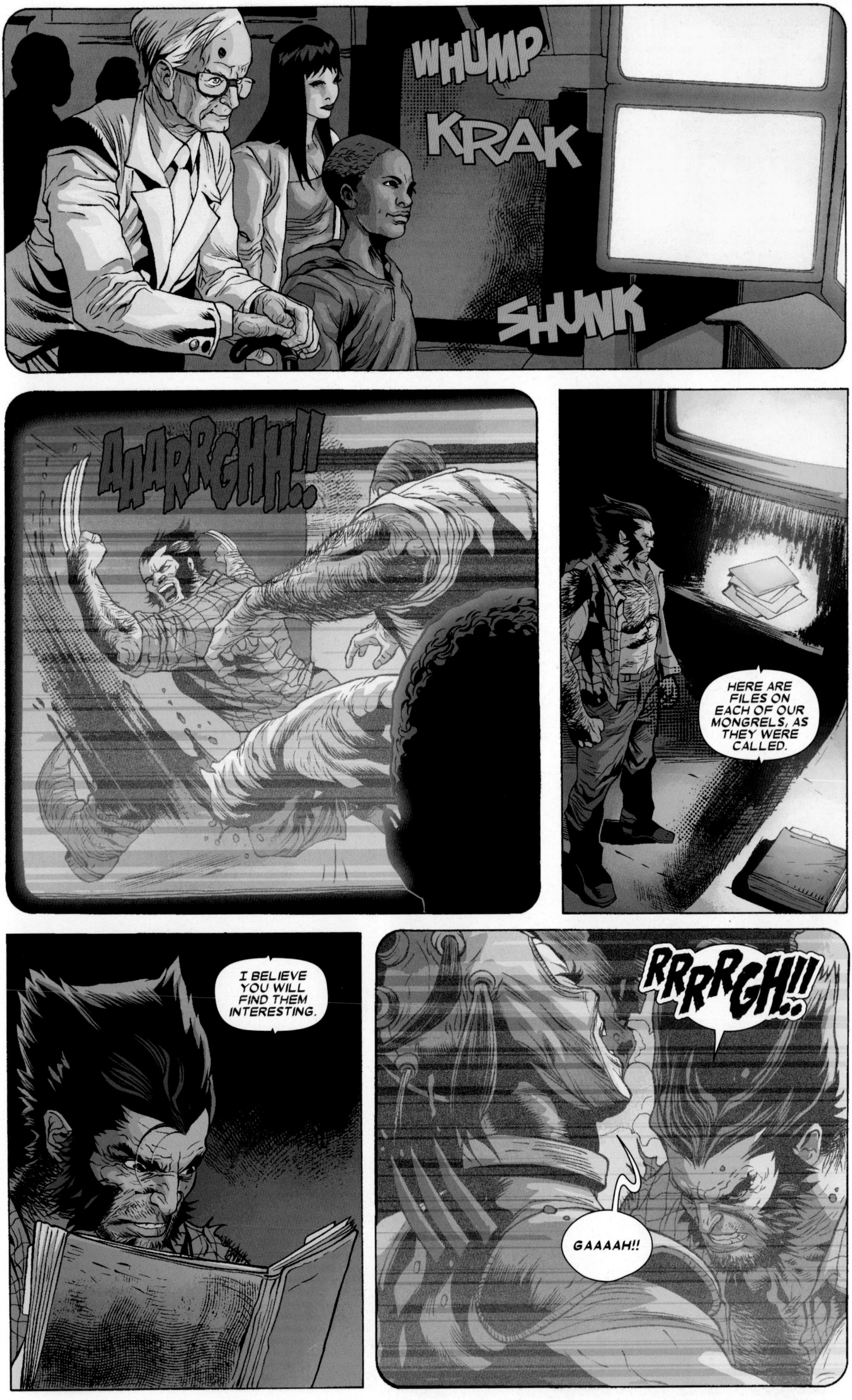
WHUMP
KRAK
SHUNK
AAARRGHH!!
HERE ARE FILES ON EACH OF OUR MONGRELS, AS THEY WERE CALLED.
I BELIEVE YOU WILL FIND THEM INTERESTING.
RRRRGH!!
GAAAAH!!

WE SPENT **YEARS** STUDYING YOU, JAMES. SEARCHING FOR WAYS TO MAKE YOU SUFFER. SOME OF US SPENT THEIR ENTIRE LIVES IN THAT PURSUIT.

DURING THAT TIME, WE LEARNED EVERYTHING THERE WAS TO KNOW ABOUT YOU. I DARESAY, WE CAME TO KNOW YOU BETTER THAN YOU KNOW YOURSELF.

"WE KNOW WHO YOU'VE KILLED AND WHO YOU'VE LOVED.

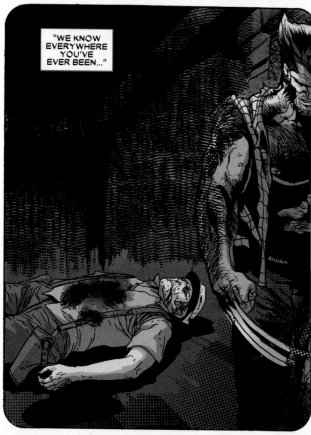

"WE KNOW EVERYWHERE YOU'VE EVER BEEN..."

AND EVERYTHING YOU'VE EVER LEFT BEHIND.

THIS... CAN'T BE TRUE.

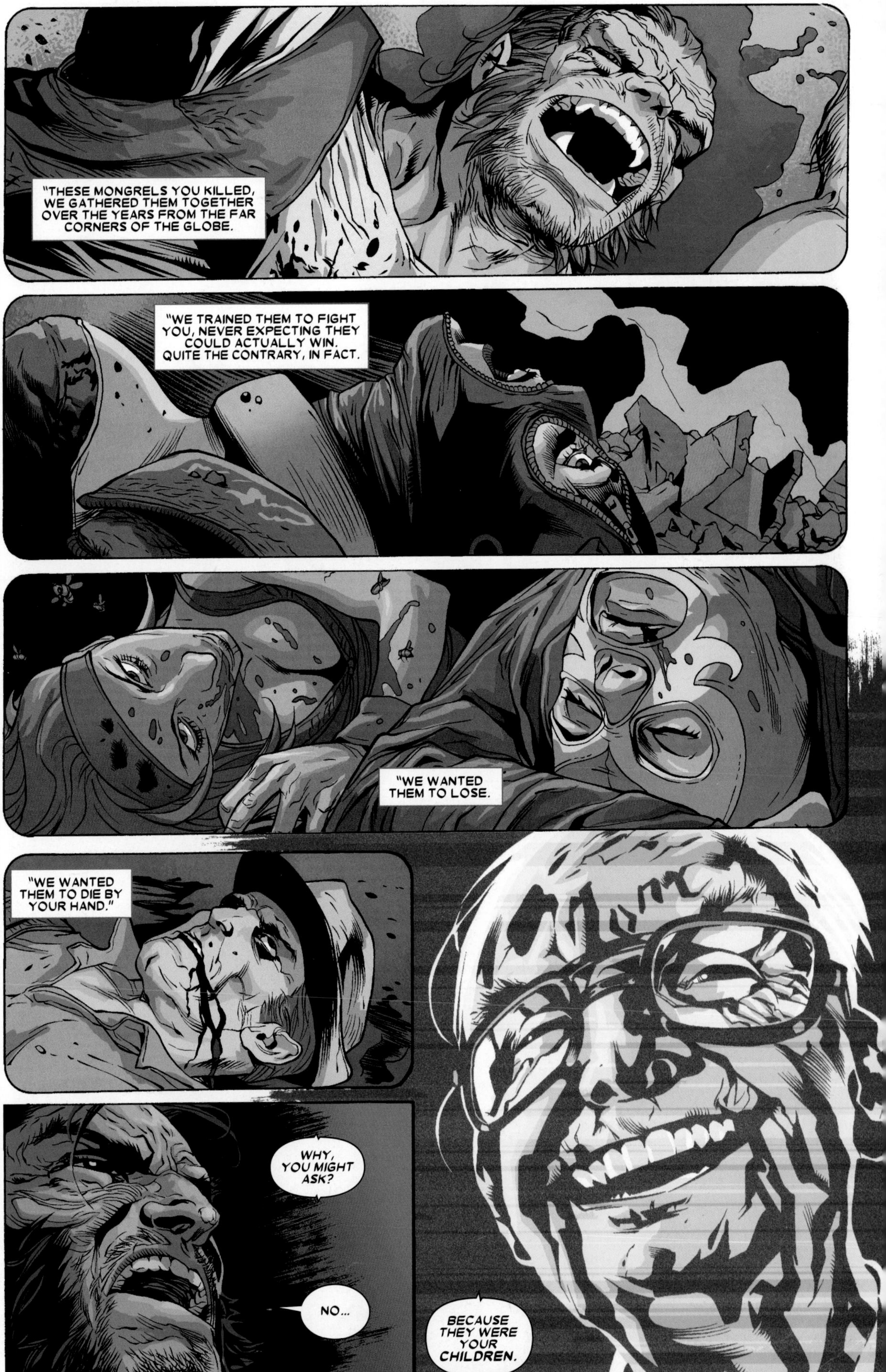
"THESE MONGRELS YOU KILLED, WE GATHERED THEM TOGETHER OVER THE YEARS FROM THE FAR CORNERS OF THE GLOBE.
"WE TRAINED THEM TO FIGHT YOU, NEVER EXPECTING THEY COULD ACTUALLY WIN. QUITE THE CONTRARY, IN FACT.
"WE WANTED THEM TO LOSE.
"WE WANTED THEM TO DIE BY YOUR HAND."
WHY, YOU MIGHT ASK?
NO...
BECAUSE THEY WERE YOUR CHILDREN.

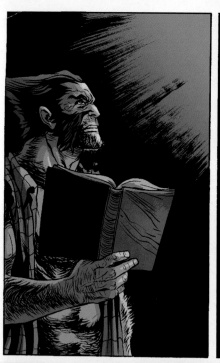

NOW, AT LAST, YOU KNOW WHAT IT IS LIKE TO BE US.

WELCOME, JAMES HOWLETT...

TO THE RED RIGHT HAND.

CLICK

HEH.

LOOK AT HIS FACE...

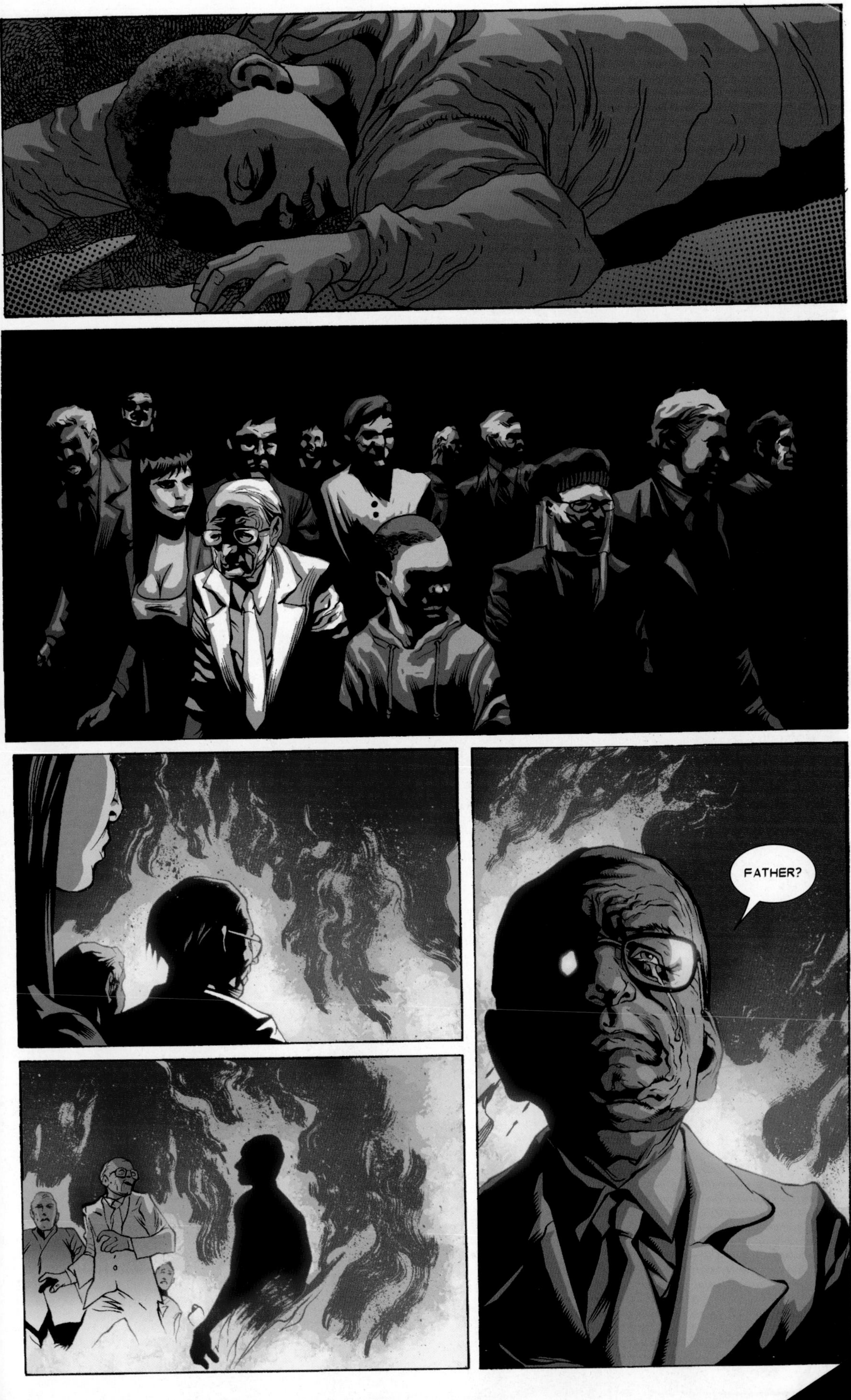
FATHER?

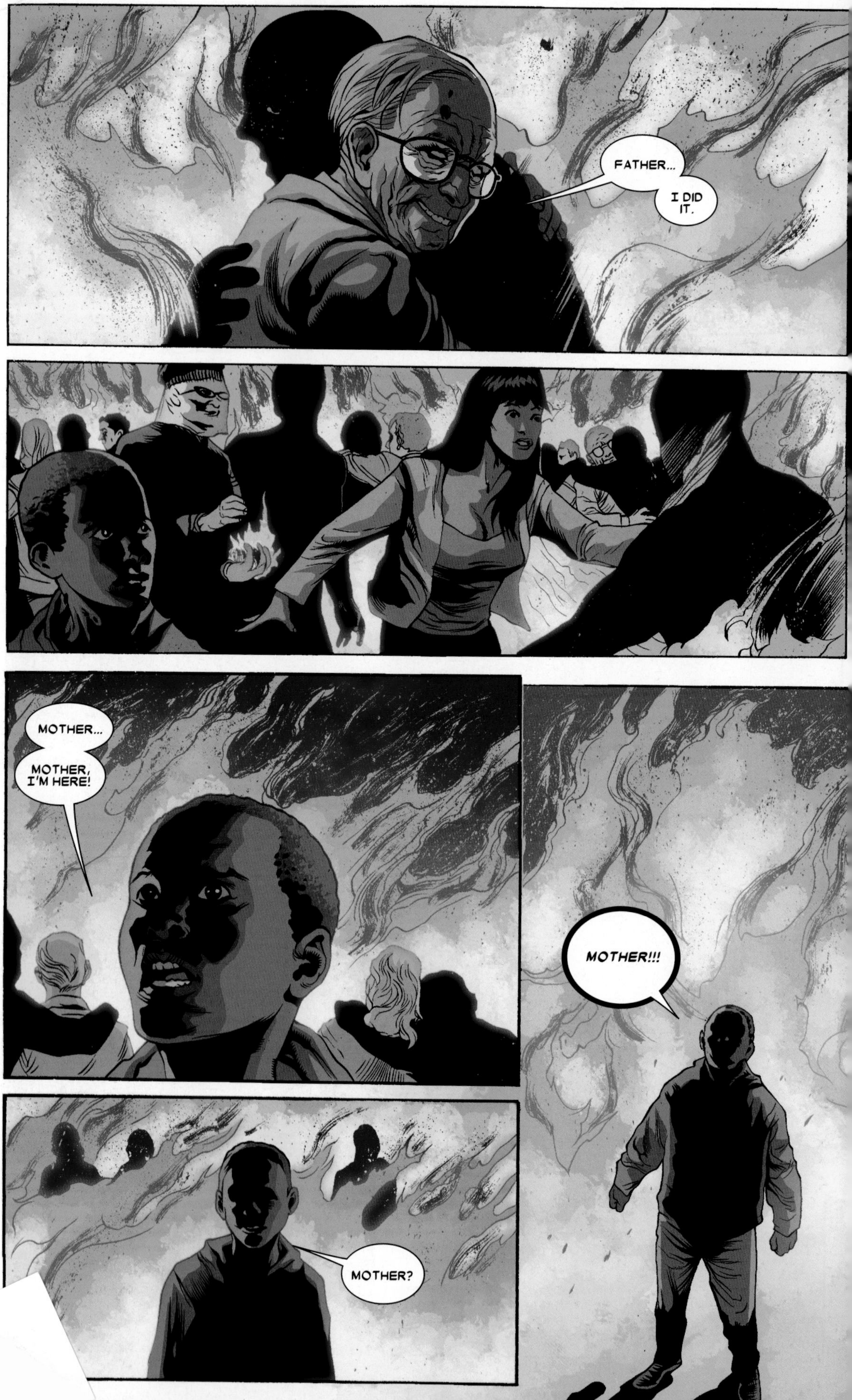

FATHER...
I DID IT.
MOTHER...
MOTHER, I'M HERE!
MOTHER!!!
MOTHER?

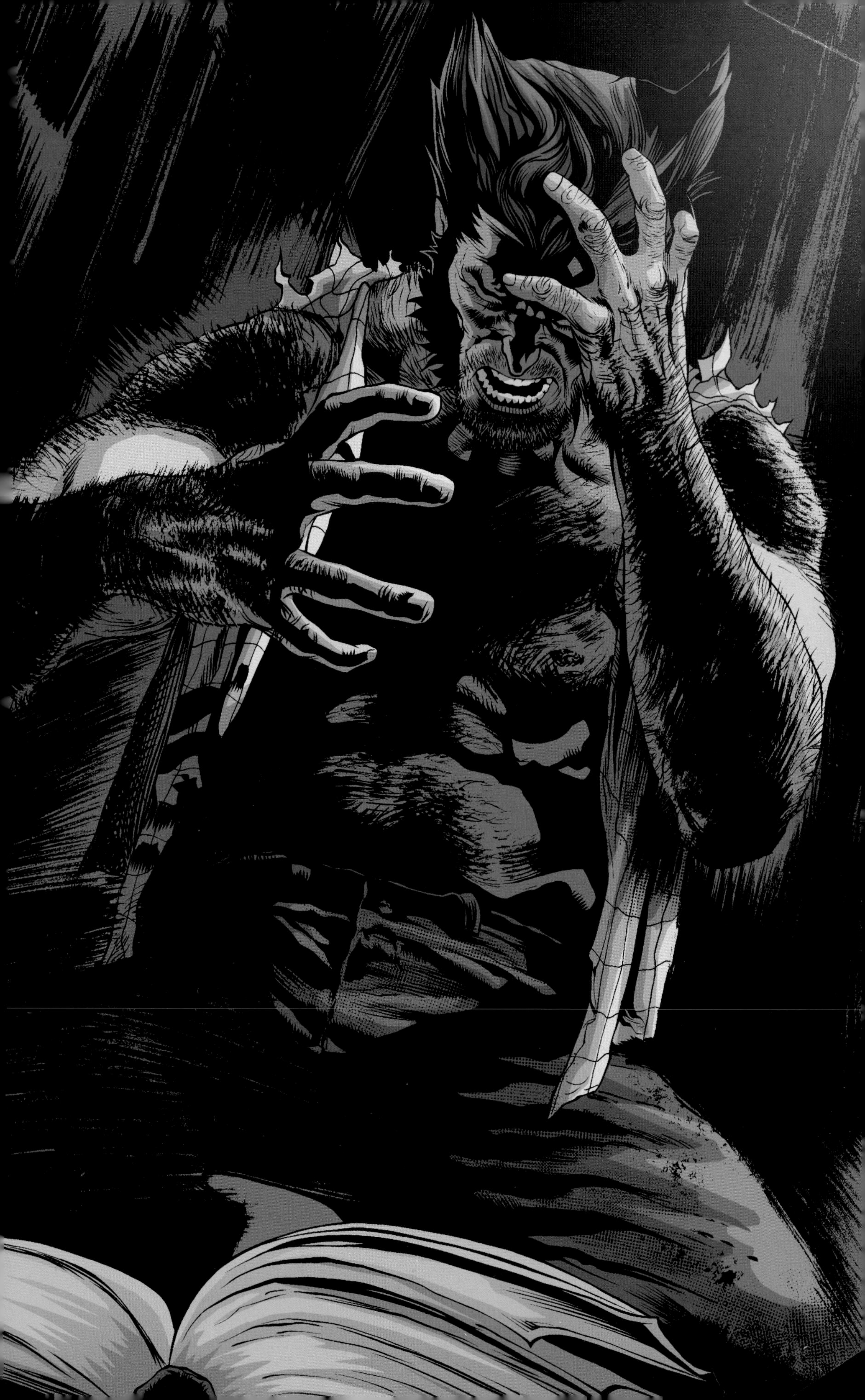

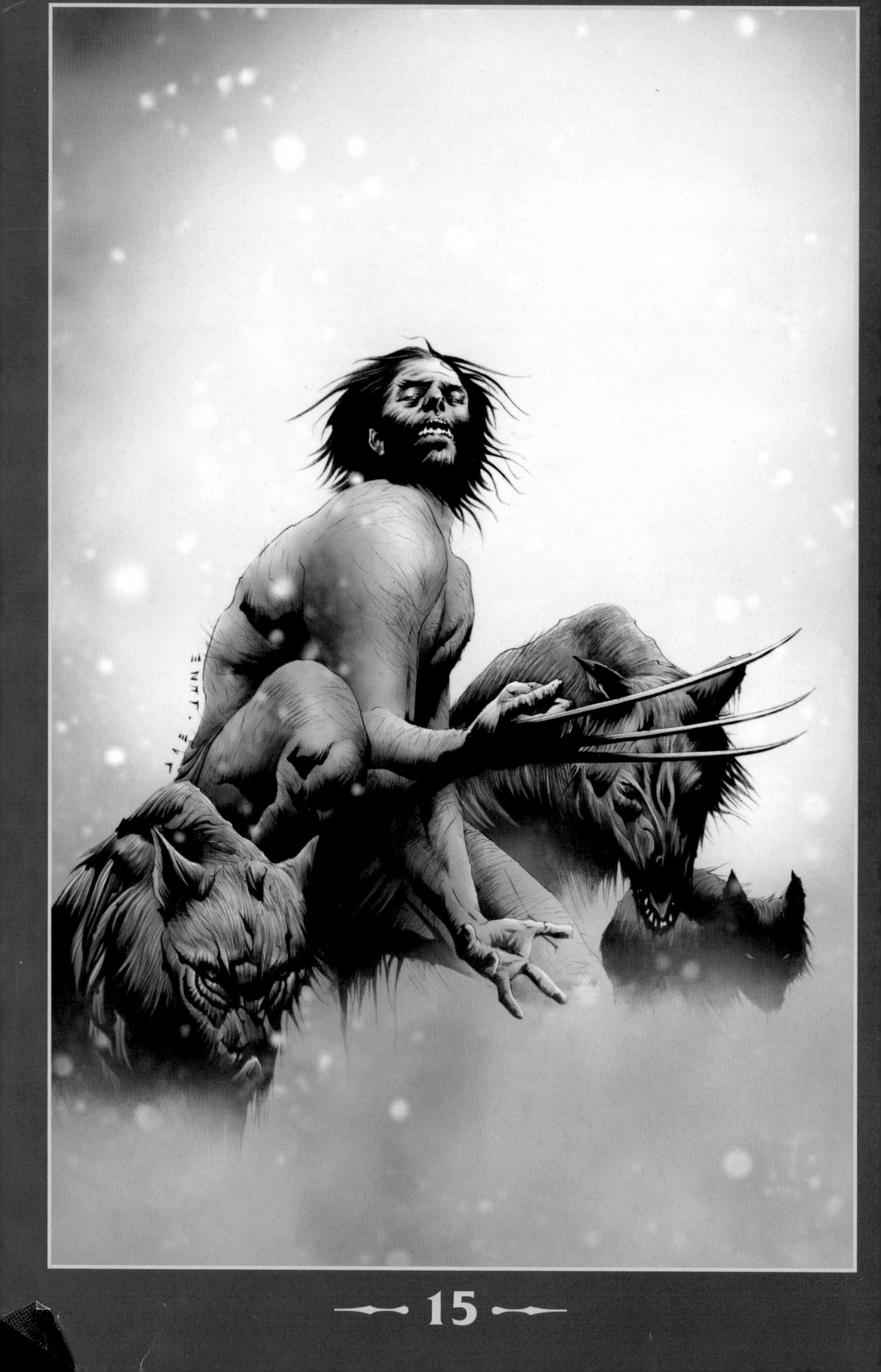

—— 15 ——

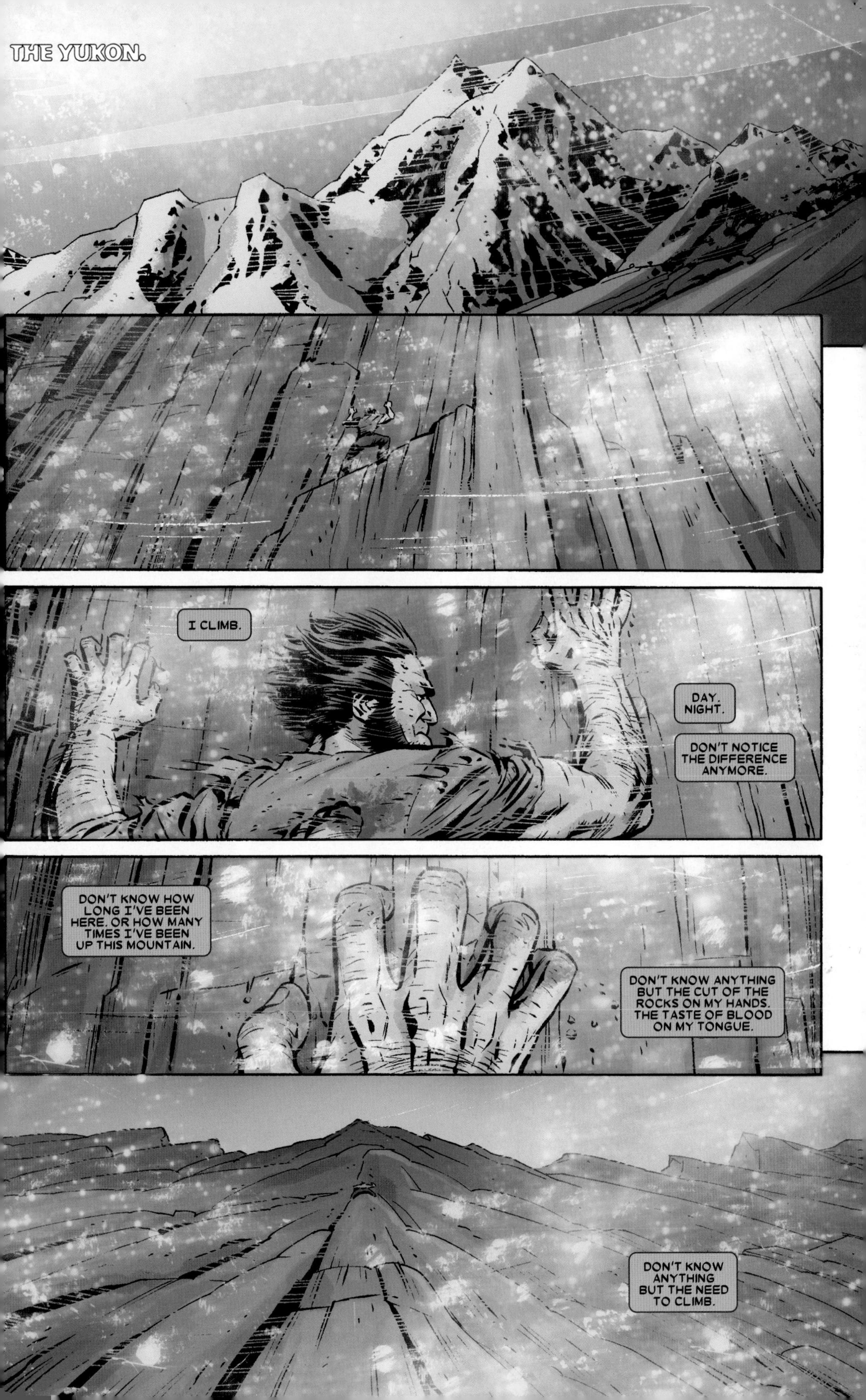
THE YUKON.
I CLIMB.
DAY. NIGHT.
DON'T NOTICE THE DIFFERENCE ANYMORE.
DON'T KNOW HOW LONG I'VE BEEN HERE. OR HOW MANY TIMES I'VE BEEN UP THIS MOUNTAIN.
DON'T KNOW ANYTHING BUT THE CUT OF THE ROCKS ON MY HANDS. THE TASTE OF BLOOD ON MY TONGUE.
DON'T KNOW ANYTHING BUT THE NEED TO CLIMB.

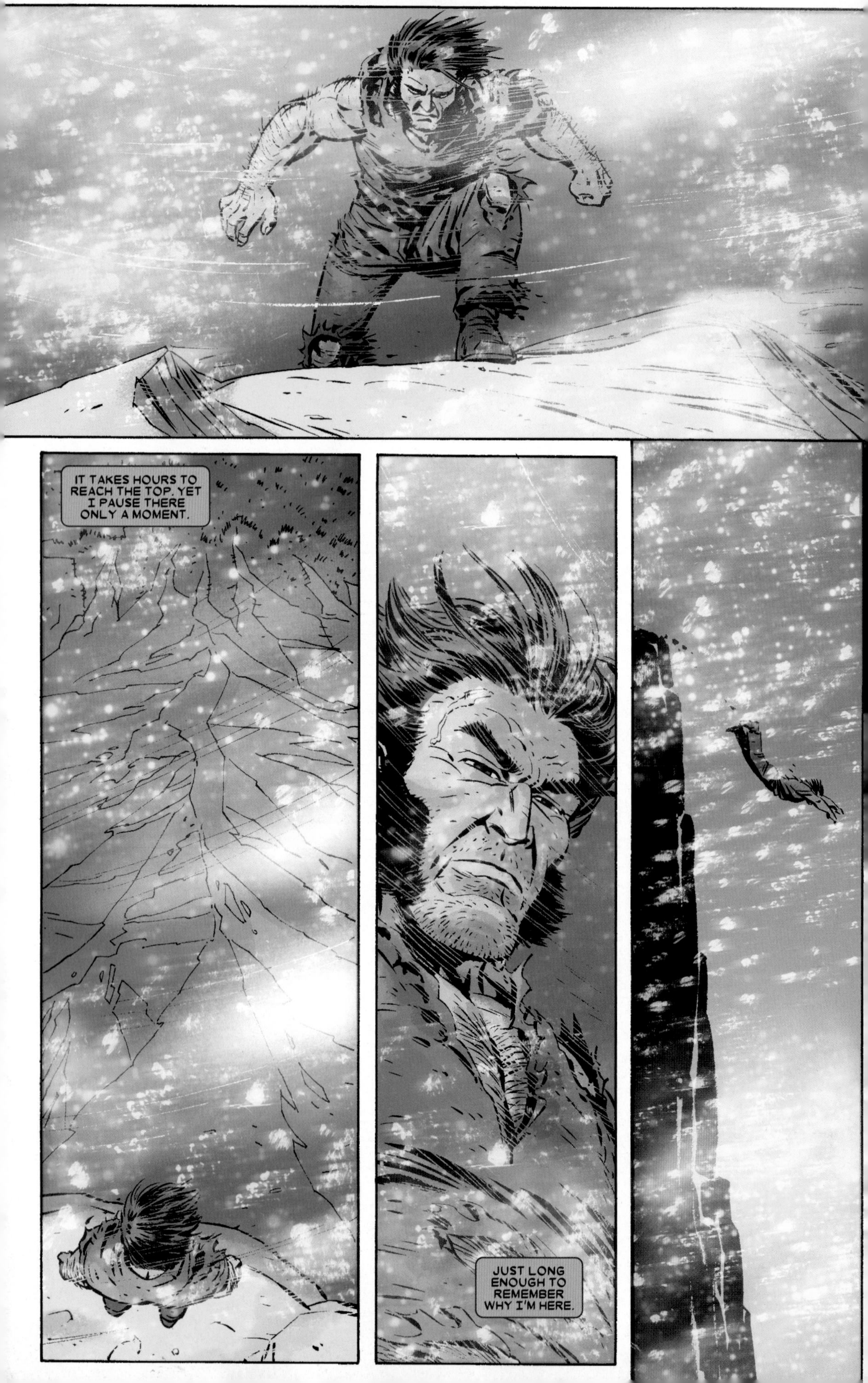
IT TAKES HOURS TO REACH THE TOP. YET I PAUSE THERE ONLY A MOMENT.
JUST LONG ENOUGH TO REMEMBER WHY I'M HERE.

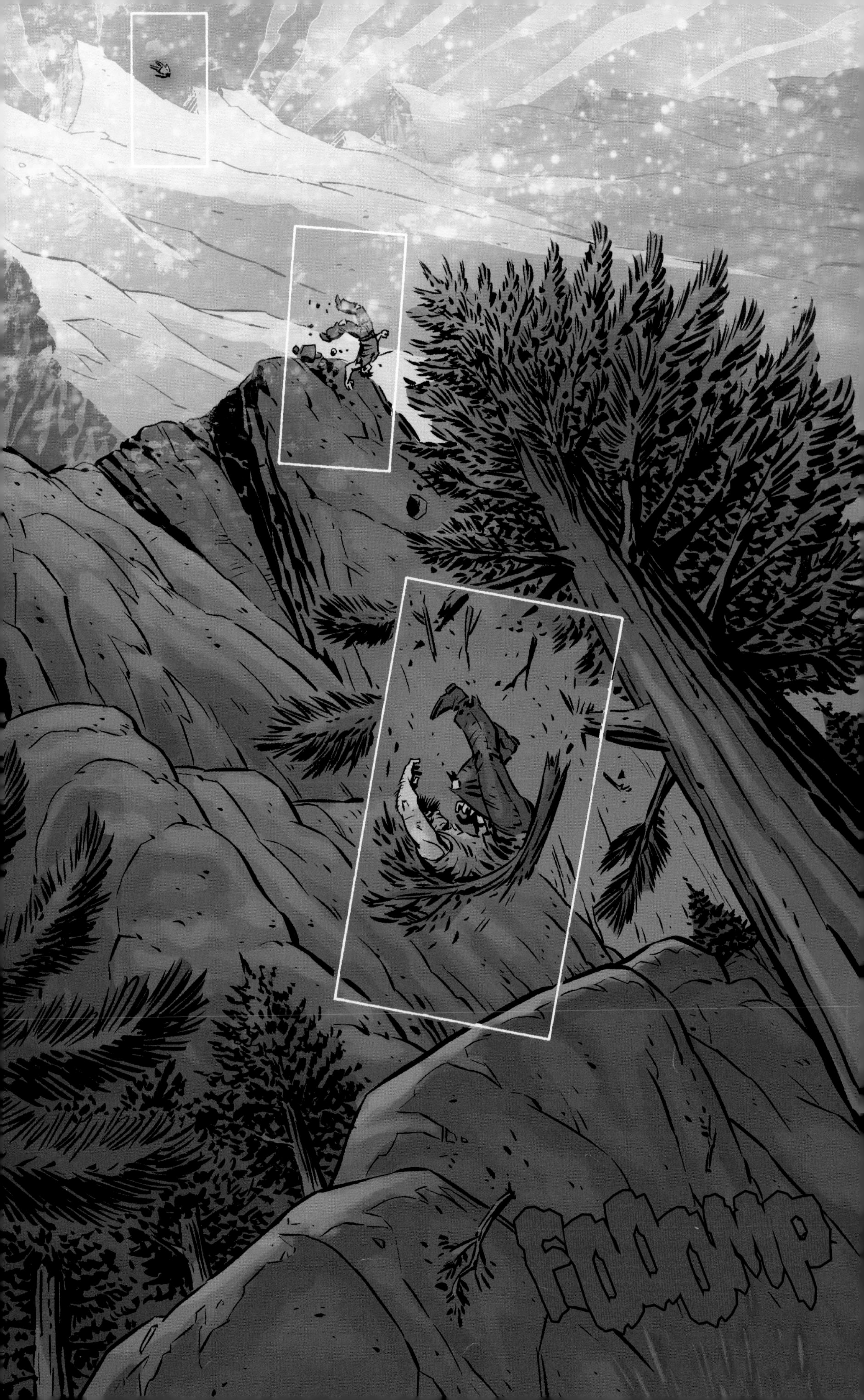
FOOOMP

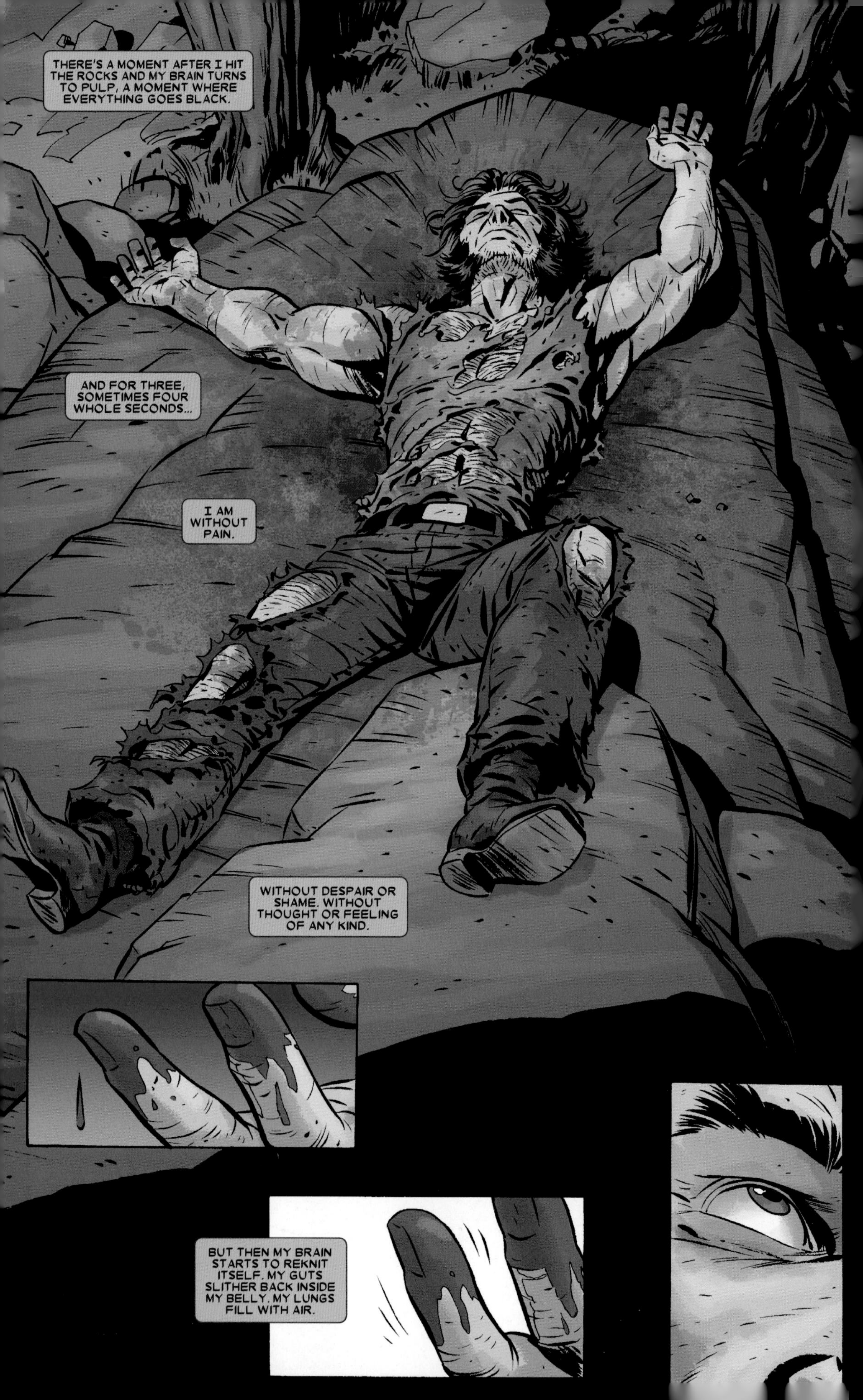

THERE'S A MOMENT AFTER I HIT THE ROCKS AND MY BRAIN TURNS TO PULP, A MOMENT WHERE EVERYTHING GOES BLACK.
AND FOR THREE, SOMETIMES FOUR WHOLE SECONDS...
I AM WITHOUT PAIN.
WITHOUT DESPAIR OR SHAME. WITHOUT THOUGHT OR FEELING OF ANY KIND.
BUT THEN MY BRAIN STARTS TO REKNIT ITSELF. MY GUTS SLITHER BACK INSIDE MY BELLY. MY LUNGS FILL WITH AIR.

AND I
GET UP.

AND CLIMB
AGAIN.

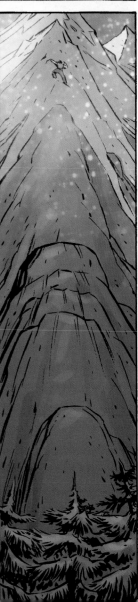

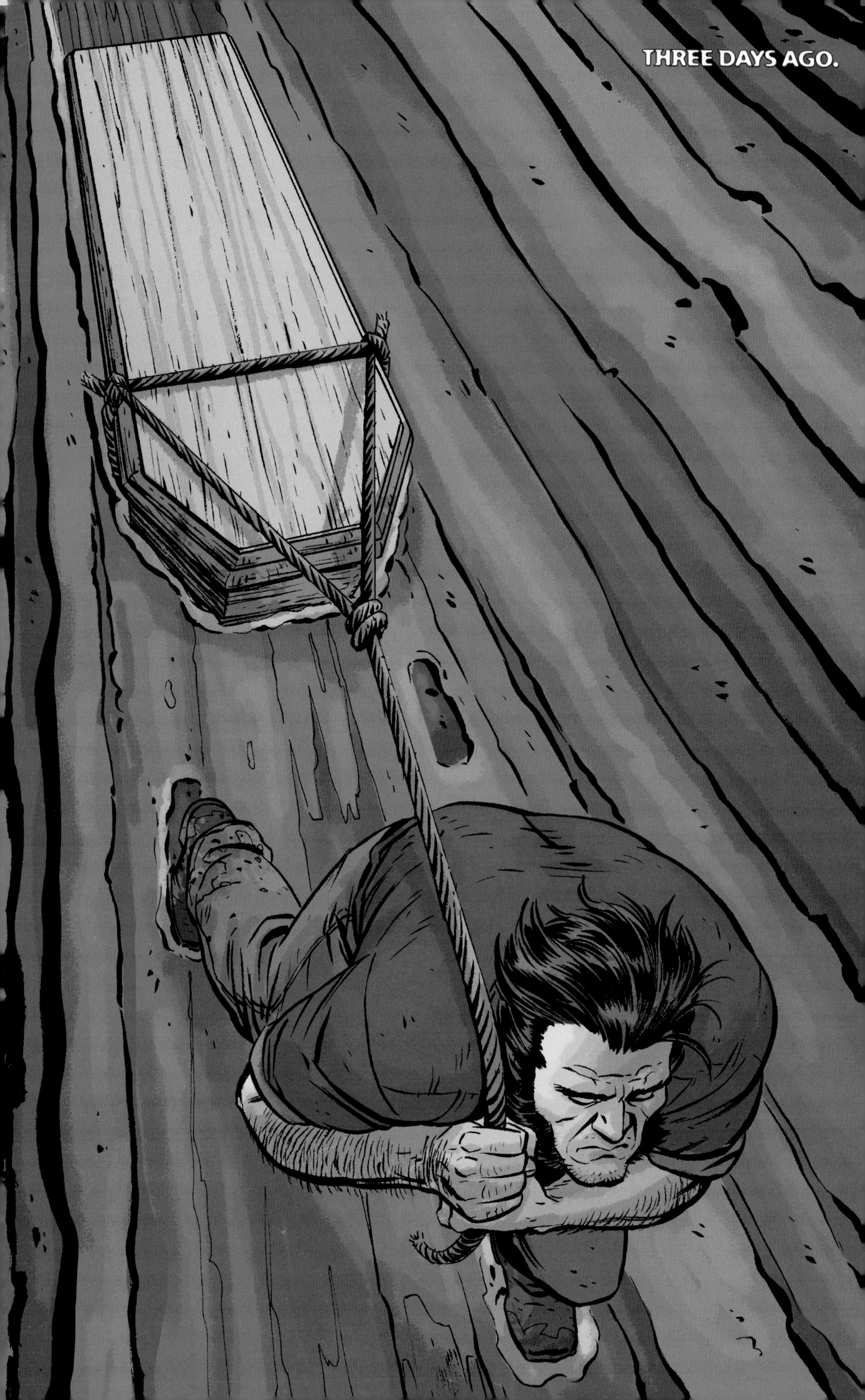
THREE DAYS AGO.

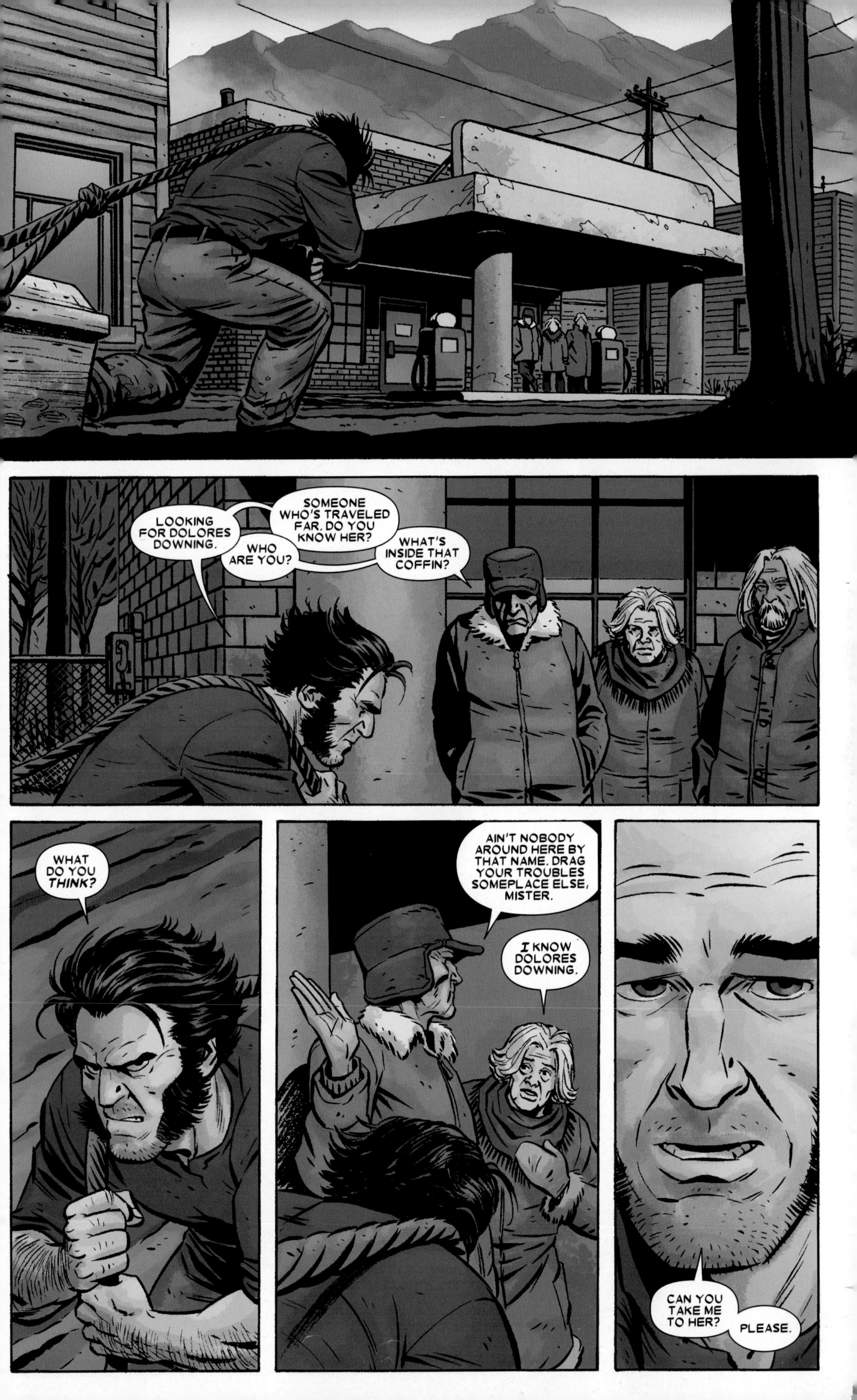
LOOKING FOR DOLORES DOWNING.
WHO ARE YOU?
SOMEONE WHO'S TRAVELED FAR. DO YOU KNOW HER?
WHAT'S INSIDE THAT COFFIN?
WHAT DO YOU *THINK*?
AIN'T NOBODY AROUND HERE BY THAT NAME. DRAG YOUR TROUBLES SOMEPLACE ELSE, MISTER.
*I* KNOW DOLORES DOWNING.
CAN YOU TAKE ME TO HER?
PLEASE.

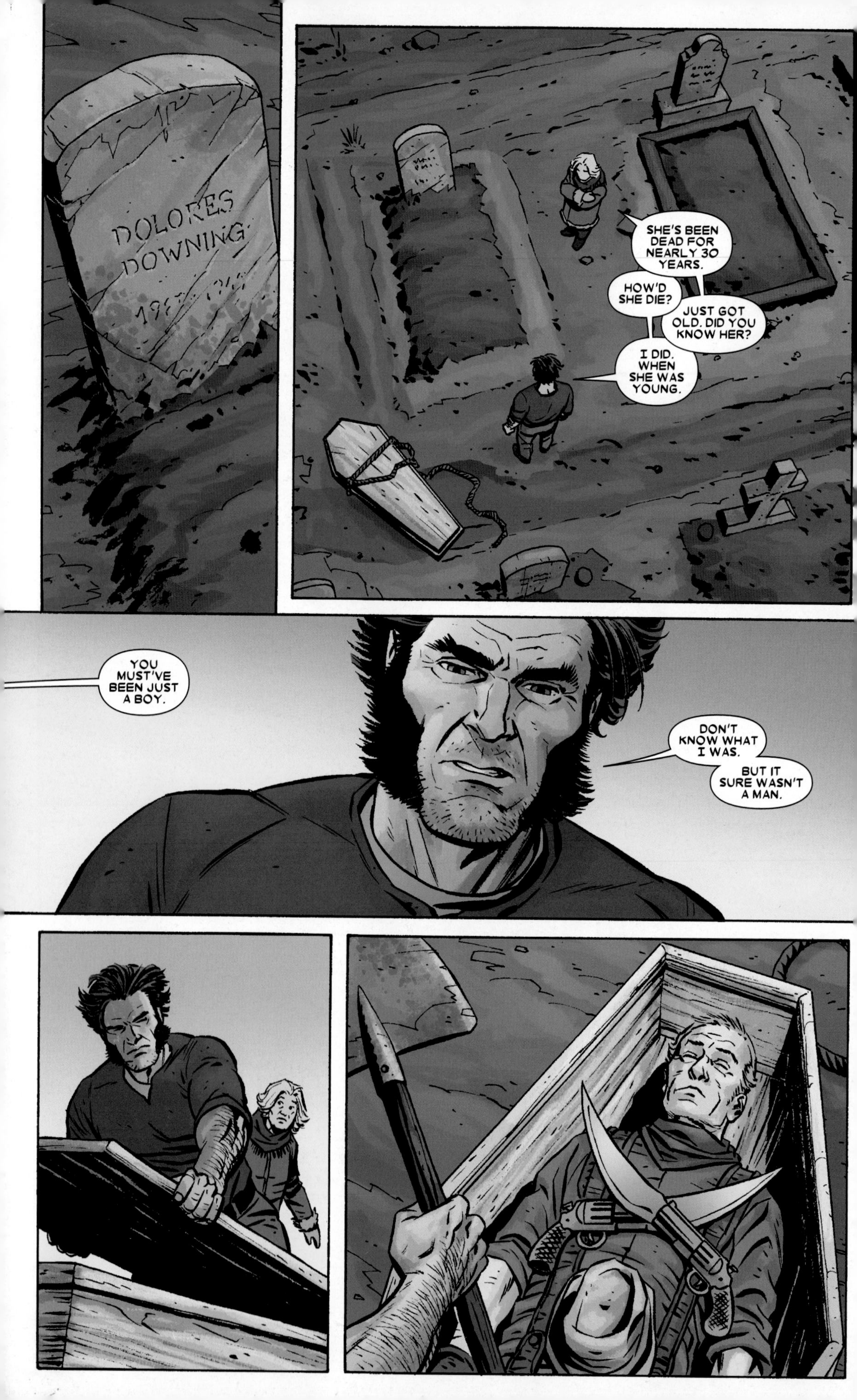
DOLORES DOWNING
SHE'S BEEN DEAD FOR NEARLY 30 YEARS.
HOW'D SHE DIE?
JUST GOT OLD. DID YOU KNOW HER?
I DID. WHEN SHE WAS YOUNG.
YOU MUST'VE BEEN JUST A BOY.
DON'T KNOW WHAT I WAS.
BUT IT SURE WASN'T A MAN.

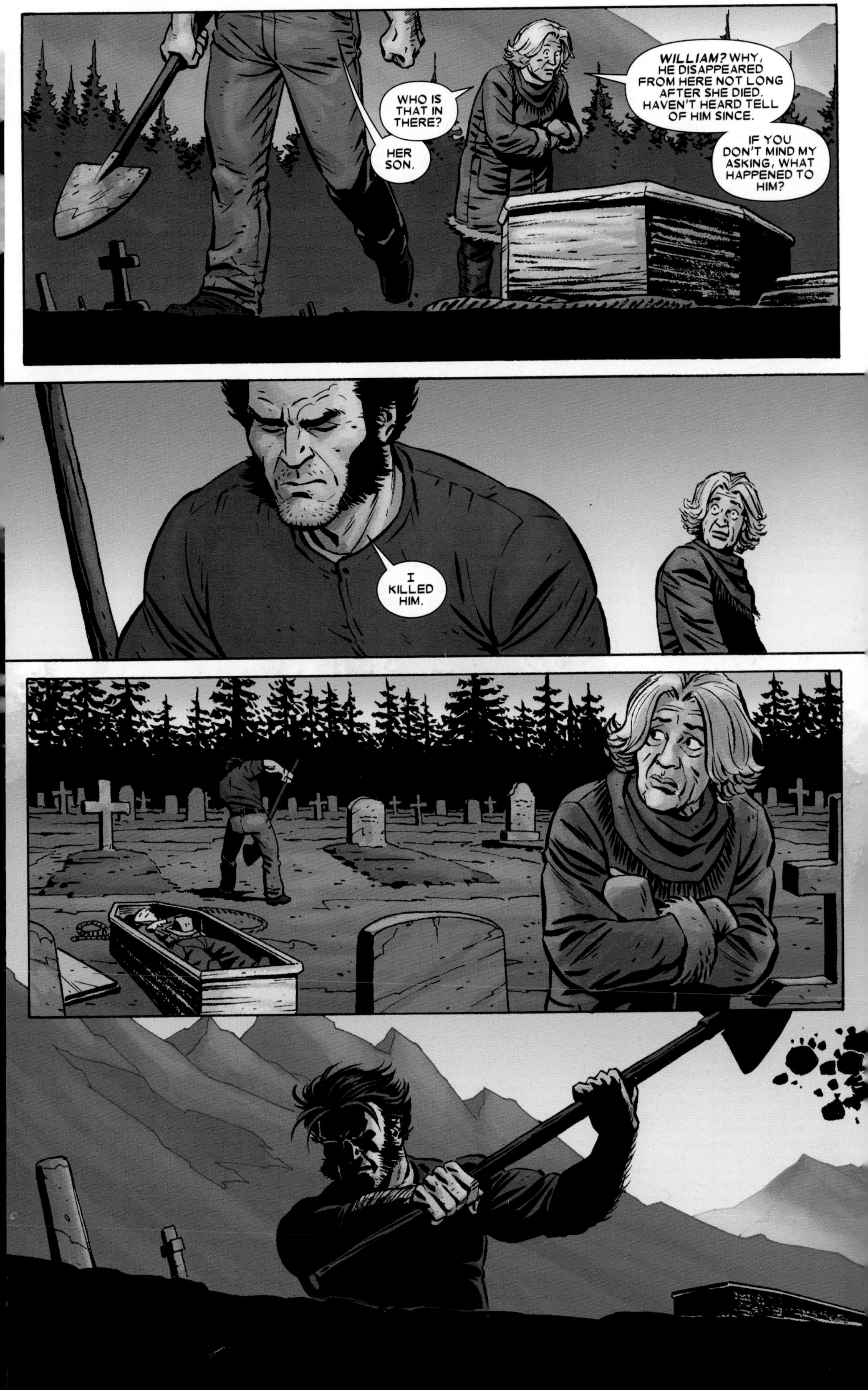
WHO IS THAT IN THERE?
HER SON.
WILLIAM? WHY, HE DISAPPEARED FROM HERE NOT LONG AFTER SHE DIED. HAVEN'T HEARD TELL OF HIM SINCE.
IF YOU DON'T MIND MY ASKING, WHAT HAPPENED TO HIM?
I KILLED HIM.

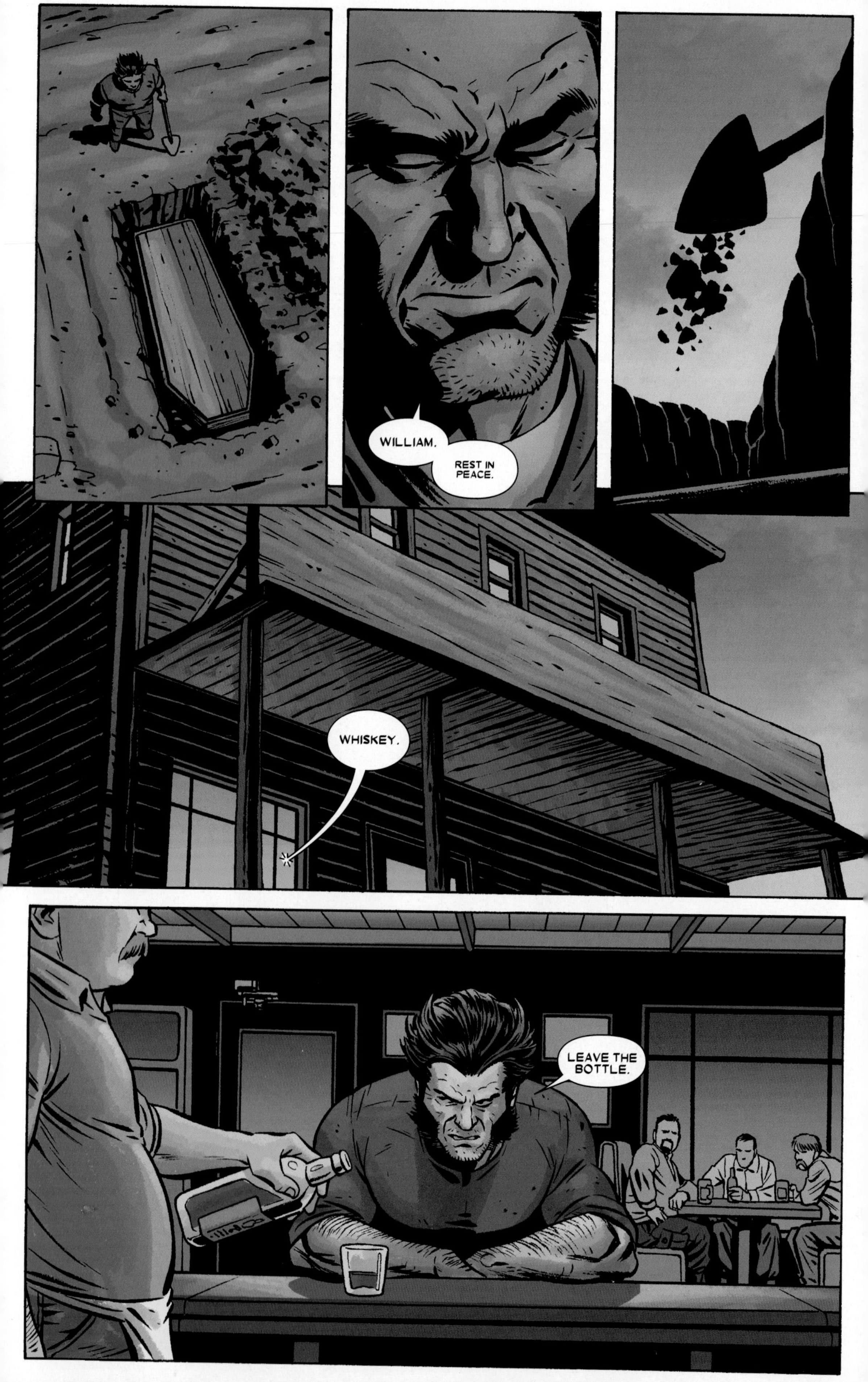
WILLIAM.
REST IN PEACE.
WHISKEY.
LEAVE THE BOTTLE.

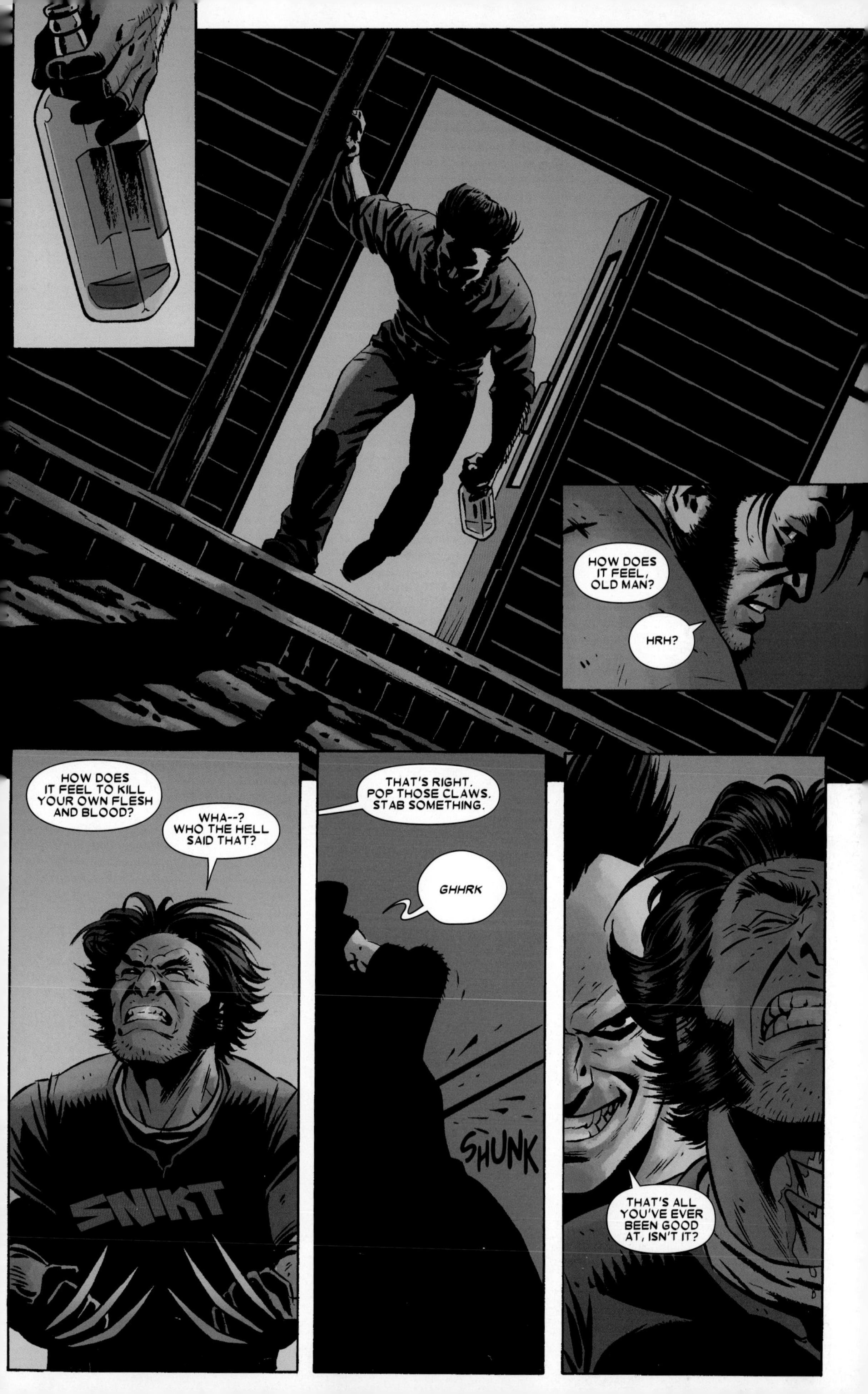
HOW DOES IT FEEL, OLD MAN?
HRH?
HOW DOES IT FEEL TO KILL YOUR OWN FLESH AND BLOOD?
WHA--? WHO THE HELL SAID THAT?
SNIKT
THAT'S RIGHT. POP THOSE CLAWS. STAB SOMETHING.
GHHRK
SHUNK
THAT'S ALL YOU'VE EVER BEEN GOOD AT, ISN'T IT?

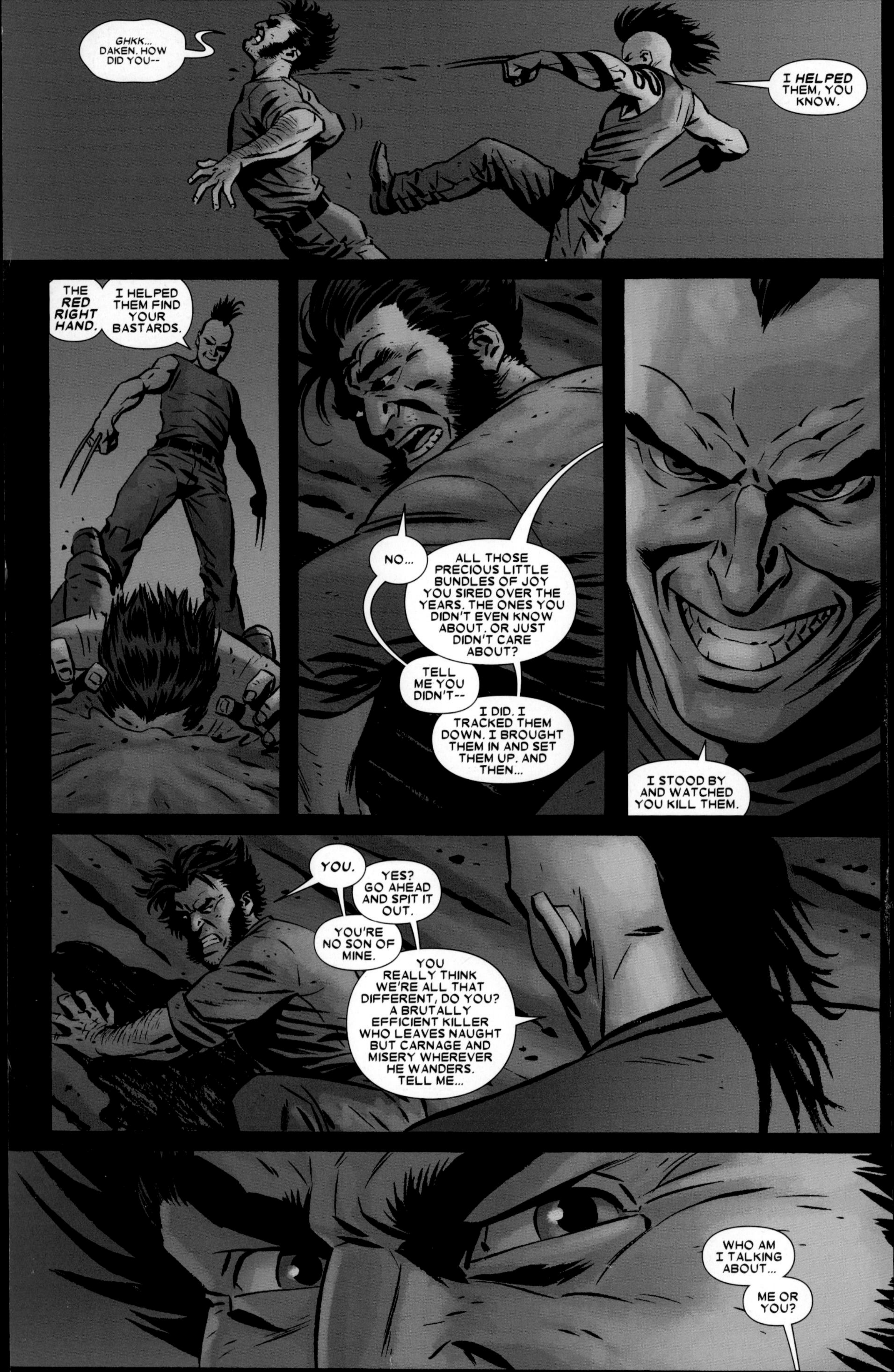
GHKK... DAKEN. HOW DID YOU--
I HELPED THEM, YOU KNOW.
THE RED RIGHT HAND.
I HELPED THEM FIND YOUR BASTARDS.
NO...
ALL THOSE PRECIOUS LITTLE BUNDLES OF JOY YOU SIRED OVER THE YEARS. THE ONES YOU DIDN'T EVEN KNOW ABOUT, OR JUST DIDN'T CARE ABOUT?
TELL ME YOU DIDN'T--
I DID. I TRACKED THEM DOWN. I BROUGHT THEM IN AND SET THEM UP. AND THEN...
I STOOD BY AND WATCHED YOU KILL THEM.
YOU.
YES? GO AHEAD AND SPIT IT OUT.
YOU'RE NO SON OF MINE.
YOU REALLY THINK WE'RE ALL THAT DIFFERENT, DO YOU? A BRUTALLY EFFICIENT KILLER WHO LEAVES NAUGHT BUT CARNAGE AND MISERY WHEREVER HE WANDERS. TELL ME...
WHO AM I TALKING ABOUT...
ME OR YOU?

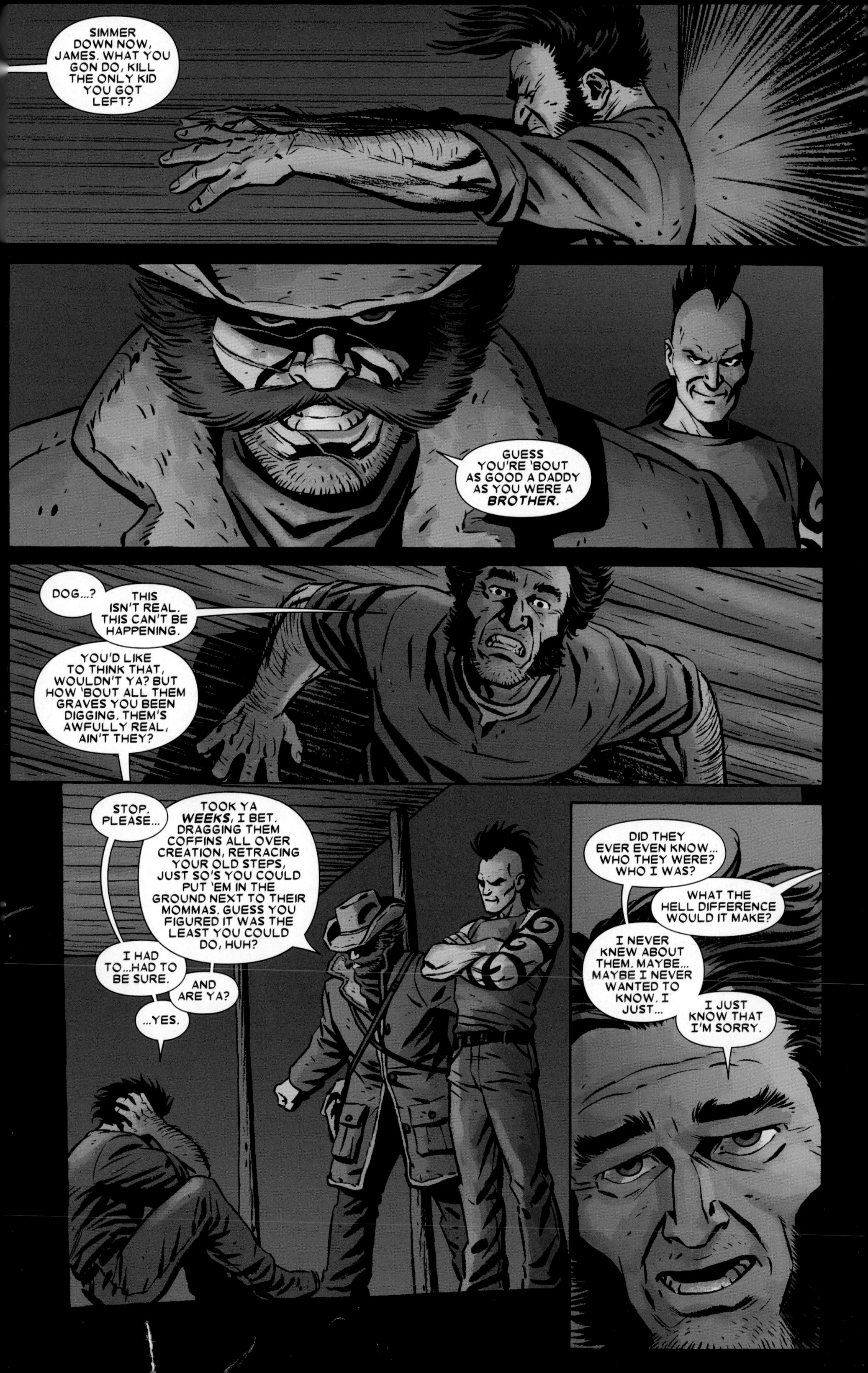
SIMMER DOWN NOW, JAMES. WHAT YOU GON DO, KILL THE ONLY KID YOU GOT LEFT?
GUESS YOU'RE 'BOUT AS GOOD A DADDY AS YOU WERE A BROTHER.
DOG...?
THIS ISN'T REAL. THIS CAN'T BE HAPPENING.
YOU'D LIKE TO THINK THAT, WOULDN'T YA? BUT HOW 'BOUT ALL THEM GRAVES YOU BEEN DIGGING. THEM'S AWFULLY REAL, AIN'T THEY?
STOP. PLEASE...
TOOK YA WEEKS, I BET. DRAGGING THEM COFFINS ALL OVER CREATION, RETRACING YOUR OLD STEPS, JUST SO'S YOU COULD PUT 'EM IN THE GROUND NEXT TO THEIR MOMMAS. GUESS YOU FIGURED IT WAS THE LEAST YOU COULD DO, HUH?
I HAD TO...HAD TO BE SURE.
AND ARE YA?
...YES.
DID THEY EVER EVEN KNOW... WHO THEY WERE? WHO I WAS?
WHAT THE HELL DIFFERENCE WOULD IT MAKE?
I NEVER KNEW ABOUT THEM. MAYBE... MAYBE I NEVER WANTED TO KNOW. I JUST...
I JUST KNOW THAT I'M SORRY.

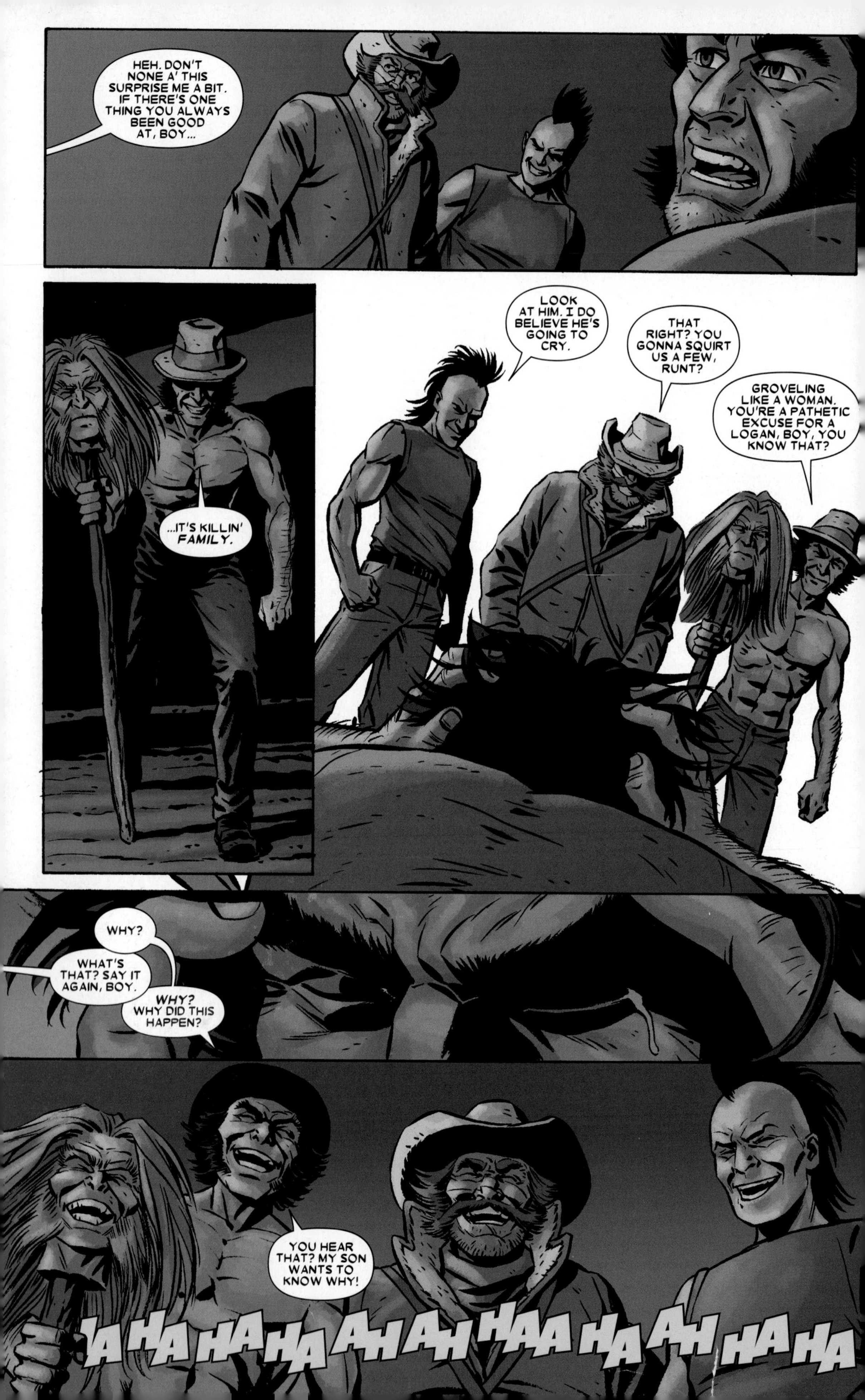
HEH. DON'T NONE A' THIS SURPRISE ME A BIT. IF THERE'S ONE THING YOU ALWAYS BEEN GOOD AT, BOY...
...IT'S KILLIN' *FAMILY.*
LOOK AT HIM. I DO BELIEVE HE'S GOING TO CRY.
THAT RIGHT? YOU GONNA SQUIRT US A FEW, RUNT?
GROVELING LIKE A WOMAN. YOU'RE A PATHETIC EXCUSE FOR A LOGAN, BOY, YOU KNOW THAT?
WHY?
WHAT'S THAT? SAY IT AGAIN, BOY.
*WHY?* WHY DID THIS HAPPEN?
YOU HEAR THAT? MY SON WANTS TO KNOW WHY!
HA HA HA HA HA AH AH HAA HA HA AH HA HA

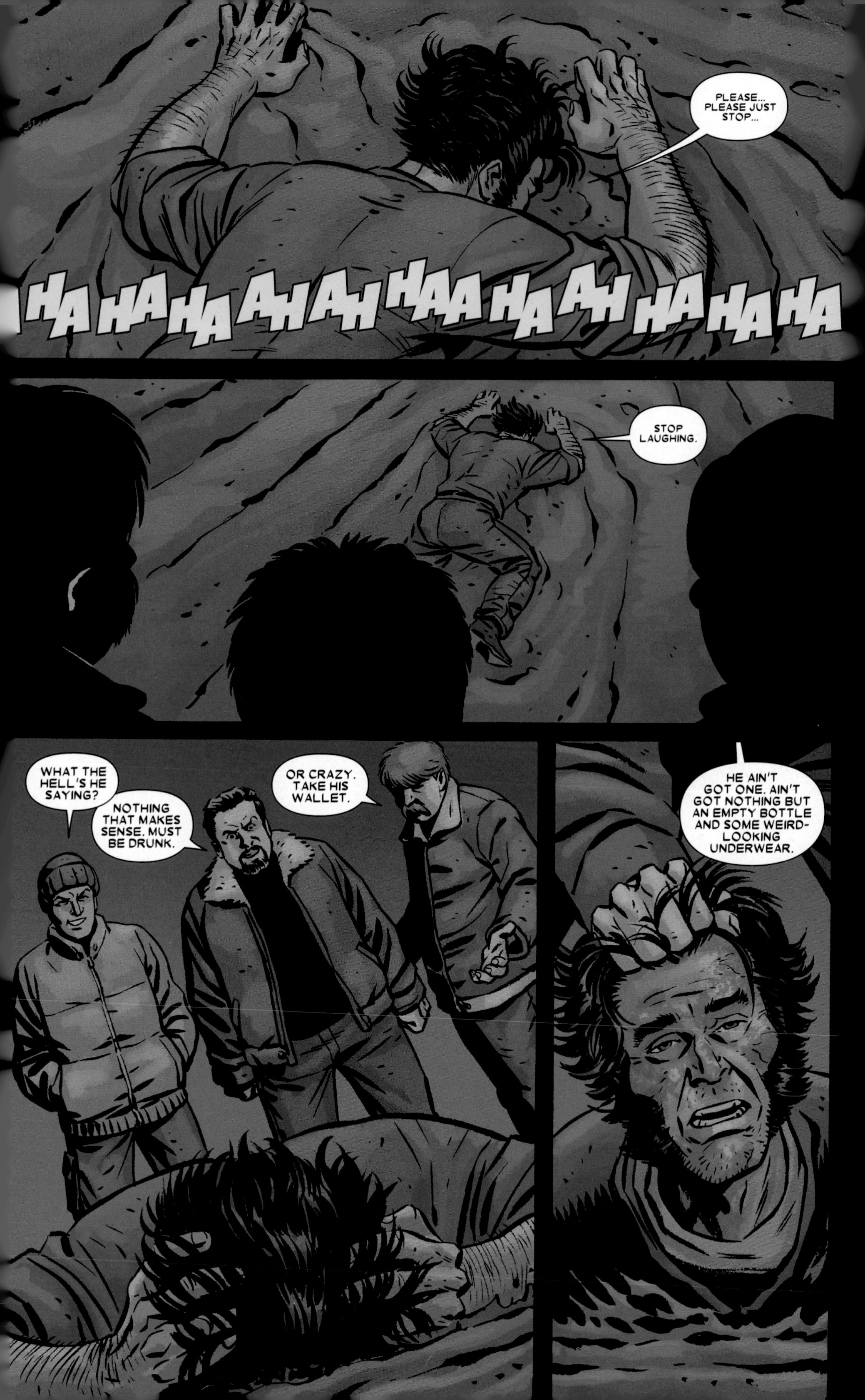
PLEASE... PLEASE JUST STOP...
HA HA HA AH AH HAA HA AH HA HA HA
STOP LAUGHING.
WHAT THE HELL'S HE SAYING?
NOTHING THAT MAKES SENSE. MUST BE DRUNK.
OR CRAZY. TAKE HIS WALLET.
HE AIN'T GOT ONE. AIN'T GOT NOTHING BUT AN EMPTY BOTTLE AND SOME WEIRD-LOOKING UNDERWEAR.

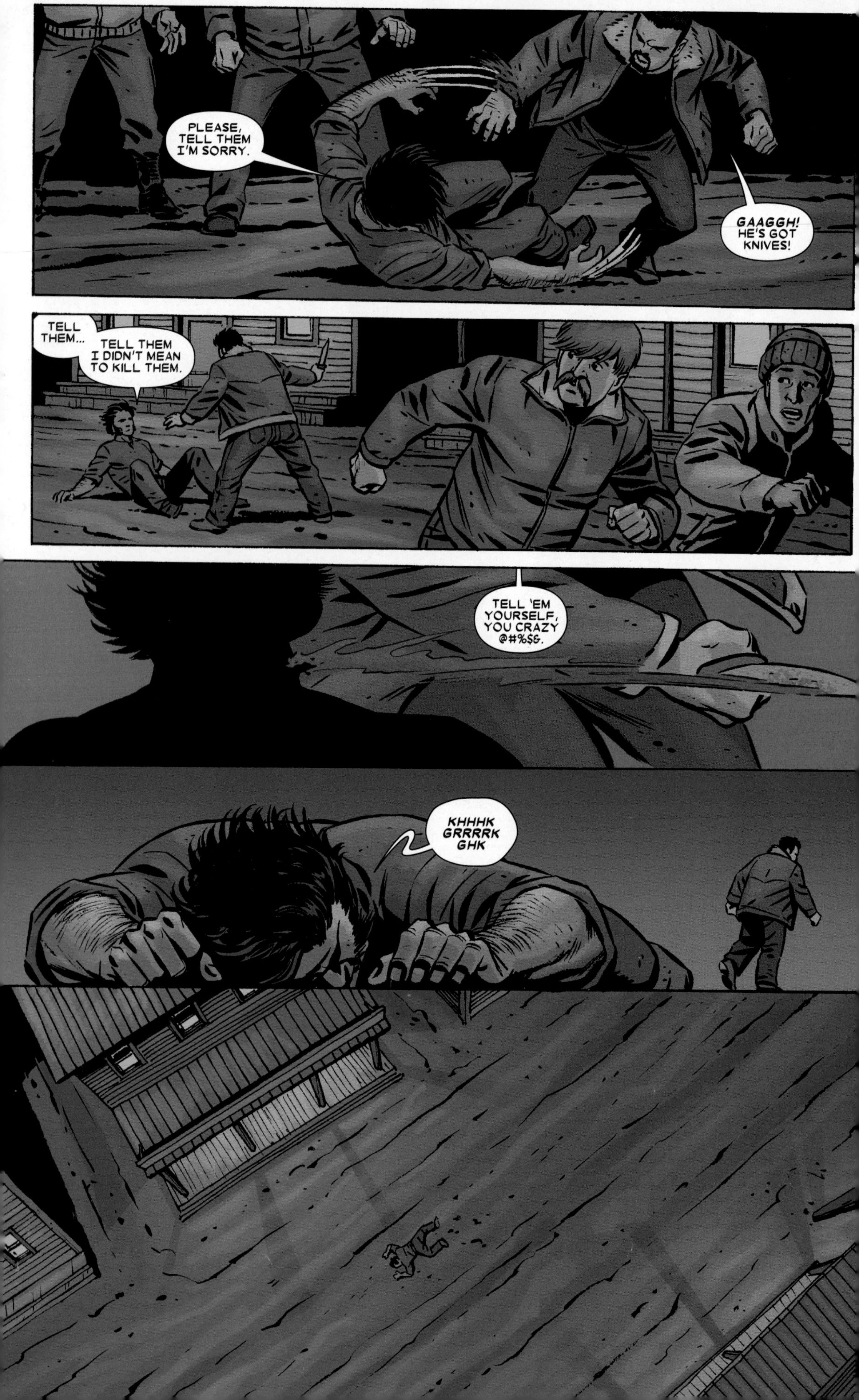
PLEASE, TELL THEM I'M SORRY.
GAAGGH! HE'S GOT KNIVES!
TELL THEM...
TELL THEM I DIDN'T MEAN TO KILL THEM.
TELL 'EM YOURSELF, YOU CRAZY @#%$&.
KHHHK GRRRRK GHK

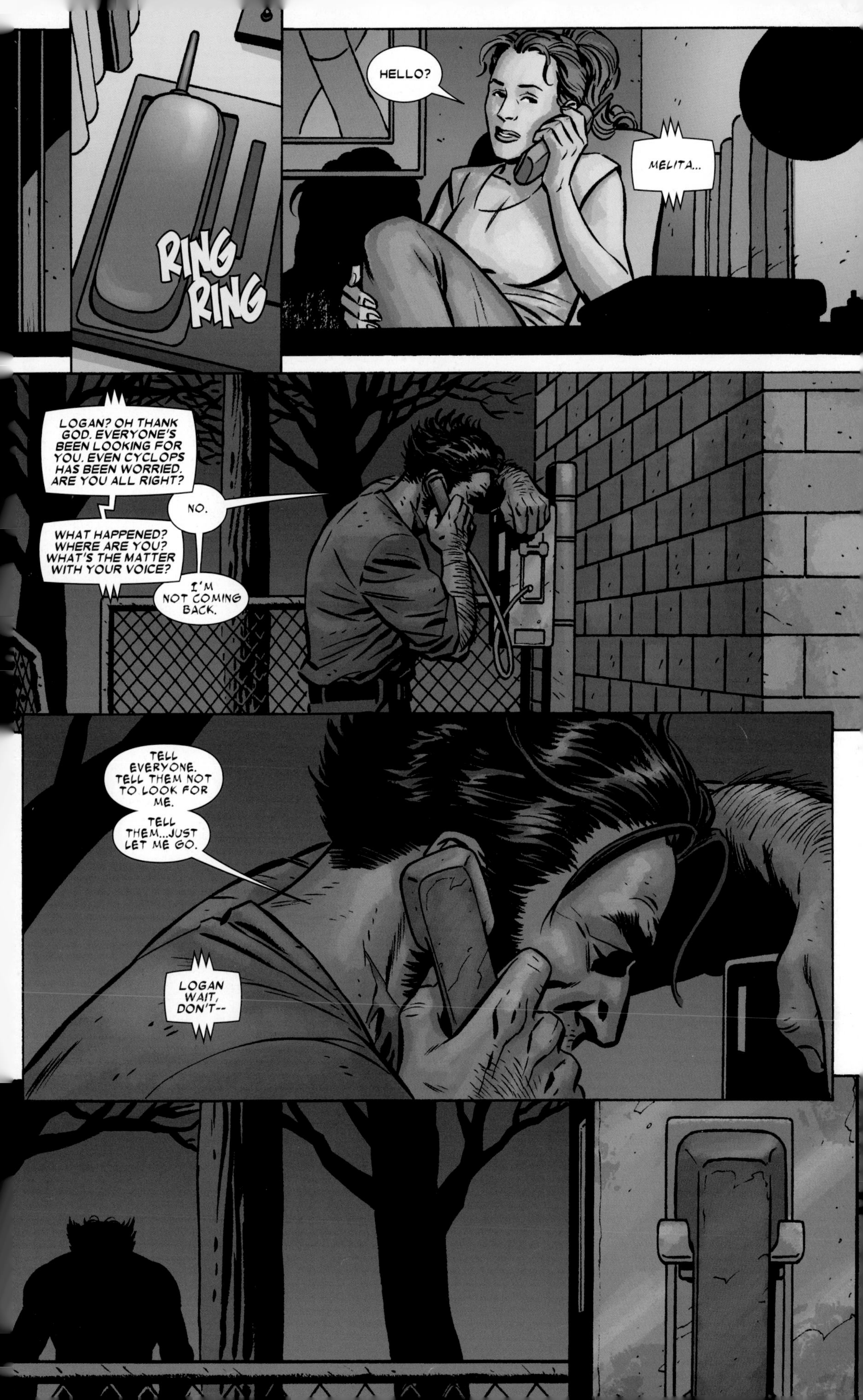
RING
RING
HELLO?
MELITA...
LOGAN? OH THANK GOD. EVERYONE'S BEEN LOOKING FOR YOU. EVEN CYCLOPS HAS BEEN WORRIED. ARE YOU ALL RIGHT?
NO.
WHAT HAPPENED? WHERE ARE YOU? WHAT'S THE MATTER WITH YOUR VOICE?
I'M NOT COMING BACK.
TELL EVERYONE. TELL THEM NOT TO LOOK FOR ME.
TELL THEM...JUST LET ME GO.
LOGAN WAIT, DON'T--

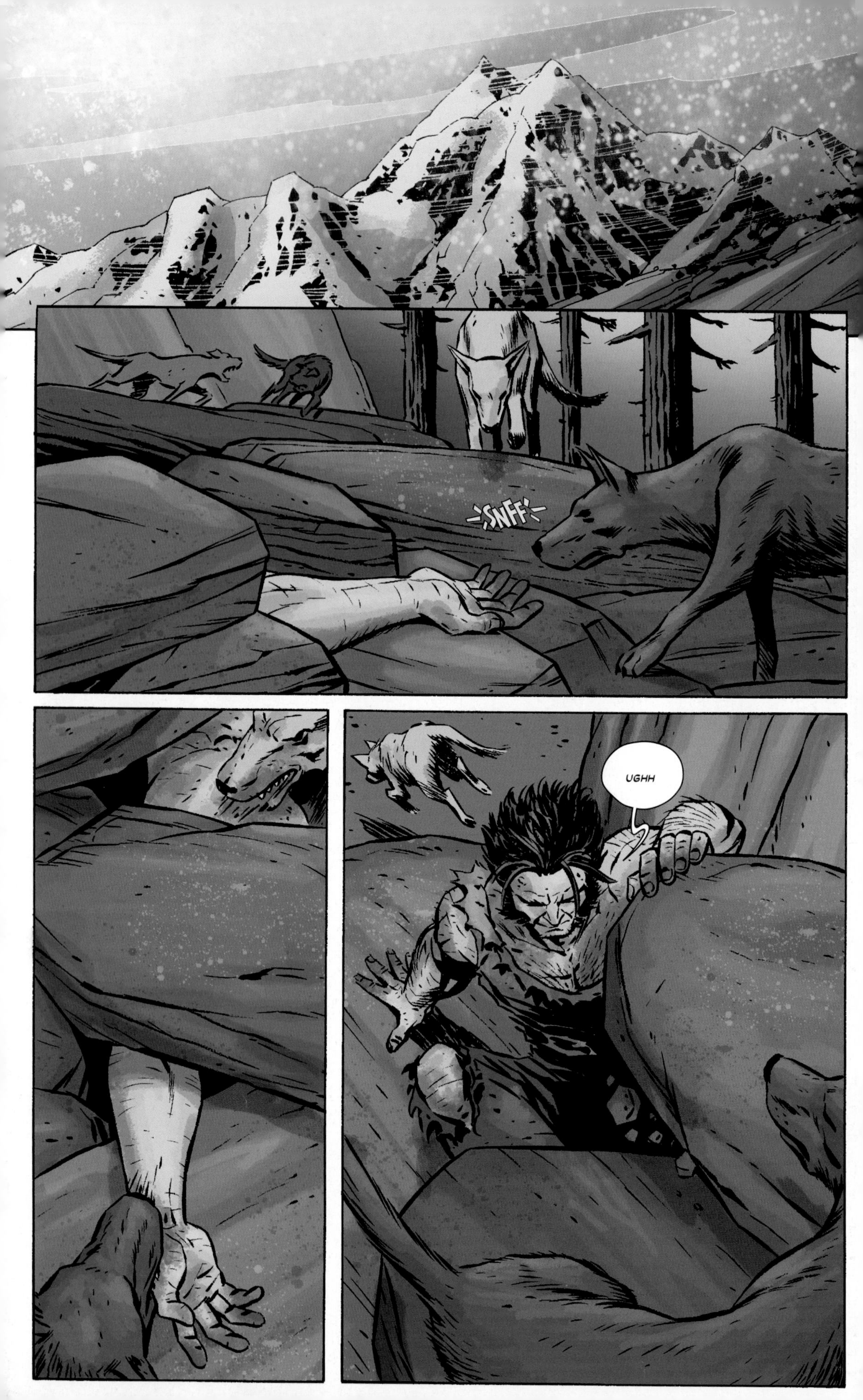
SNFF
UGHH

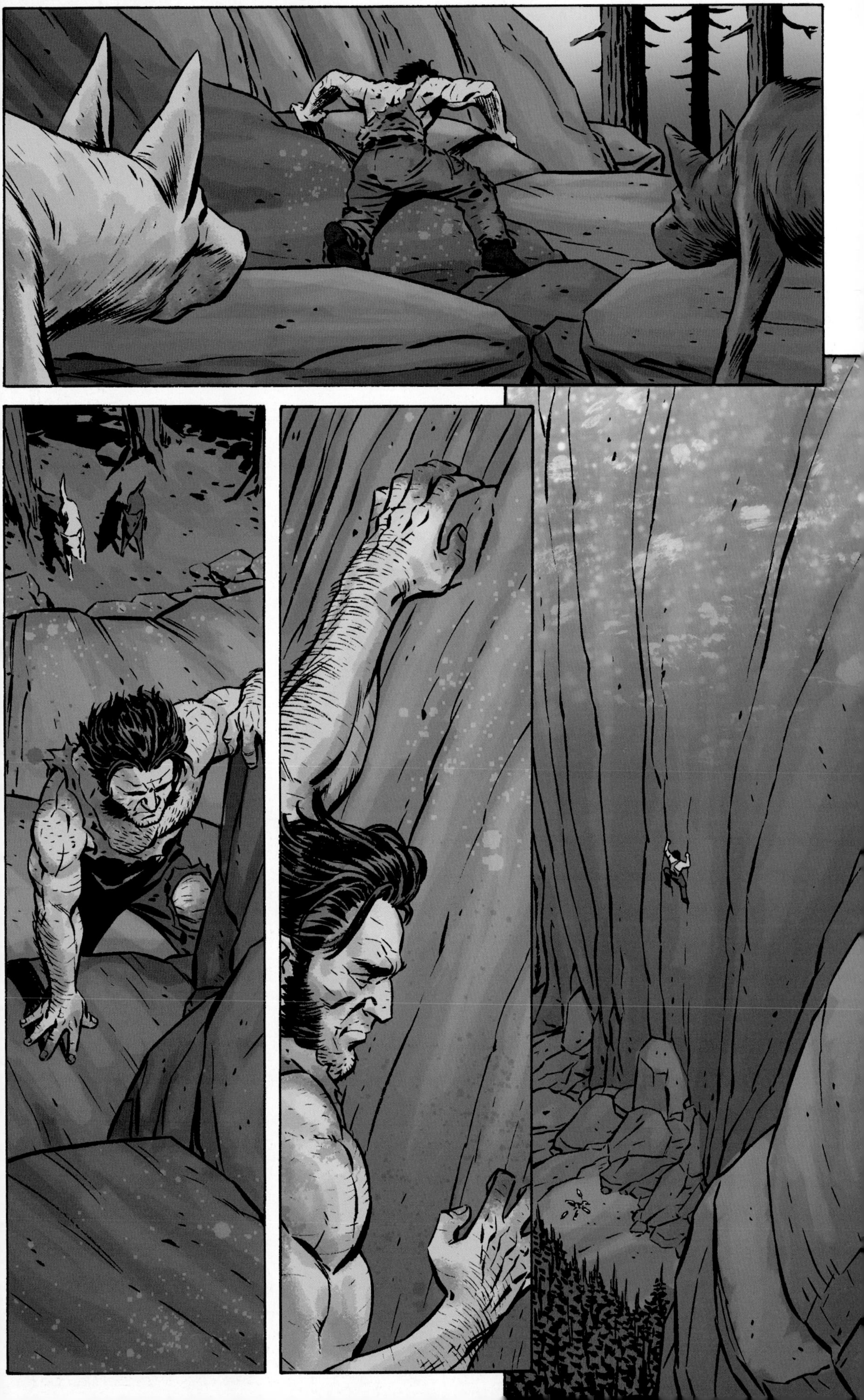

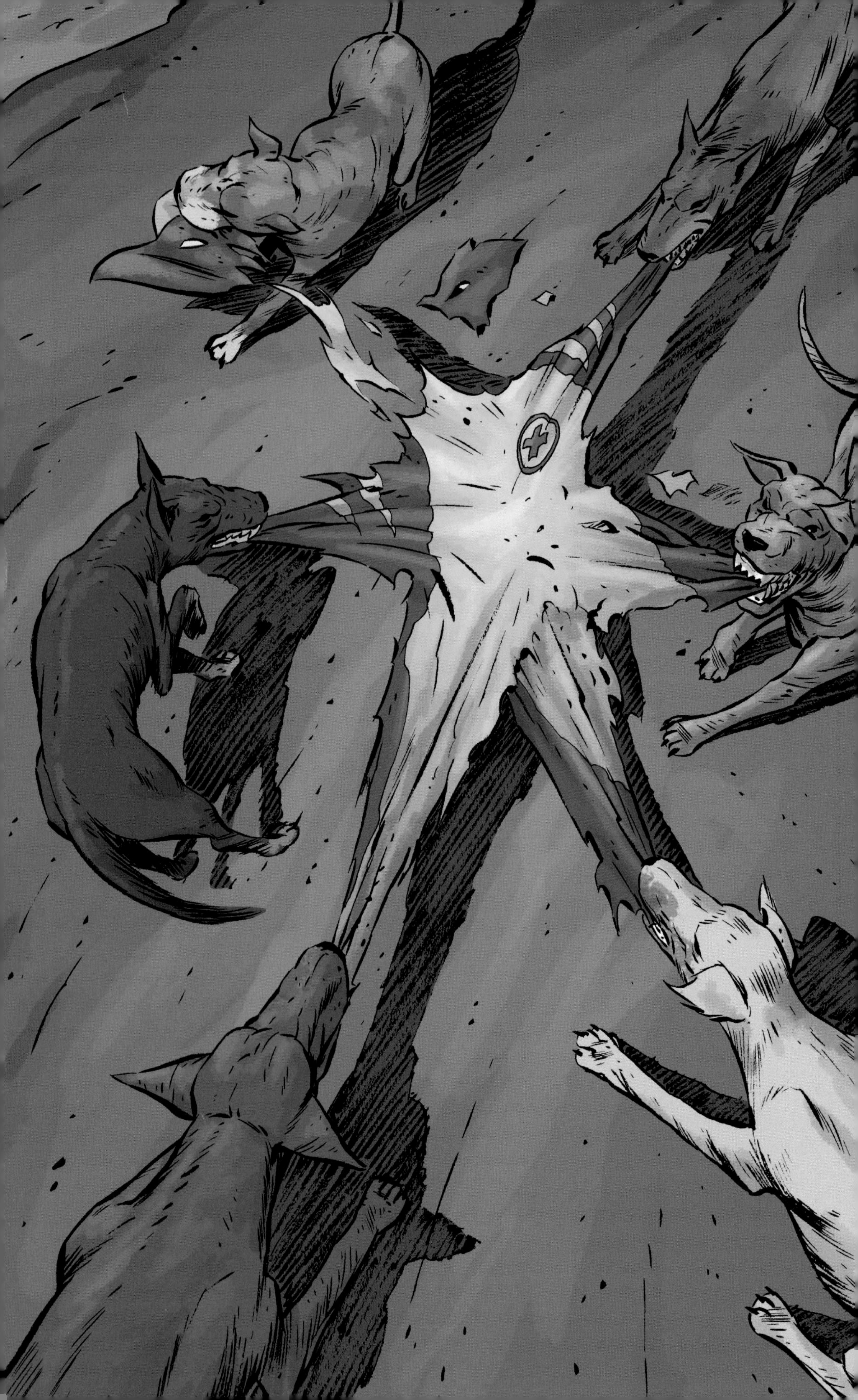

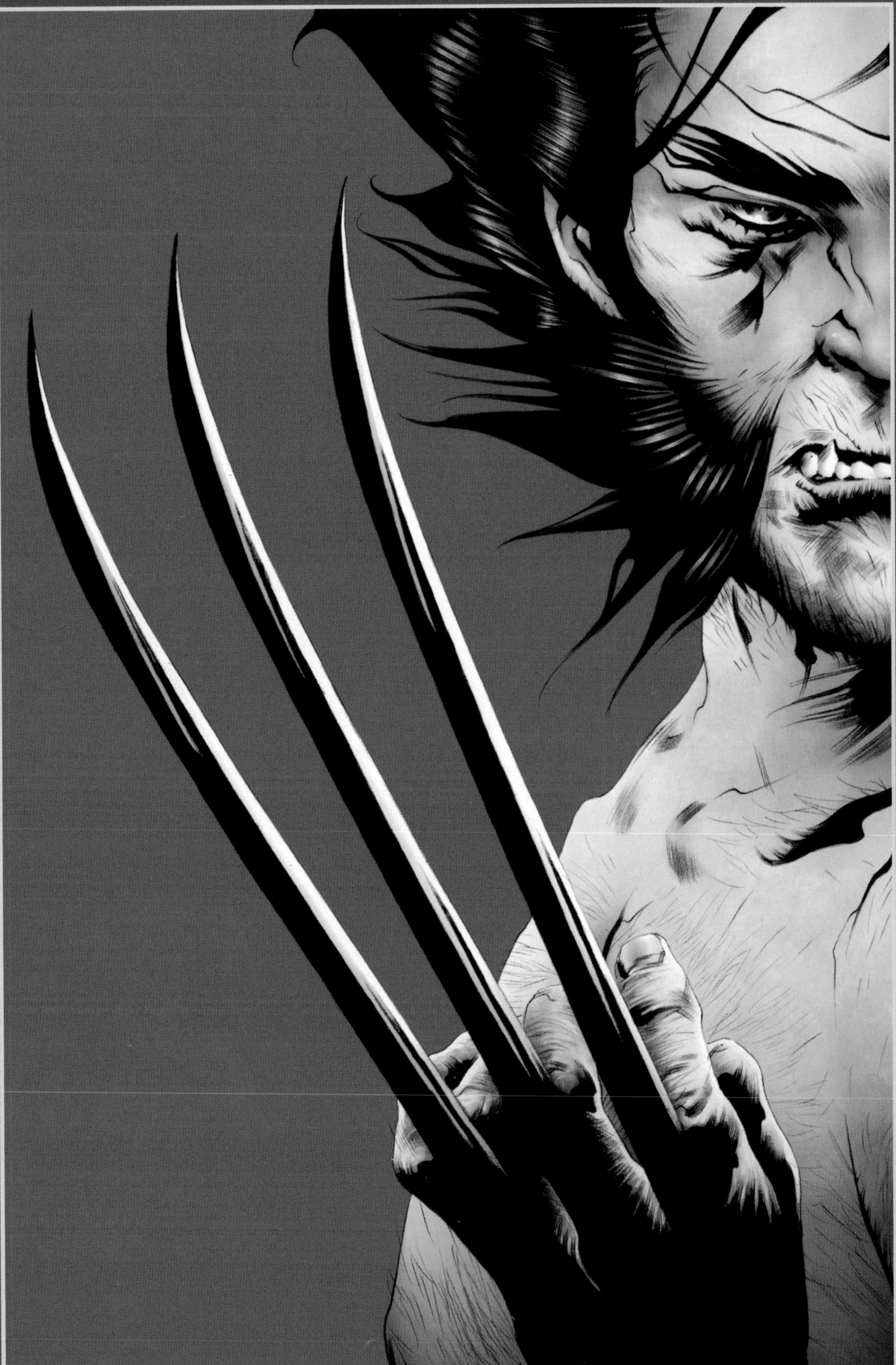

# 16

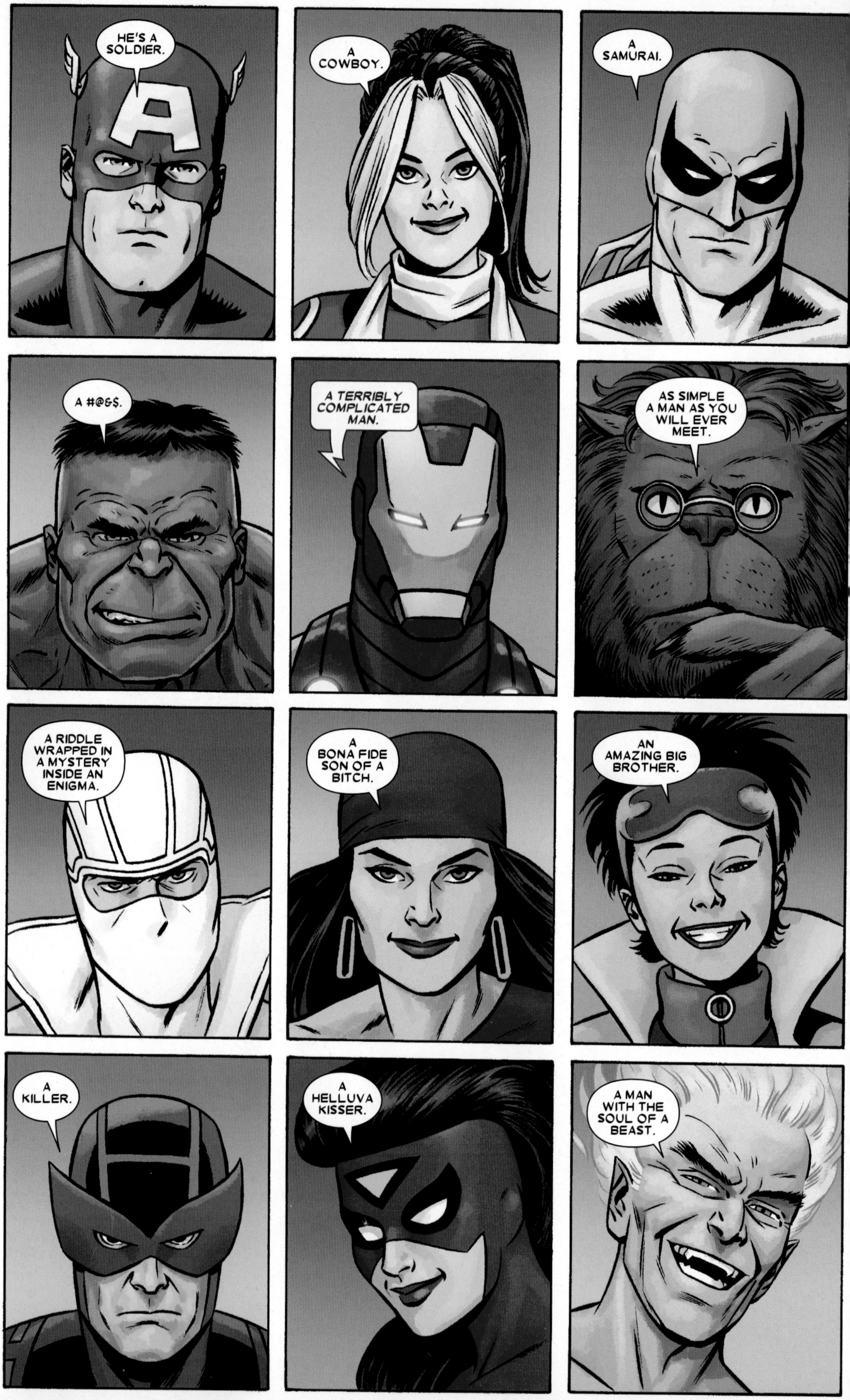
HE'S A SOLDIER.
A COWBOY.
A SAMURAI.
A #@&$.
A TERRIBLY COMPLICATED MAN.
AS SIMPLE A MAN AS YOU WILL EVER MEET.
A RIDDLE WRAPPED IN A MYSTERY INSIDE AN ENIGMA.
A BONA FIDE SON OF A BITCH.
AN AMAZING BIG BROTHER.
A KILLER.
A HELLUVA KISSER.
A MAN WITH THE SOUL OF A BEAST.

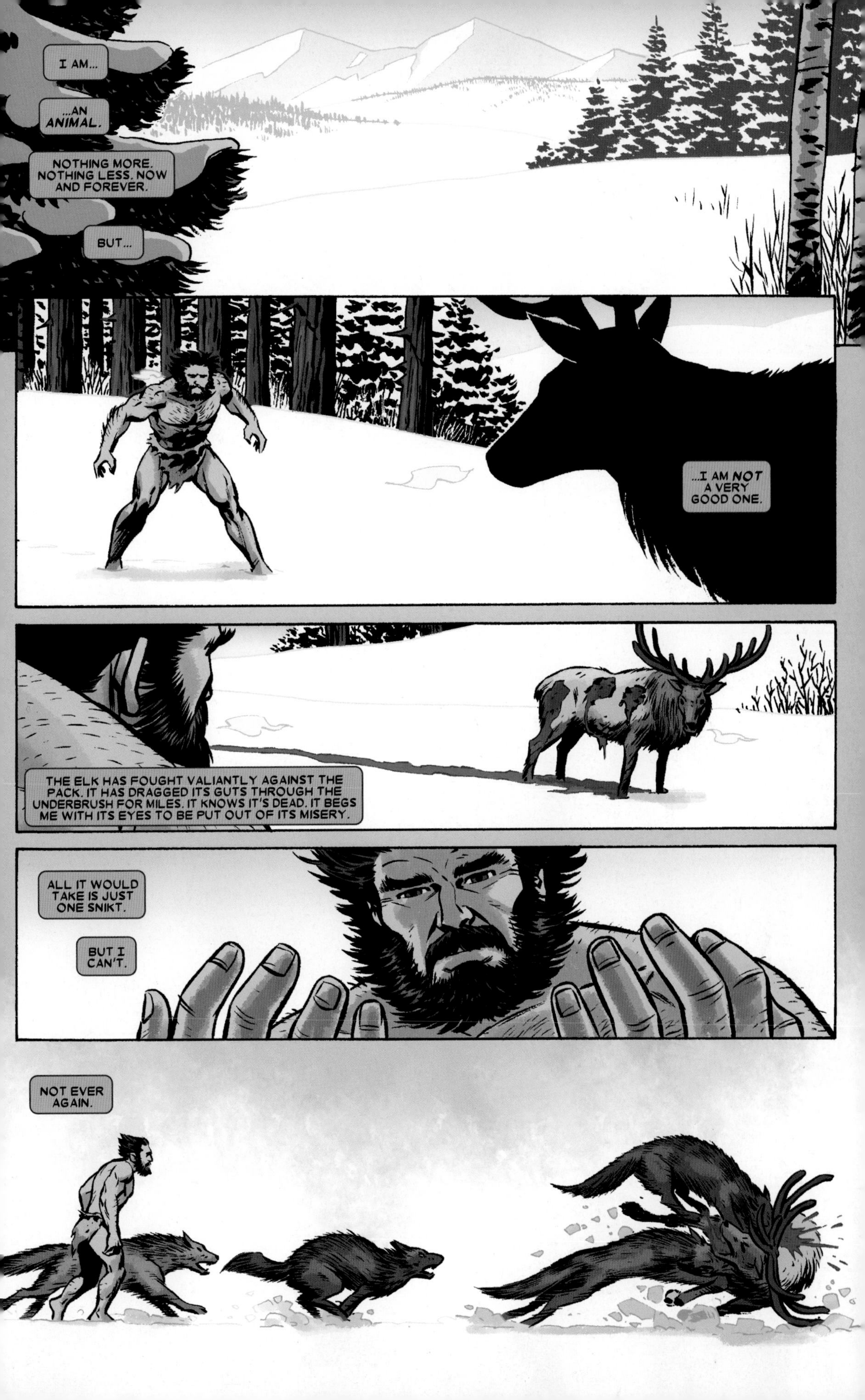
I AM...
...AN *ANIMAL.*
NOTHING MORE. NOTHING LESS. NOW AND FOREVER.
BUT...
...I AM *NOT* A VERY GOOD ONE.
THE ELK HAS FOUGHT VALIANTLY AGAINST THE PACK. IT HAS DRAGGED ITS GUTS THROUGH THE UNDERBRUSH FOR MILES. IT KNOWS IT'S DEAD. IT BEGS ME WITH ITS EYES TO BE PUT OUT OF ITS MISERY.
ALL IT WOULD TAKE IS JUST ONE SNIKT.
BUT I CAN'T.
NOT EVER AGAIN.

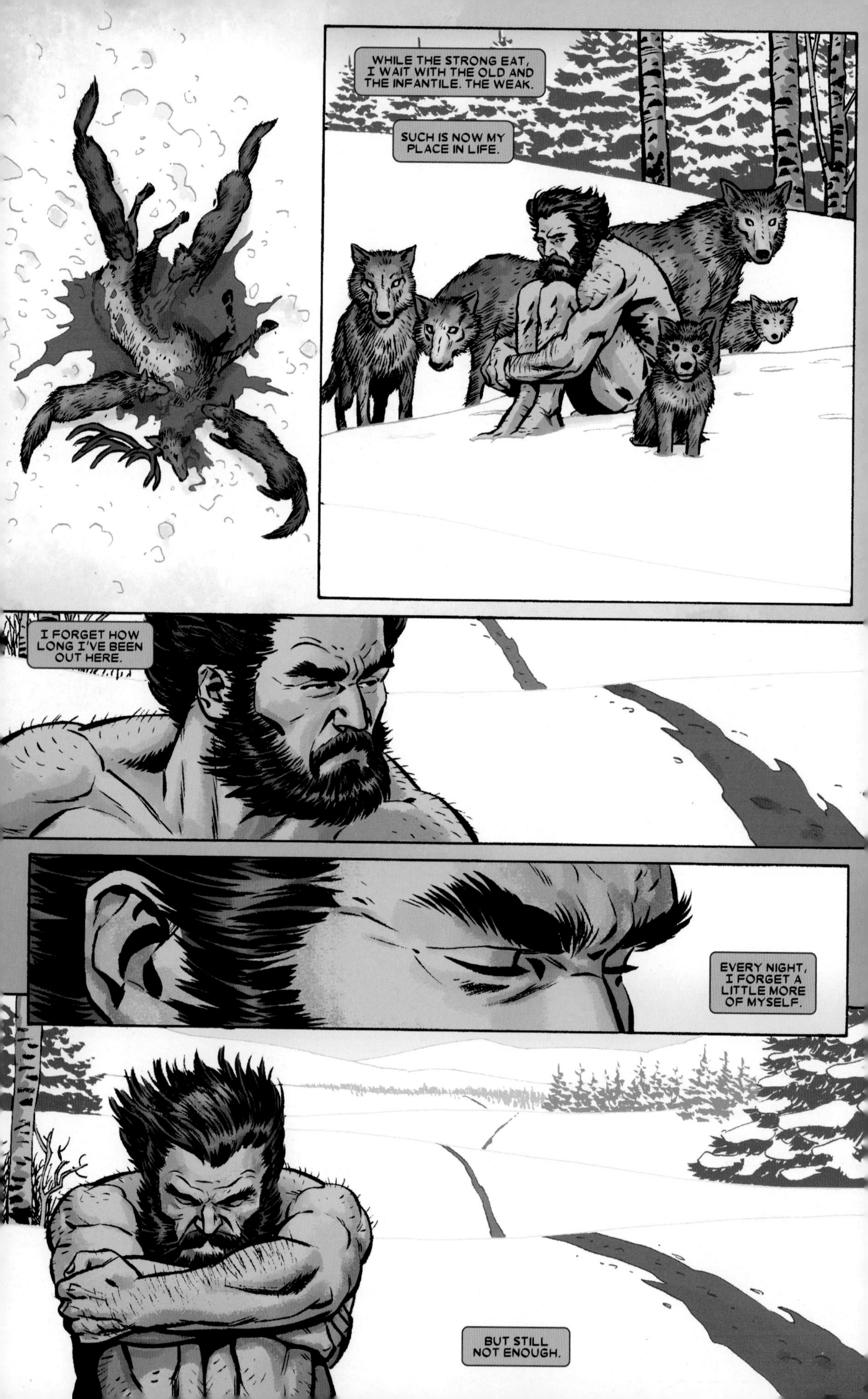
WHILE THE STRONG EAT, I WAIT WITH THE OLD AND THE INFANTILE. THE WEAK.
SUCH IS NOW MY PLACE IN LIFE.
I FORGET HOW LONG I'VE BEEN OUT HERE.
EVERY NIGHT, I FORGET A LITTLE MORE OF MYSELF.
BUT STILL NOT ENOUGH.

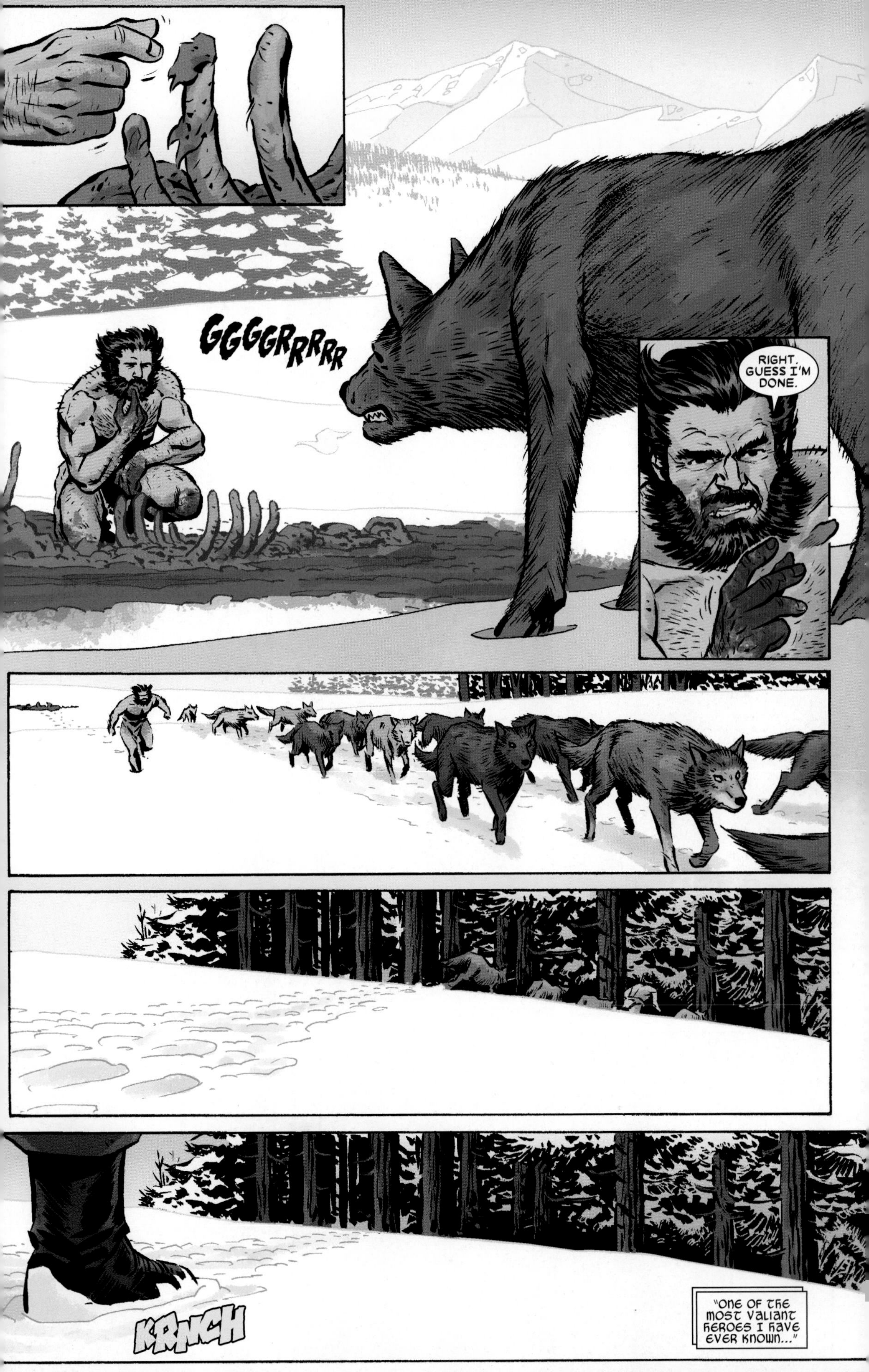
GGGGRRRRR
RIGHT. GUESS I'M DONE.
KRNCH
"ONE OF THE MOST VALIANT HEROES I HAVE EVER KNOWN..."

...EVEN IF HE HIMSELF WOULD NEVER ADMIT IT.

THE FIERCEST OF ENEMIES.

A LEADER. AND A DAMN GOOD ONE. EVEN IF HE DOESN'T REALIZE IT.

THE SCARIEST MAN I HAVE EVER MET.

AND I HAVE *LITERALLY* SHAKEN HANDS WITH THE DEVIL.

THE *SECOND* TOUGHEST CANADIAN I KNOW.

A THOROUGHLY UNTRUSTWORTHY FELLA WHO I'D TRUST MY LIFE TO ANY DAY OF THE WEEK.

A WORSE SWIMMER YOU WOULD NOT WANT TO MEET.

A BIT OF A JERK.

A DAMN *CARD CHEAT*, I DON'T CARE WHAT HE SAYS.

TALK ABOUT YOUR LAUGH RIOTS...

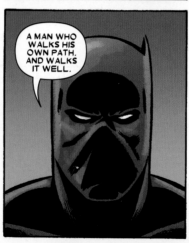

A MAN WHO WALKS HIS OWN PATH. AND WALKS IT WELL.

A WARTHOG. HE SMELLS *EXACTLY* LIKE A WARTHOG.

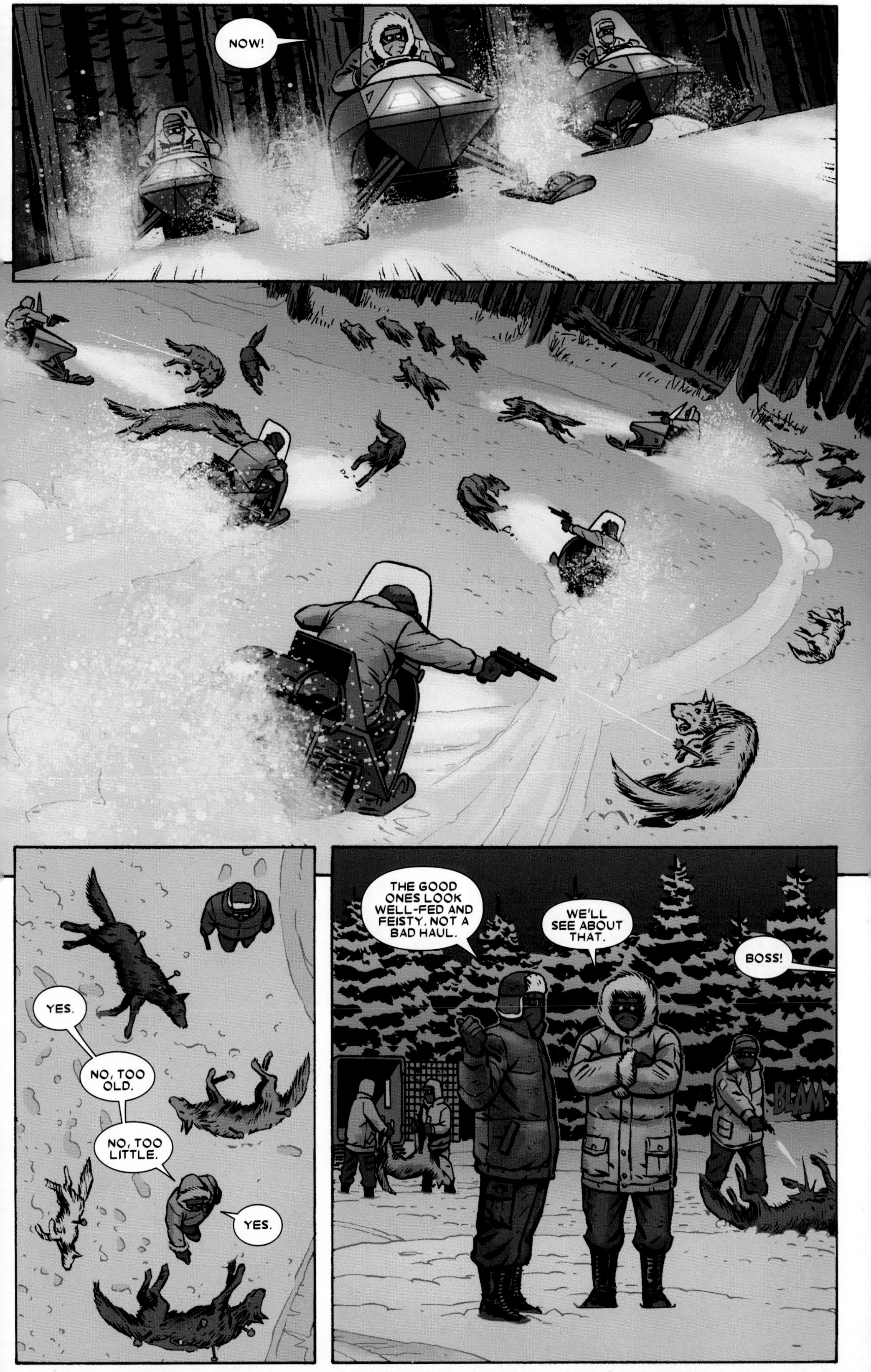
NOW!
YES.
NO, TOO OLD.
NO, TOO LITTLE.
YES.
THE GOOD ONES LOOK WELL-FED AND FEISTY. NOT A BAD HAUL.
WE'LL SEE ABOUT THAT.
BOSS!
BLAM

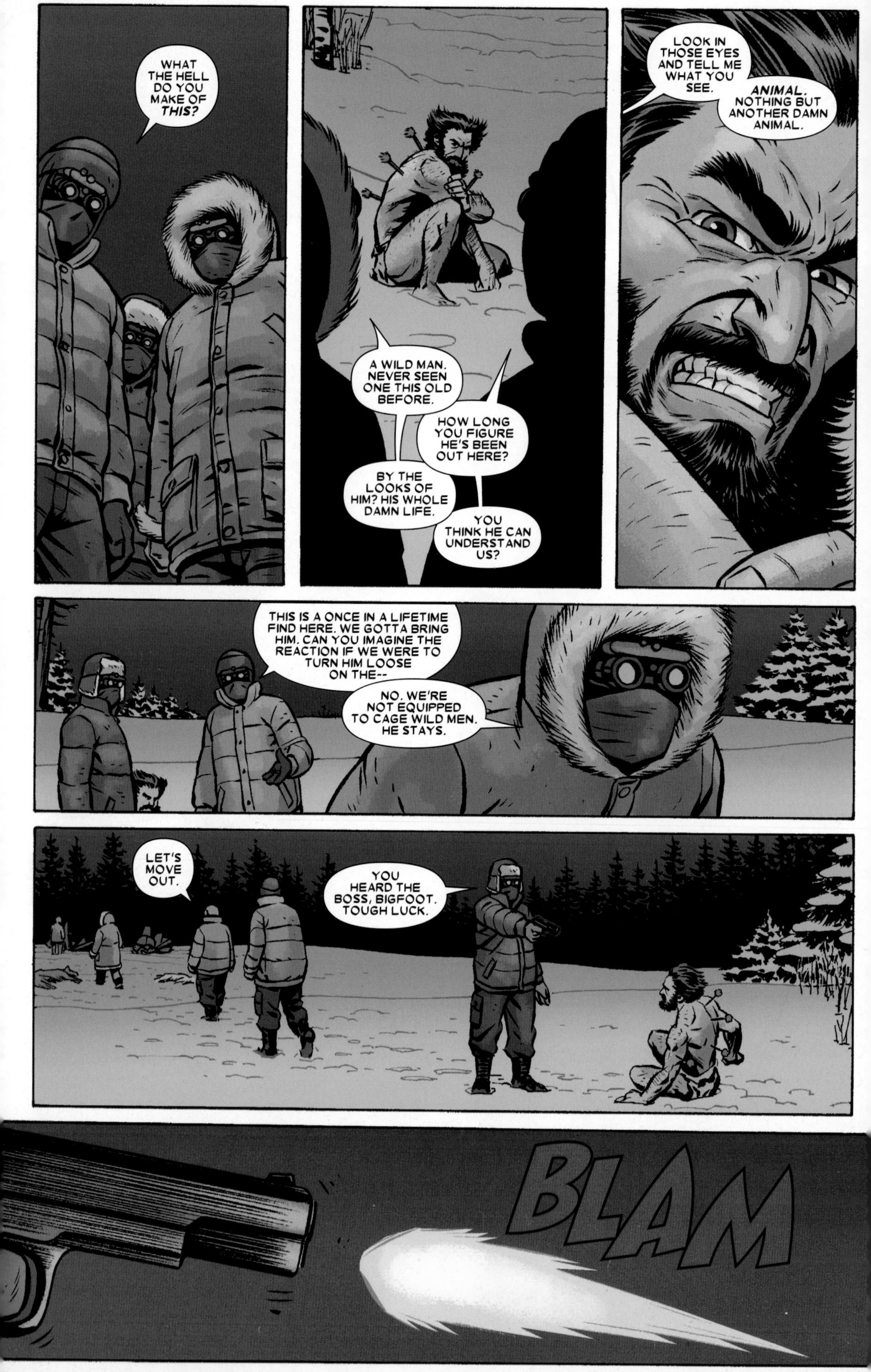
WHAT THE HELL DO YOU MAKE OF *THIS?*
A WILD MAN. NEVER SEEN ONE THIS OLD BEFORE.
HOW LONG YOU FIGURE HE'S BEEN OUT HERE?
BY THE LOOKS OF HIM? HIS WHOLE DAMN LIFE.
YOU THINK HE CAN UNDERSTAND US?
LOOK IN THOSE EYES AND TELL ME WHAT YOU SEE.
*ANIMAL.* NOTHING BUT ANOTHER DAMN ANIMAL.
THIS IS A ONCE IN A LIFETIME FIND HERE. WE GOTTA BRING HIM. CAN YOU IMAGINE THE REACTION IF WE WERE TO TURN HIM LOOSE ON THE--
NO. WE'RE NOT EQUIPPED TO CAGE WILD MEN. HE STAYS.
LET'S MOVE OUT.
YOU HEARD THE BOSS, BIGFOOT. TOUGH LUCK.
BLAM

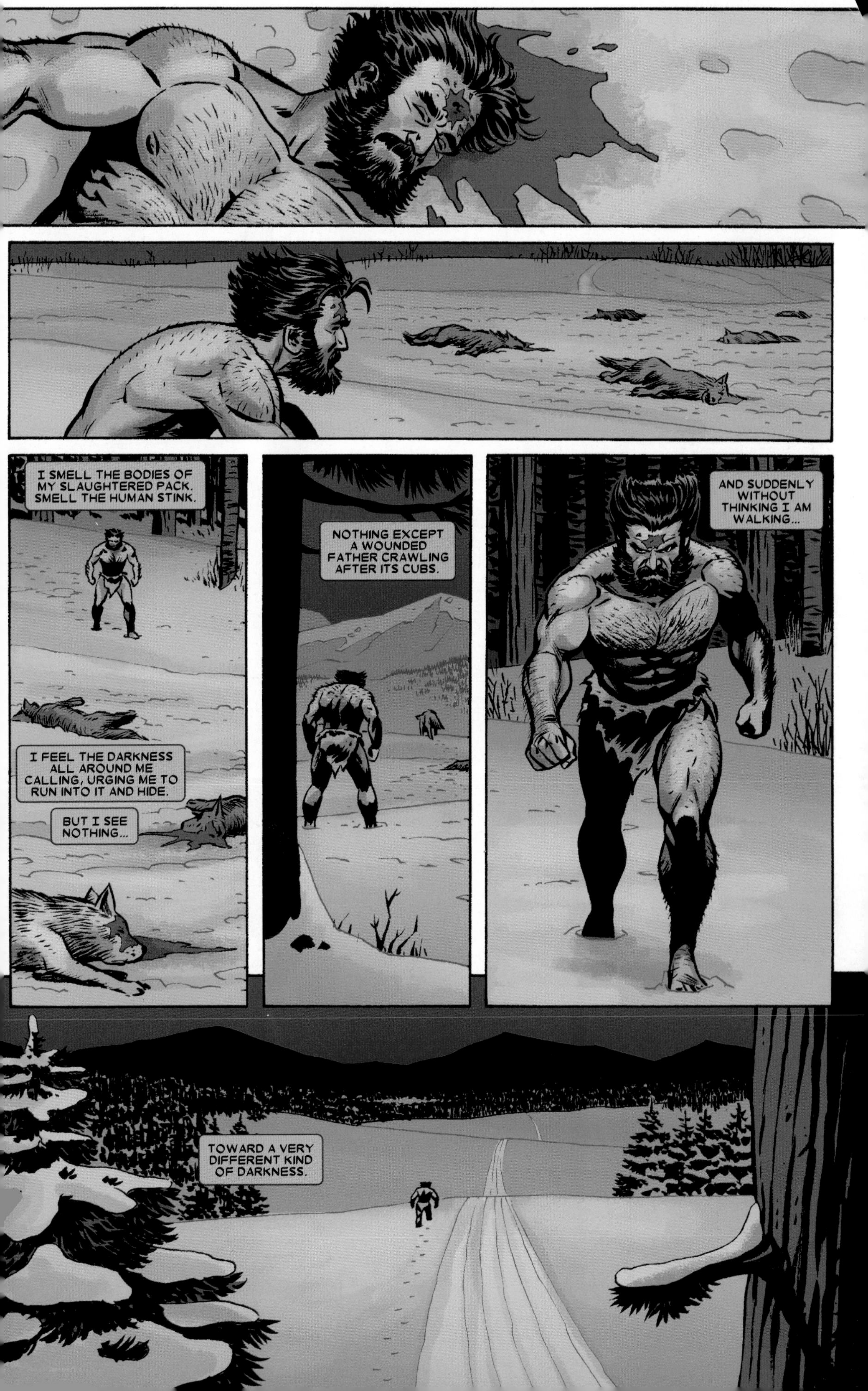
I SMELL THE BODIES OF MY SLAUGHTERED PACK. SMELL THE HUMAN STINK.
I FEEL THE DARKNESS ALL AROUND ME CALLING, URGING ME TO RUN INTO IT AND HIDE.
BUT I SEE NOTHING...
NOTHING EXCEPT A WOUNDED FATHER CRAWLING AFTER ITS CUBS.
AND SUDDENLY WITHOUT THINKING I AM WALKING...
TOWARD A VERY DIFFERENT KIND OF DARKNESS.

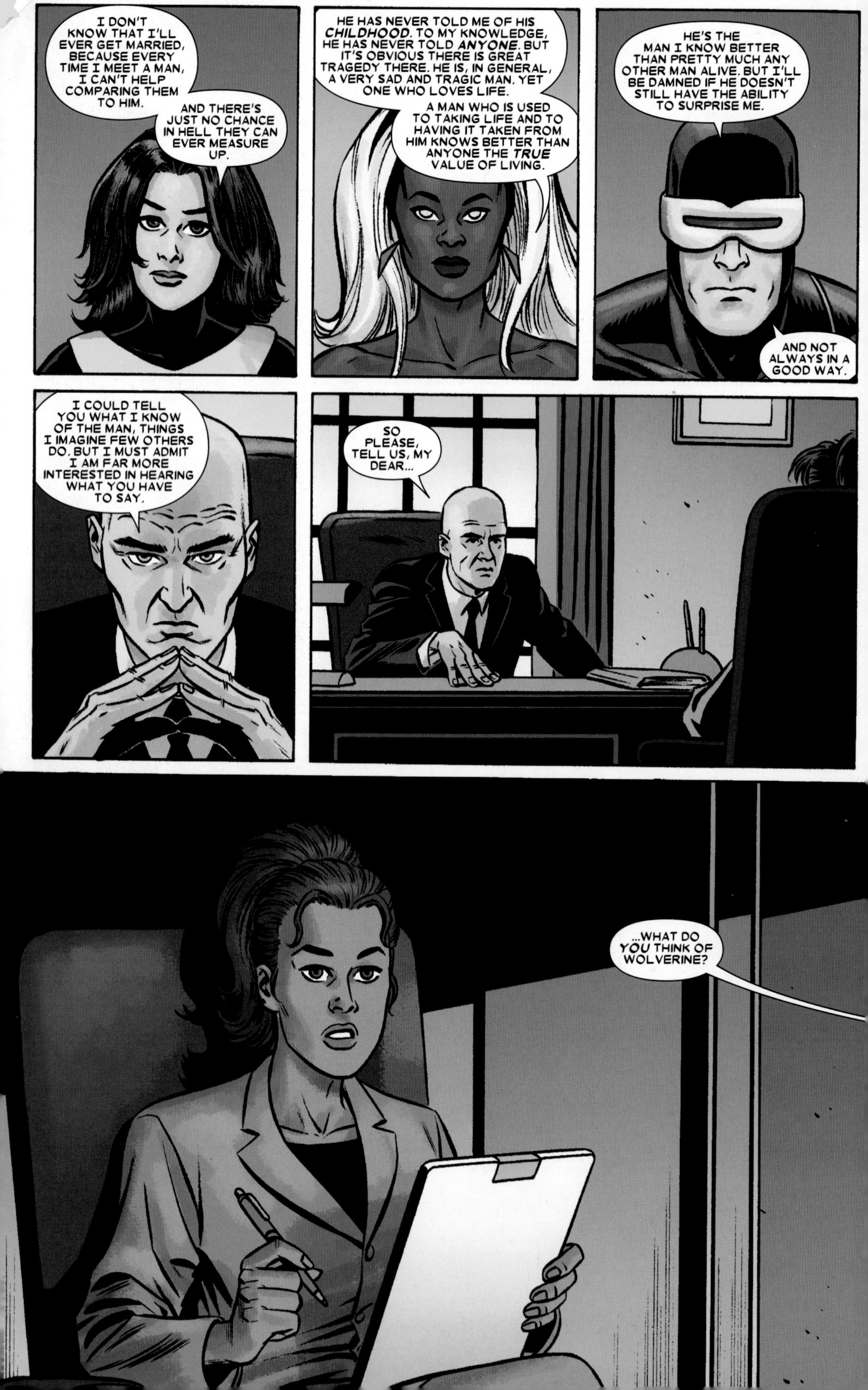
I DON'T KNOW THAT I'LL EVER GET MARRIED, BECAUSE EVERY TIME I MEET A MAN, I CAN'T HELP COMPARING THEM TO HIM.
AND THERE'S JUST NO CHANCE IN HELL THEY CAN EVER MEASURE UP.
HE HAS NEVER TOLD ME OF HIS *CHILDHOOD*. TO MY KNOWLEDGE, HE HAS NEVER TOLD *ANYONE*. BUT IT'S OBVIOUS THERE IS GREAT TRAGEDY THERE. HE IS, IN GENERAL, A VERY SAD AND TRAGIC MAN. YET ONE WHO LOVES LIFE.
A MAN WHO IS USED TO TAKING LIFE AND TO HAVING IT TAKEN FROM HIM KNOWS BETTER THAN ANYONE THE *TRUE* VALUE OF LIVING.
HE'S THE MAN I KNOW BETTER THAN PRETTY MUCH ANY OTHER MAN ALIVE. BUT I'LL BE DAMNED IF HE DOESN'T STILL HAVE THE ABILITY TO SURPRISE ME.
AND NOT ALWAYS IN A GOOD WAY.
I COULD TELL YOU WHAT I KNOW OF THE MAN, THINGS I IMAGINE FEW OTHERS DO. BUT I MUST ADMIT I AM FAR MORE INTERESTED IN HEARING WHAT YOU HAVE TO SAY.
SO PLEASE, TELL US, MY DEAR...
...WHAT DO *YOU* THINK OF WOLVERINE?

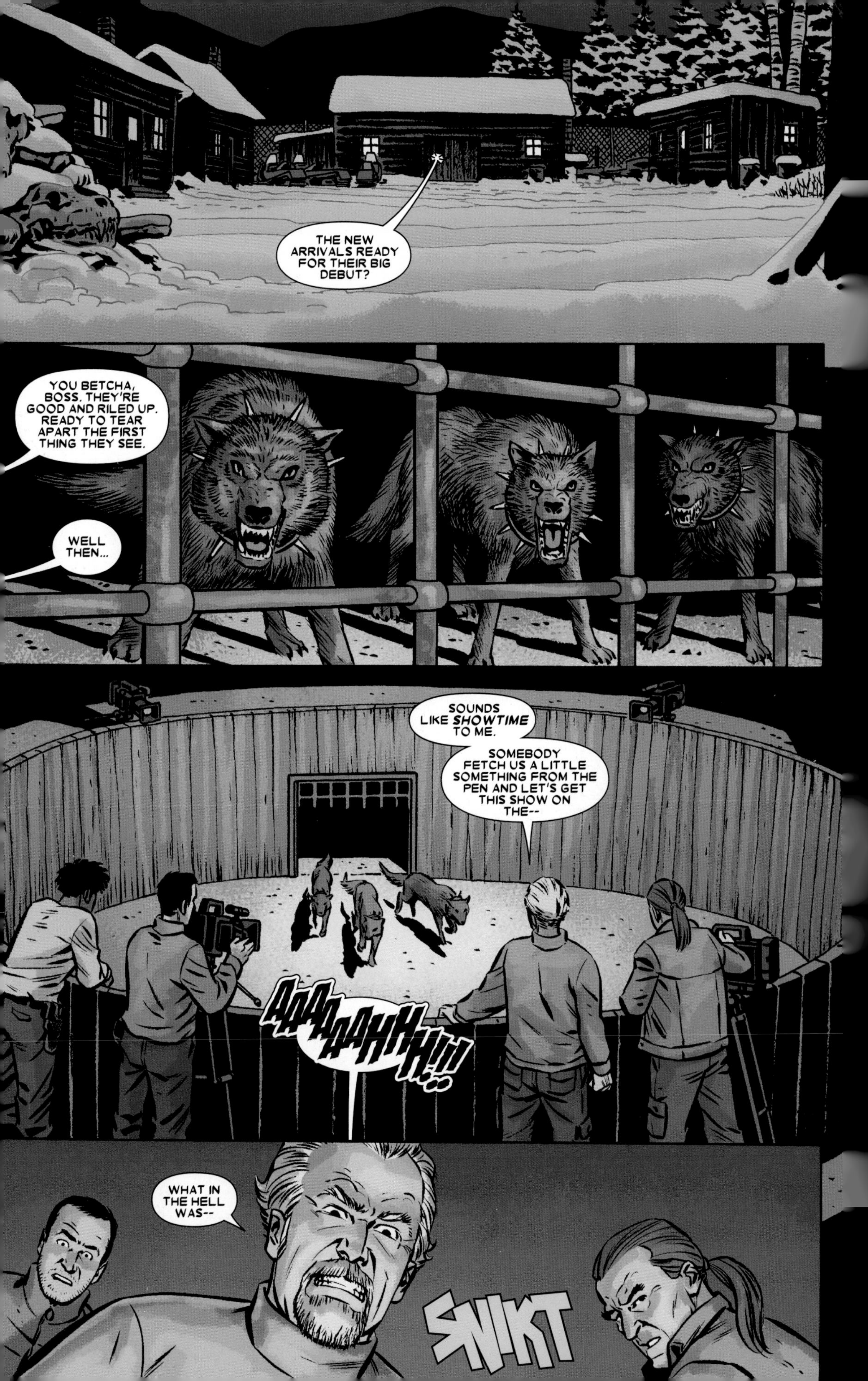
THE NEW ARRIVALS READY FOR THEIR BIG DEBUT?
YOU BETCHA, BOSS. THEY'RE GOOD AND RILED UP. READY TO TEAR APART THE FIRST THING THEY SEE.
WELL THEN...
SOUNDS LIKE *SHOWTIME* TO ME.
SOMEBODY FETCH US A LITTLE SOMETHING FROM THE PEN AND LET'S GET THIS SHOW ON THE--
AAAAAAHHHH!!!
WHAT IN THE HELL WAS--
SNIKT

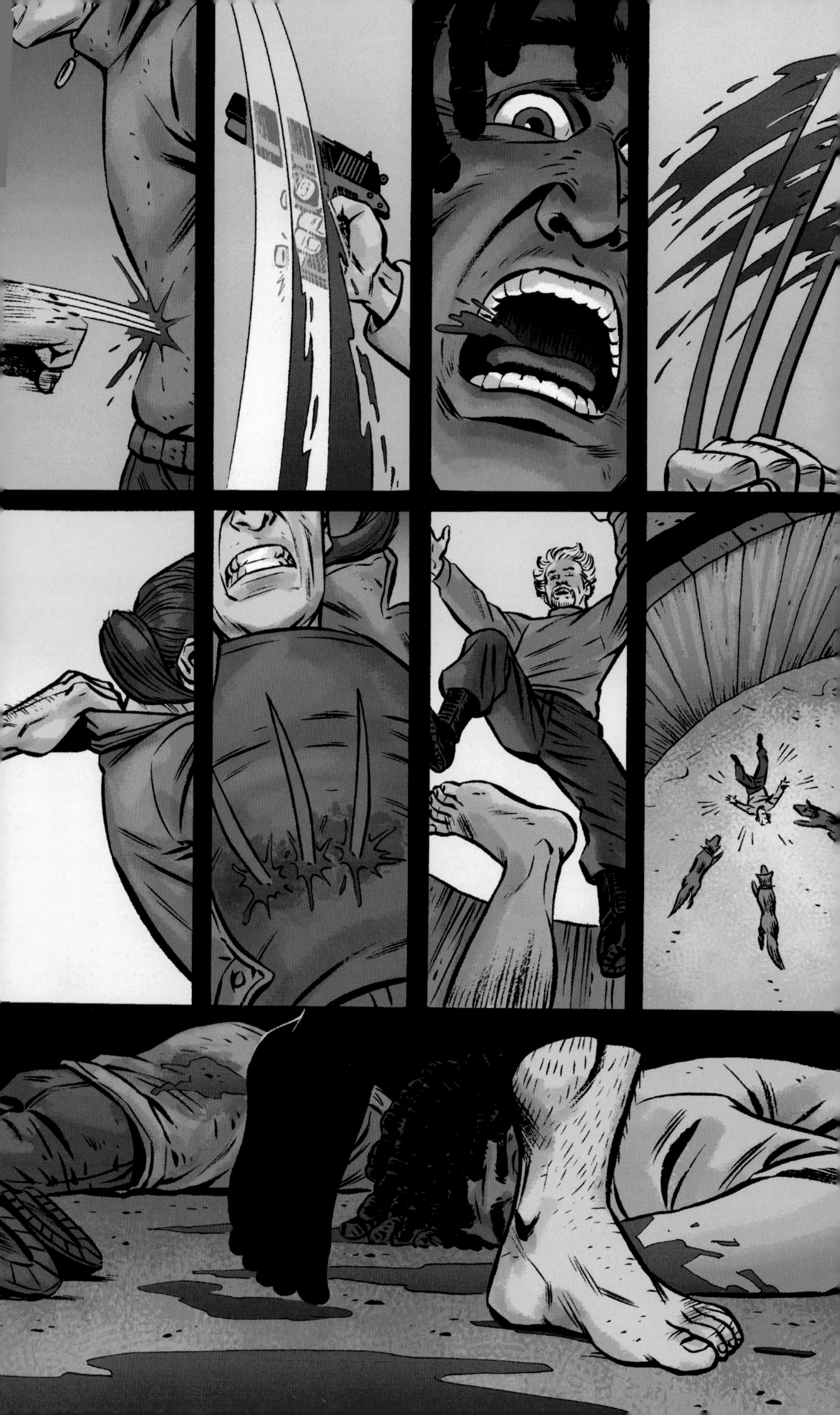

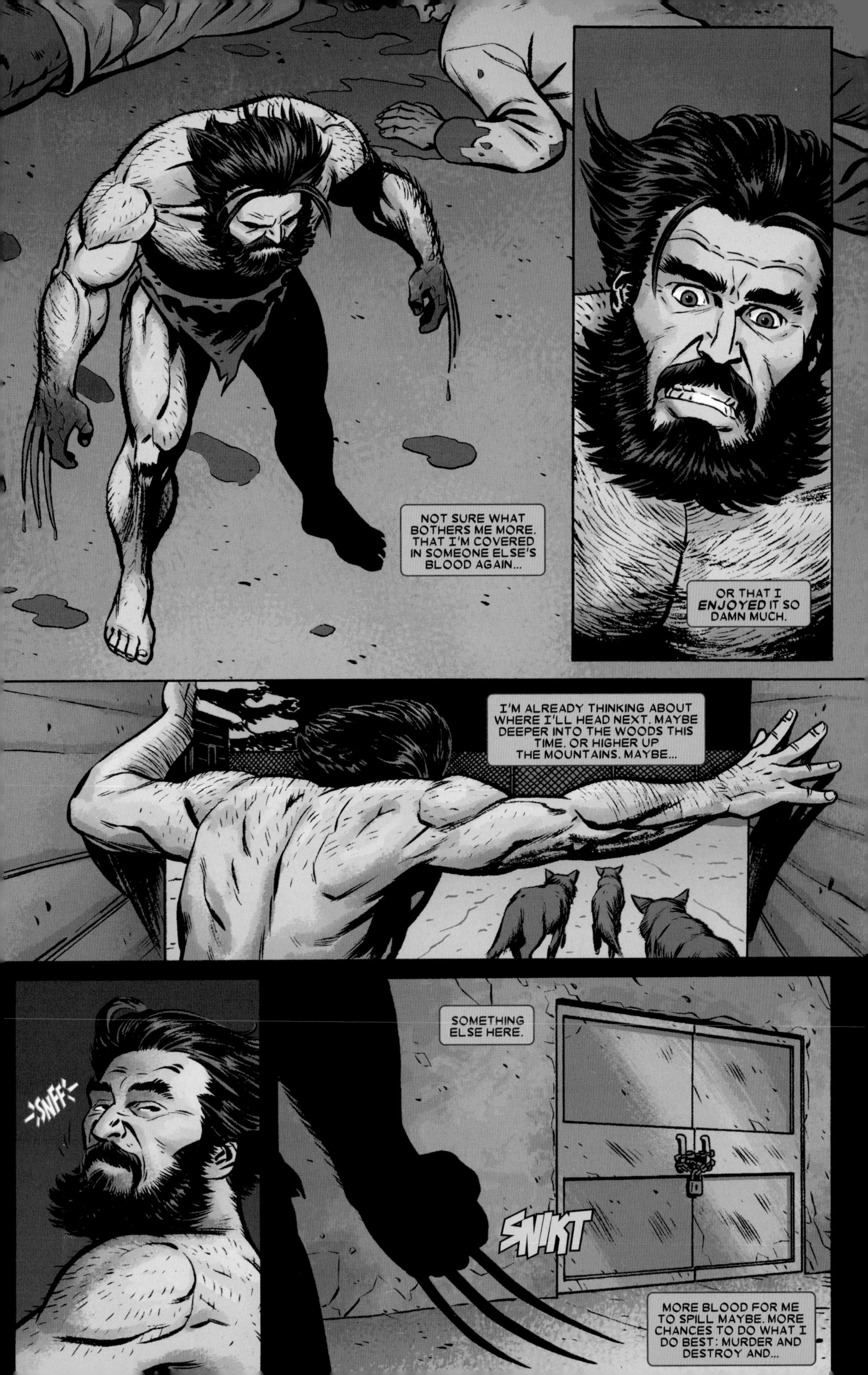
NOT SURE WHAT BOTHERS ME MORE. THAT I'M COVERED IN SOMEONE ELSE'S BLOOD AGAIN...
OR THAT I *ENJOYED* IT SO DAMN MUCH.
I'M ALREADY THINKING ABOUT WHERE I'LL HEAD NEXT. MAYBE DEEPER INTO THE WOODS THIS TIME. OR HIGHER UP THE MOUNTAINS. MAYBE...
SNIFF
SOMETHING ELSE HERE.
SNIKT
MORE BLOOD FOR ME TO SPILL MAYBE. MORE CHANCES TO DO WHAT I DO BEST: MURDER AND DESTROY AND...

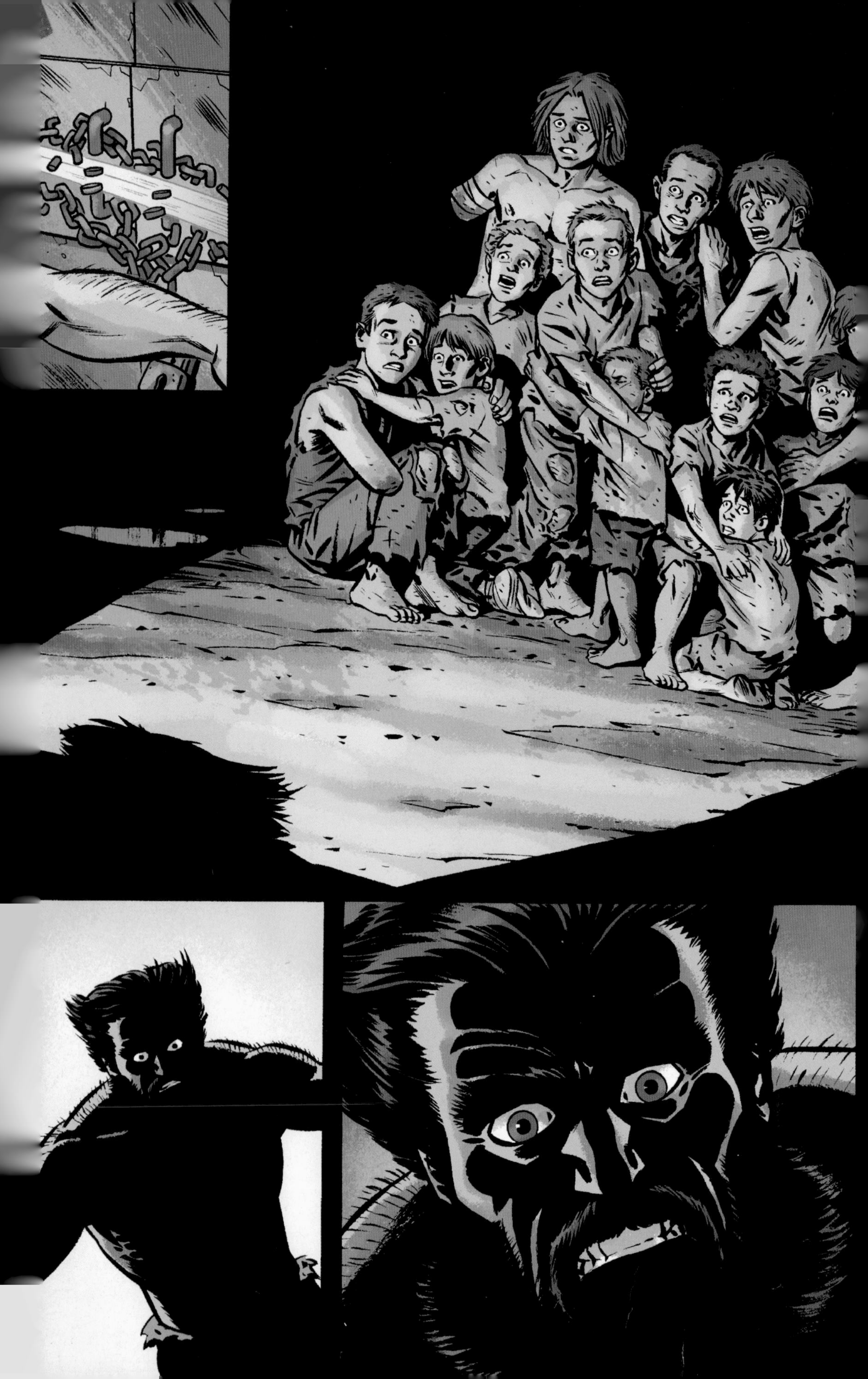

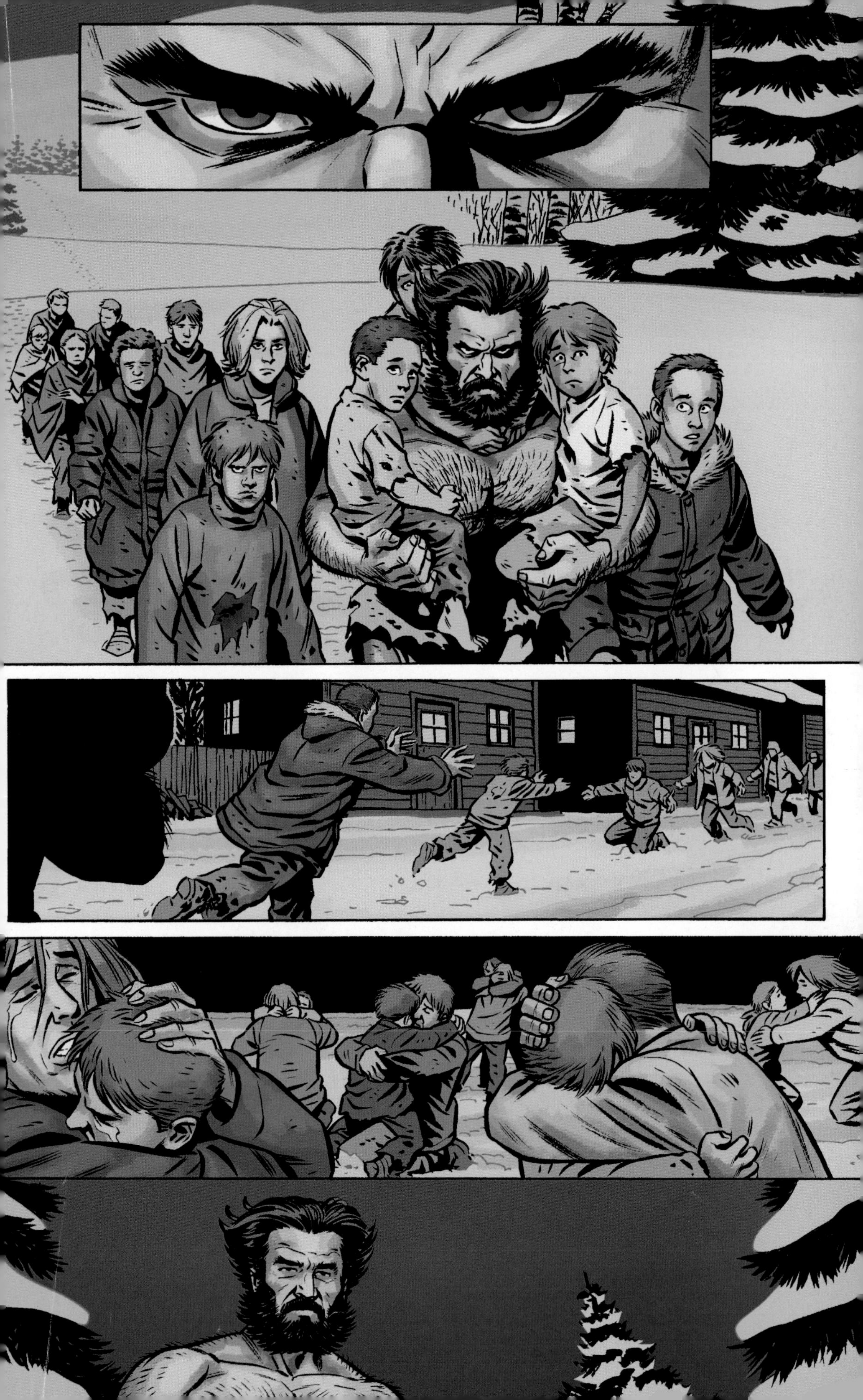

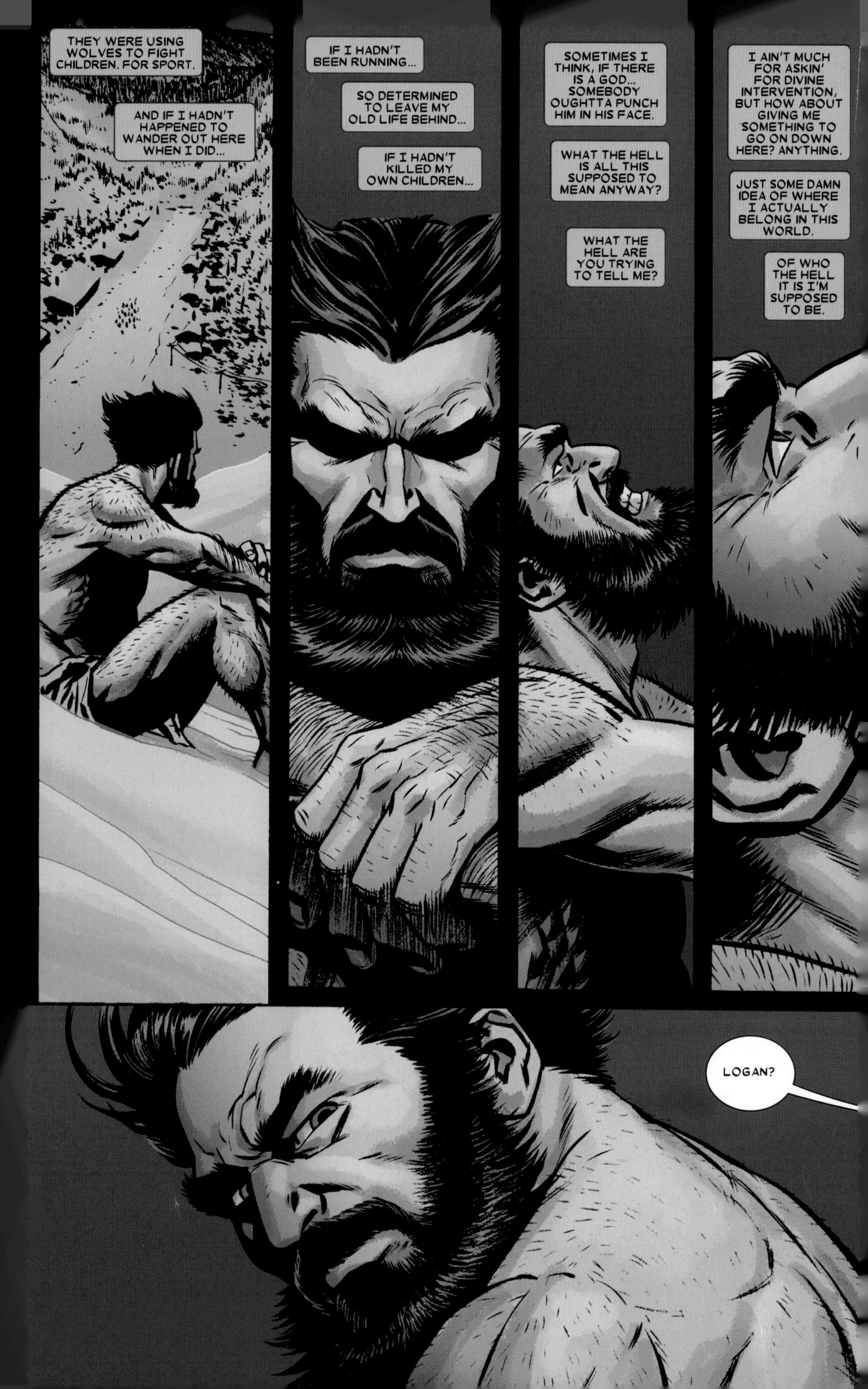
THEY WERE USING WOLVES TO FIGHT CHILDREN. FOR SPORT.
AND IF I HADN'T HAPPENED TO WANDER OUT HERE WHEN I DID...
IF I HADN'T BEEN RUNNING...
SO DETERMINED TO LEAVE MY OLD LIFE BEHIND...
IF I HADN'T KILLED MY OWN CHILDREN...
SOMETIMES I THINK, IF THERE IS A GOD... SOMEBODY OUGHTTA PUNCH HIM IN HIS FACE.
WHAT THE HELL IS ALL THIS SUPPOSED TO MEAN ANYWAY?
WHAT THE HELL ARE YOU TRYING TO TELL ME?
I AIN'T MUCH FOR ASKIN' FOR DIVINE INTERVENTION, BUT HOW ABOUT GIVING ME SOMETHING TO GO ON DOWN HERE? ANYTHING.
JUST SOME DAMN IDEA OF WHERE I ACTUALLY BELONG IN THIS WORLD.
OF WHO THE HELL IT IS I'M SUPPOSED TO BE.
LOGAN?

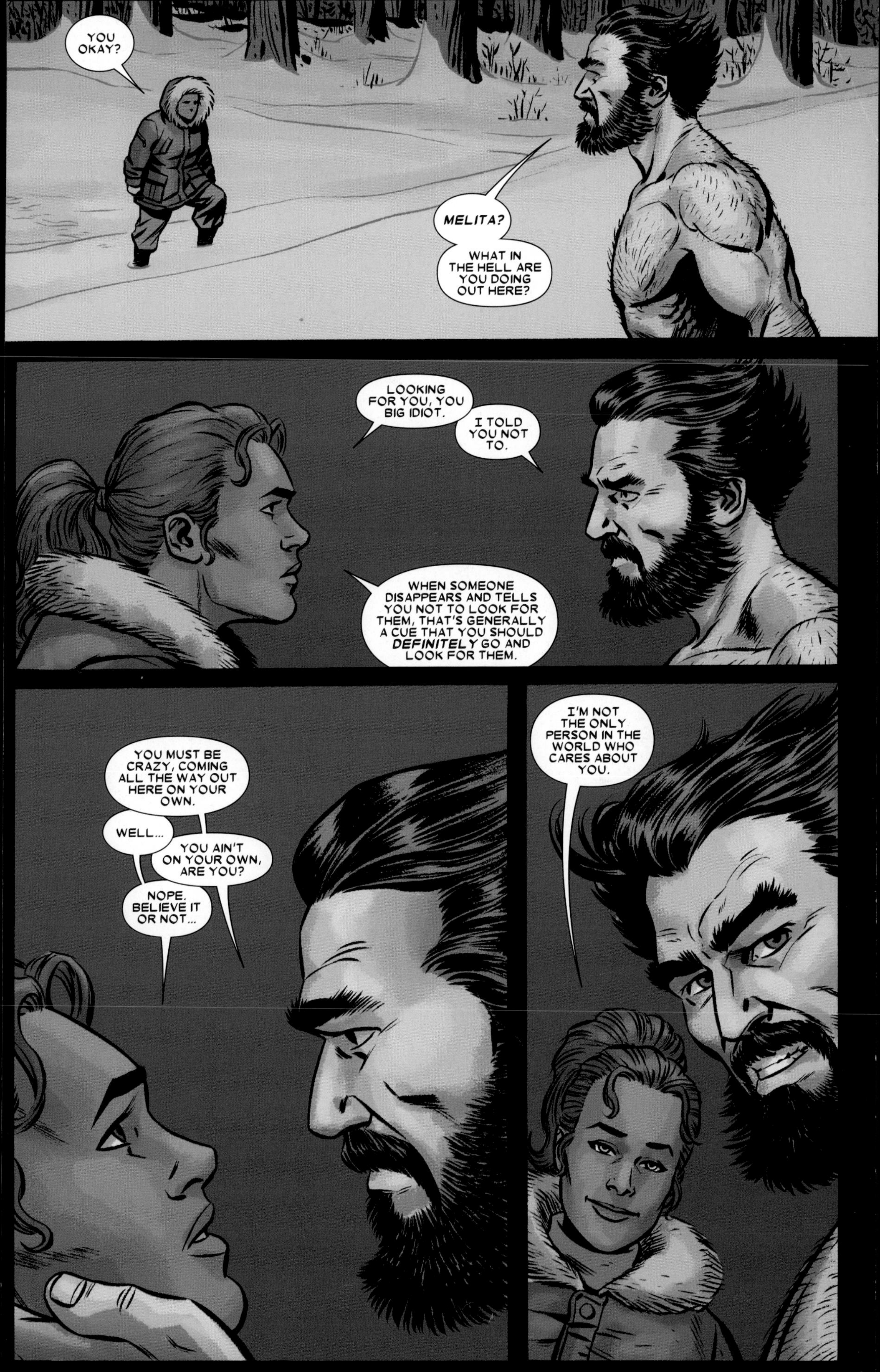
YOU OKAY?
MELITA?
WHAT IN THE HELL ARE YOU DOING OUT HERE?
LOOKING FOR YOU, YOU BIG IDIOT.
I TOLD YOU NOT TO.
WHEN SOMEONE DISAPPEARS AND TELLS YOU NOT TO LOOK FOR THEM, THAT'S GENERALLY A CUE THAT YOU SHOULD DEFINITELY GO AND LOOK FOR THEM.
YOU MUST BE CRAZY, COMING ALL THE WAY OUT HERE ON YOUR OWN.
WELL...
YOU AIN'T ON YOUR OWN, ARE YOU?
NOPE. BELIEVE IT OR NOT...
I'M NOT THE ONLY PERSON IN THE WORLD WHO CARES ABOUT YOU.

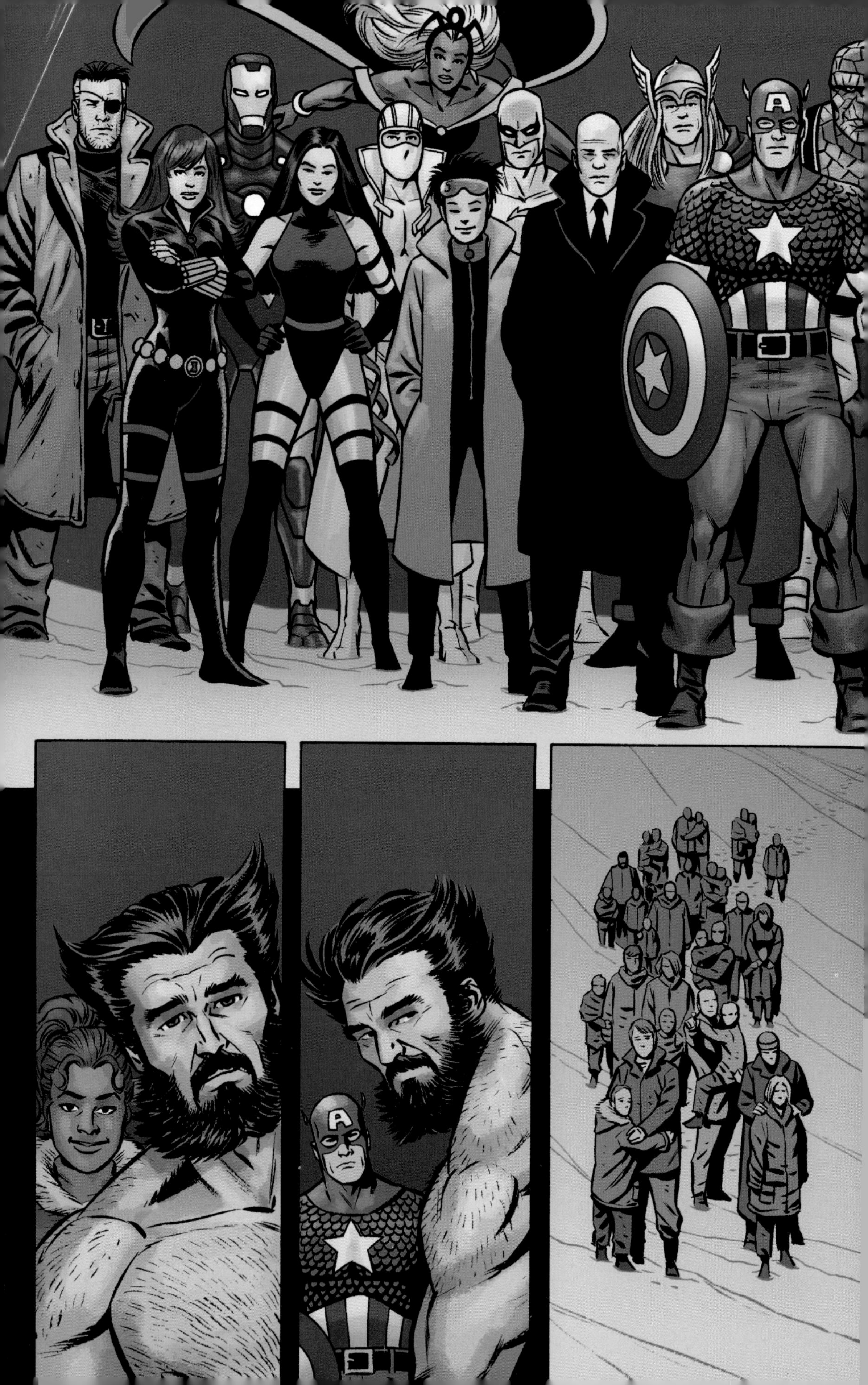

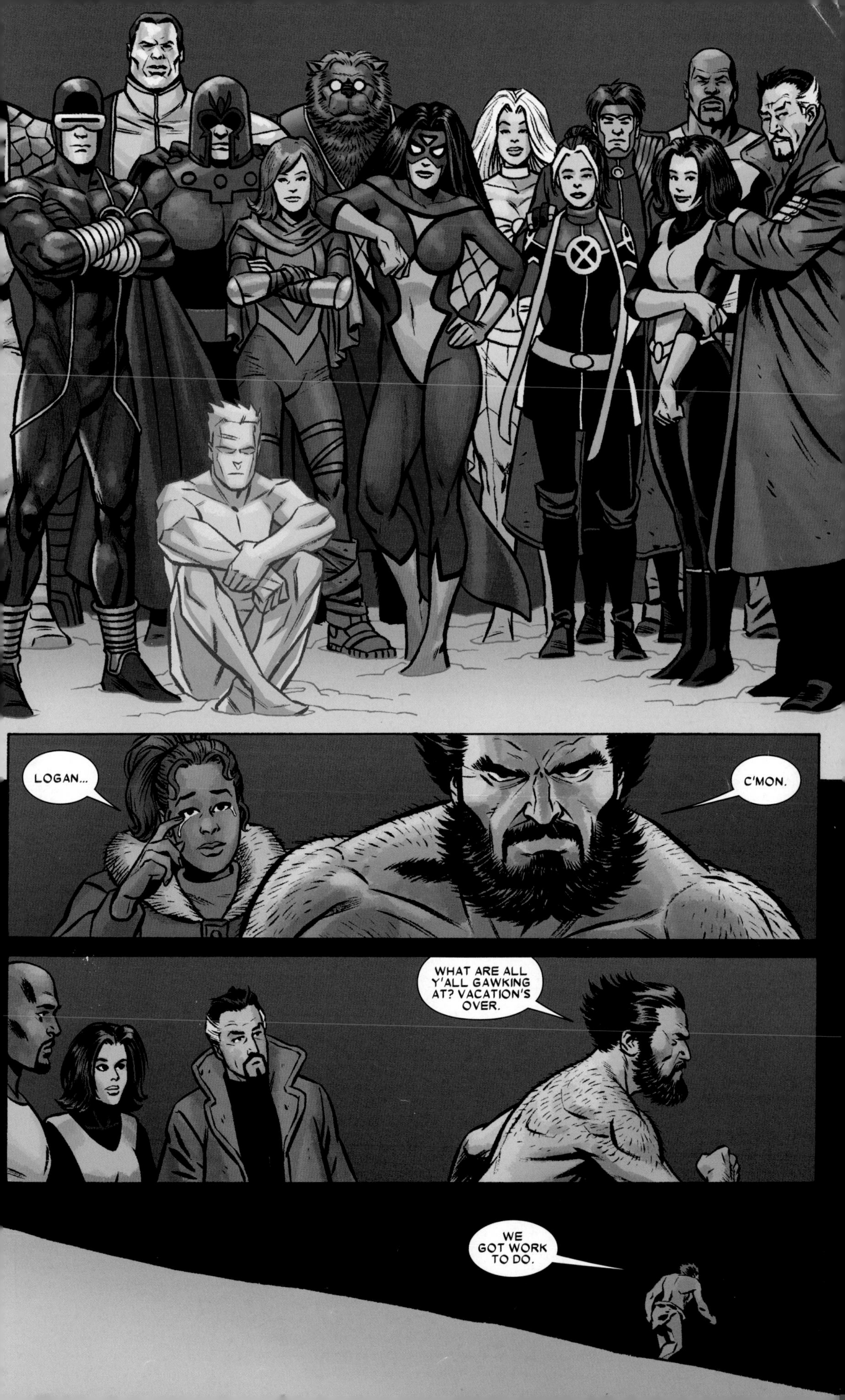
LOGAN...
C'MON.
WHAT ARE ALL Y'ALL GAWKING AT? VACATION'S OVER.
WE GOT WORK TO DO.

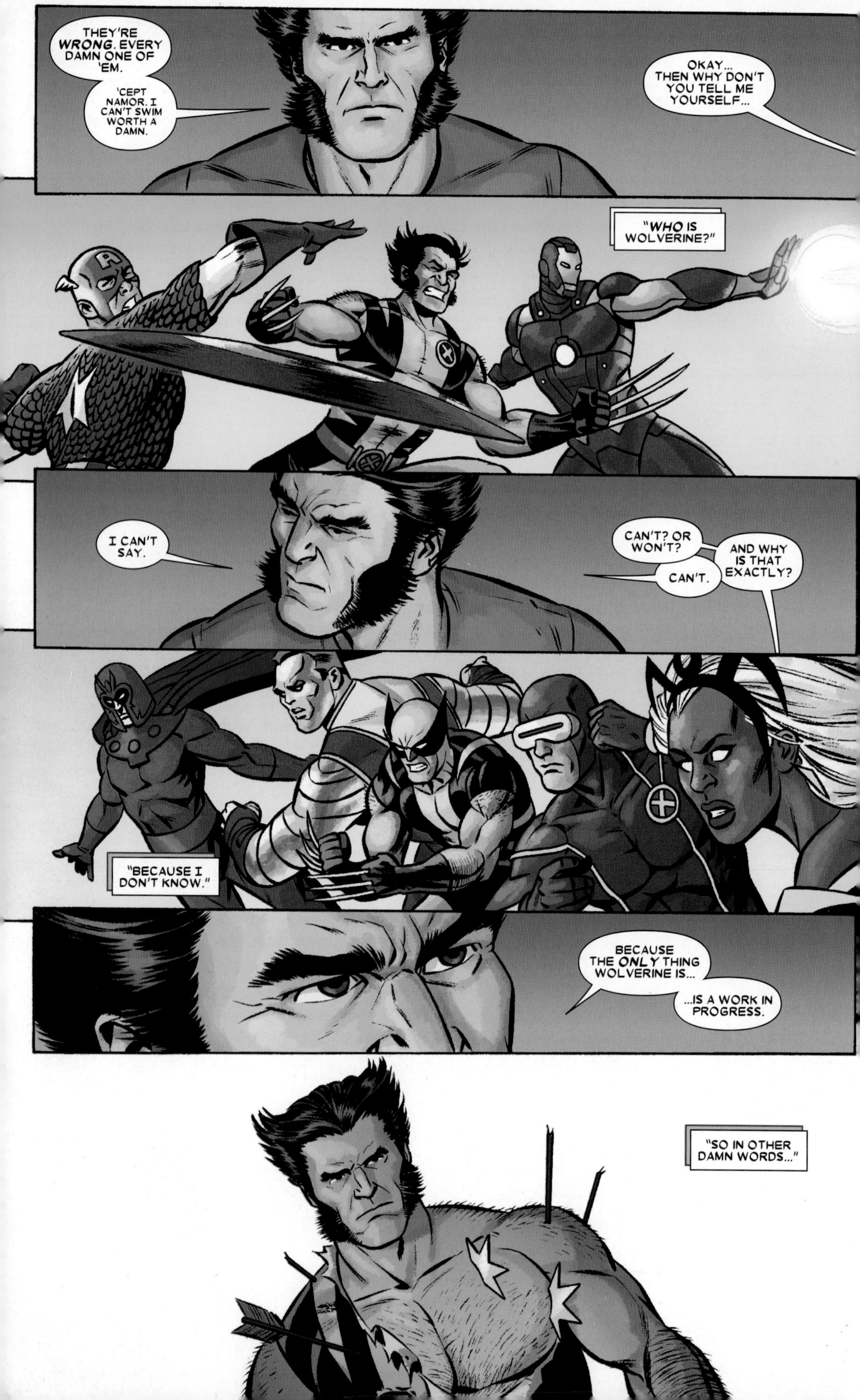

THEY'RE WRONG. EVERY DAMN ONE OF 'EM.
'CEPT NAMOR. I CAN'T SWIM WORTH A DAMN.
OKAY... THEN WHY DON'T YOU TELL ME YOURSELF...
"WHO IS WOLVERINE?"
I CAN'T SAY.
CAN'T? OR WON'T?
CAN'T.
AND WHY IS THAT EXACTLY?
"BECAUSE I DON'T KNOW."
BECAUSE THE ONLY THING WOLVERINE IS...
...IS A WORK IN PROGRESS.
"SO IN OTHER DAMN WORDS..."

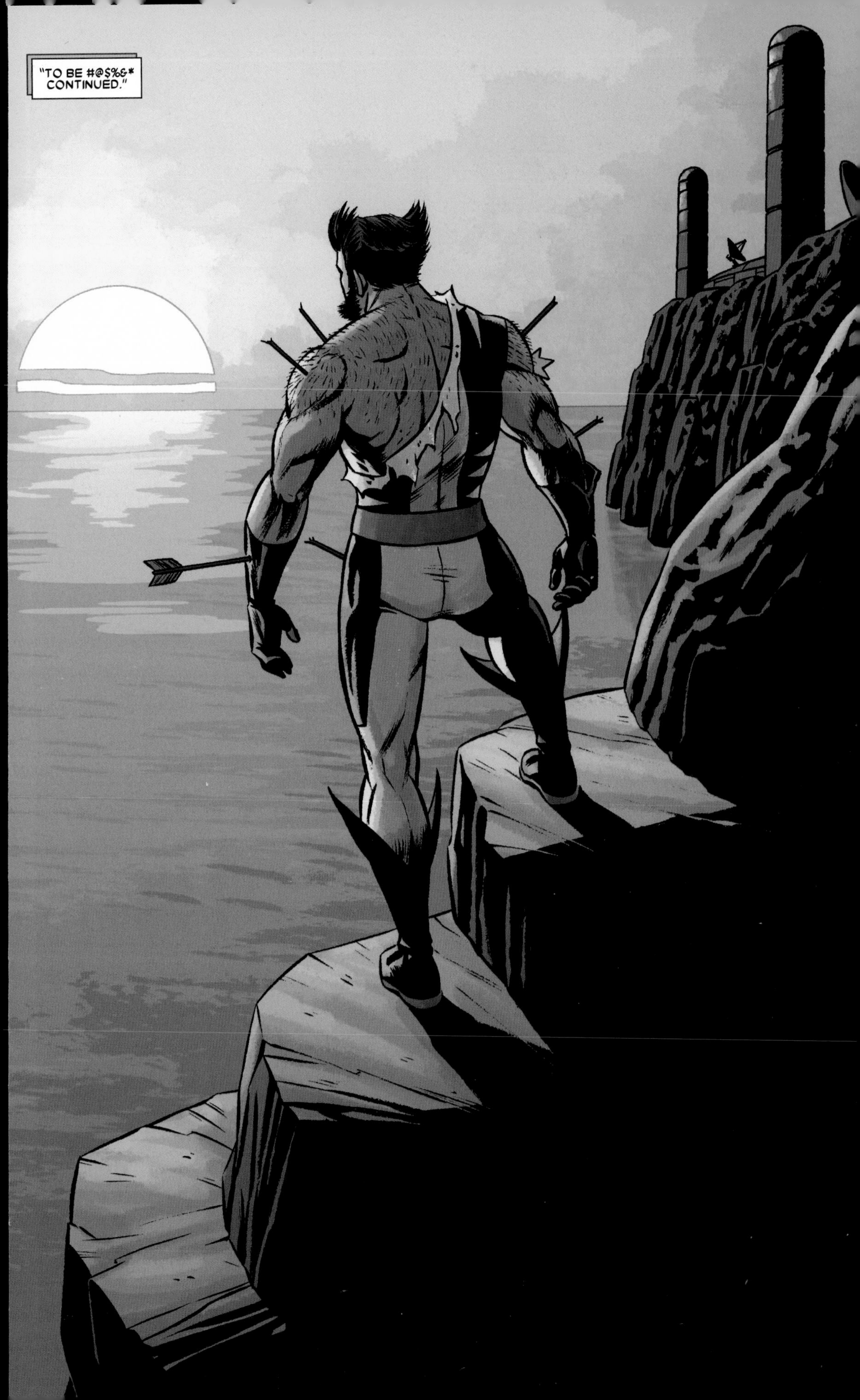
"TO BE #@$%&* CONTINUED."

**#12 I AM CAPTAIN AMERICA VARIANT**
**BY JOE QUESADA, DANNY MIKI & RICHARD ISANOVE**

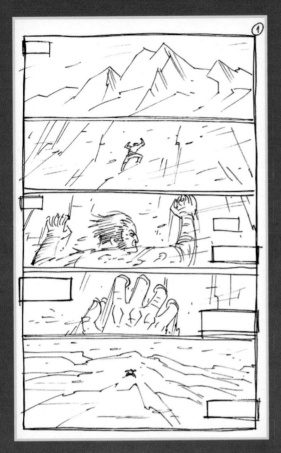

**#15 PAGE LAYOUTS**
**BY GORAN SUDZUKA**

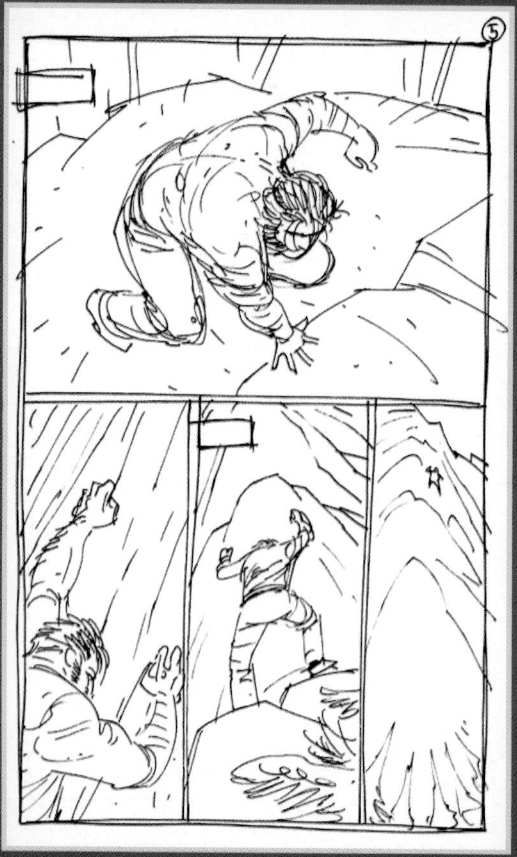
5

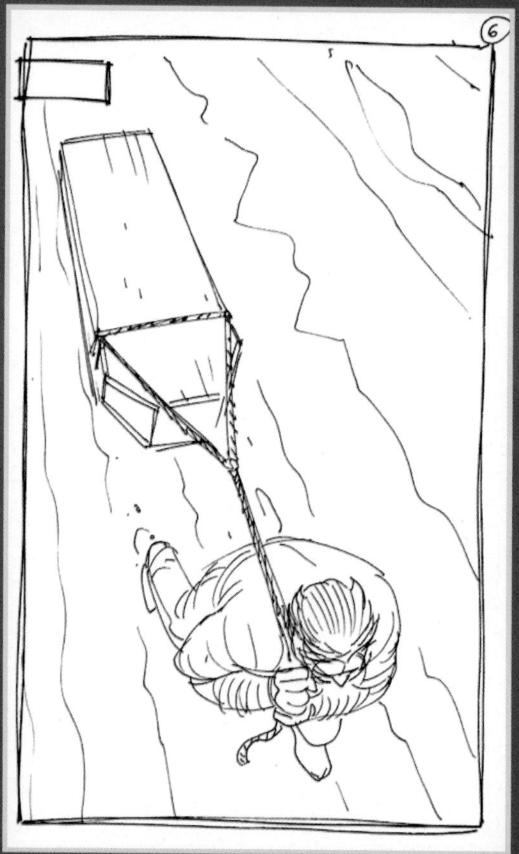
6

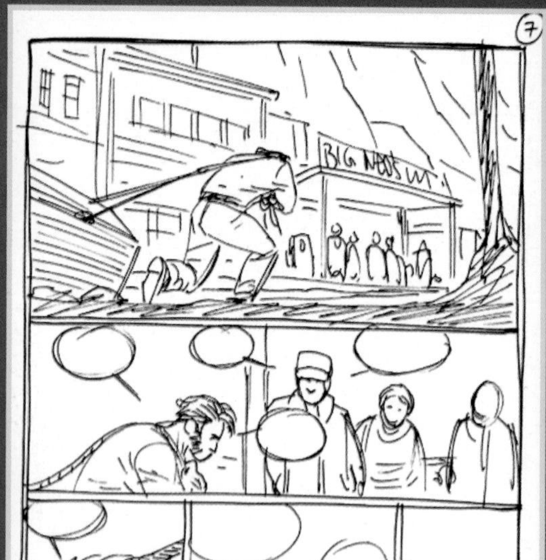
7
BIG NEWS

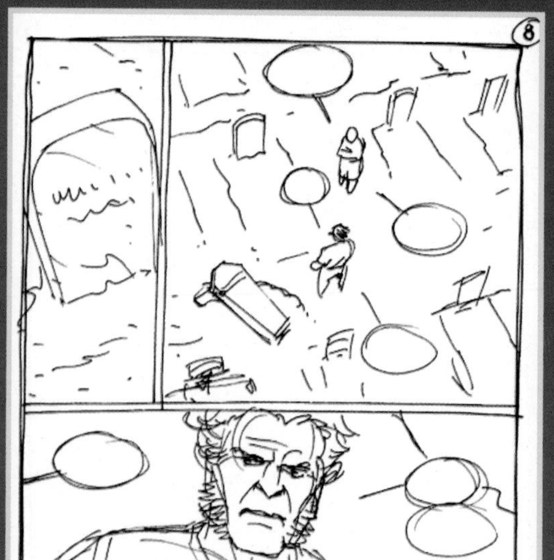
8

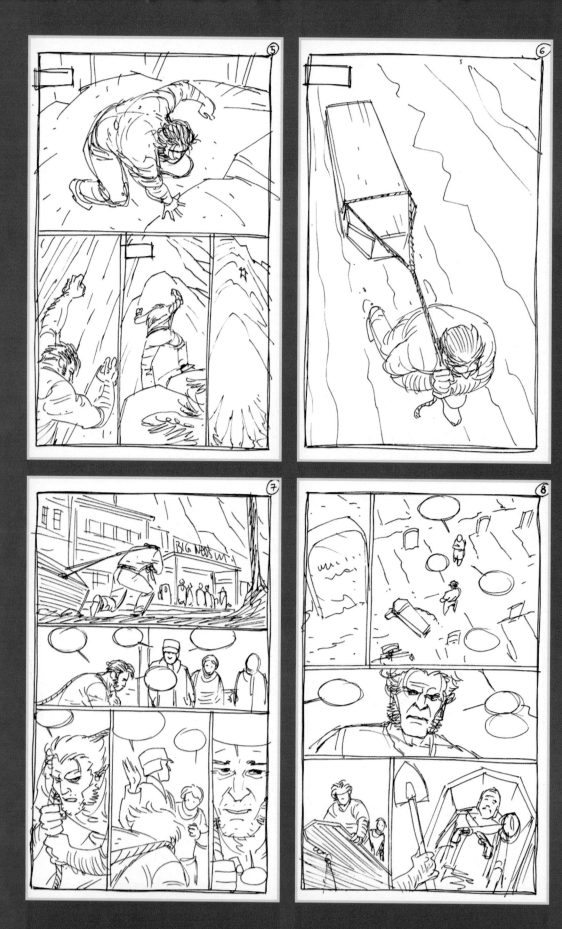

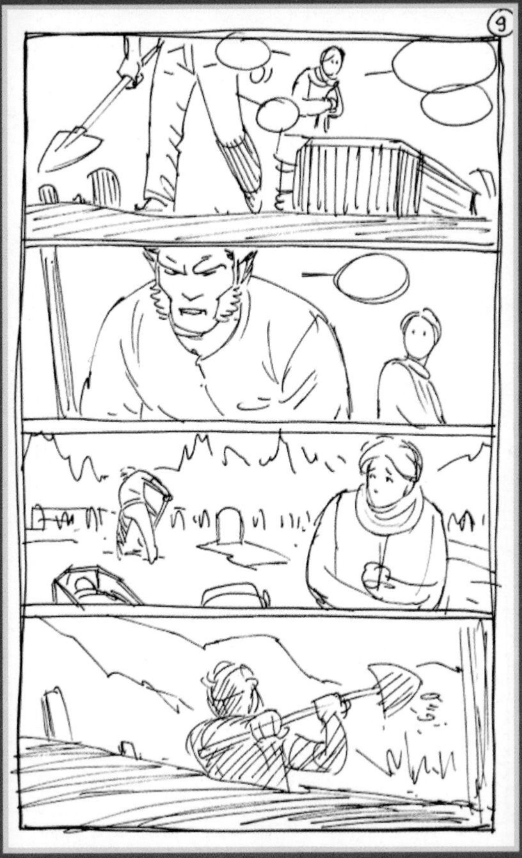
9

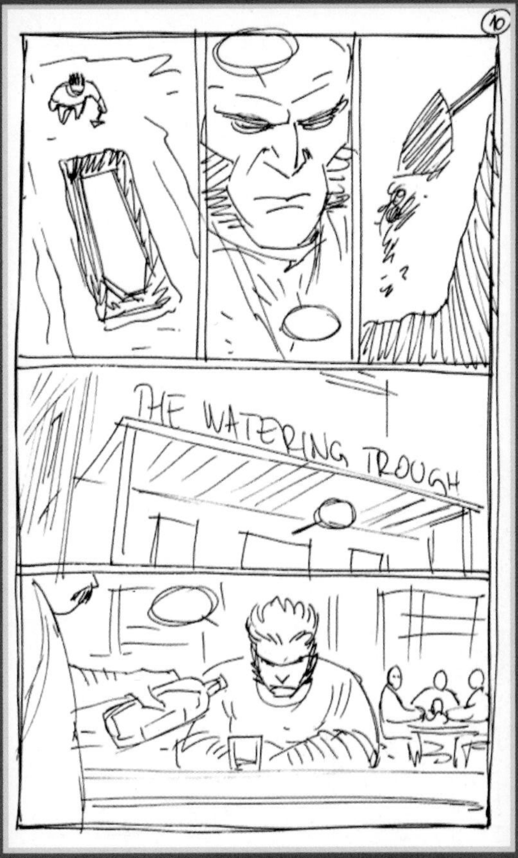
10
THE WATERING TROUGH

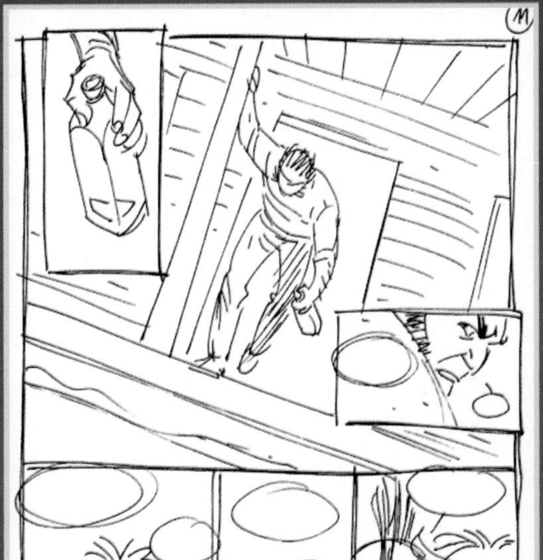
11

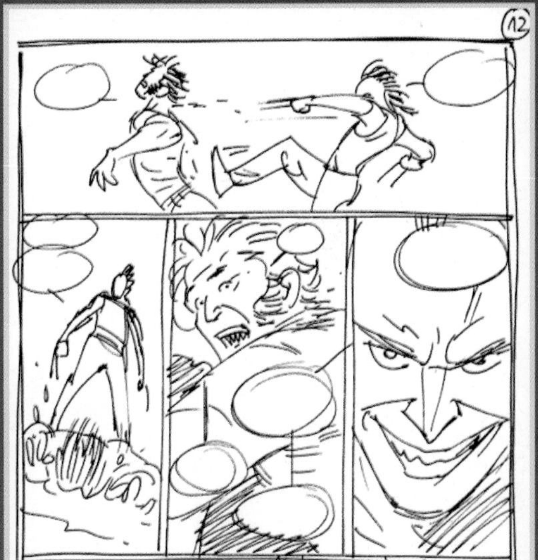
12

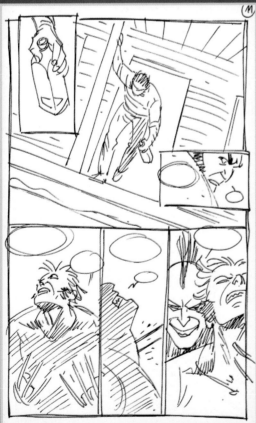

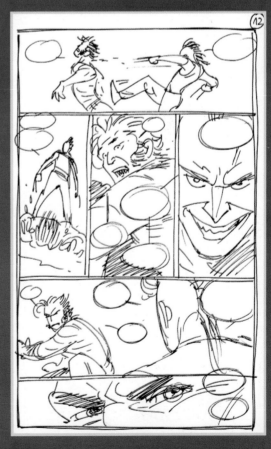

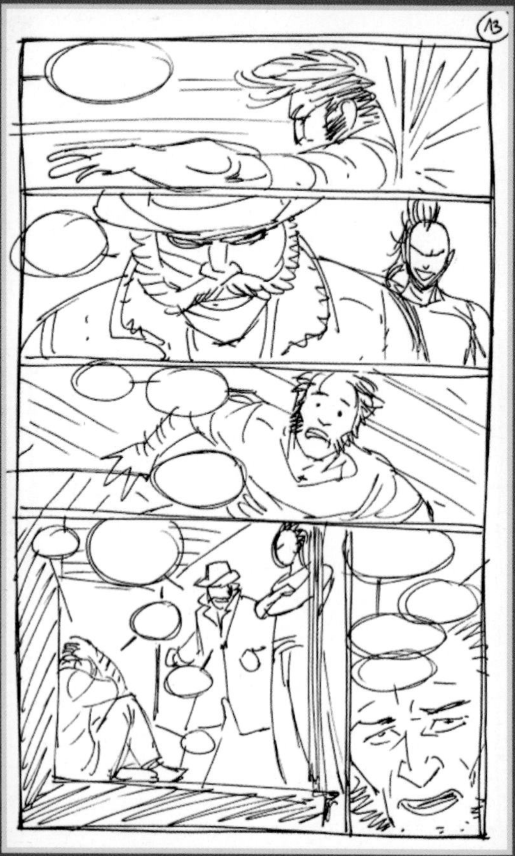
13

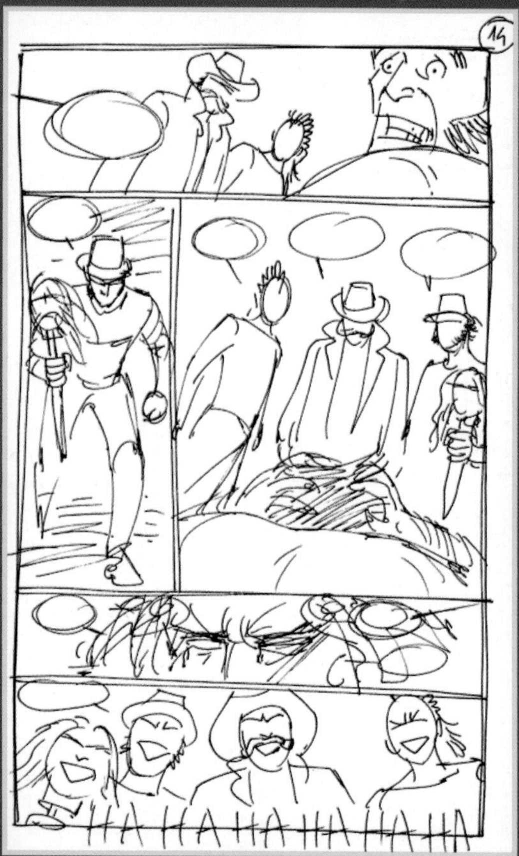
14
HA HA HA HA HA HA HA HA

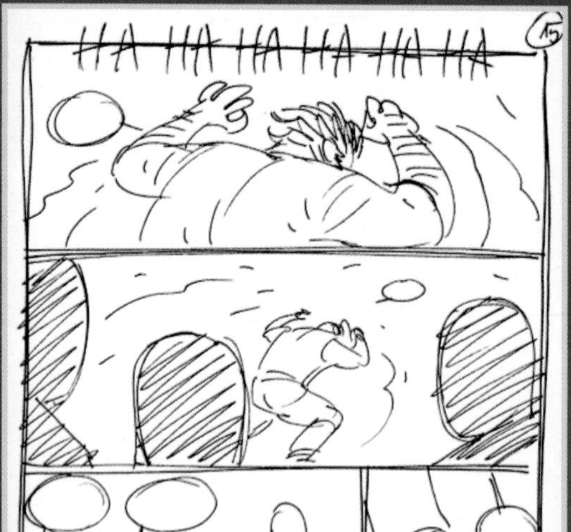
15
HA HA HA HA HA HA HA

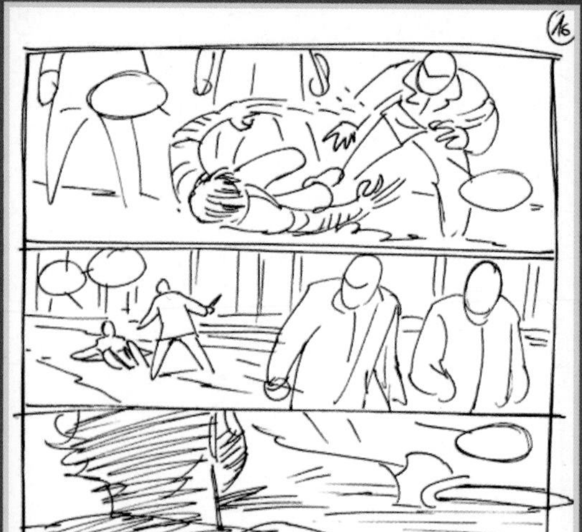
16

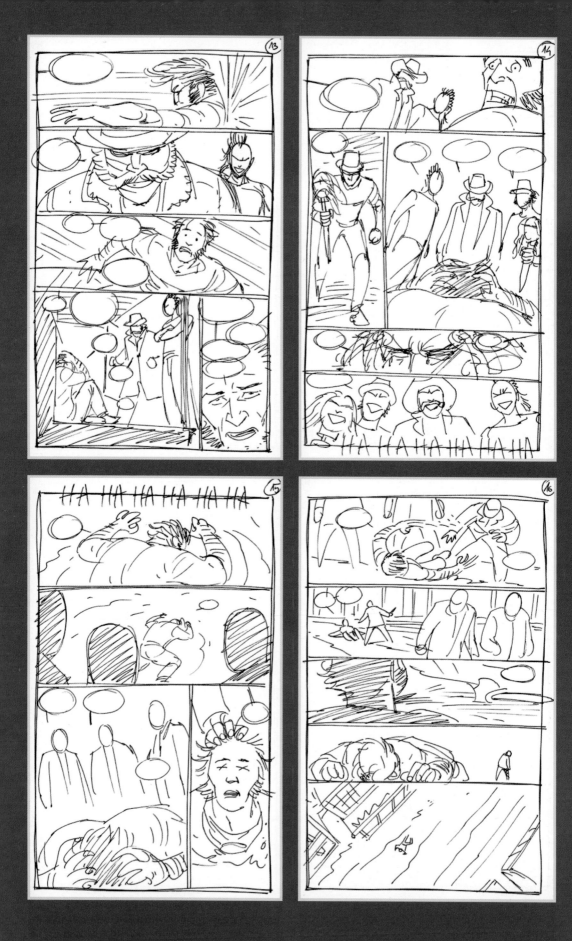

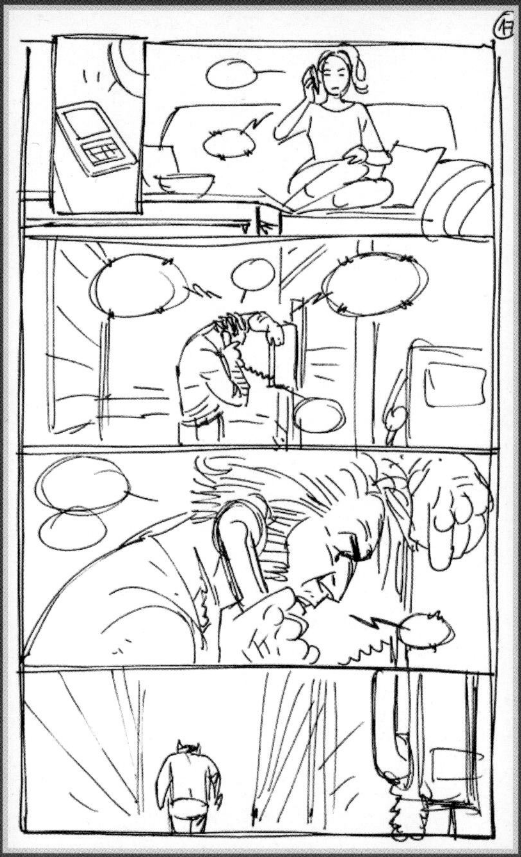

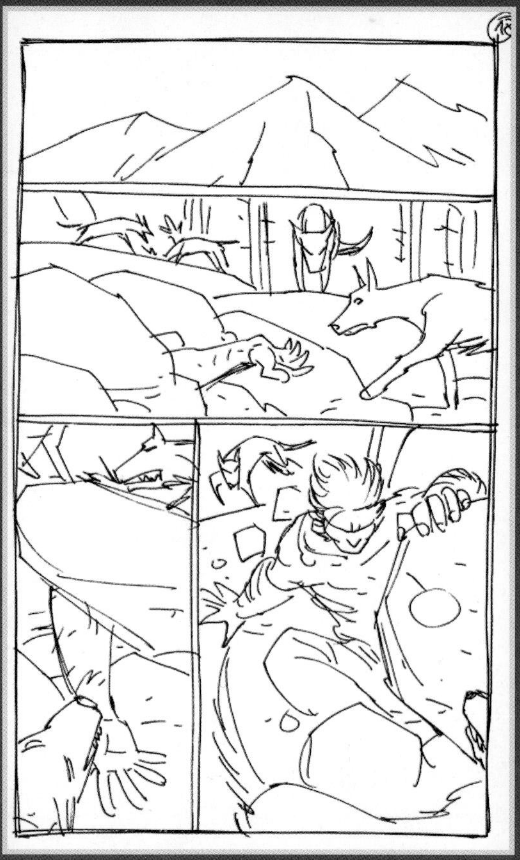

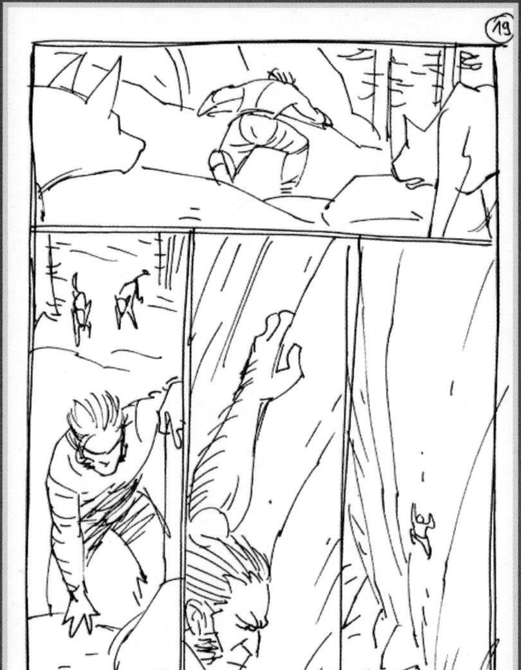
19

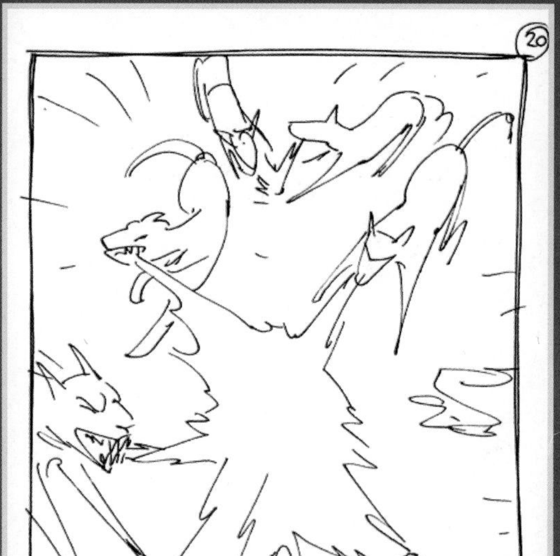
20

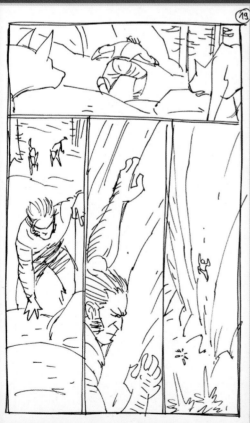

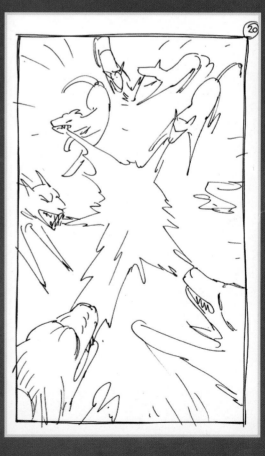

**#15 COVER SKETCH
BY JAE LEE**